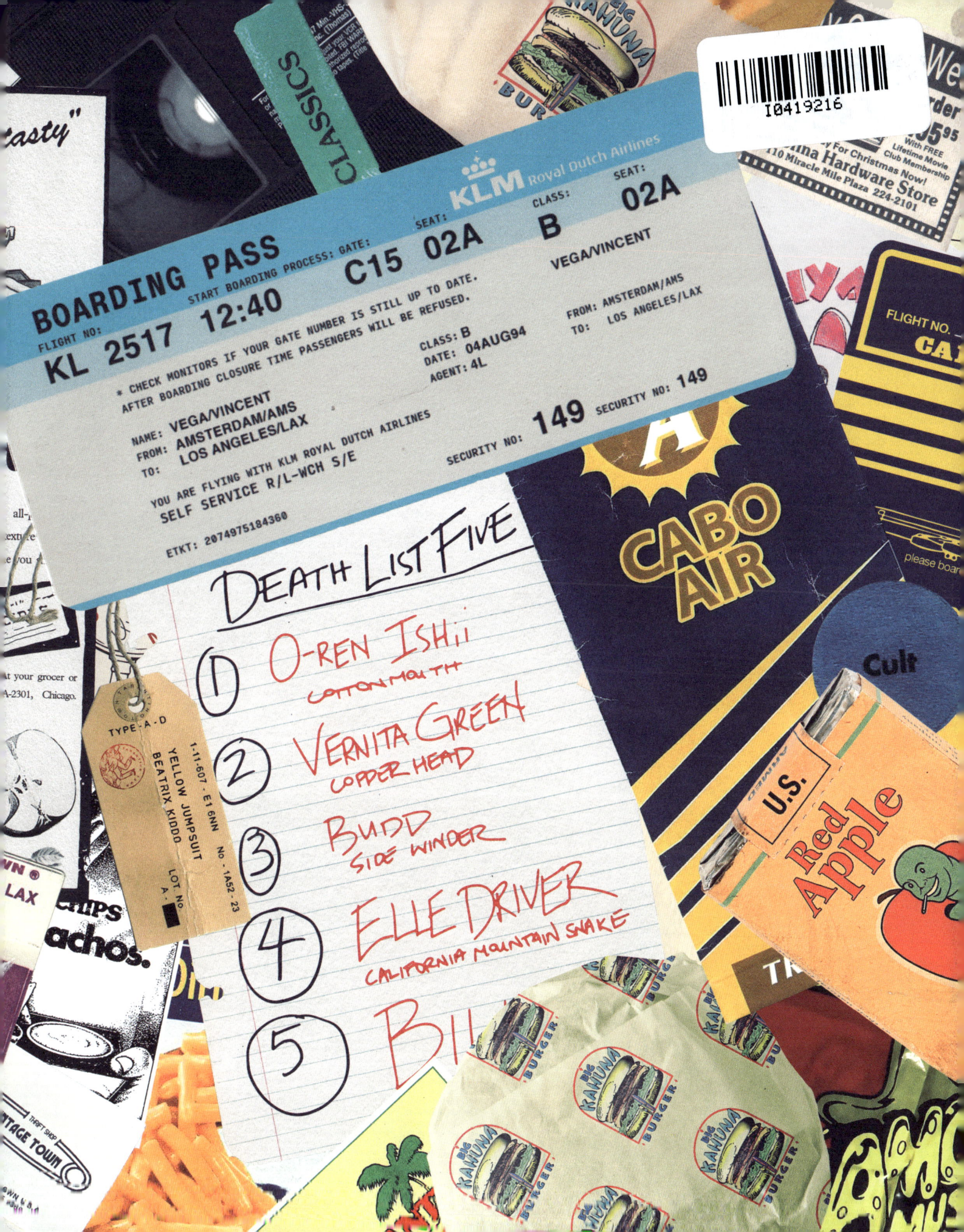

In memory
of Rick Dalton
1933–2023

Written and directed by
Camille Mathieu & Johan Chiaramonte

TARANTINO TOWN

PRESTEL

MUNICH · LONDON · NEW YORK

Tarantino Town	
CONTENTS	
Script	C. Mathieu
	J. Chiaramonte

200 pp.

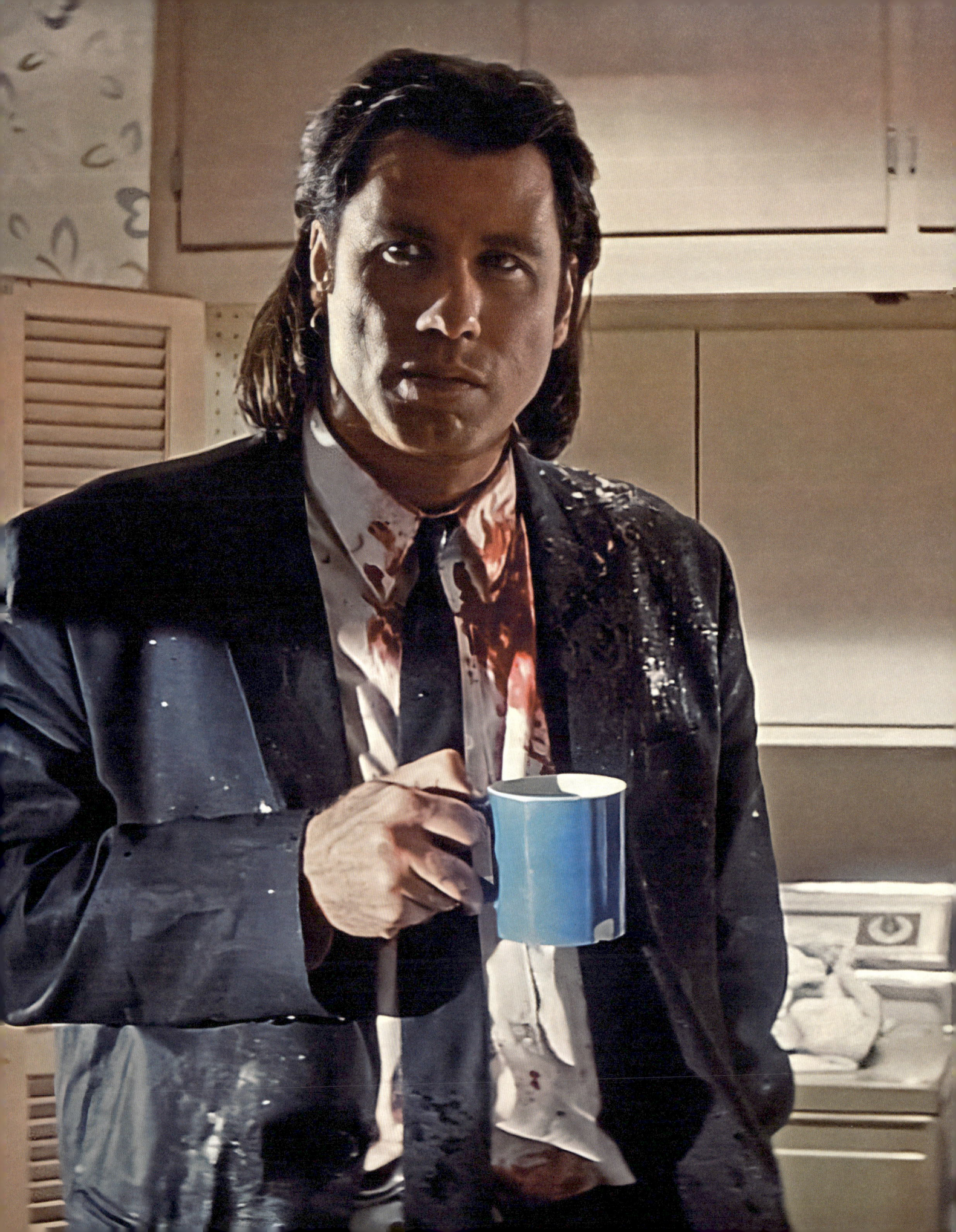

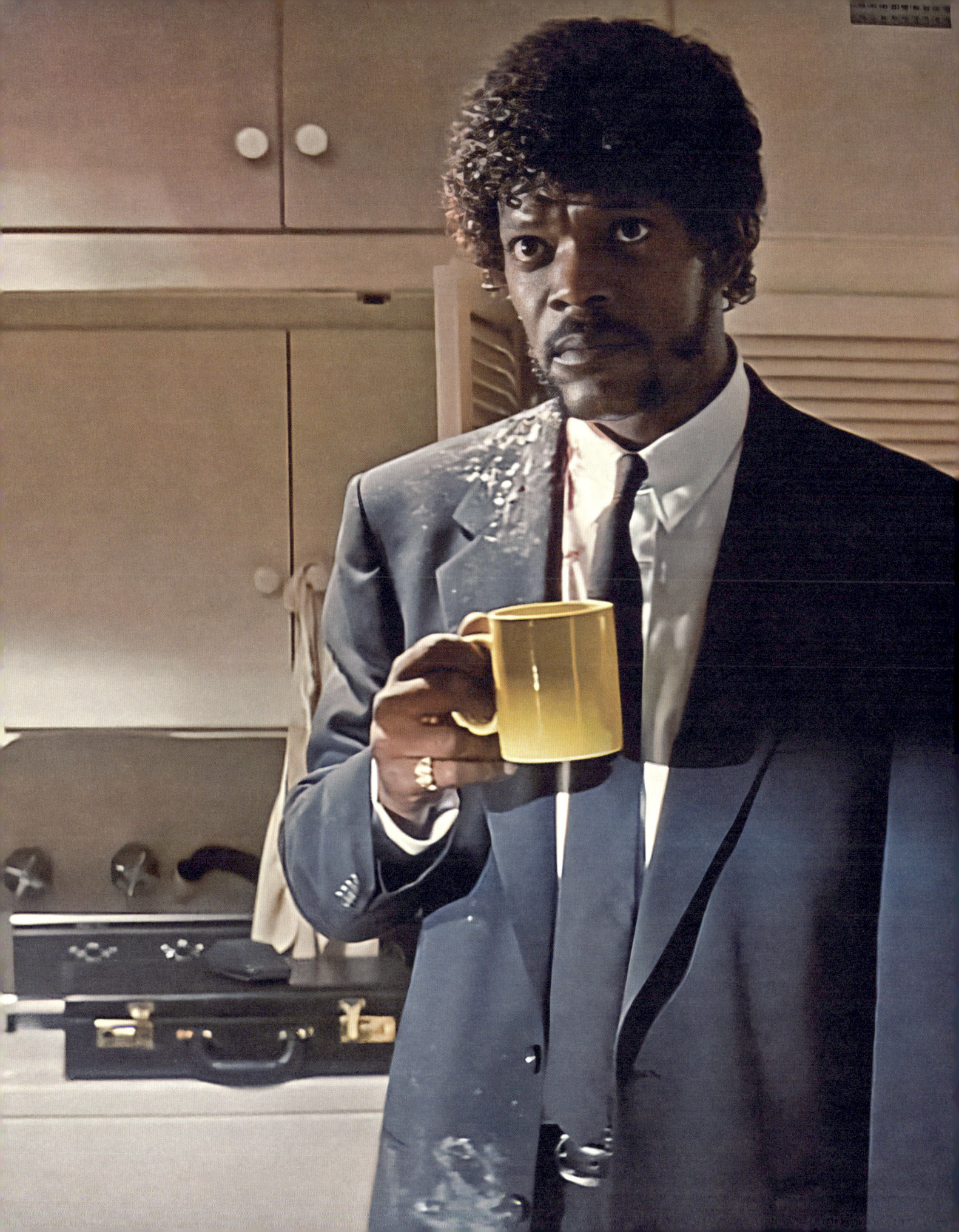

WELCOME!

★ ★

Welcome to Tarantino Town!

After driving for hours along a road bristling with spiky cactuses and agave plants, kicking up a cloud of dust behind you, here you are in Tarantino Town. It's a modest little town of several thousand inhabitants, smack in the middle of the desert a couple hundred miles from the City of Angels. Cut off from time by the heavy ring of desert around it, our town might come across as a little outdated to modern visitors, but it has all the conveniences you will need (the rooms in the motel are all equipped with state-of-the-art VCRs). While you're here, there are some must-see places to visit: Slide yourself onto one of the vinyl benches in the diner and tuck into a juicy Big Kahuna Burger, push open the door of the neighborhood bookstore or record store, slip into the movie theater to watch a single or double feature, or if you'd rather, hang around at the video store and see if you can unearth a couple of gems to shoot the breeze about with the local movie buffs. But before you go anywhere else, you'll need to pass by the only motel in town to check in for your stay. Don't be surprised if you bump into some familiar figures by the ice machine—these guys are regulars here…

Tarantino Town invites you to take an imaginary stroll through Quentin Tarantino's world so that you can start to map it out, crisscross your way through it, explore its furthest reaches, and perhaps unravel some of its mysteries. A fanatical movie buff all his life, from his days behind the counter in a video store in Hermosa Beach to present-day Hollywood Hills, Quentin Tarantino has created a body of work that is truly pop, iconoclastic, awash with references which see exploitation movies sit alongside cinema greats.

To help guide you through the maze of scenes, details, and influences that fill the director's work, *Tarantino Town* throws open the doors of an imaginary town devoted to it.

The volume you are holding in your hands is a guidebook
to Tarantino Town. Pick up a map from the tourist office,
but don't worry: You won't have any trouble finding
your way around our little town. Don't hesitate to ditch
our suggested itinerary and wander freely from one point
to another, because just like the director himself,
here in Tarantino Town we don't have any qualms about
upsetting chronological order. Here, what we're interested
in is two-piece suits, dodgy gangsters, old pulp fiction
books, videocassettes, Japanese pop, packs of cigarettes,
vanilla milkshakes, Elvis Presley, and America—
and most importantly of all, film.

But don't let us hold you up any longer on the outskirts
of town. Turn on the ignition, insert your best retro
mixtape into the cassette player, and head off
on a trip you won't forget in a hurry!

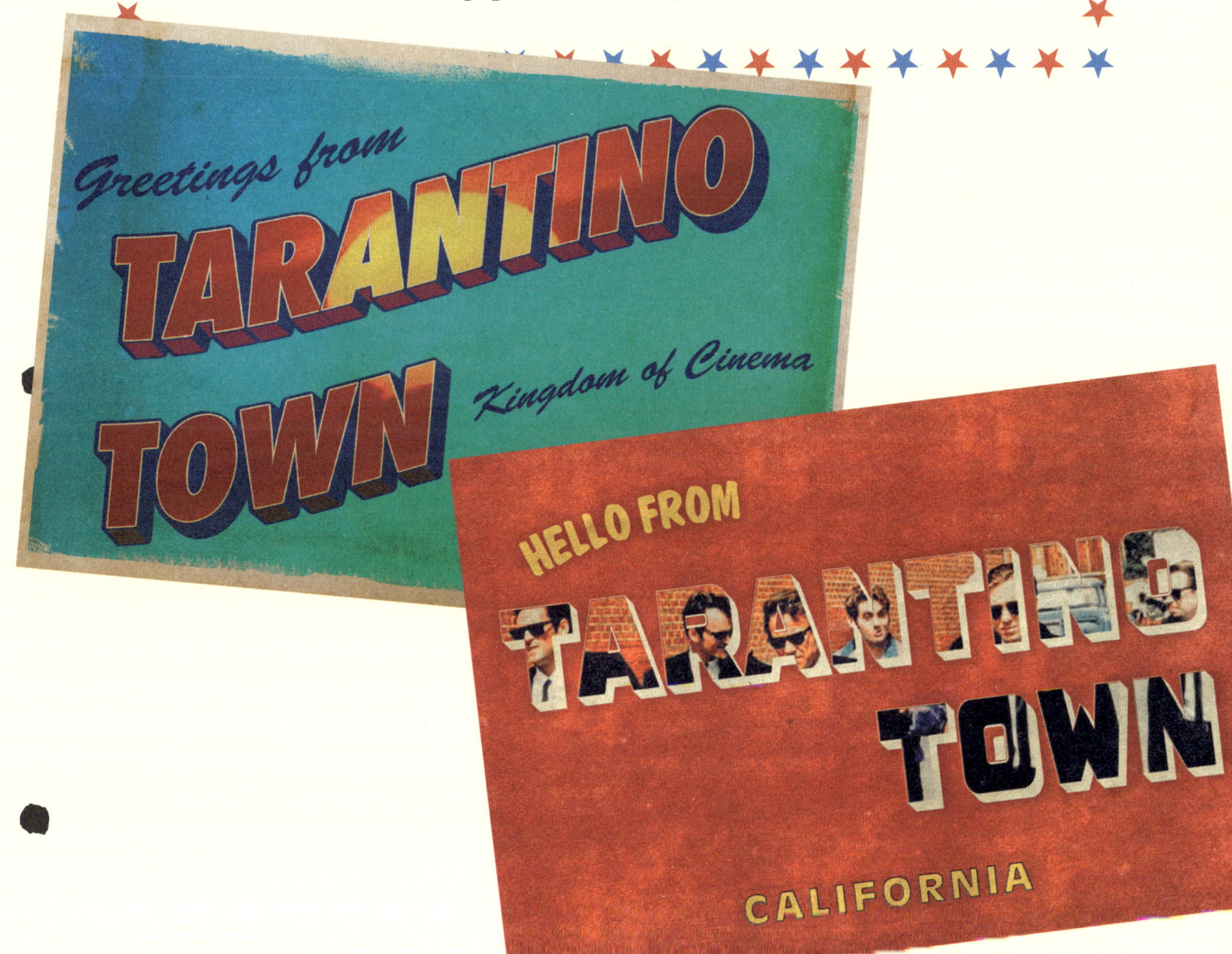

I
The Thrift Store

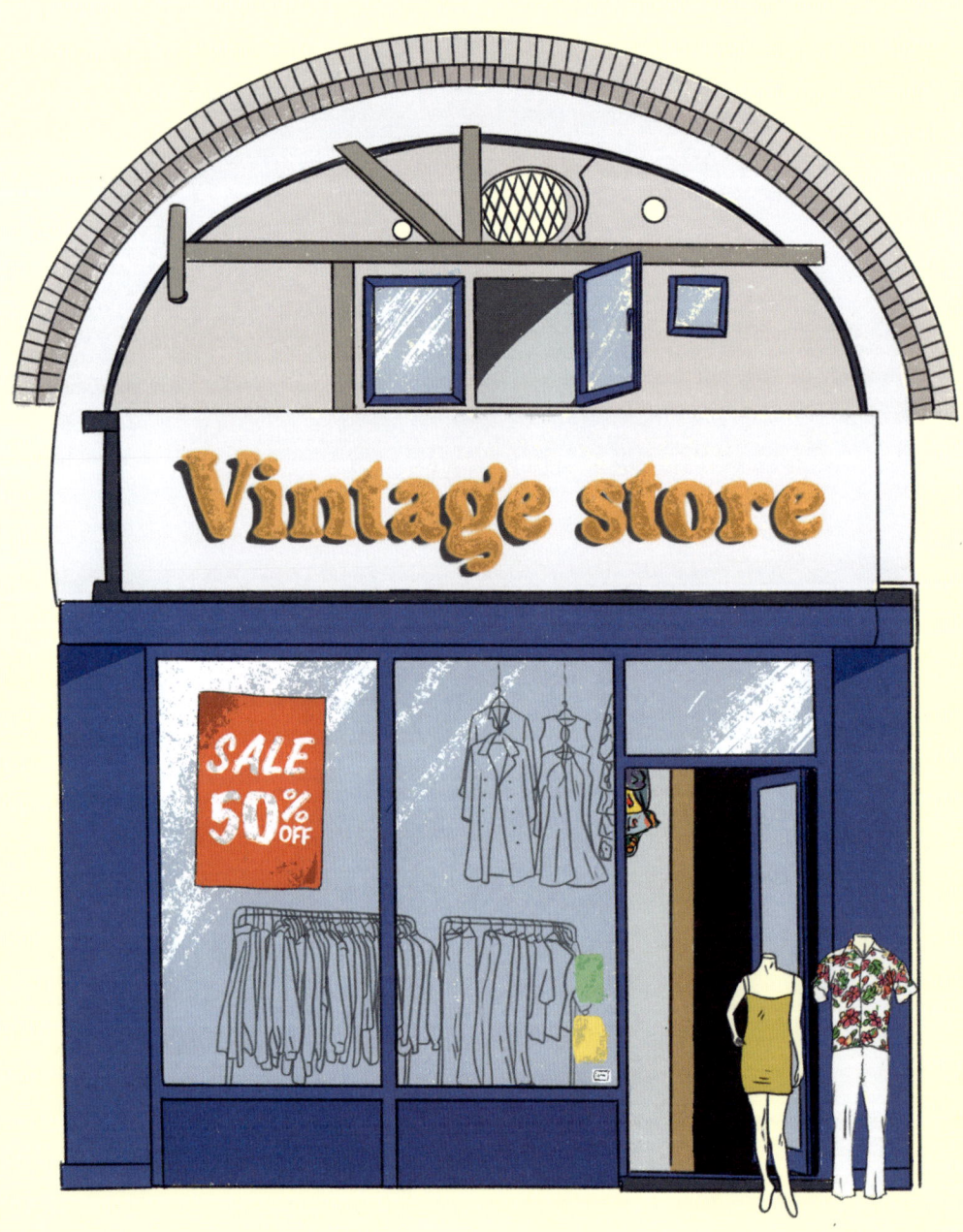

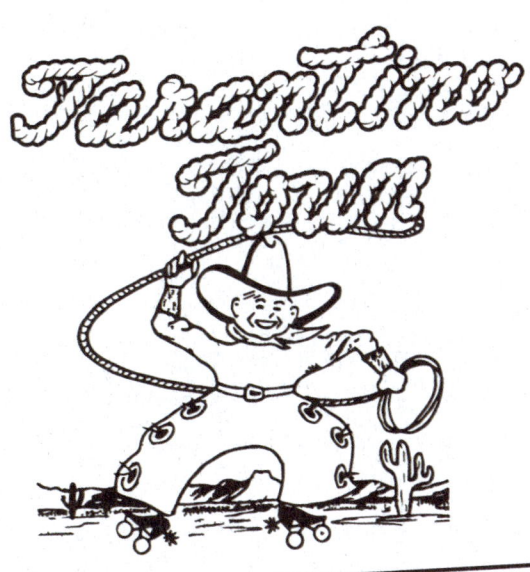

Telephone Bi. 6-2301

VINTAGE STORE
11000 VICTORY BLVD.
NORTH TARANTINO TOWN
U.S.A

BELTS - BOOTS

BUCKLES - HATS

SUITS - JACKETS

When you first arrive in Tarantino Town, there is one place you simply have to stop by. You'll find everything you need to blend in with the local color here: quality fabrics, accessories, more or less matching suits, Hawaiian shirts, and, hanging between a couple of T-shirts with nerdy slogans, an iconic yellow jumpsuit. Even though everything is secondhand and may not have been ironed in a while, the selection on offer is sharp and carefully chosen. There's nothing random about the way Quentin Tarantino dresses his characters: He builds in references with the precision of the Bride wielding her sword, conjuring up iconic outfits that immediately enter pop culture's hall of fame. *"None of my costume designers have ever been nominated for an Oscar,"* the director complained before his first costume design nomination in 2020. *"But we do have something else: We have Halloween parties… To tell you the truth, I've always considered that maybe the greatest award."*[1] Luckily, in Tarantino Town, there's no need to wait until Halloween to dress up like Mia Wallace or play at being "reservoir dogs." Here, everyone dresses Tarantino-style: It may not always be the height of fashion, but you can be sure to look the part when you're out strutting your stuff on the sidewalk. As Jules Winnfield would say, there's nothing like it for getting into character.

1- Nigel M. Smith, "Quentin Tarantino Complains the Oscars Never Recognise His Film's Costumes," *The Guardian*, February 24, 2016.

THE RESERVOIR DOGS SUITS

Dressed to Kill

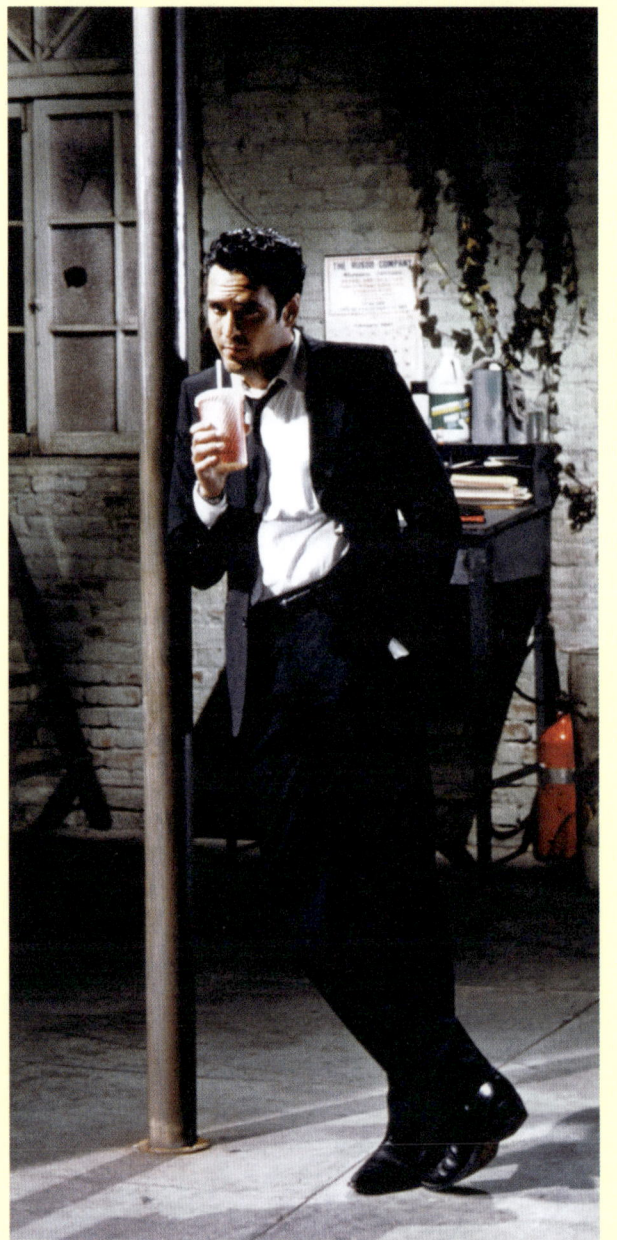

These are Quentin Tarantino's men in black. After a breakfast scene full of talk, Tarantino's first movie opens with this pack of "reservoir dogs" stepping out jauntily to the cool rhythm of an old George Baker Selection hit, "Little Green Bag," resurrected from 1969 to be given a dose of cult status. The characters were immediately "iconized"—and not only as a result of the combined effect of the slow motion and the incomparable baseline of the soundtrack, but also thanks to the image these tall figures cut in their black suits, which even went so far as to inspire the logo for Quentin Tarantino's production company.

When our gangsters finally stop their gassing and step outside, they walk with an easy, nonchalant gait, slipping on their shades, chewing idly on a toothpick or spewing out wreaths of cigarette smoke. With their suits and ties, close formation, and casual air, they recapture the image of the Rat Pack walking toward the final credits in *Ocean's Eleven* (1960), in which Frank Sinatra, Dean Martin, Sammy Davis Jr., and their associates played another gang of robbers—one targeting casinos rather than diamond dealers. But there aren't any rats here (or perhaps there is one, in the "sneak" sense of the word). Rather, it's a whole pack of dogs who have yet to show their teeth. They're impassive, displaying the cold-blooded composure of killers through the

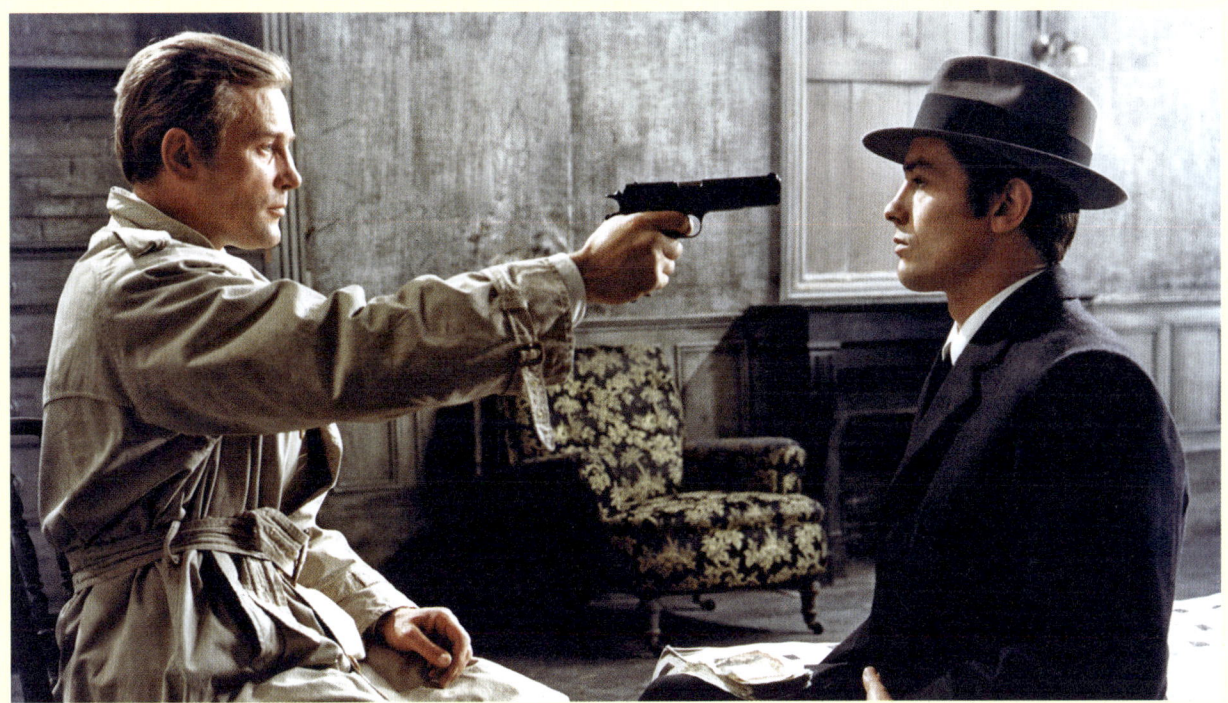

killer suits they've got on, "*their armor*," as Tarantino likes to call it. By donning these black suits they're dressing up as professional criminals. Our characters constantly go on about professionalism, laying down codes of behavior for gangsters and proudly protecting their reputations. The secret is to keep a clear head. However, Mr. White never misses a chance to make a blunder, and as the one who ought to be the most accomplished of the lot, he proves in the end to be the most fallible.

Backstage, Tarantino would shower his costume designer, Betsy Heimann, with pictures from French-style film noir movies featuring cool, impeccably turned-out gangsters, like Alain Delon in Jean-Pierre Melville's films. Recognizing the almost fetishistic power of the outfits, Tarantino was eager to incorporate this quintessentially devilish Melville ingredient, as John Woo had done before him in the 1980s, in a kind of backward homage to the man they called "*the most American of French directors.*" "*I like the way certain directors approach genre and try*

and mythologize it and make it their own," the director declared. "*Jean-Pierre Melville… he'd take genre stories from Warner Brothers' heyday and then kind of do it in his French style… He had a sense of style for his characters, with their snap-brim fedoras, their trench coats and their raincoats. Yeah, Bogart wore that kind of stuff, but man, when you see Belmondo wear it and when you see Alain Delon wear it, wow, OK, it has this specific look, and that became the suit of armor for his characters. And then… we had John Woo doing his version of gangster stuff and yeah, he's taking from Melville… but… John Woo's characters had their own suit of clothing, and their own glasses, and the way they would put a match in their mouth or whatever. So when I came along, it was my thing… to establish my own sense of style and my own sense of… a coat of armor for them. And mine was the black suits.*"[1]

The choice of costume was not based purely on aesthetics, of course. With a limited budget of ten thousand dollars, Betsy Heimann was pragmatic: "*We're talking about*

1- "Quentin Tarantino on 'The Black Suits of Armor' in His Films," *American Film Institute*, YouTube, 2010.

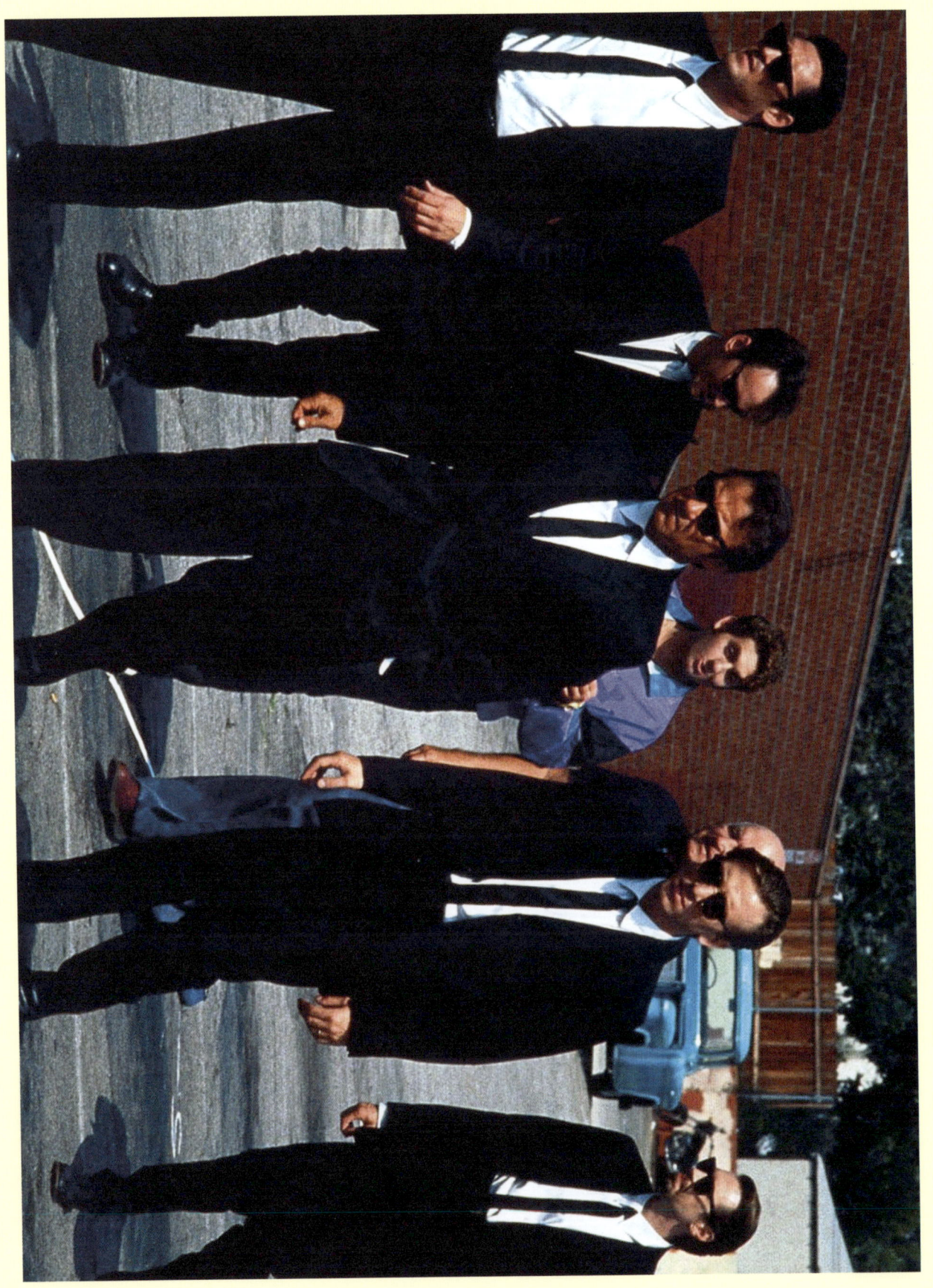

guys who have just got out of jail and want to be anonymous. What can they do? They could go to a thrift store, buy a black suit, a white shirt and a tie, and they could afford it."[2] To dress all these fine people—and to include extra suits to allow for all the costumes that were going to end up soaked in blood— Heimann rummaged through the thrift stores and dime stores in West Hollywood. She scoured the aisles, picking up individual pieces which she put together to create suits, or sometimes what might pass at first glance as a suit, but was actually a pair of black jeans and a navy-blue jacket. Only Harvey Keitel, who knew the fashion designer Agnès B. personally, was given a suit worthy of the name, which confirmed his status on the screen as leader of the pack. There is an almost narrative element to the differences in the characters' suits which speaks to the director's intuitive approach to characterization. The elegant Mr. White establishes himself at the top of the hierarchy as the father figure in the group. Mr. Pink (Steve Buscemi) sports a secondhand jacket and black denim pants, further highlighting the fact that he's broke, hinted at in his grudging reluctance to leave a tip a few minutes before. The oversize shoulders on the jacket Mr. Brown (Tarantino) wears underline his loud, flashy character, incapable of keeping a low profile. By contrast, Vic Vega, alias Mr. Blonde (Michael Madsen), projects a calm appearance which masks a wild temper. This ambivalence is hinted at in the fact that he wears cowboy boots with his suit, which is enough to conjure up the image of an outlaw. There is a similar touch of the cowboy in the bolo tie Vega's presumed brother Vincent wears in *Pulp Fiction,* while Jules Winnfield's narrow collar conversely casts him rather as a preacher. A few details, and the broad lines of the characters are already there.

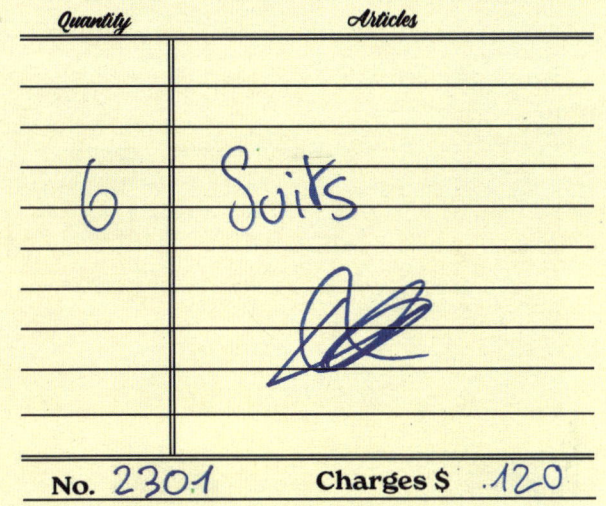

In *Reservoir Dogs,* however, these differences diminish and disappear in the face of the group effect. For a few seconds, captured in slow motion rather than in the heat of the action—as if to intimate to us that what transpires will have everything to do with the characters' personalities and precious little to do with the robbery, which, by the way, is studiously avoided—they form a single unified group. Of course, the apparent harmony is deceptive, as much in form, with their mismatched costumes, as in substance, since the movie is a vast exercise in breaking down the unity of the group. But what does it matter in this moment if there are traitors among the faithful? Here they are, all of them bound together by the strength of their armor. And yet there most definitely is a wolf hidden in the middle of the pack of dogs. His suit is as black as those of his comrades, his tongue as ready as theirs, his expression just as cool behind his shades, and his shirt as immaculately white. For now, at least. •

2- Nick Pope, "'Reservoir Dogs' and 'Pulp Fiction': The History Behind the Iconic Black Suits," *Esquire,* October 23, 2019.

THE FLIGHT ATTENDANT'S UNIFORM

Power Games

In the aisles of the Tarantino Town thrift store, sandwiched between two men's-cut black suits and sitting neatly on its hanger, is a bright royal-blue woman's suit. Jackie Brown, the eponymous heroine of Tarantino's movie, wears this suit with conventional elegance. Her thick hair is impeccably styled, a scarf with orange stripes is modishly tied around her neck, and she has unremarkable pearl earrings, classic bright-red polished nails, and mid-heel shoes: Everything about Jackie's uniform is conventionally feminine, controlled, and reassuring. With its pencil skirt and jacket with padded shoulders (albeit a long way from the excessive shoulder pads which epitomized power dressing in the previous decade), the uniform is designed to accomplish two contrasting objectives: on one hand, to ensure that the flight attendant is immediately recognizable at all times amid the throngs of travelers in transit, and on the other, to do the opposite and downplay her as a woman, making her blend into the background. It is probably not a coincidence that in the movie's opening sequence the azure blue of her uniform merges with the blue of the mosaic lining the airport halls. Jackie Brown comes across to us from the start as a woman who has been rendered invisible as much by her uniform as by the color of her skin or her age—holding up a mirror, perhaps, to the Hollywood movie industry, which is always so quick to discount its actresses. But Jackie plans to make good use of this general disregard.

She's in trouble: Having been exploiting her appearance as a flight attendant to play at cash smuggling, she finds herself pinioned between a dangerous arms trafficker and a pair of determined cops. Caught red-handed, manipulated from all sides, she will have to choose between going to jail and collaborating with the forces of law and order—and potentially paying a high price. Rather than choose the lesser of these two evils, she decides to dupe the lot of them. Fortunately for her, Jackie has a couple of tricks up her sleeve: She thinks on her feet, is as cool as a cucumber, and is constantly underestimated by her opponents.

Embroidered on the left sleeve of her uniform is a coral-red sun in a yellow circle with "CA" written across it in big white letters. This is the badge of the fictional airline she works for, Cabo Air, "*the shittiest little shuttle-fucking piece of shit Mexican airline that there is,*" as the LAPD cop comments. "*You didn't exactly set the world on fire, did you, Jackie?*" he quips sarcastically when she tells him how much she makes as a flight attendant for the airline. The humiliating interview carries on, with the other cop telling her, "*if I were a forty-four-year old Black woman desperately clinging on to this* one shitty little job I was fortunate enough to get, I don't think that I'd think I had a year to throw away [in prison]." For the two cops, Jackie is nothing more than a washed-up flight attendant, a pawn in a huge chess game who's going to help them bring down Ordell Robbie. Without ever giving the game away, Jackie sets about turning the tables on them.

In the power game she's playing, the handover scene in the Del Amo Mall is pivotal. The turning point is highlighted in a symbolic switch in Jackie's outfit. At the height of the operation, while she's cleverly manipulating both cops and gangsters, she allows herself the luxury of a change of style, going into a fitting room in the Billingsley department store and slipping on a black suit with slightly flared pants, a fitted jacket, shoulder pads, and a wide-collared white shirt. She comes out of the fitting room triumphant, and is met by the admiring salesclerk, who predicts that she will be the "*badass in the room.*" She looks at herself in the mirror, incredulous at the transformation she sees. In her flight attendant's uniform, Jackie fit into a mold, conforming out of necessity to outside expectations and images of her, underestimated, invisible, accepting her role as what people saw her as being. When she puts on this "black suit of armor" that Tarantino talks about, she embarks on a symbolic transition, affirming her own power in a world run by men. In her suit, the female equivalent of the Tarantino gangster uniform, Jackie no longer has any need to envy the gangsters in *Reservoir Dogs* or other hard-boiled characters in the director's world: She's now one of the pack. "*I decided to wear the suit,*" she tells the salesclerk, her old blue uniform bundled into her bag. Power has well and truly changed hands. •

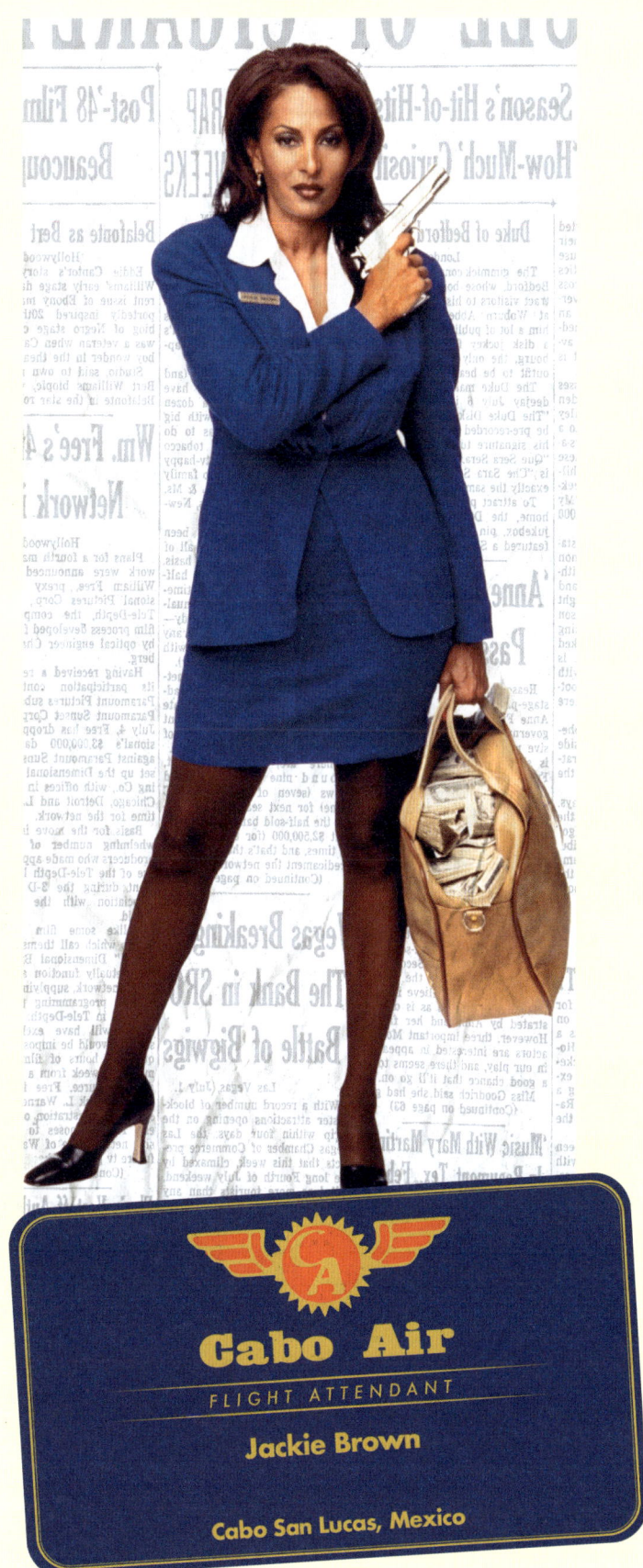

Cabo Air

FLIGHT ATTENDANT

Jackie Brown

Cabo San Lucas, Mexico

THE KILL BILL JUMPSUIT

The Bride Wore Yellow

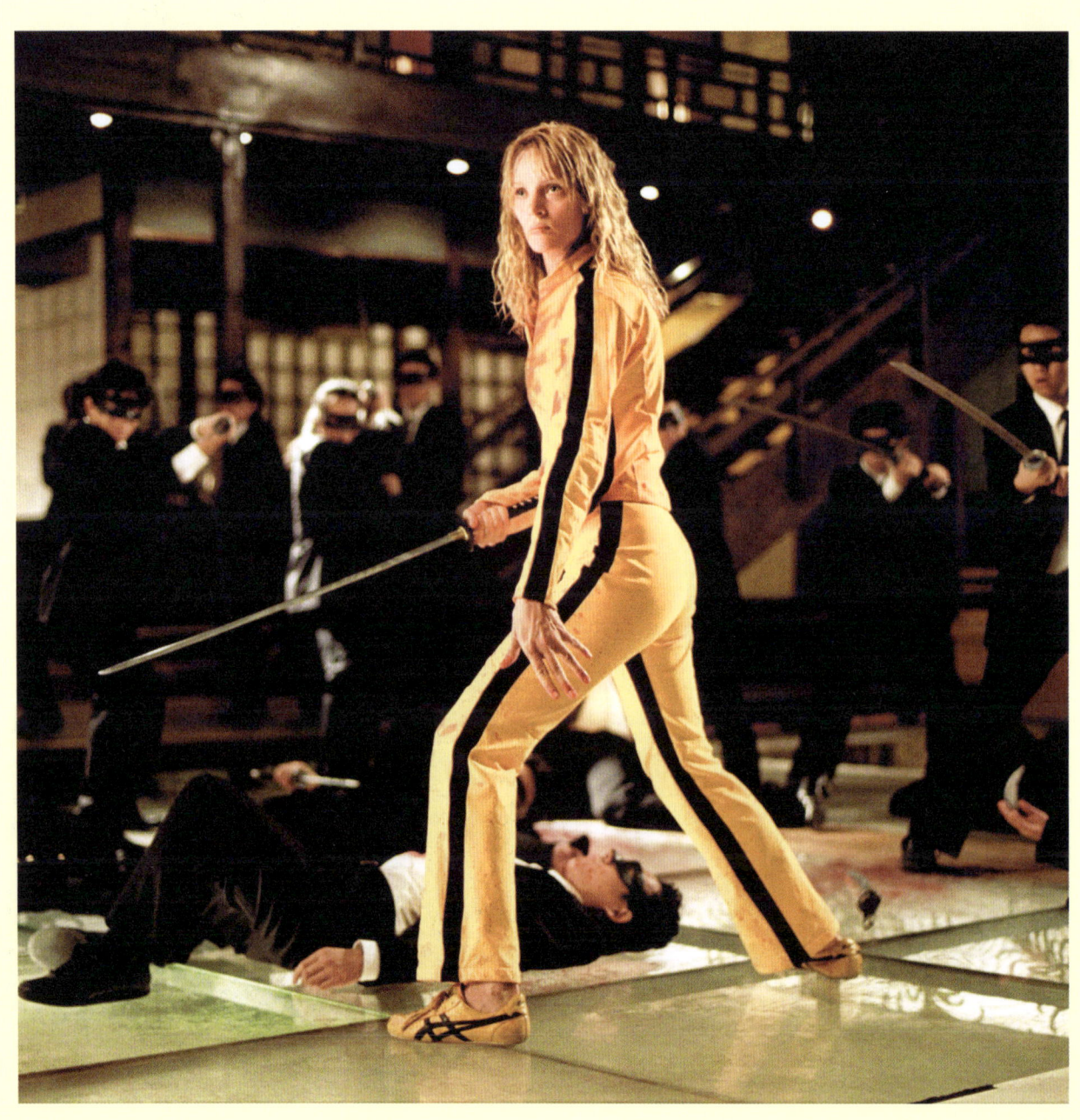

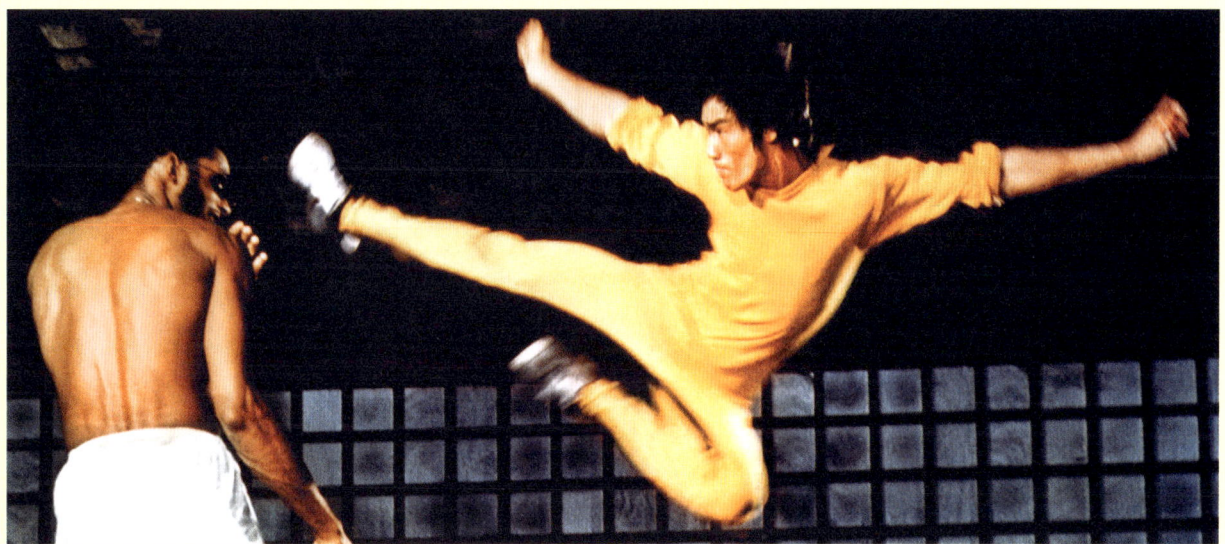

*K*ill Bill boasts perhaps the biggest icon to be found in any of Quentin Tarantino's movies. We're not talking about Uma Thurman, but about the lethal yellow outfit which Beatrix Kiddo puts on like a second skin before throwing herself into one of the most unrealistic fight sequences in Tarantino's oeuvre. First off, there is the unforgettable yellow leather motorcycle suit with its patches, which is given a starring role on the poster for the movie. Once in the arena, the leathers give way to the iconic yellow tracksuit with broad black stripes, borrowed straight from none other than Billy Lo—Bruce Lee—in *Game of Death*. On her feet (highly fetishized here, as elsewhere in Tarantino's films), she has a matching pair of light Onitsuka Tiger Mexico 66 shoes that are in every way identical to the ones worn by the "Little Dragon" in his posthumous movie. The Japanese brand had stopped production of these sneakers but resurrected them because the movie required them. Nothing here is in any way random. Armed with her lethal katana, Beatrix dons her tracksuit as a warrior does his armor: turned into a two-piece suit rather than Lee's original one-piece and given slightly flared sleeves but otherwise barely altered,

this androgynous outfit more than holds its own in a sea of catsuit-clad heroines and offers a less obviously gendered take on female action heroes. What interests costume designer Catherine Thomas here is the idea of reappropriating what is supposedly a male form of power: "*There's definitely this trope of the female hero that's always in this very sexy, badass [outfit]. I kind of wanted to play with the gender part of it—her embodying the boys club and borrowing from the boys, and taking that strength and using it… Borrowing from the boys can be really powerful because you're taking something as a woman, and you're switching it around.*"[1]

A warrior's battledress is also a powerful manifestation of their standing. In this way, battle begins even before the first blow is struck. By adopting Lee's most iconic outfit, Beatrix is declaring that what is coming is a yellow kung fu fight. Over and above any fetishistic value it may have for Tarantino, the tracksuit has the force of a movie relic and exemplifies the enormous power Tarantino confers on visual imagery. Steeped in such referential force, the costume acts as a totem. Confronting the Bride are the Crazy 88, O-Ren Ishii's personal army,

1- Hannah Jackson, "Why the *Kill Bill* Costumes Still Hit, 20 Years Later," *Vogue*, October 10, 2023.

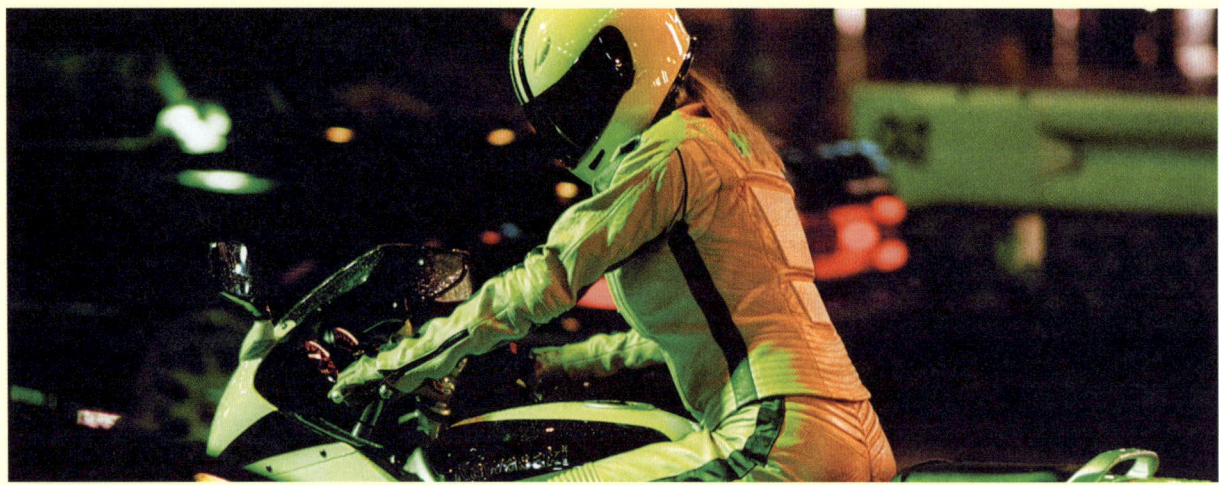

who adopt another item associated with Lee: the black mask Kato wears in the *Green Hornet* series. Effectively, then, this is a face-off between two different incarnations of Bruce Lee. On one hand is Kato—eternal lieutenant and sidekick to the vigilante after whom the series is named—who dates back to an early point in Lee's career and appears here multiplied eighty-eight-fold—or perhaps not quite that, since Bill tells us later that the Crazy 88 don't actually run to that many. On the other is Billy Lo, the hero of Lee's unfinished movie, *Game of Death*, and obviously his final screen appearance, who remains an unbeaten champion forever immortalized in his yellow tracksuit, undoubtedly foreshadowing the outcome of the fight which grips us here.

This yellow outfit is arguably one of the most direct allusions in a movie which blends traditions and references liberally, drawing from Spaghetti Westerns one minute and from Japanese *Chambara* sword-fighting movies, kung fu, or anime the next, collaging them together as only the director knows how. In the two-parter *Kill Bill* we are thrust into Quentin Tarantino's movie-movie universe, cast adrift from the shores of reality to which his previous films belonged and left to navigate the depths of pure movie fiction. We find ourselves immersed in the world of movies, in a realm of images where blood spurts in great sprays of crimson, sound effects are outrageously stylized, there is no limit to the way genres can be twisted, and all cinema legends are invited to join the party.

So when the Bride shows up at the House of Blue Leaves, it's as a killer bee—a metaphor Bill takes up again later—in that showy outfit, soon to be soaked in blood. And yet, just like a black mamba dangerously slithering close to the ground, Beatrix knows how to approach her prey silently. On her first stop in Japan, she uses her best acting skills to get through to the great man from Okinawa, Hattori Hanzō, and extract one of the mightiest of Japanese swords from him. Posing as an innocent tourist, she tops off her act by wearing a T-shirt emblazoned with "Okinawa Japan," of the kind we can readily imagine being peddled to eager holidaymakers en masse. This allows her to stay under the radar. But this evening, at the House of Blue Leaves, discretion is no longer the order of the day. The black mamba rears intimidatingly, head high, ready to strike. As she steps forward, we catch a glimpse of the underside of her yellow and black sneaker. Stamped on the rubber sole is a message—a creed, it could be said, which guides Beatrix Kiddo throughout her quest for revenge: "*Fuck you.*" •

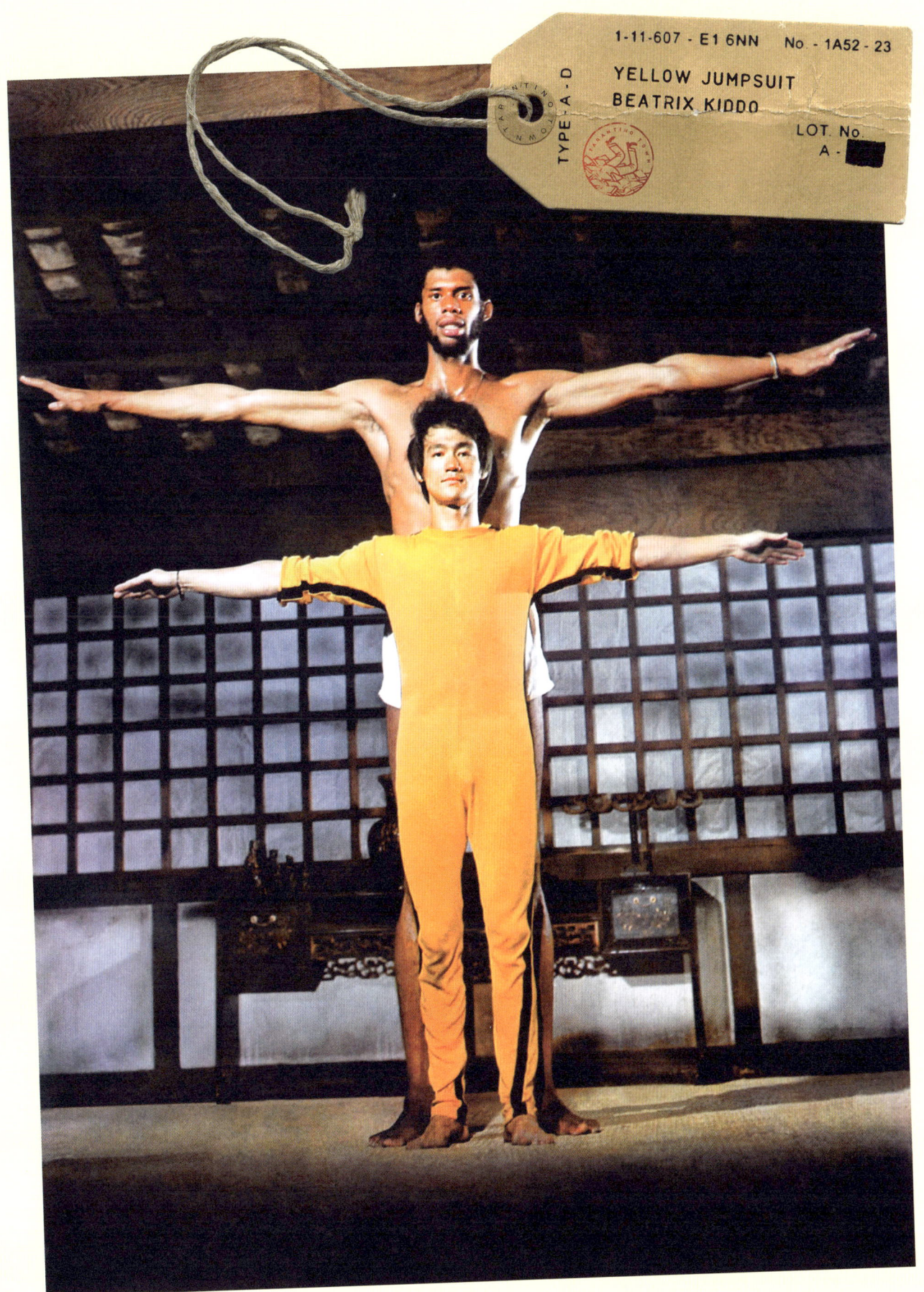

YELLOW JUMPSUIT
BEATRIX KIDDO

1-11-607 - E1 6NN   No - 1A52 - 23

TYPE-A-D

LOT. No.
A -

19

THE HAWAIIAN SHIRT

Tropical Fever

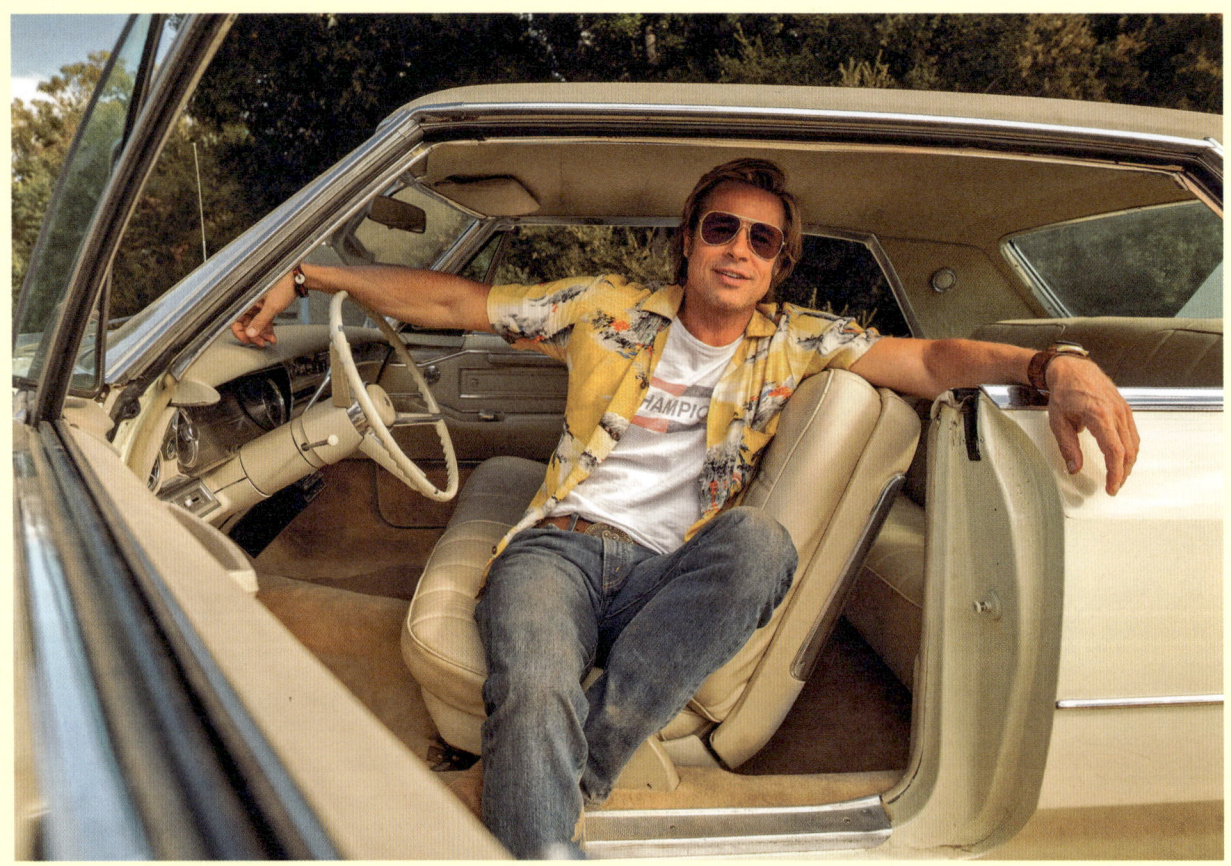

Deep red, ultramarine, with hibiscus flowers, birds of paradise, surfers, and coconut palms: The Hawaiian shirt comes in all colors and designs. It has carved out a special place for itself in the collective imagination and is still very much out there making a splash. Quentin Tarantino is not about to suggest that this should change. Short-sleeved, loose fitting, made of light cotton with a low-cut collar, designed to suit the bright California sun, Hawaiian shirts are not perhaps the most obvious choice for the gangsters and small-time hoodlums who inhabit our movie-buff director's world. And yet they appear regularly in QT's filmography. In *Reservoir Dogs*, Mr. Pink opts for a pale yellow version adorned with palm trees; in *True Romance*, Clarence wears a red one

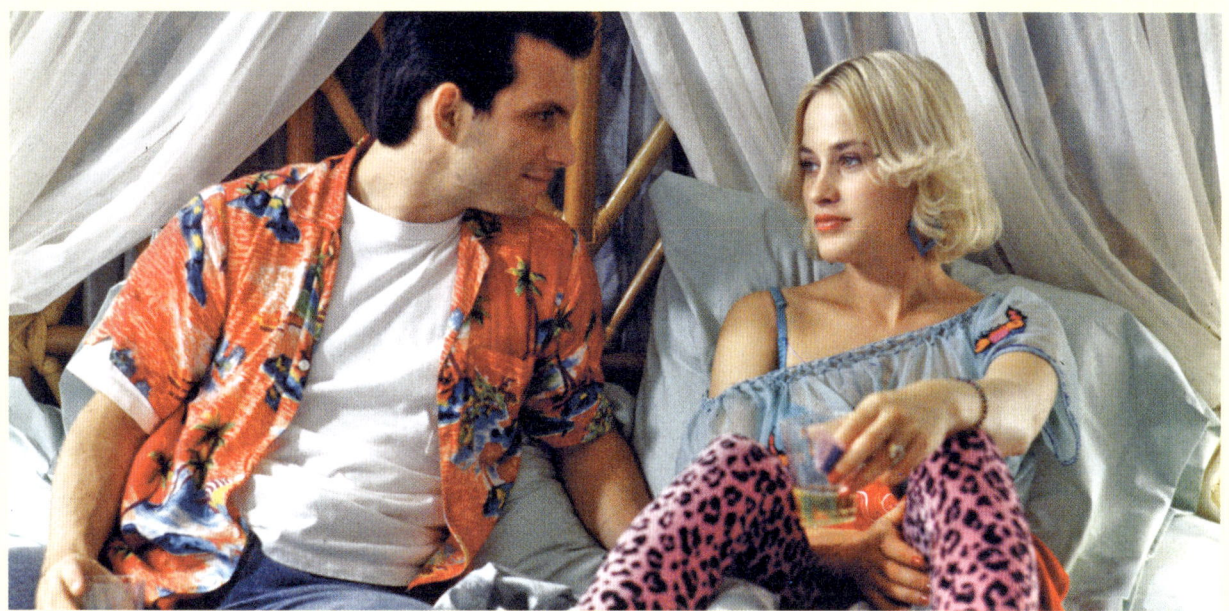

covered with idyllic beaches; at the start of *Pulp Fiction*, "Pumpkin" sports one during a spur-of-the-moment holdup. It's a thread that runs right through to *Once Upon a Time… in Hollywood*, where a Hawaiian shirt is Cliff Booth's go-to outfit, although he prefers his with quieter Japanese motifs. But make no mistake about it: There is more to these shirts than just a bit of vintage styling.

At the end of World War II the American imagination was captured by all things to do with the Pacific. The Hawaiian shirt definitely belongs to the "tiki pop" fever which took hold of the country in the fifties and sixties. As early as 1951, President Truman himself appeared on the cover of *Life* magazine looking as proud as a peacock in a Hawaiian shirt covered with birds. In everything from architecture to cooking, interior design to fashion, cultural appropriation boomed. Everyone wanted their bit of the Polynesian dream, so much so that Tiki deities gradually

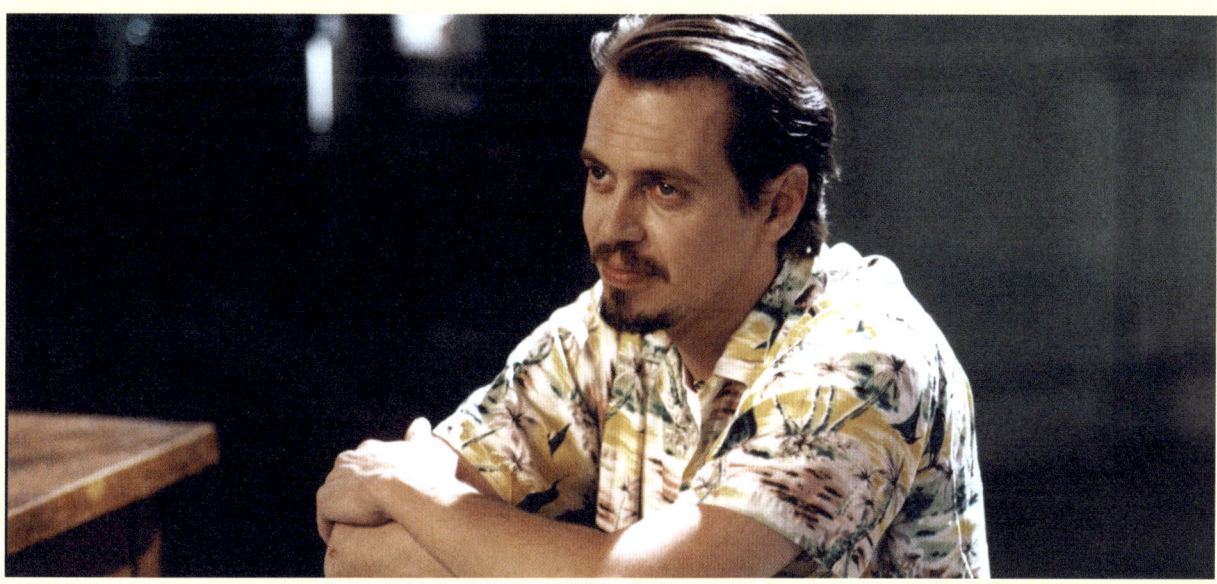

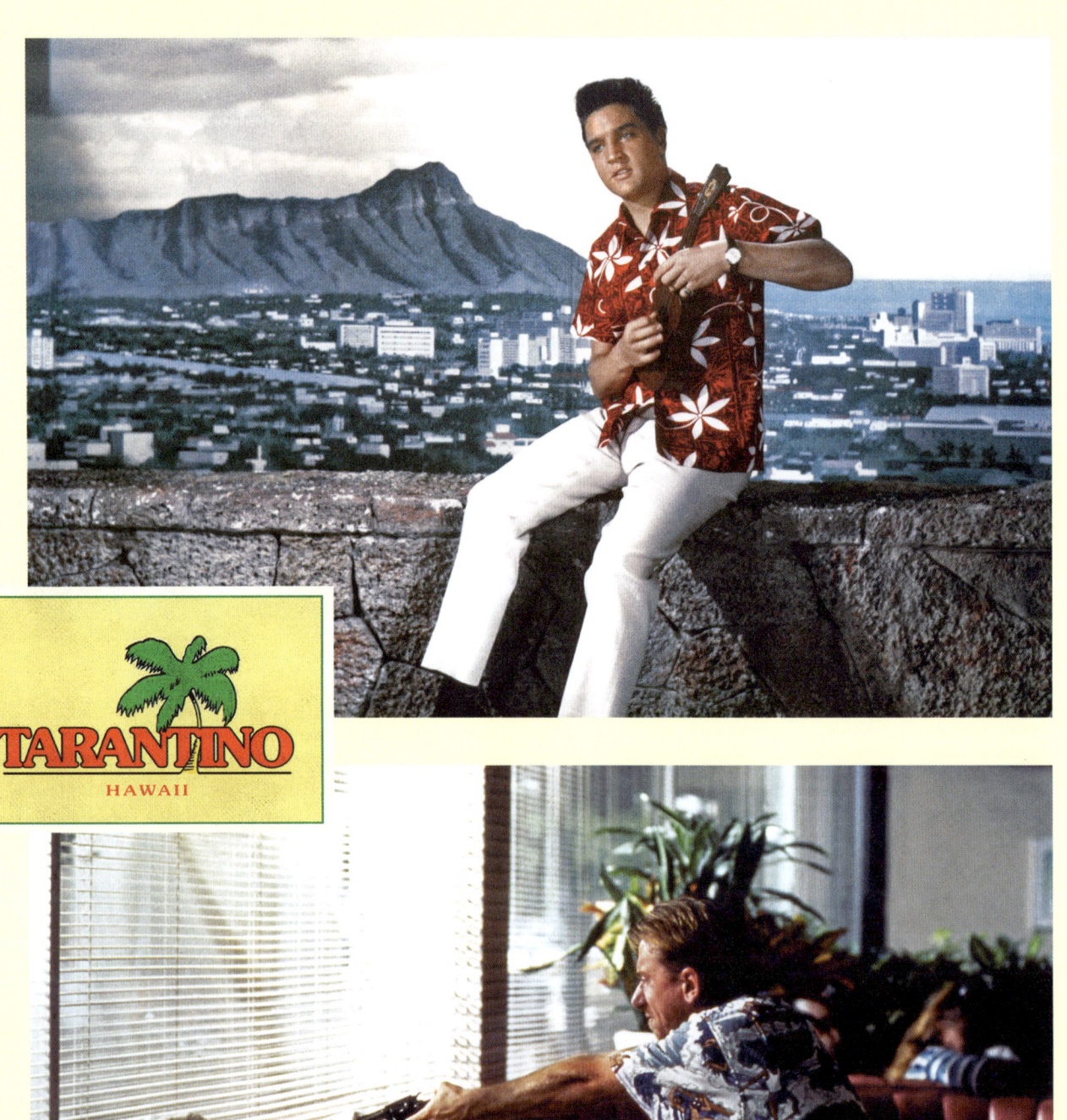

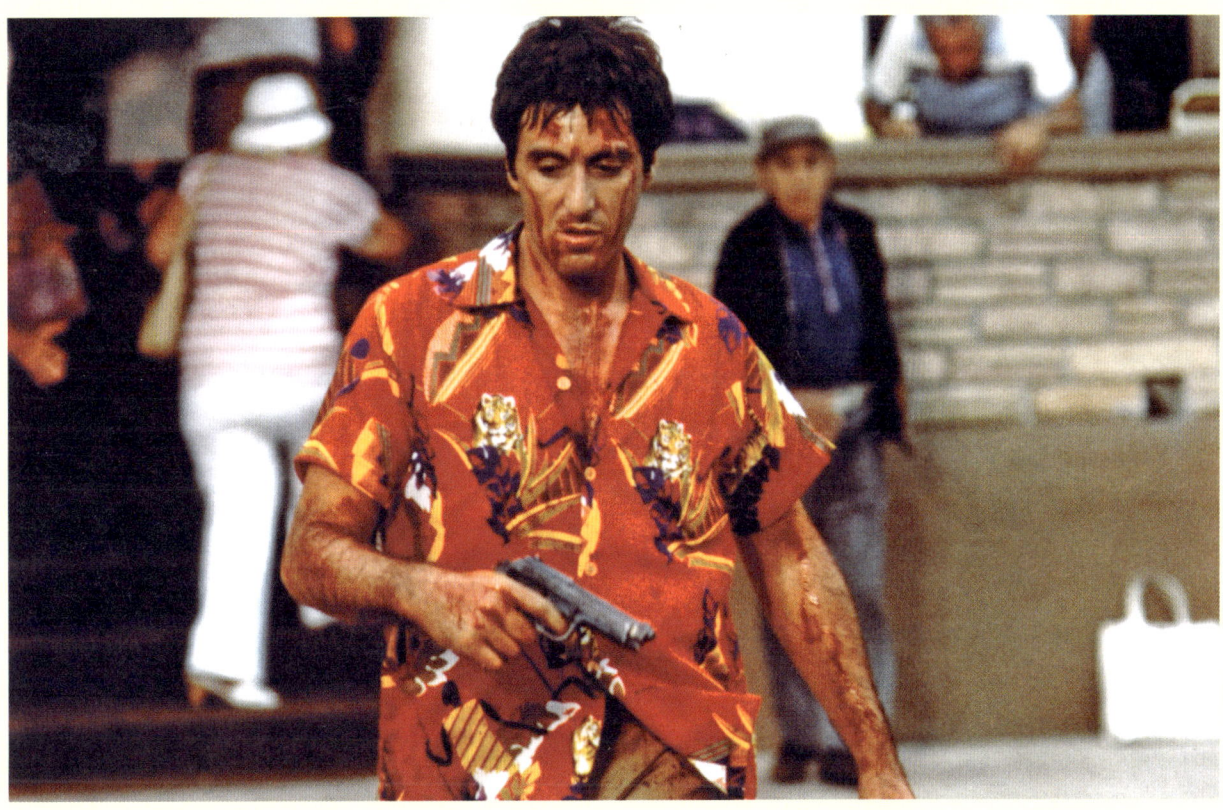

became tantamount to consumerist gods on the other side of the Atlantic. Amid the proliferation of imitation objects, what caught people's eye was the Hawaiian shirt. Hawaii's entry into the United States as the fiftieth state did nothing to lessen the fever. In 1961's *Blue Hawaii*, Elvis Presley sported a shirt with a little more panache than President Truman had, pairing it boldly with a flower garland and a ukulele, the embodiment of a postwar American ideal of leisure combined with a touch of the exotic. But the rise of counterculture movements in the sixties and seventies heralded the end of "tiki" style, which now seemed over-artificial and tinged with colonialism.

Once the squeaky-clean embodiment of a particular form of American good humor, the Hawaiian shirt had become somewhat cheesy by the turn of the eighties (despite private investigator Magnum's best efforts to rehabilitate it). Against all odds, it found its way into the wardrobes of mafiosi, crooks, and losers of all kinds. Sported by the likes of Max Cady in *Cape Fear* and Tyler Durden in *Fight Club*, not to mention the hallucinating duo in *Fear and Loathing in Las Vegas*, the Hawaiian shirt became increasingly disreputable. The figure of Tony Montana, who blasted his way into the eighties under the direction of Brian De Palma, was undoubtedly primarily to blame. Bent on profoundly distorting the idea of the American dream, *Scarface* appropriated this wholesome, carefree motif and tarnished it for good.

On Tony Montana's shoulders, the once clean-cut Hawaiian shirt is disheveled and soaked in blood, a clear metaphor for a paradise lost, never to be regained. It is ready, in short, to enter Tarantino's universe, full of all these magnificent losers and oddballs, where the American dream is constantly repeated, alluded to, chewed over ad infinitum, and both shattered and celebrated in a single movement. •

STUNTMAN MIKE'S JACKET

Old School

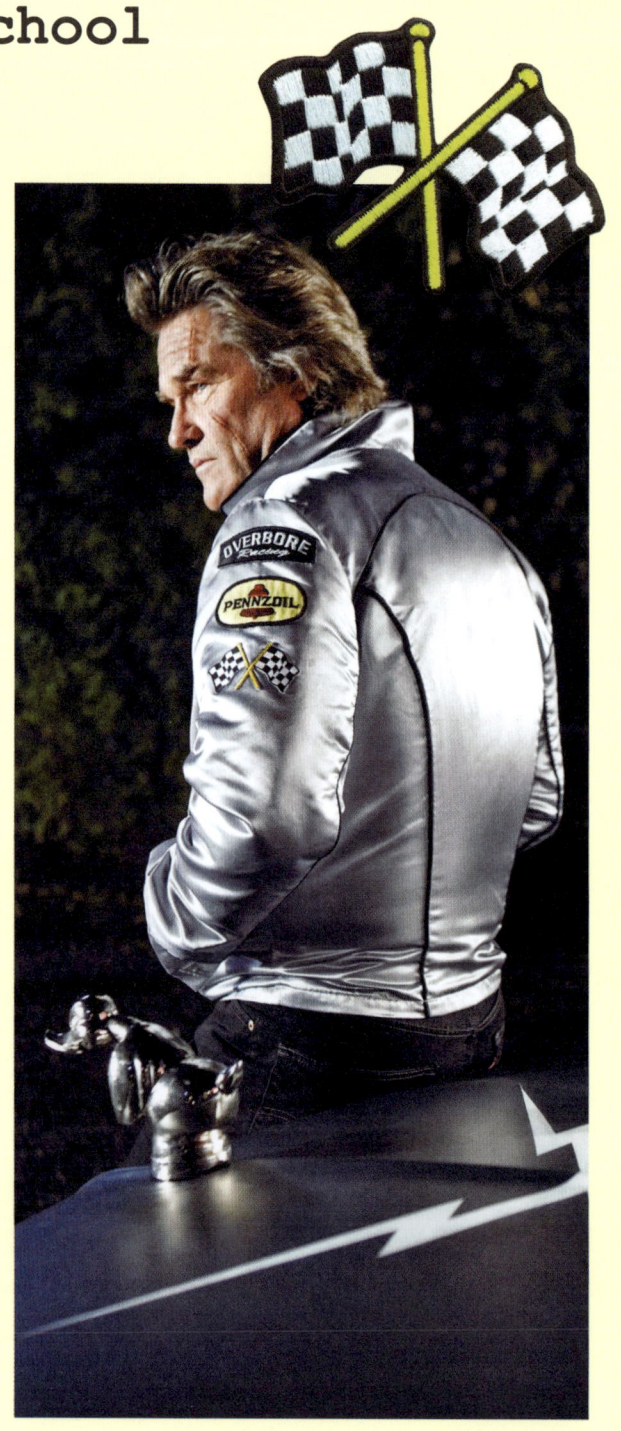

It's a narrow-cut jacket made of gray satin shot with silver, reminiscent of old race car drivers' jackets, covered with patches and sponsors' logos of all kinds. Like those earlier racing jackets, Stuntman Mike's jacket has patches sewn all over it with the names of gas companies—Husky, Pennzoil, Derby—or interlocking checkered racing flags. On the back of the jacket a broad badge with the words "ICY HOT" runs across the stuntman's shoulders in letters that go from icy blue to fiery red. It's the logo of an ointment for muscle pain relief which Stuntman Mike probably applies liberally between stunts, but it could equally well tell us something about his dangerously ambivalent nature…

Under his jacket, which he wears with the collar proudly turned up, he sports a body-hugging black T-shirt tucked into a pair of dark jeans, set off with flashy matching turquoise jewelry, a leather cuff watch, and a pair of boots. Everything about the way Stuntman Mike looks, from his outdated outfit to his lion-like head of hair streaked with gray, reads old-school virility of a kind that has long since been consigned to history by the group of kids fooling around at the back of the Texas Chili Parlor in *Death Proof*. This tough display of manliness verging on cheesy takes on a darker hue when a shaft of light reveals the long scar which runs down the left side of Stuntman Mike's face, over his steely blue eye.

Propped at the bar on his own, our man is a jarring presence amid the local wildlife. From a safe distance, two boys make fun of him, venturing loud, derogatory remarks about his appearance, comparing him to the trucker hero of a dated TV series, *B. J. and the Bear*, and suggesting that he must have gouged his face falling off his time machine. When Pam, rather more charitably, compares him to a cowboy, Stuntman Mike replies with a touch of satisfaction: "*I'm not a cowboy, Pam. I'm a stuntman. But that's a very easy mistake to make.*" But the stranger's old-school charm doesn't cut it: Pam is not taken with the idea of flirting with this man who is "*old enough to be [her]*

dad." Even when the stuntman recites his humble list of film appearances to the assembled company of young women, they are far from impressed, confessing that they've never heard of any of them. The clash between the two generations is even more clearly epitomized when Stuntman Mike waxes lyrical about the glory days of live stunts to Pam, who has been brought up on a diet of digital special effects.

It's no coincidence that Jungle Julia rechristens him "Stuntman Burt." The references to actor Burt Reynolds come thick and fast, from *Stroker Ace* to *The Cannonball Run* and *Hooper*. In these three films directed by Hal Needham (a former stuntman himself), Reynolds stars variously—and aptly—as a race car driver and stuntman making a comeback.[1] He

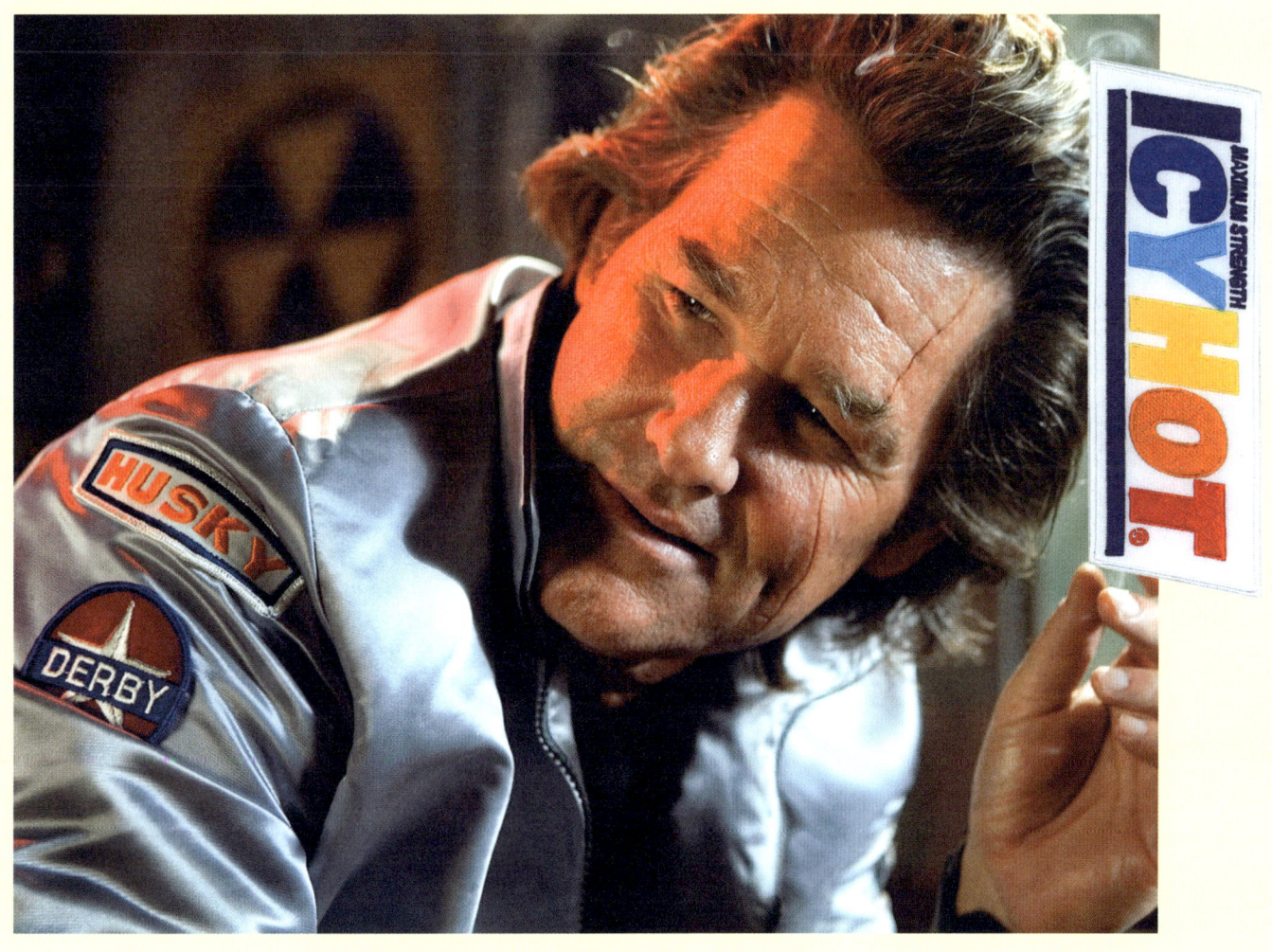

1- In *Stroker Ace* (1983), Burt Reynolds plays a race car driver who is sick of being ridiculed for the fried chicken brand which sponsors him. In *The Cannonball Run* (1981), he takes part in an illegal race across the country. In *Hooper* (1978), he plays a stuntman growing old.

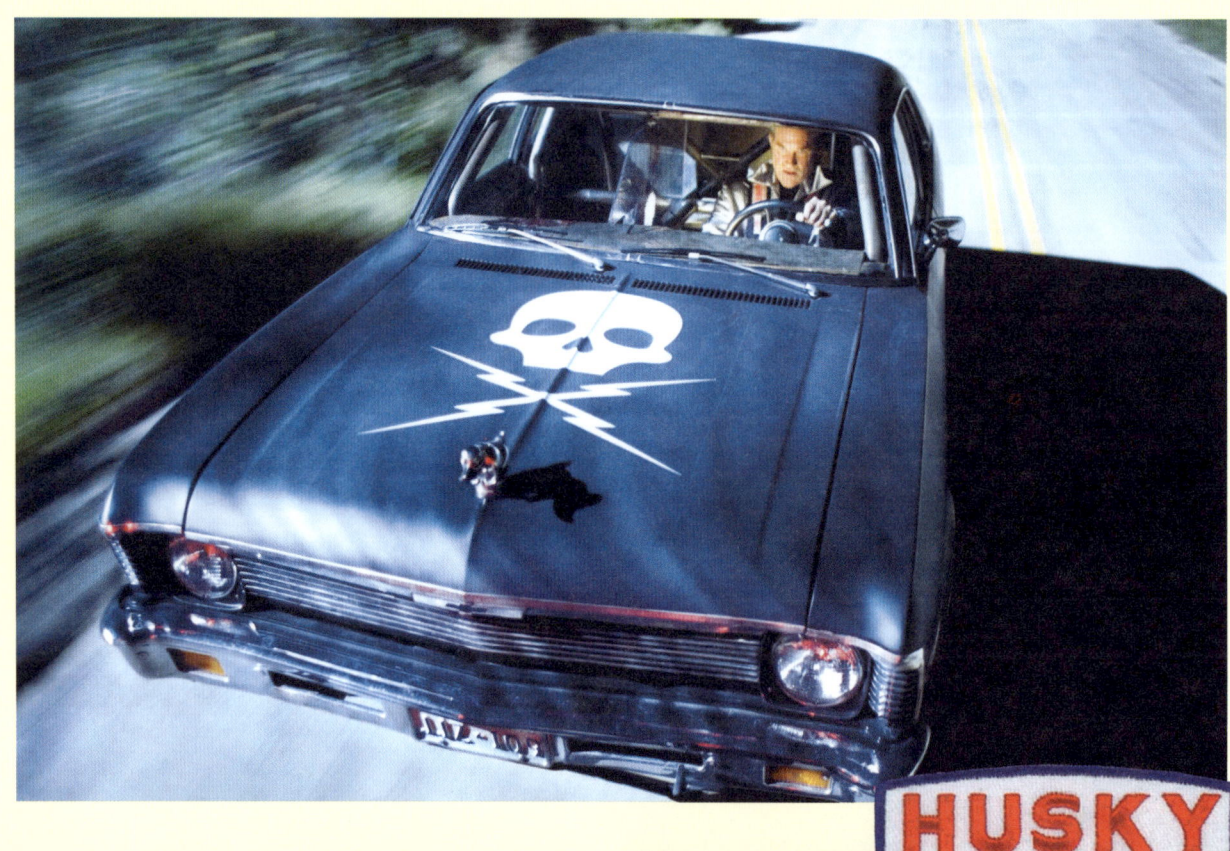

HUSKY

portrays the quintessential dominant American male, a paragon of outdated virility. Reynolds cultivated this macho image with a great sense of self-mockery. This is not so very far from some of the roles Kurt Russell himself has notably played under the director John Carpenter—as Snake Plissken, for instance (*Escape from New York*, *Escape from L.A.*), or the braggart and oafishly virile Jack Burton of *Big Trouble in Little China*. Unsurprisingly, we see Burton's tank top hanging up at the back of the Texas Chili Parlor.

By wearing his jacket both on set and in real life, Stuntman Mike wants to be seen for what he is: a stuntman, a man of action. The boundary between what he *does* and what he *is* has become so blurred that his job and his name have merged into a single moniker. His vocation condemns him to live in the wings: His profession is largely invisible and he only exists as someone else's shadow. But his work as a stunt double finally demands the recognition he believes he has been deprived of, for the physical sacrifices he's made, evidenced in his enduring scar, for his dangerous virility, his power… even if that means punishing these modern young women for not believing in him, not seeing him. The sheriff convincingly sums up the sexual nature of his crimes: "*It's probably the only way that diabolical degenerate can shoot his goo.*" To Tarantino, "*what he was doing was a rape murder, his act of sex. He does it in such a way that it looks like an accident, so he gets away with it. Then we wait until he recovers and, like a serial killer, he goes to another state and does it again.*"[2] While the film highlights the symbolic link between the "accident" and the act of sex, what is also clearly at play here is Stuntman Mike's impotence. Even when he approaches the group of girlfriends and they invite him to join them, the stuntman finds himself unable to do so: He is seized by a sudden need to sneeze so bizarre and ridiculous that he retreats, humiliated and looking uncomfortable. Armed with his indestructible Chevrolet Nova SS, Stuntman Mike appeases his wrath toward the female sex and assuages his perverted desire, at least for a time. The girls in Lebanon recognize the same impotence in Stuntman Mike later: When he tries to make an impressive exit, screeching his tires, they unleash an emasculating tirade at him and make "little dick" gestures with their pinky fingers. By not being duped by his macho posturing, the girlfriends foreshadow their ability to defend themselves against the killer.

Under his satin jacket, Stuntman Mike is indeed a bogeyman slasher, ready to terrify the most rebellious of young women. But his golden age is well and truly over by the time of *Death Proof*, and the stuntman will learn to his cost that girls are no longer afraid to go and hunt down the monsters under their beds. •

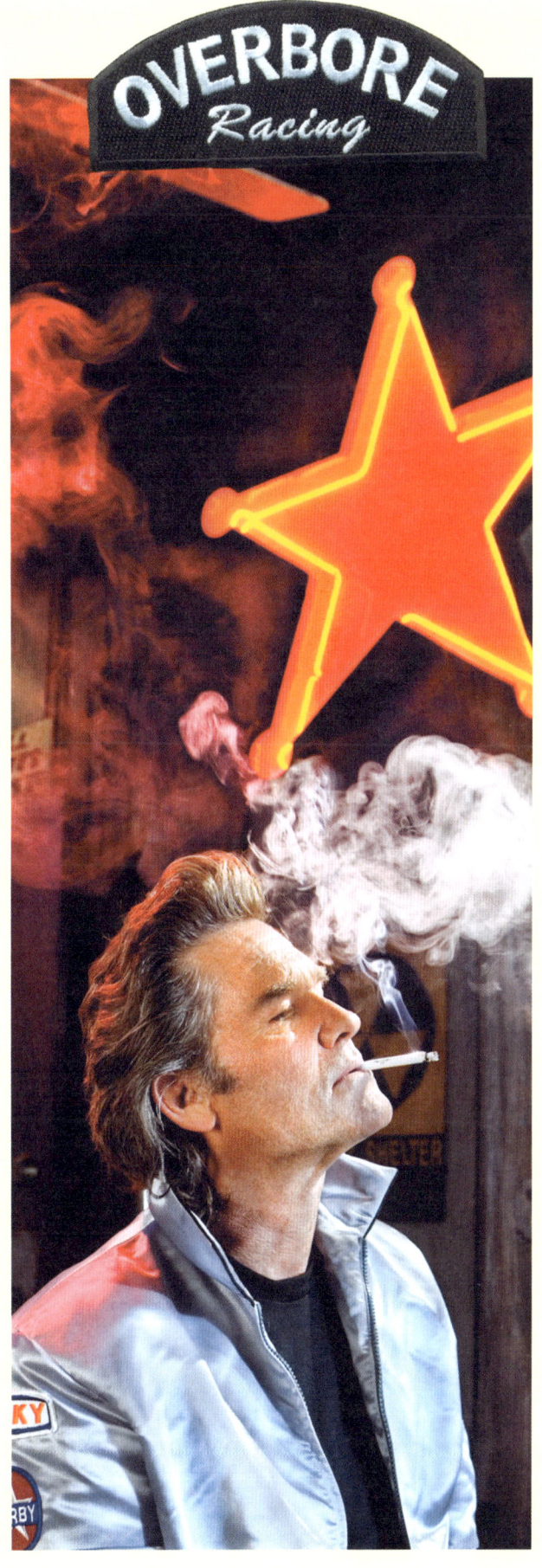

2- Nick James, "Tarantino Bites Back: An Interview," *Sight & Sound*, February 2008.

ORDELL ROBBIE'S BERET

Influencer

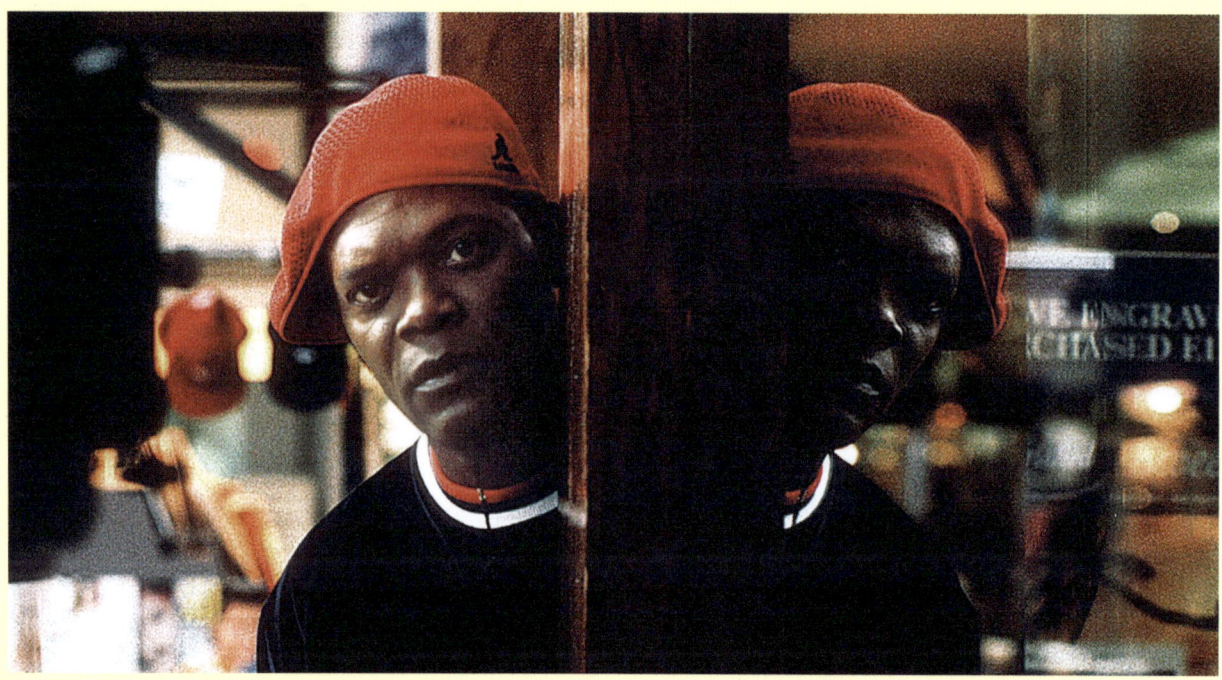

He is without a doubt one of the worst bastards in a universe full of them. When it comes to pure evil, of course, Ordell Robbie cannot hope to compete with the slave owner Mr. Candie or Nazi Colonel Hans Landa, who are each in a league of their own. But if he doesn't exactly reign supreme in that field, there's one area where he truly does: he's the undisputed king of bad fashion.

It's quite simple: From his head to his toes, nothing Ordell Robbie wears works. A modest arms trafficker who likes nothing better than to play at being a gangster, Ordell takes great care with his appearance. And the star of the show, his signature accessory, is the Kangol beret he owns in a whole range of colors and which he unfailingly coordinates with the rest of his outfit. The brand with the kangaroo logo became a must-have in the hip-hop scene of the eighties. The image of Kangol hats, which were once worn by the Beatles and Princess Diana, was reinvented. Now they were honing their street cred and gracing the heads of the likes of rapper LL Cool J and Wesley Snipes's character in *New Jack City*, directed by Mario Van Peebles, which came out in 1991. It's not surprising, therefore, to find one perpetually glued to Ordell Robbie's head in *Jackie Brown*. Perhaps it is a way of hiding the relentless balding process stripping away at his head of straightened hair, which he wears tied back in an unfortunate ponytail. This is not even his biggest fashion mistake. Moving down his hairless face a little, we come to a thin little braided goatee about four inches (10 cm) long, enough to make anyone who sees it want to whip out their sharpest scissors and lop off the foul appendage. Ordell Robbie could have left it at that, but this gangster doesn't shy away from anything, whether it's breaking the law or

indulging in bad taste. Judge for yourself: a heavy gold chain bracelet and signet ring, an assortment of colored berets, electric blue pants, T-shirts with zippers, golf polo shirts, low-necked Lycra sports shirts, and a canary yellow jacket—not to forget, of course, that wide-collared leopard-print shirt he wears under a white jacket. It's not a getup you'd easily overlook on a street corner, making it a strange choice for an arms trafficker, who would surely do better to err on the side of caution. But not Ordell Robbie.

Perhaps we should look at Ordell in a different light, change our perspective, think outside the box. What if, rather than being a low-grade little trafficker, Ordell was really what we would today call a fashion influencer? You have to admit that kind of getup calls for a certain kind of confidence, a certain taste for showing off and performing. One can readily envisage Ordell Robbie in front of the mirror, choosing what to wear with his own particular rigor and sense of style. Because it is obvious that somewhere within this great wardrobe chaos is an order with strict rules and laws—which means that this bad taste somehow ends up "making sense." There are no errors in Ordell Robbie's look, just dubious choices. Rather than judge him, we envy his sheer nerve and can even begin to imagine ourselves donning a Kangol beret like his, sporting a goatee and a leopard-print shirt. That's when the truth hits us, irrefutably: If we dressed like Ordell, we would look ridiculous. So we have to recognize the undeniable: that in the entire Tarantino universe, Ordell Robbie is without a doubt the character with the best style, the one who can wear what no one else could. Why? Because neither you nor we are Samuel L. *fucking* Jackson, the one and only. Let us bow down and take our hats off to him. •

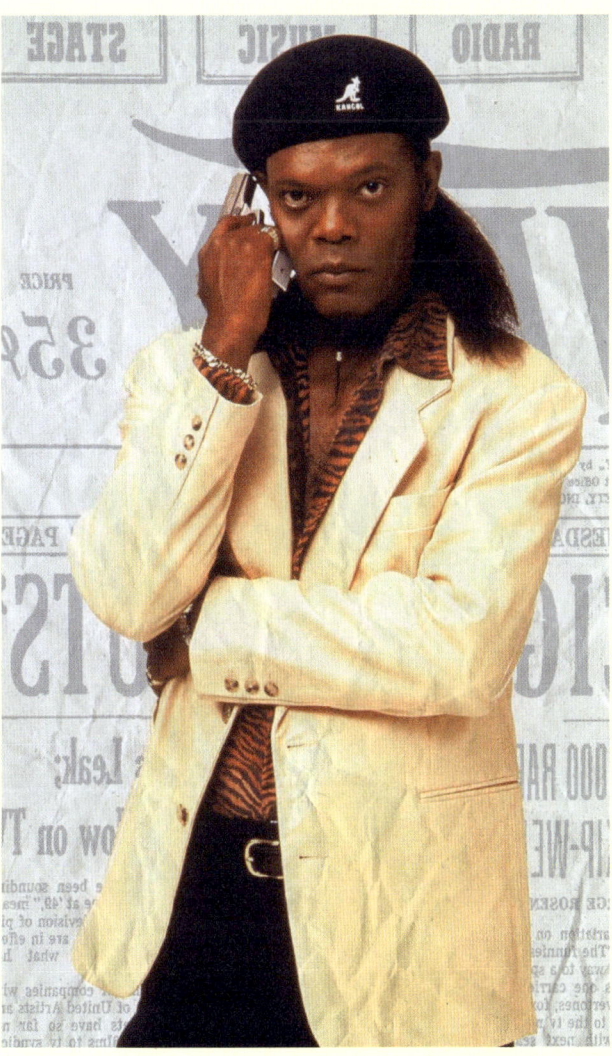

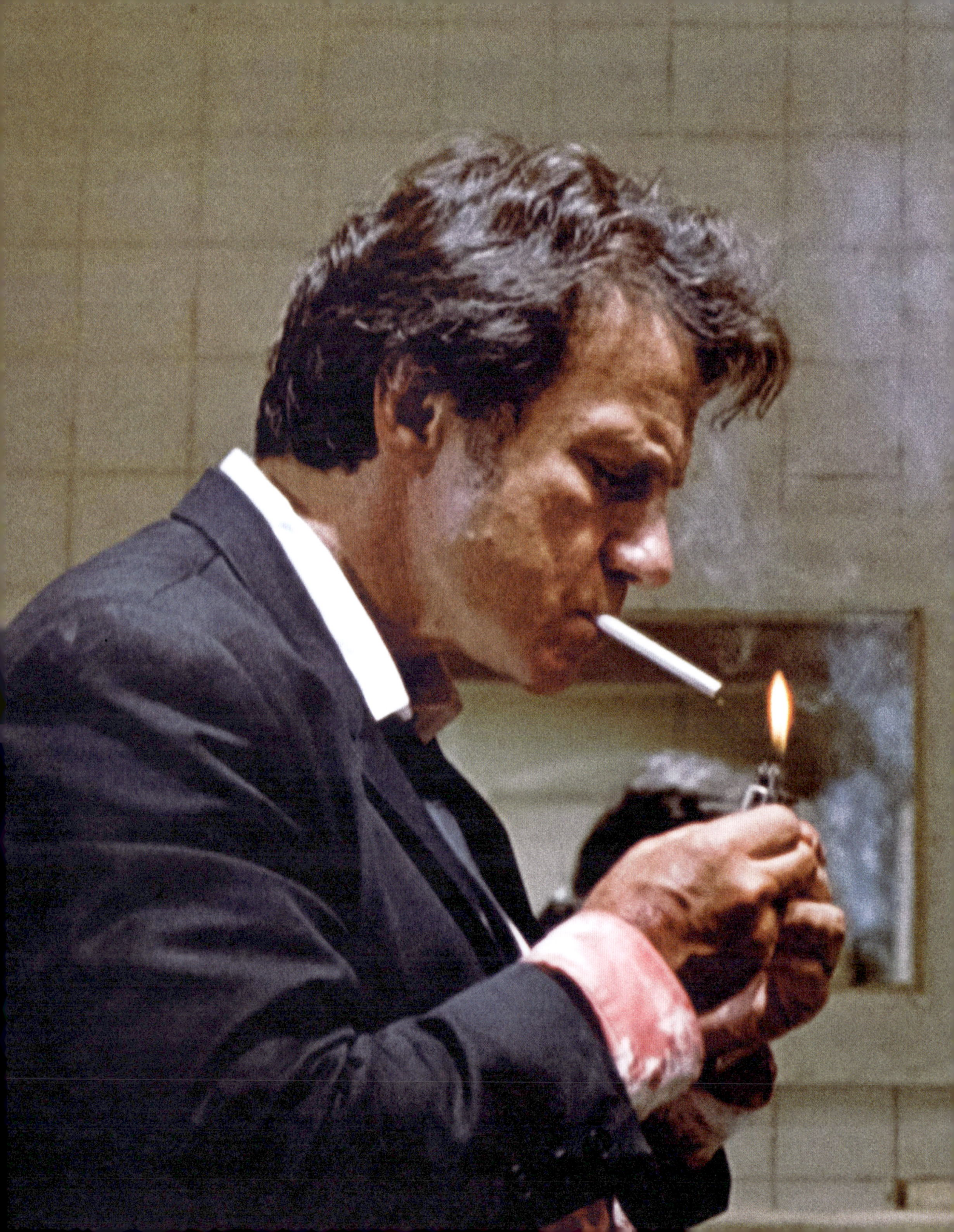

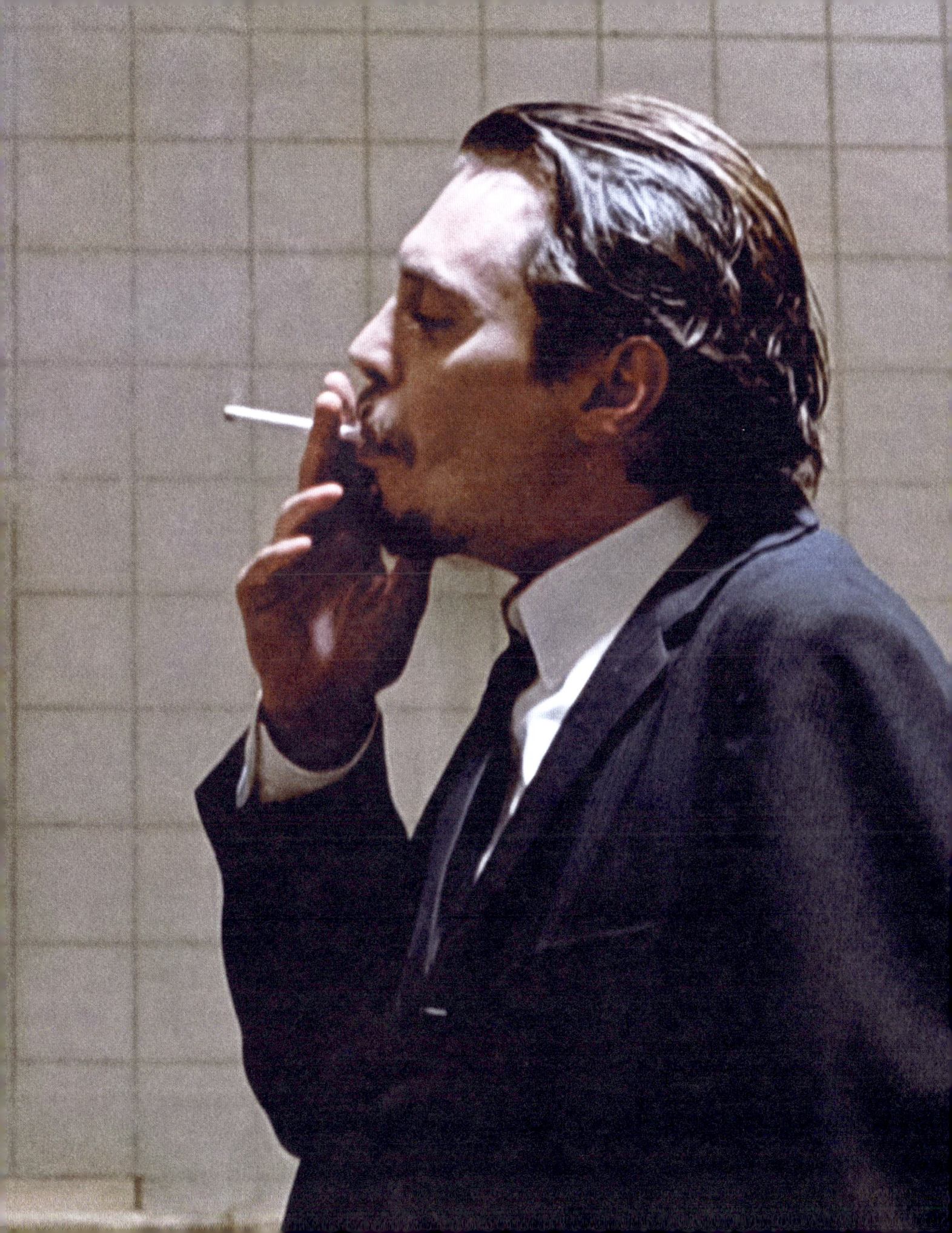

11
THE MOTEL

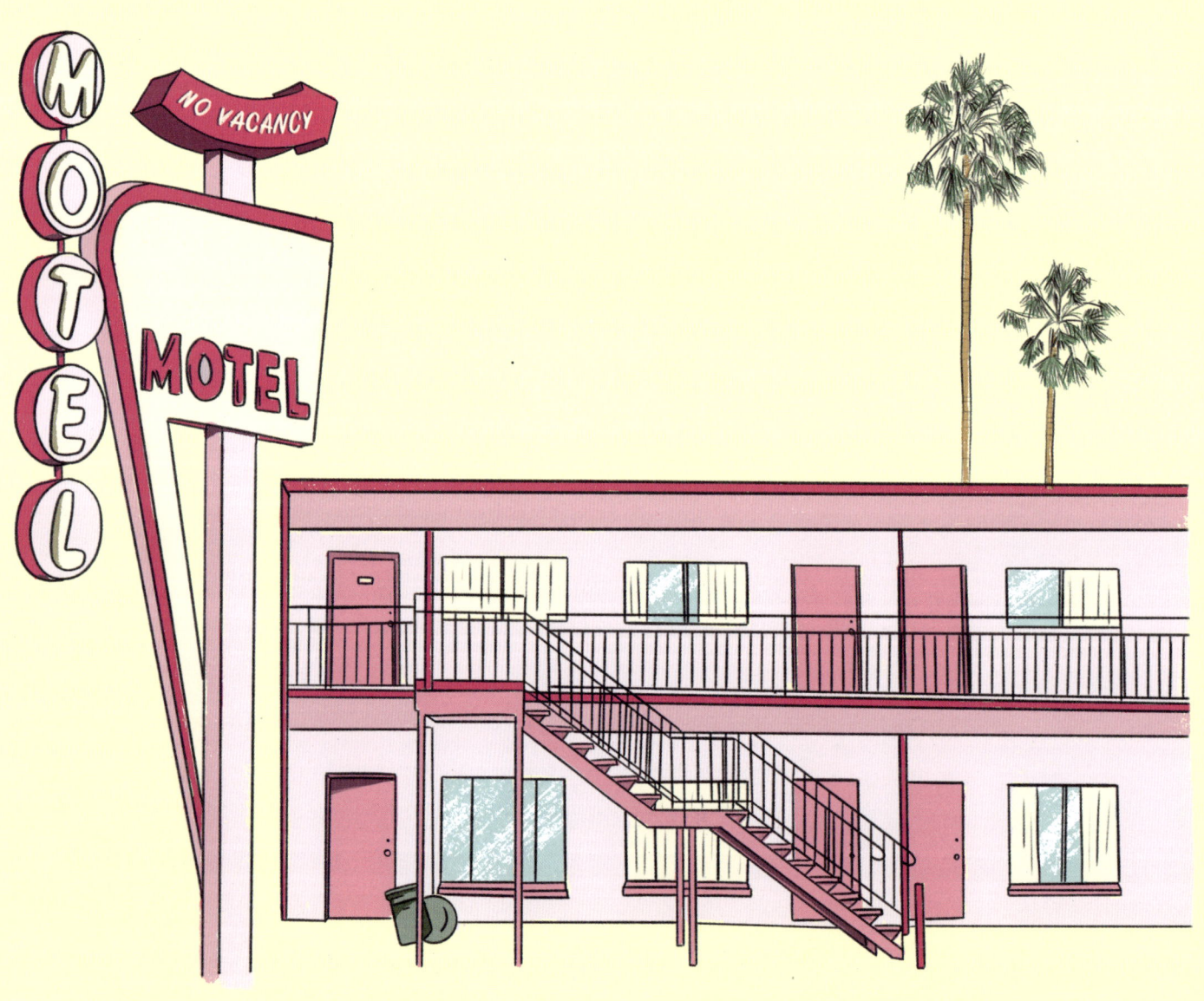

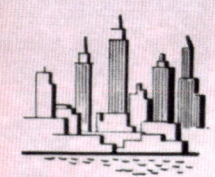

The Tarantino Motel

A NEW MODERN MOTOR HOTEL

SWIMMING POOL
TV AND VCR
COMPLETELY AIR CONDITIONED

711 FAST HIGHWAY 66
TARANTINO TOWN
U.S.A

Cut the engine. Here you are, parked outside the Tarantino Town Motel, a mandatory stop for our visitors. You will have had to drive for hour after hour across the desert, beyond Palm Springs and Death Valley, to get to our dear old town. After all that time at the wheel in the heat of the afternoon, tuned into "Super Sounds of the Seventies" on K-Billy's radio station, it's time to take a much-needed and well-deserved break at the local motel. The comforts may be on the basic side, and the pink paint is a little faded, but the television, the scrap of a swimming pool, and the air conditioning are likely to make you a happy guest. What's more, the rates are very reasonable. And with a bit of luck, you'll run across a few of the characters who inhabit Quentin Tarantino's universe as they philosophize endlessly, lounging on pool chairs or loitering in the motel hallways. You'll catch a whiff on the air, too, that will tell you one of those legendary cigarette machines is just behind the building, ready to cater to our guests' needs… We'll let you get your bags and head to reception. Please don't forget to deposit your key when you go out, even for just a couple of hours. It will be much appreciated by the management.

VINCENT VEGA & JULES WINNFIELD

Thick as Thieves

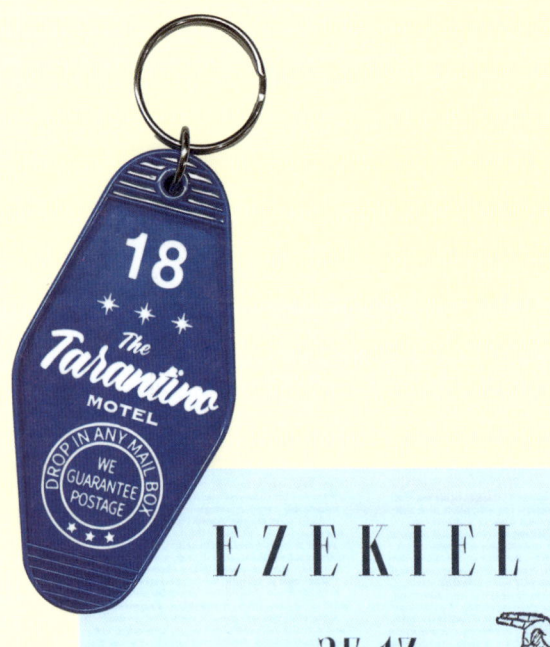

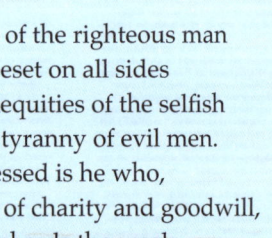

E Z E K I E L

25:17

The path of the righteous man
is beset on all sides
by the inequities of the selfish
and the tyranny of evil men.
Blessed is he who,
in the name of charity and goodwill,
shepherds the weak
through the valley of the darkness.
For he is truly his brother's keeper
and the finder of lost children.
And I will strike down upon thee
with great vengeance and furious anger
those who attempt to poison
and destroy my brothers.
And you will know my name is the Lord
when I lay my vengeance upon thee.

It's impossible to confuse Vincent and Jules, and yet if you listen to them with your eyes closed, you can easily lose track of who is who. Of all the duos in Quentin Tarantino's films, they are undoubtedly the most enduring: Marsellus Wallace's guard dogs, a twin-headed Hydra you would do well not to attempt to tickle. Whether in their hitman suits or surfing shorts and T-shirts ready to hit the beach, the two gangsters always stay cool. On the surface, at least…

Vincent has just come back from Amsterdam—where Tarantino himself spent time after the release of *Reservoir Dogs*—his pockets crammed with stories of the Old World. When he meets up with Jules, their conversation ranges from Quarter Pounders with cheese to hashish to the way people in Holland slather their french fries with mayonnaise. "*Yuck!*" comments Jules.

How could we possibly guess from this interaction that our two friends are on their way to commit the unthinkable? They can be quietly discussing the metric system and what it really means to give someone a foot massage (is it sexual or not sexual?) one minute, and launch into a murderous shooting spree the next, with sips of nice cold soda in between. To do this, all they need are the magic words: "*Come on, let's get into character.*"

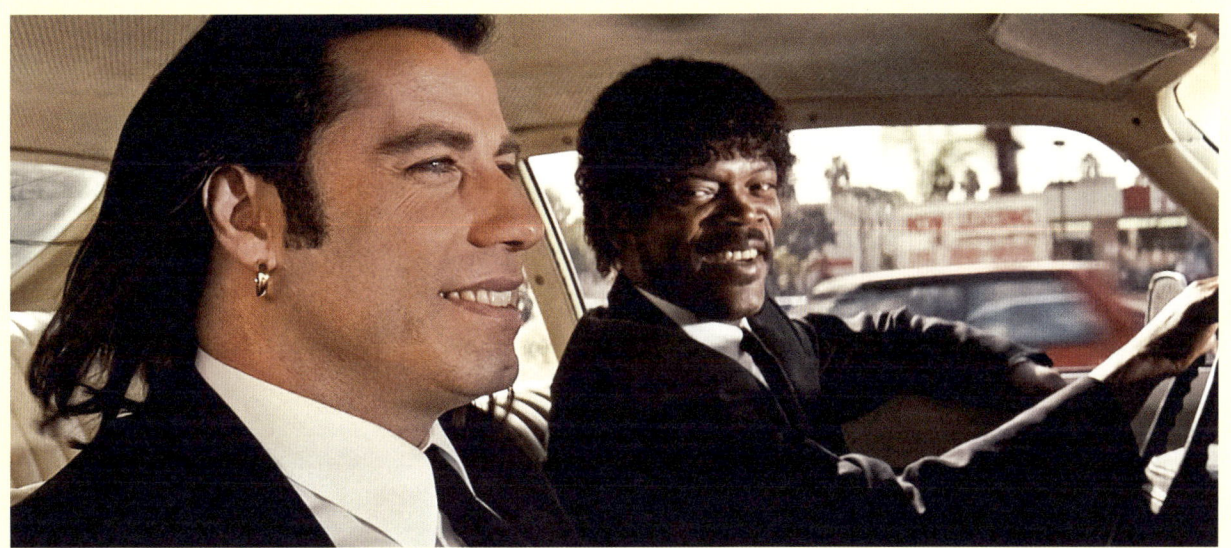

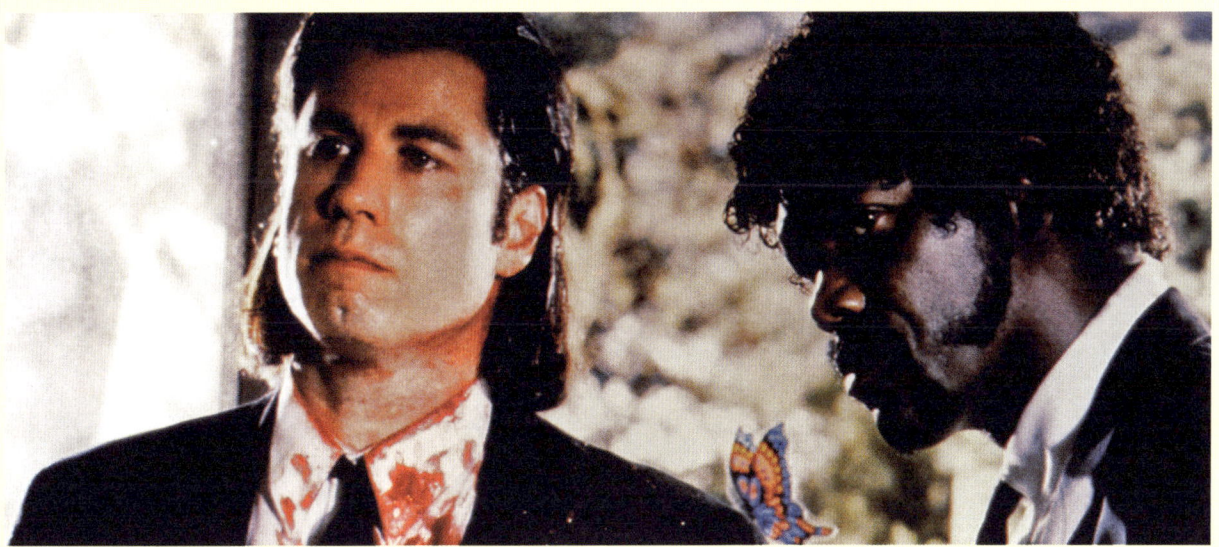

This idea of playing a part runs all the way through Tarantino's filmography: Mr. Orange rehearses in front of a mirror, Jackie Brown takes everyone around her for a ride, King Schultz teaches Django never to break character, and even the *Basterds* go undercover at the big movie premiere. The theme reaches its peak in *The Hateful Eight*, which is a real game of charades until good old Marquis Warren takes control of the movie and starts to play Hercule Poirot. Half actors, half stage managers, the characters seem, just like their own director, to have watched a few too many movies.

Jules and Vincent are "*a cross between criminals and actors and children playing roles*," states Tarantino. "*It was never a conscious decision, playing on the idea of big men are actually little boys with real guns, but it kept coming out and I realized as I was writing* Pulp, *that actually fits.*"[1] Don't go thinking, however, that these two are "playing pretend" at being gangsters: A couple of greenhorns who took liberties with Marsellus Wallace paid the price, if you remember. But rather than display the meticulous professionalism we might expect, Vincent and Jules are perfectly normal, not to say average,

1- Gavin Smith, "Interview: Quentin Tarantino," *Film Comment*, July–August 1994.

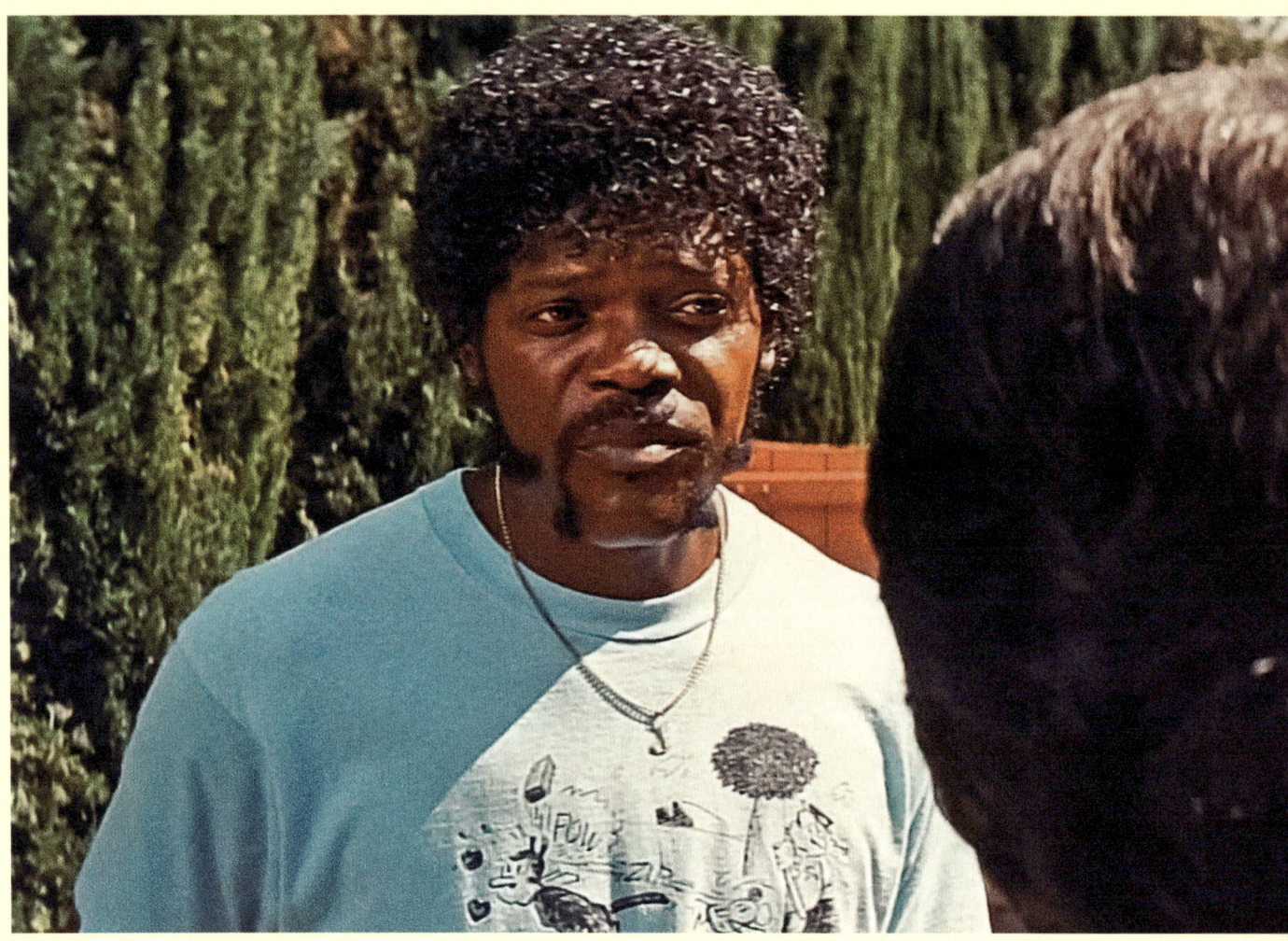

guys who make mistakes, take offense, grab a snack, and spend too much time gassing. By dwelling on these "side" characters, Tarantino bypasses an entire mythical movie world inhabited by taciturn, methodical killers and makes *Pulp Fiction* into a movie stuffed full of comic mishaps, shifts in tone, and mismatches. Vincent is quintessentially banal: He always misses the best part of the action because he's in the john and ends up riddled with bullets when the toaster betrays him.

Between contracts, Jules and Vincent are not the kind to let themselves go hungry: Breakfast is as serious a business for them as a target with a price on their head. Vincent is the mellower of the two, a decent type with long hair, a couple of principles, and a bolo tie. He's an Elvis fan and a quiet kind of guy, provided you don't bark at him. This makes him the calmer of the Vega brothers, quite different from the highly unstable Vic Vega in *Reservoir Dogs*. As for Jules, he is perhaps the more dangerous, but also the more thoughtful, the more spiritual of the two, prone to seeing his life as an episode out of the series *Kung Fu* and fond of reciting the Bible in a familiar way every time he gets ready to fire off his gun. A mystic in his spare time, he perceives signs the rest of us do not see. Between two cups of coffee, Jules, who can recognize when God is speaking to him, decides it's time to hang up his gun and change his way of life.

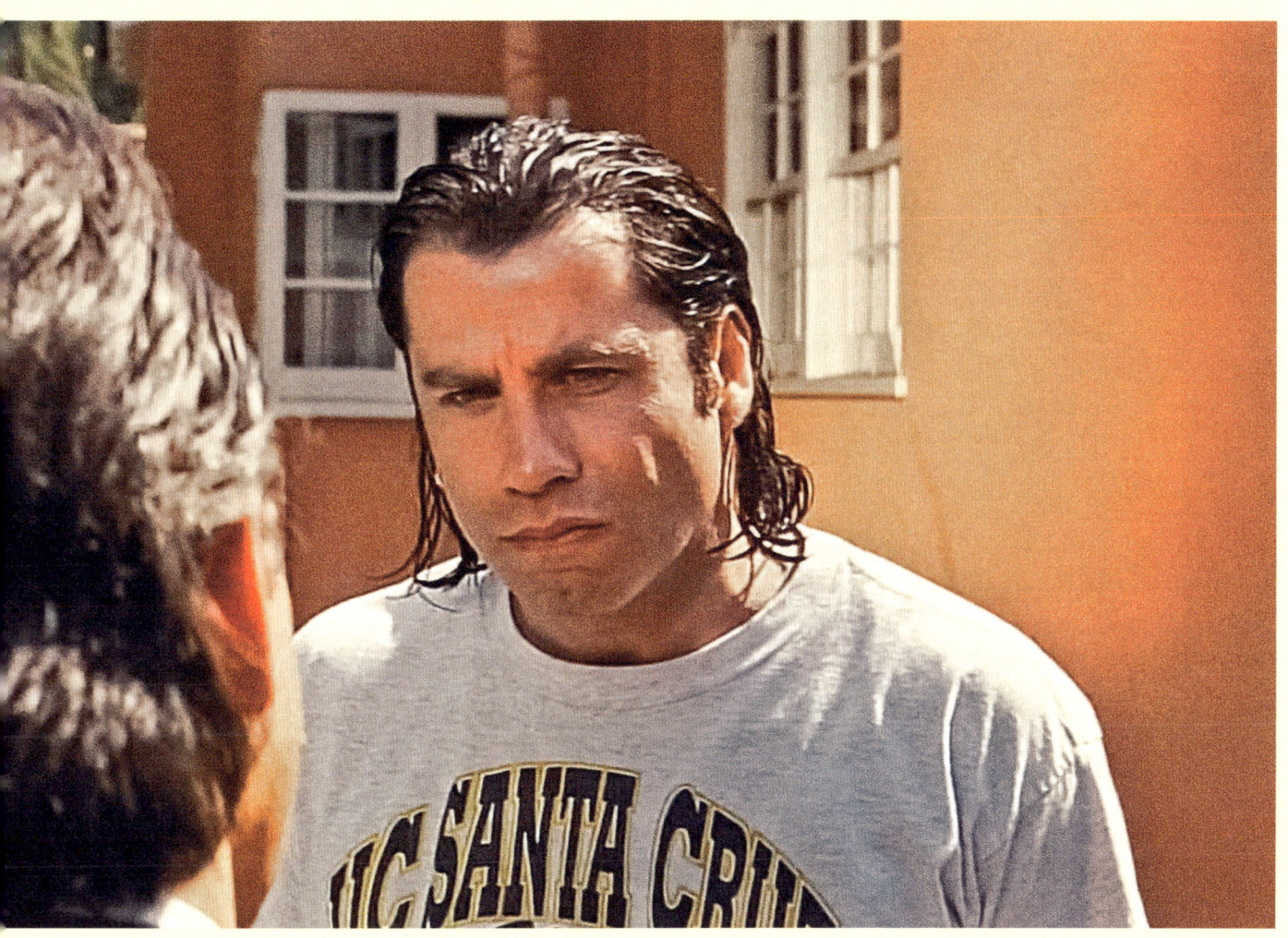

To seal his transformation, he spares two lives, while Vincent, ever the rationalist, has every intention of killing anyone who gets in his way. It's a *matter of principle,*" as he says.

To cut a long story short, one could say that Jules and Vincent are two sides of the same coin, a suburban Los Angeles yin and yang, with sun and palm trees thrown in for good measure. One can imagine them driving calmly along the boulevards, engaging in an allegorical discussion about the ephemeral nature of existence, couched in terms of the average time it will take them to finish their pancakes that morning. You've got it: Vincent and Jules are not really hitmen. They're modern-day philosophers.

After all the time we've spent in their company, we surely recognize something of these two lovable thugs in ourselves, and our hearts go out to them both in turn—those same hearts that break every time we see Vincent motionless in that goddamn bathtub… Bitch of a toaster. Luckily for us, *Pulp Fiction* is digested in a chaotic order. At the end of the movie, then, we can leave Jules and Vincent tucking their guns into their board shorts and leaving the diner with their bellies full and their hearts light, carrying Marsellus's mysterious briefcase, and we can imagine them living on for as long as possible, which is to say forever. Amen. •

WINSTON WOLF

The Guy You Can Count On

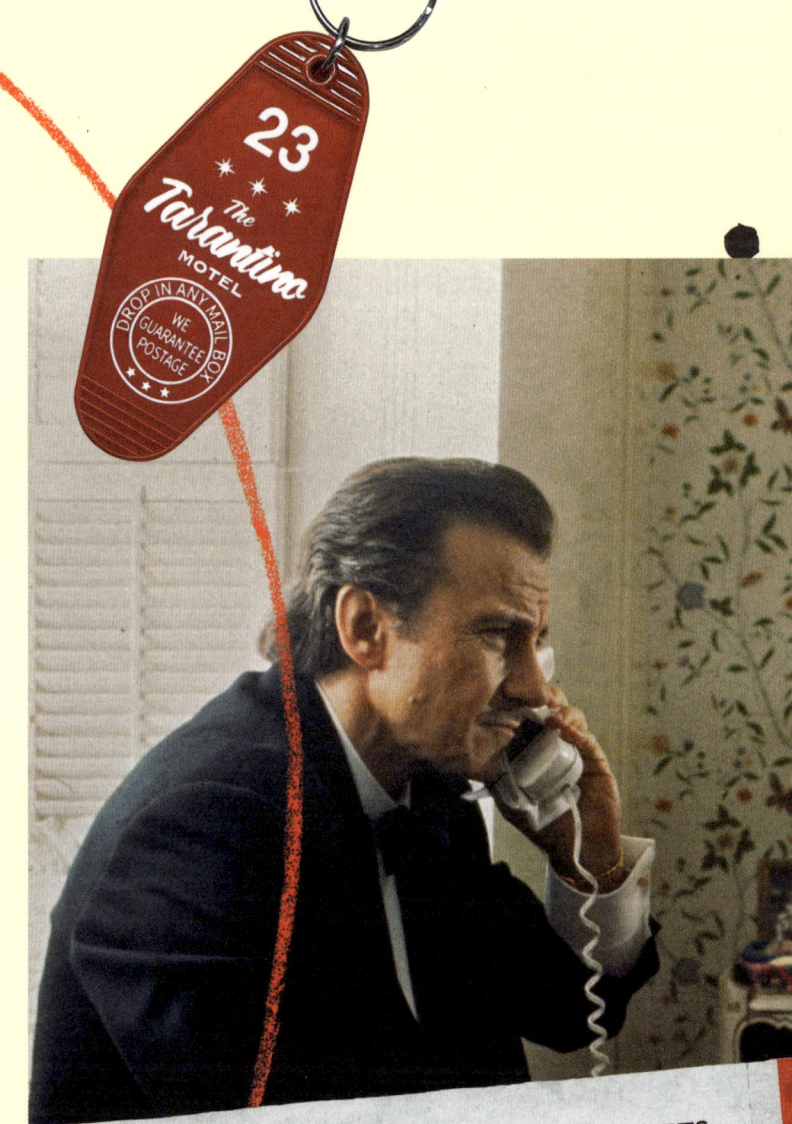

With these few words, in less than the time it takes to blink, Marsellus Wallace, Los Angeles millionaire and organized crime boss, placates a heated Jules Winnfield, who is not expecting the response he gets. Marsellus is not just sending in the cavalry, but the cavalry as encapsulated in a single name guaranteed to take the heat out of the most explosive situations: the Wolf. The Wolf is the man to sort out the present unfortunate incident: the rogue shot from Vincent Vega's gun that brought young Marvin's life to a premature end and repainted the entire interior of the car red.

Winston Wolf is the man to call to "solve problems," to fix the situation for anyone with a blot on their CV—or, more particularly, their criminal record. Ducking out of an event on the strength of a call from Marsellus, Wolf is thirty minutes away and so will be there in under ten. His reputation precedes him—when he gets to the scene of the "problem," he is addressed as "Mr." and offered the best coffee in the house. And we watch the master at work. One hand in the pocket of his elegant double-breasted suit, a mug of piping hot coffee in the other, his hair neatly

MONSTER JOE'S

USED AUTO PARTS
555-7908 555-7909

MARSELLUS WALLACE: "You ain't got no problem, Jules. I'm on the motherfucker. Go back in there and chill them ▇▇▇▇ out and wait for the Wolf who should be coming directly."

38

slicked back, his mustache trimmed with laser sharpness, and his bowtie knotted with millimeter precision, Winston Wolf remains a gentleman whatever the circumstances. Having reviewed the situation, he needs only a few seconds to decide how to proceed. He is, after all, the ultimate problem-solver, a Special Forces team in his own right, precision-engineered and guaranteed to execute an operation without a hitch.

The plan is amazingly simple: Clean the car, stash the corpse in the trunk, and cover the seats. Elementary, you may say. Perhaps,

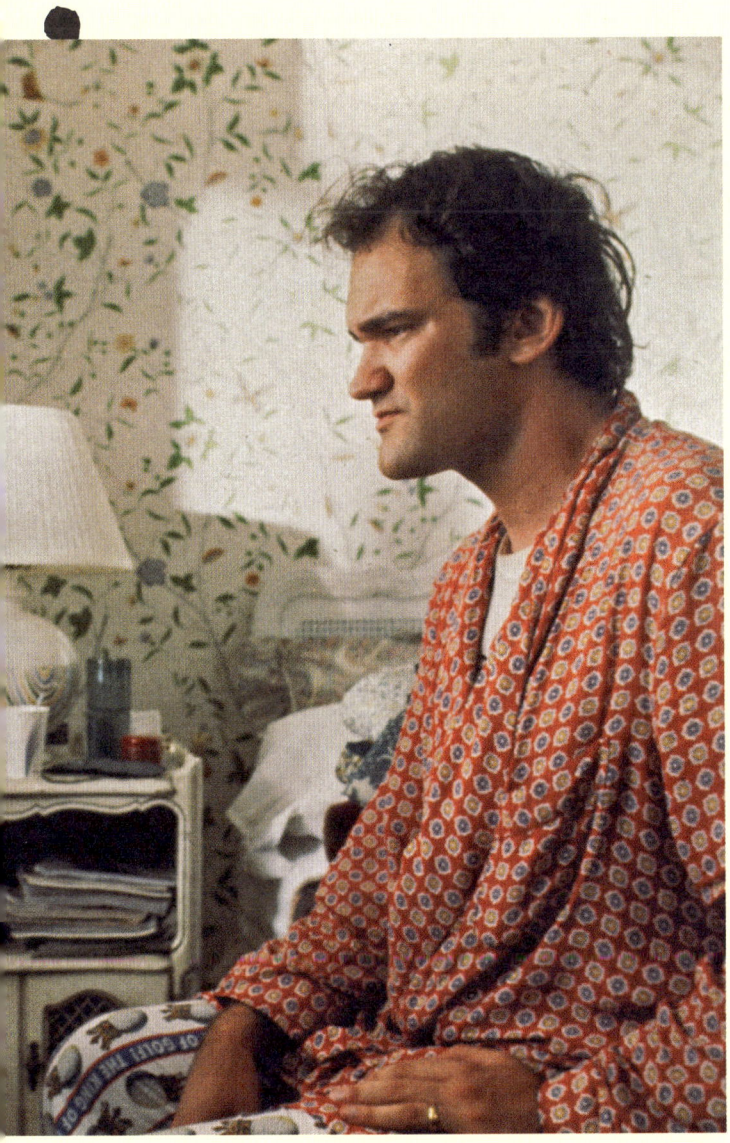

but Jules and Vincent are more predisposed to gab than scrub, and it takes all of Winston Wolf's poise, composure, and best military tone to bring them into line. No one says a word, apart from Vincent, who complains that he doesn't like *"people barking orders"* at him, only to find himself torn into. It's not a question of orders, but efficiency: The clock is ticking and Winston Wolf's time is precious. With Wolf, you hold your tongue, you listen, and you get on with it. This is in everybody's interest, but particularly in Marsellus Wallace's. Even Jimmie, who owns the suburban house where Vincent and Jules have gone to ground, complies with Wolf's demands, giving up the bedspread he and his wife received as a wedding gift. Uncle Marsellus is a millionaire, Wolf reminds him, and will happily furnish him with a whole new bedroom set if need be. The operation is well executed all the way through to the very end at Monster Joe's auto parts yard in North Hollywood, where Jules and Vincent's car, poor Marvin's body, and the old aunt's bedspread all find their final resting place.

And while Winston Wolf doesn't actually do anything in a practical sense other than sip a cup of coffee, he does it with the kind of paternalistic, old-school authority and calm professionalism to which Mr. White, also played by Harvey Keitel, aspires in *Reservoir Dogs*. As soon as the "problem" is solved, he takes off with Raquel, who one day will inherit the car graveyard, playing the old charmer and sermonizing to her as they go. *"Respect for one's elders shows character,"* he declares as he gets into his car. It's the parting precept of a character who traverses *Pulp Fiction* at lightning speed, with the precision of a 9mm pistol and all the elegance of James Bond, minus the Queen and Perfidious Albion. •

THE DEATH PROOF GIRLS

Cool Chicks

In room 28 of our motel, the atmosphere is cheerfully chaotic. The television crackles, there's a half-drunk can of Big Red lying around, a bottle of nail polish has rolled onto the carpet, and shouts, shrieks of laughter, and the odd torrent of colorful language find their way into the corridor.

If things are a little hectic on the second floor, it's because Kim, Zoë, Abernathy, and Lee are a real bunch of Tarantino-style girls. In other words, they yak randomly, in truly great Tarantino tradition. When *Death Proof* isn't straying into the realm of a slasher, revenge, or road trip movie, it's a hangout movie—a description Tarantino uses for the kind of movies it's good to hang out with on account of the great company and terrific conversation they provide. So, of course, when the director introduces us to the coolest girls in Lebanon, Tennessee, there's only one thing we want to do: be one of them.

However, *Death Proof* opens about nine hundred miles (1,400 km) down the road, in the city of Austin, Texas, in the company of another group of young women. On their way to a girls' weekend away, Shanna, Jungle Julia, and Arlene stop off at Güero's Taco Bar for a couple of quick margaritas before ending up at the Texas Chili Parlor, where some

boys are waiting for them. Everything starts off as we might expect in a typical hangout movie of the kind the director is so fond of, with a clutch of loudmouthed girlfriends, especially Jungle Julia, a local radio DJ star. The conversation rattles along merrily, with Tarantino planting references all over the place the whole time: in a line, on the walls of Julia's apartment—which feature a picture of a reclining Brigitte Bardot alongside a poster for *A Quiet Place to Kill*, directed by Umberto Lenzi[1]—down to a prophetic branded T-shirt promoting the film *Faster, Pussycat! Kill! Kill!*, directed by Russ Meyer. But our friends' road comes to a sudden end as they get hunted down by a maniac.

Their fate may be sealed, but not because their pursuer conforms to archetypal slasher stereotypes, driven by a puritanical impulse to exact punishment on female characters who are overly bold or enterprising. Nor will the "final girl" ultimately left standing be glorified as the most modest and deserving. In avoiding these tropes, Tarantino has taken stock of much of the criticism leveled at the genre, citing Carol Clover (*Men, Women, and Chain Saws*) and applying her teaching.[2]

The girls' empowerment is not at issue here: what is, rather, is the concept of power they pursue. Instead of overthrowing the patriarchy, they

1- *A Quiet Place to Kill* (original title: *Paranoia*), directed by Umberto Lenzi (1970), opens with a female racer crashing on a racetrack.
2- Nick James, "Tarantino Bites Back: An interview," *Sight & Sound,* February 2008.

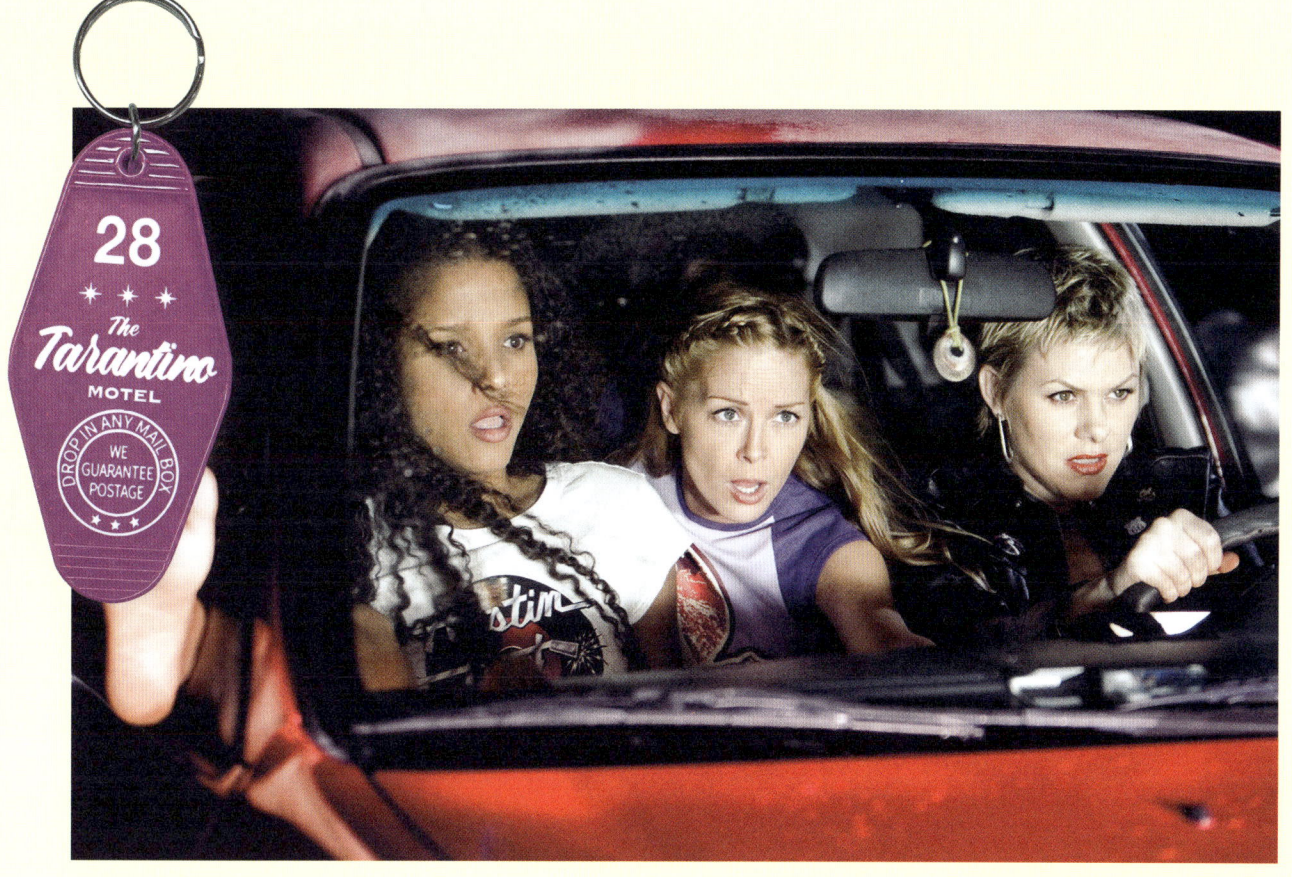

appropriate male attitudes, worrying about the symbolic implications of who takes the dominant sexual position ("*Who was on top?*"), setting traps for men, and treating them with scorn. Their male friends don't deserve any better, acting like predators as they do by trying to hoodwink the girls into drinking too much. But above all, our girlfriends are scared of looking "gutless," displaying an almost male kind of pride. When Stuntman Mike threatens to write her name down under the "chickenshit" category in his little red book, Arlene succumbs to his puerile provocation and falls into the stuntman's trap. Thinking she is regaining control, she takes up the challenge and dances for the stranger. She plays the dominatrix in an unforgettable lap dance scene, setting her foot squarely between his outspread thighs as he sits in his chair, inches from his genitals, in a deliberately emasculating gesture. The dance comes to an abrupt stop as the film strip apparently jumps, cutting the cheap eroticism of the scene dead. A few minutes later, the

car crash hits the screen in a flash of gore, with the director repeating the moment of the fatal impact and its effect on each of the bodies in turn.

Death Proof is a movie which tells a twin story. Repetition is key to its structure as the movie follows the paths of two groups of girls who are targeted by the stuntman, whose only way of satisfying his sexual desire is through blood and twisted metal. When the first group gets mown down by the killer, Tarantino restarts the movie with a new team. Kim, Zoë, Abernathy, and Lee are presented from the very start as quintessential female Tarantino heroes, with all the appropriate trappings. They drive a car in the Bride's colors, yellow and black, with a Pussy Wagon sticker; Abernathy's cell phone has a "Twisted Nerve" ringtone, a direct reference to Elle Driver's menacing whistle in *Kill Bill*; and Lee's cheerleader outfit even says "Viper," an allusion to the assassination squad in the same movie. Alongside the abundant nods to *Kill Bill*—the two movies share a theme of female revenge, after all—another reference surfaces. When the girls are eating in the restaurant, the scene is filmed in a long sequence shot. The camera moves around the group sitting and chatting at the table, evoking another diner scene: the one at the start of *Reservoir Dogs*. The movie does not merely adopt the same format as the earlier scene, but uses it to achieve the same ends, letting the dialogue, which flits from politics to pop culture, build the different characters and solidify their little community for us. From the slew of references it is clear that this new band of girls scoop all the prizes in the director's book. An actress, a makeup artist, and a pair of stuntwomen, they are a part of the movie world, the "movie family" to which QT belongs and to which he

pays homage by casting a real stuntwoman, Zoë Bell (*Kill Bill*), to play the part of Zoë.

Having been chased in their turn, the girls turn on their attacker, switching from prey to predator. While it previously leaned toward a slasher movie, in the end the film abandons the final girl trope and comes down instead on the side of revenge by proxy. Our four friends aren't feminist vigilantes, however, as evidenced by the fact that one of them is left alone with a lecherous redneck. Rather than championing a cause, *Death Proof* is a movie which reflects on the conventions of its own genre, aware of slasher films' inherently highly gendered gaze and the impact this might have on its appeal, likely limiting it to a uniquely

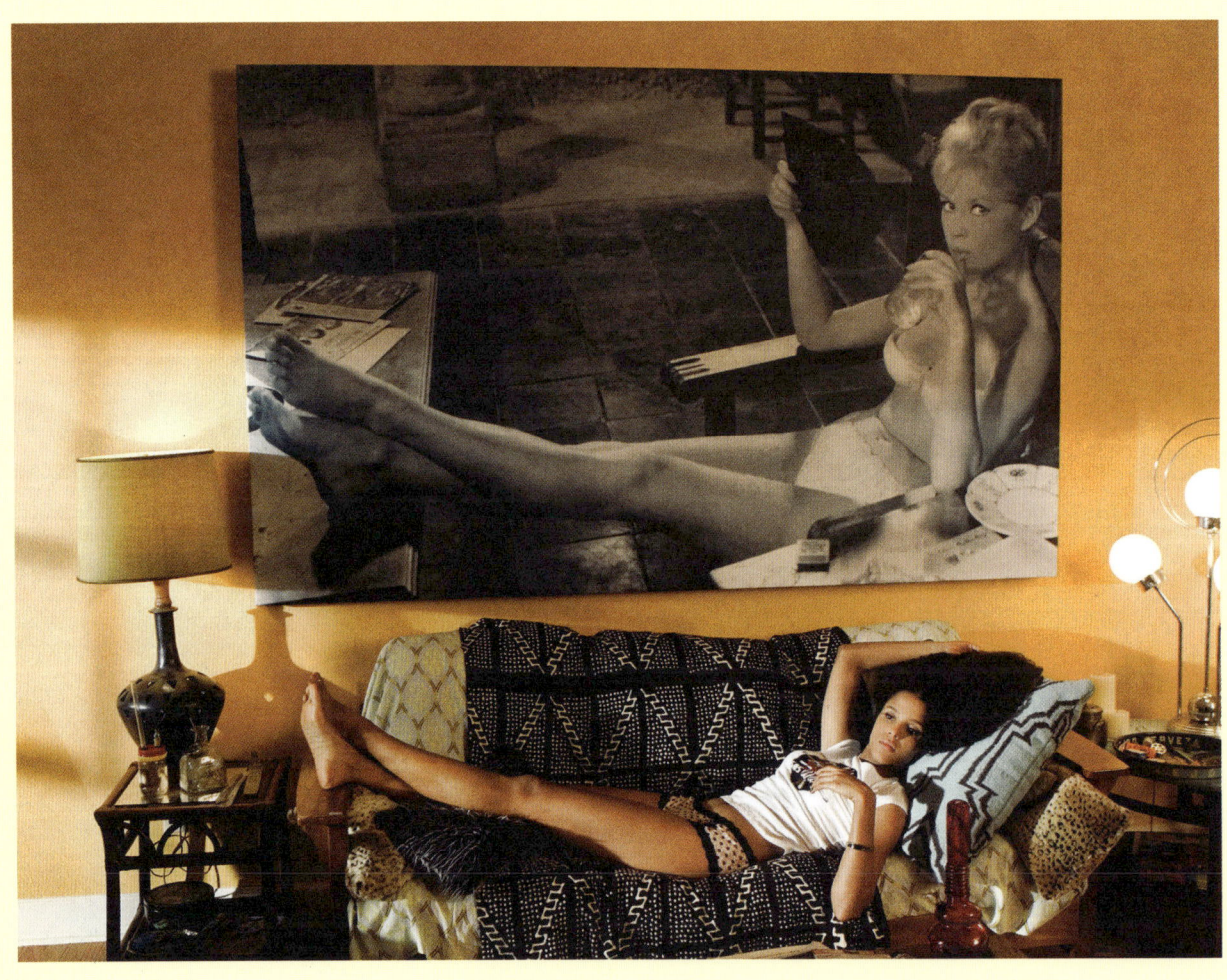

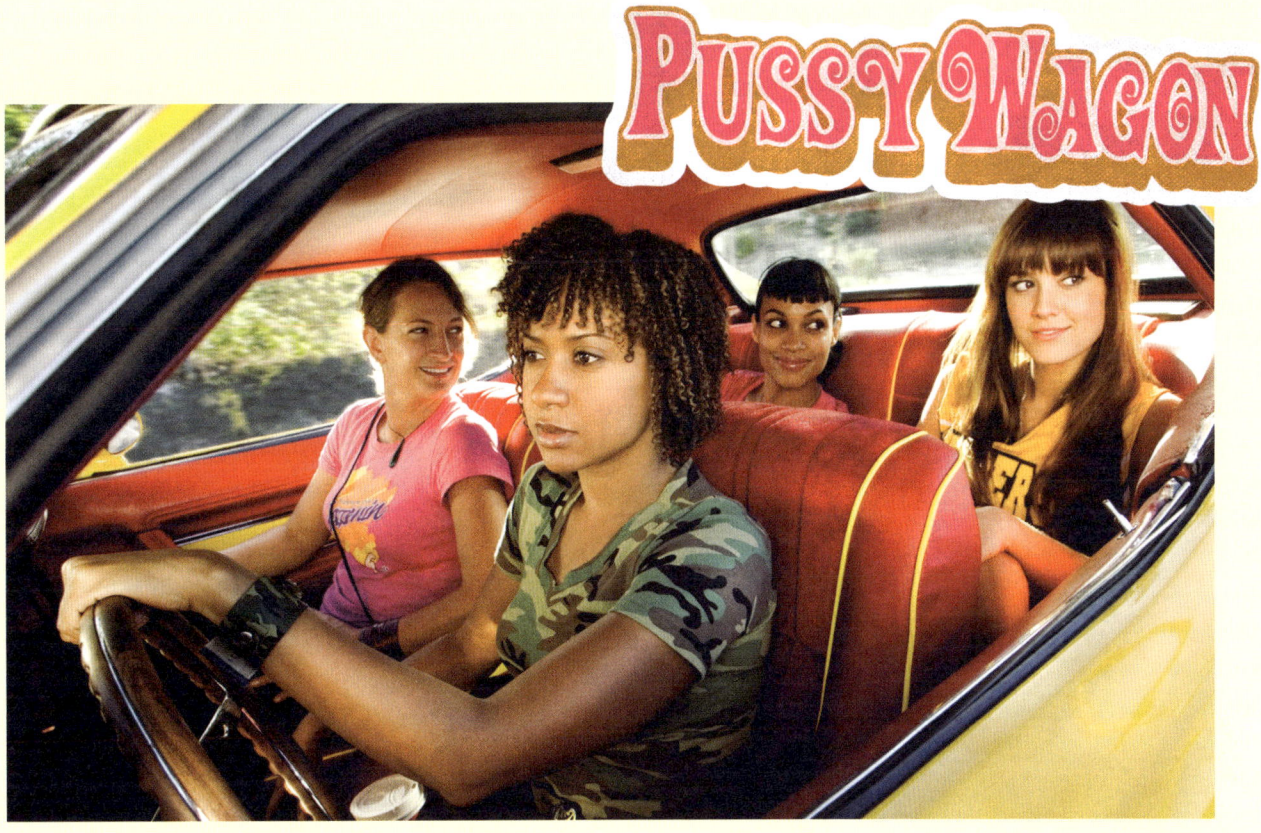

PUSSY WAGON

male audience. "*So this was my girl movie, my way to write girls now, not me remembering what girls were like in college. It became my version of* The Women *[George Cukor, 1939]. But I directed it like an exploitation film. Every other movie I've ever done, I've always been a gentleman about how I shot women. Not in that movie. I was a leering bastard in that one.*"[3] Operating in collusion with the audience, the film adopts the conventions of grindhouse movies in order to examine them, deliberately working within a genre that features women but never addresses them.

Abernathy, in particular, protests against the limiting stereotypes imposed by the genre. At dinner the two stuntwomen talk about the movie *Vanishing Point* (Richard C. Sarafian, 1971), asserting categorically that "*most girls wouldn't know* Vanishing Point," unlike John Hughes's sugary teen movies, as they mockingly tell their friend. "*Excuse me, most girls? What the fuck are you two?*" Abernathy retorts. Later, when they tell her she can't take part in the action because

her status as a mother is incompatible with the heavy-duty car chase about to take place, she objects. "*You know we're supposed to be this big posse, but that's the excuse that you guys use whenever you want to exclude me from something,*" she says, before insisting on her place in the upcoming adventure.

Kim, Zoë, and Abernathy are road warriors, throwing themselves into their punitive mission at the wheel of their white Dodge Challenger like real modern-day Amazons. What commands our attention here is not the inversion of polar female and male opposites, but the way our female heroes participate fully in a genre we might have thought irredeemably mired in contradiction for a large swathe of its potential audience. Through violence, whether dressed in combat gear or rose-pink T-shirts, the three girlfriends storm their way into an entire movie mythology where previously they had been seen but not noticed. •

3- Ella Taylor, "Quentin Tarantino: The *Inglourious Basterds* Interview," *The Village Voice*, August 18, 2009.

HANS LANDA

The Chess Player

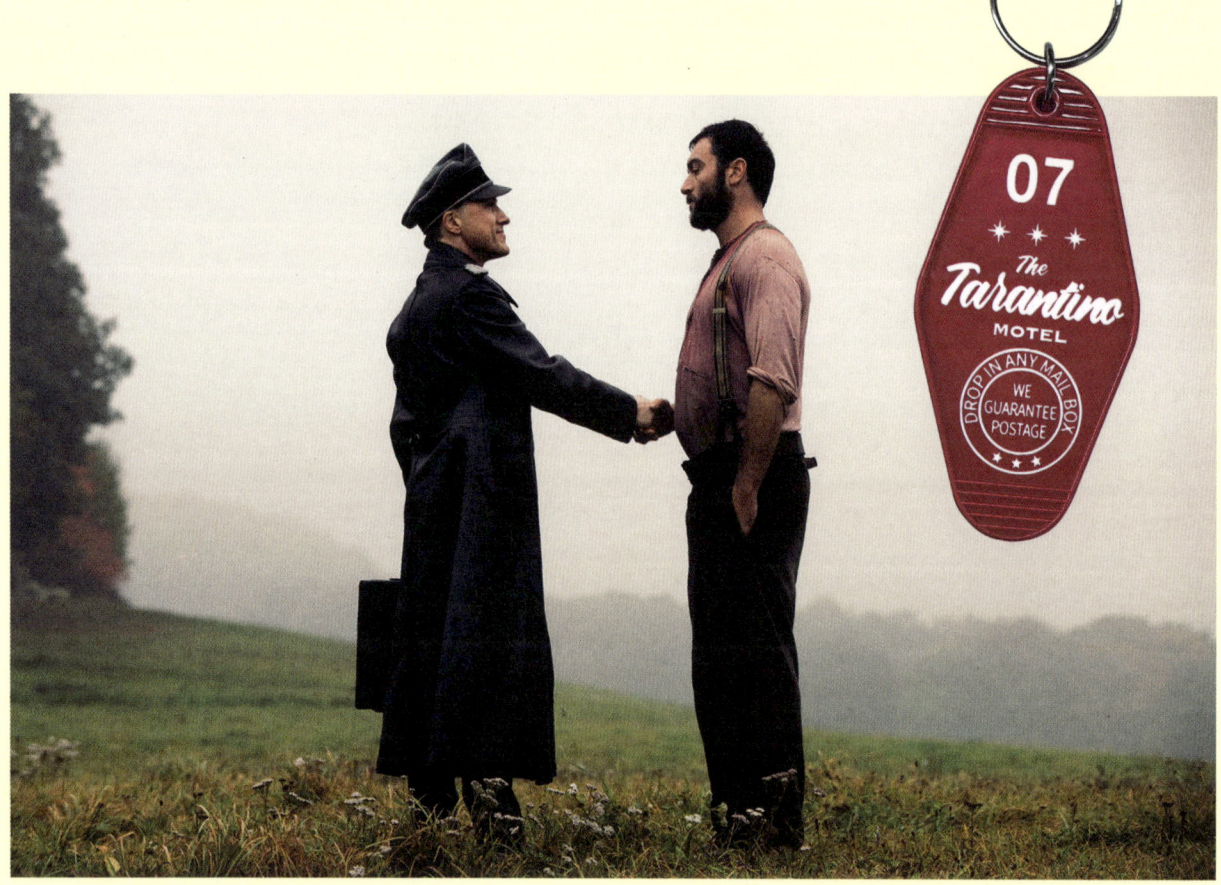

In 1941, in the heart of the French countryside, a man and his daughters are going about their business on their farm when a motorcade appears in the distance. A car stops near the little house and out steps Colonel Hans Landa, a high-ranking official in the Nazi regime, dressed from head to toe in leather. A lover of milk and pastries, Landa strikes us as a cheerful, good-natured type whose politeness borders on flattery.

Expressing himself in truly remarkable French, betrayed only by his Austrian accent, he invites himself into the LaPadite family farmhouse. From the start, his bonhomie and incessant chatter make him an unsettling character, his likableness disturbing under his SS uniform.

As he gets out his pen and his files, Landa could be mistaken for a zealous bureaucrat, a modest administrator in the Nazi regime, in an echo of what

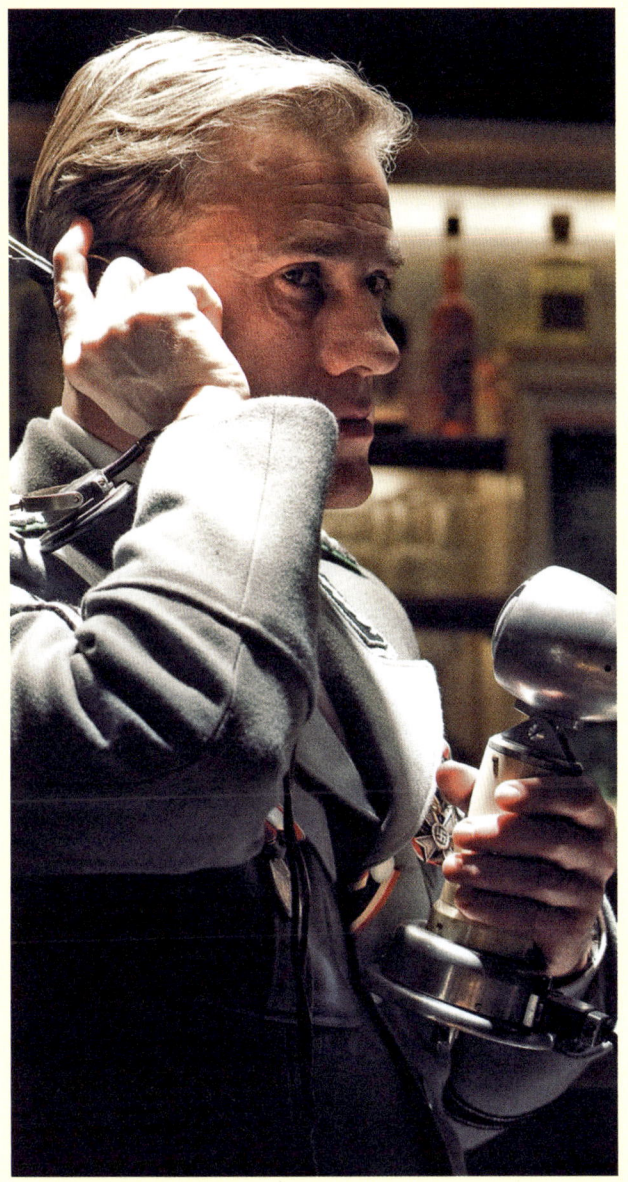

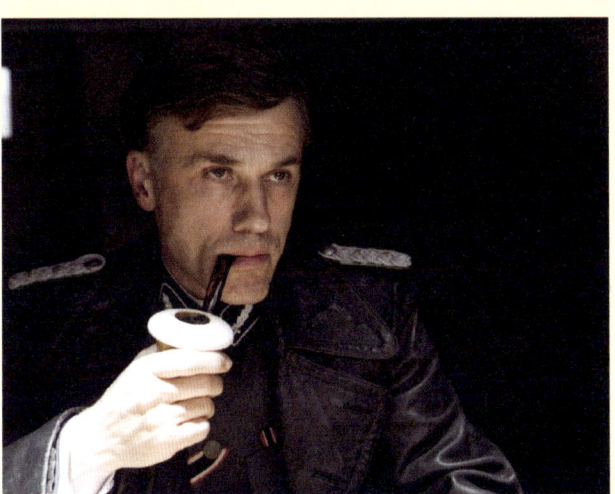

Hannah Arendt dubbed "the banality of evil," in which barbarism can sometimes hide in the seemingly ordinary, in the tiniest cog in a vast guilty structure. Might Hans Landa simply be a pen-pushing bureaucrat sent out to seal the fate of a few innocent people with his rubber stamp? Impossible, because Christoph Waltz, who was at the time largely unknown to the general public, plays him with too much style and panache. We weren't wrong about his sinister appearance: behind that affable manner of his lurks a monster. The reputation of the man they call "the Jew Hunter" precedes him. Perrier LaPadite knows it: The wolf is among the sheep. The tension rises and all of Landa's false ploys to defuse it only increase the unease—not least the enormous pipe, practically bigger than he is, which he suddenly pulls out of his coat as if for comic relief. For Tarantino, the grotesquely huge calabash pipe is a pure movie prop, designed as much to allow Landa to lighten the atmosphere and mimic LaPadite as to inject a touch of Sherlock Holmes—style theatricality into the interrogation. Like a good many of the sadistic characters in Tarantino's world, Hans Landa shows himself to be a consummate stage director. Without exhibiting any violence or raising his voice, the colonel contrives to push the farmer to admit to hiding Jews as the camera winds around the pair, encircling the scene.

Landa has a particular talent, it transpires. "*As opposed to most German soldiers, I can think like a Jew,*" he explains casually to LaPadite. This alleged understanding of the Jewish people doesn't engender any form of empathy in him. But his real gift is for language. He weaves webs of words around his victims, luring them in until they are caught in the spider's trap he has set for them and end up betraying themselves. His intelligence is matched by an unswerving cynicism, because Hans Landa is a man who is not wedded to any cause, save his own. He defines himself simply as a detective. "*A damn good detective*," as he declares lightheartedly to Lieutenant Aldo Raine. "*Finding people is my specialty so naturally, I work for the Nazis finding people and yes, some of them were Jews. But Jew Hunter? That's just a name that stuck.*" Landa is the ultimate pragmatist, a relativist of the worst kind, and the swastika, that sad little hooked cross which decorates the uniforms and flags of the Third Reich, doesn't mean much to him. Indeed, when the time comes, he won't hesitate to ditch his Nazi jacket in order to pass himself off instead as a killer of Nazis and take credit for eliminating the Führer. He dictates his terms to the American secret service in a single telephone call, coolly negotiating a rewriting of history which will see him absolved of all guilt, allowing him to go down in the history books as one of the victors. History, he knows, is always written by them. The only ideology Landa subscribes to is opportunism, and the only instinct which drives him

is the survival of the fittest, which makes him a perfect piece of scum and one of the most monstrous characters in the Tarantino universe. An animal like him richly deserves the fate reserved for him by the director's killer pen: to have that terrible symbol carved onto his forehead, to be branded forever with his disgrace when he thought he could simply wipe it away and set himself on the right side of history.

Hans Landa looks at the world with the eyes of a lone chess player, treating those around him as mere pawns. Normally, Tarantino likes nothing better than a duo, however odd a pair the two might be. Even Mr. Candie finds his sidekick in the end in Stephen, an old Black house slave who serves a destructive White cause. In *Inglourious Basterds*, though, Colonel Landa does not have an equal. It's an aspect some movie critics have seen as a limitation: "*Landa simply has no equal in the film, no counterpart who can match him*

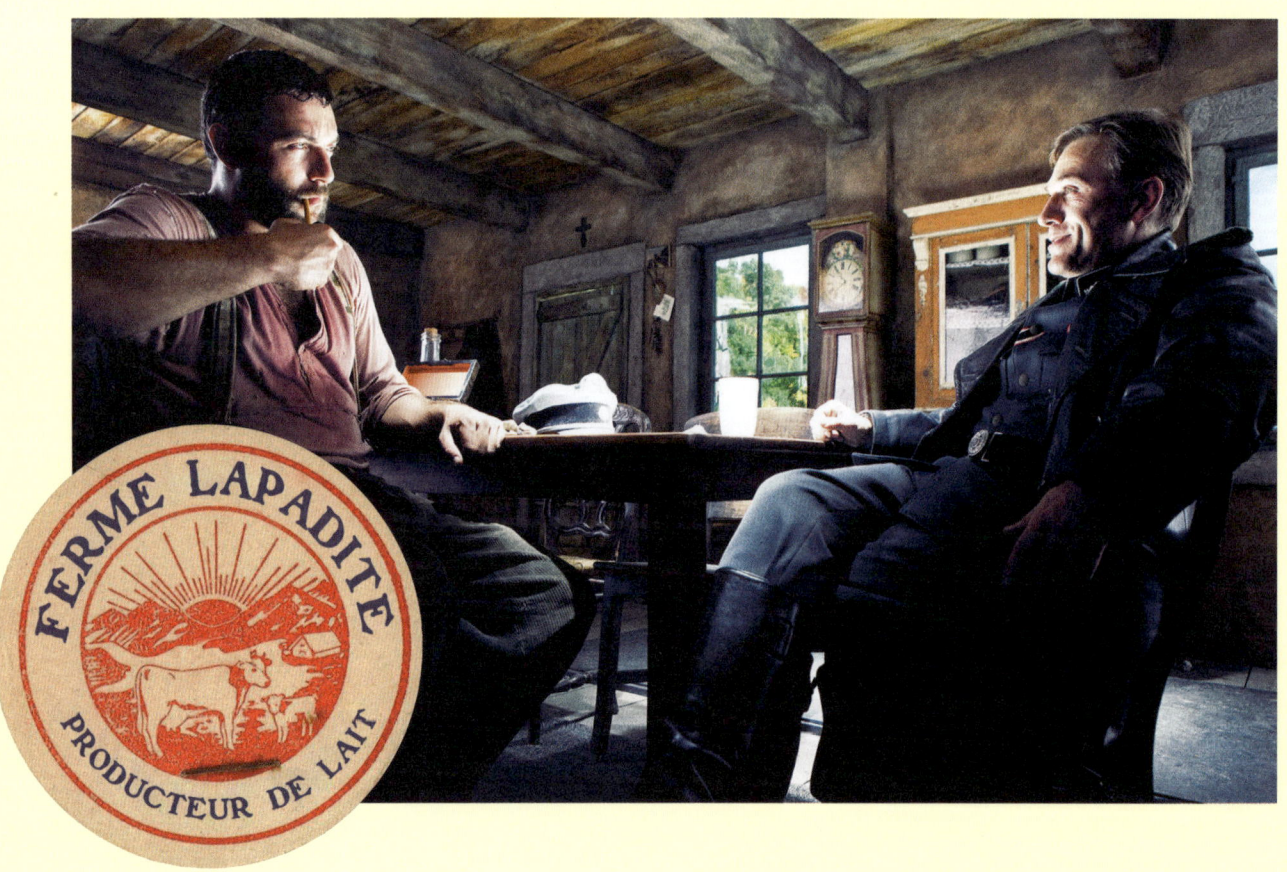

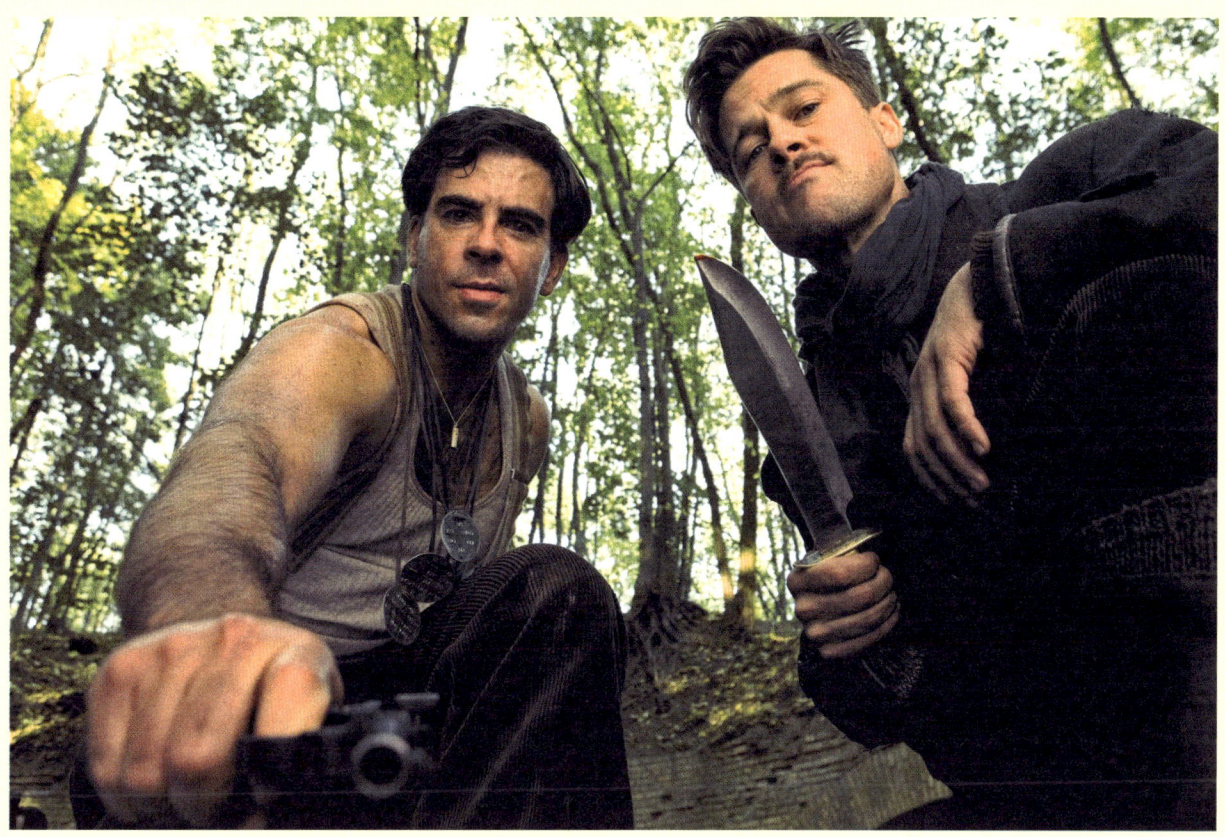

*in verbal dexterity and charisma,
who can be the Jules Winnfield and
Mia Wallace to his Vincent Vega.*"[1] But
perhaps that is the whole point of the
movie: Against the brilliant, depraved
Hans Landa, Tarantino deliberately
chooses to set the boorish, coarse
figure of Aldo Raine, who has been
parachuted in behind enemy lines
from his native Kentucky. A far cry
from Landa and his mind games, "Aldo
the Apache" is a thug who scalps,
tortures, and kills, or is happy to
watch a Nazi being beaten to death
with a baseball bat while he munches
a sandwich without any loss of
appetite.

It's a bit of leap, but it's worth
remembering what Isaac has to say
about how to be done with Nazis in
Woody Allen's movie *Manhattan*: "*We
should go down there, get some guys
together, y'know, get some bricks
and baseball bats and really explain
things to them… Well, a satirical
piece in the* Times *is one thing,
but bricks and baseball bats really
gets right to the point.*" When one
of his fellow diners says that a good
dose of satire is better than force,
Isaac replies: "*No, physical force is
always better with Nazis. It's hard
to satirize a guy with shiny boots.*"
Leaving all moral considerations
aside, when it comes to effectiveness,
would Hans Landa's sheer brilliance
really trump the crude brutality
Aldo Raine displays on his missions?
The eventual triumph of well-directed
violence over intelligence is implicit
from the start, in the film's title,
Inglourious Basterds. With its many
mistakes, the title rides roughshod
over the use of language, which
is, after all, the colonel's great
strength. Hans Landa thought he could
play a formidable game of chess
according to the strict rules which
govern his world. Aldo Raine, on the
other hand, is far less subtle, simply
laying into the chessboard with his
bat and smashing it up. Checkmate. •

1- Manohla Dargis, "Tarantino Avengers in Nazi Movieland," *The New York Times*,
August 20, 2009.

BILL

The Snake Charmer

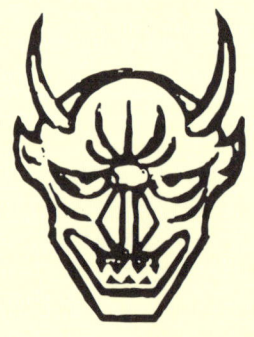

Of all the pieces of scum that inhabit Tarantino's universe— and they are legion—none likes to stage an entrance more than old Bill. After six years away from the limelight, from the release of *Jackie Brown* to that of the first volume of *Kill Bill*, Tarantino can afford to build up the suspense… And so, although the big bad wolf of *Kill Bill* does appear in the first volume of the Bride's adventures, it's only in tiny glimpses, snippets, and teasers. He is no more than a deep voice, a powerful hand wearing a ring with a green stone resting on the handle of a sword or tenderly wiping Beatrix's blood-stained face. Bill is both the underlying cause and the effect of the action in this achronological tale, but he remains elusive for a long time. And yet the interwoven chapters all lead to his inevitable fate, heralded in the directive in the very title of the movie: Bill must die.

With *Kill Bill*, we plunge headlong into Tarantino's movie-movie universe, a celluloid world full of jostling visual movie references ranging from echoes of Spaghetti Westerns to figures out of kung fu or yakuza- eiga movies. Quentin Tarantino blends genres here as freely as if "*a tornado*

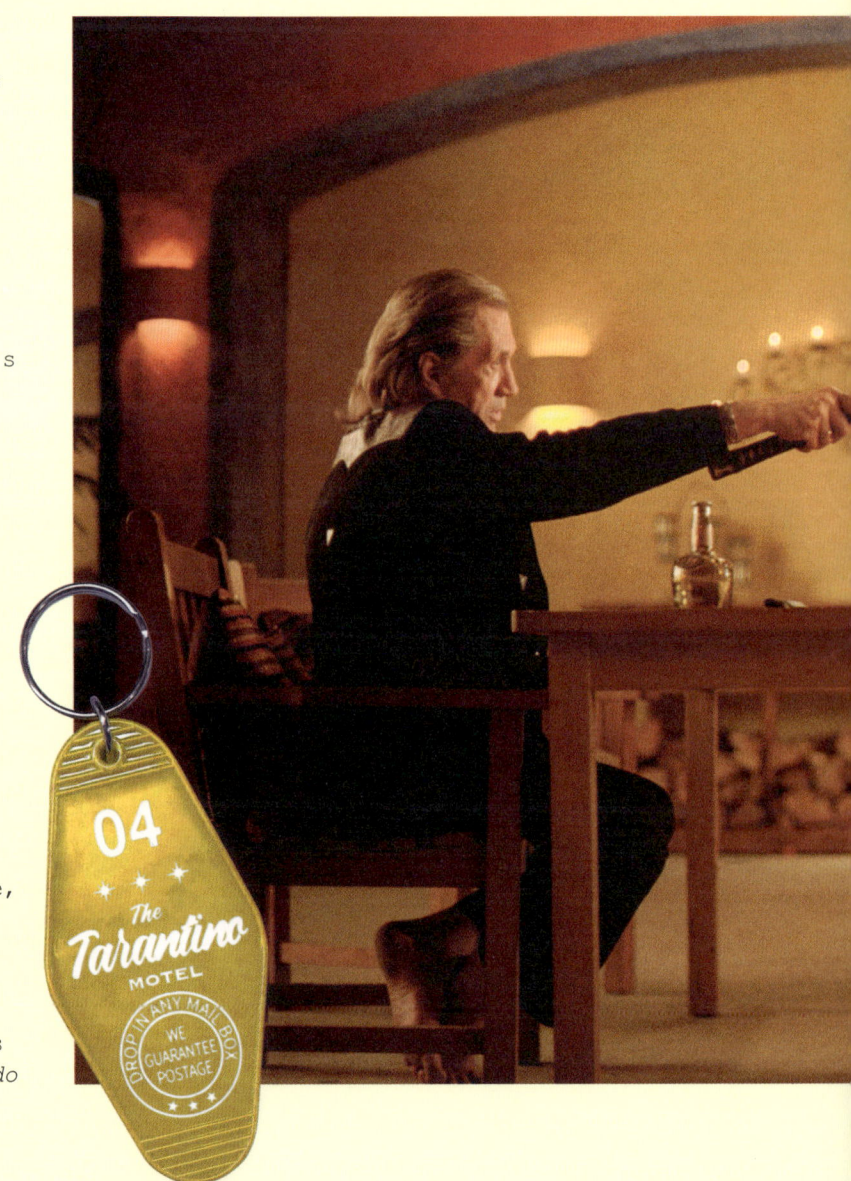

had torn through Video Archives scattering tapes in all directions," as Ian Nathan puts it.[1]

Amid this vast maelstrom of references, Bill has to stand supreme. He is after all, none other than the "final boss," the last name Beatrix has to cross off her death list. After the torrent of violence in the first movie, the second part brings an expected moral depth to the *Kill Bill* story, concentrating on the roots and repercussions of revenge. When he was writing the script, Tarantino initially thought of the actor Warren Beatty as Bill, imagining the character as more suave, more dangerously deductive, a tailor-

made villain. But Warren Beatty's commitment to the project wavered. The director turned instead to David Carradine, who starred in the 1970s TV series *Kung Fu*, in which he played a Shaolin monk—a role for which Bruce Lee was passed over in favor of Carradine—before gradually fading from memory. An inveterate movie buff, Tarantino was highly sensitive to the actor's persona, which was laden for him with a whole world of references. The *Kung Fu* series was a loose blend of Western and basic Buddhist elements, and its hero, Caine, became the archetypal peaceful warrior. In making Carradine his new Bill, Tarantino lent the character a distinctly different quality: "*With Warren, Bill would have been much more of the sexy old lion, a James Bond character—James Bond as a villain. David has a mystical quality and that became more important at the end [of the movie],*" he declared.[2]

Tarantino takes Carradine's persona and turns it on its head, transforming a warrior who never seemed to use his power in anything other than the cause of peace into the polar opposite. Unlike Caine, Bill sows death wherever he goes, yet he retains aspects of the actor's previous incarnations in both the *Kung Fu* series and the movie *Circle of Iron*, carrying them on like mythical relics: the asceticism, the pebble-snatching test, the flute. Straddling two genres, Bill is both a wild man of the West and a warrior monk, combining two fictional icons of the West and the East. But instead of subverting his hero and turning him into a classic movie villain, Tarantino gives him a horribly human motive: His thirst for revenge is driven by his pain at having been left by his lover, and this makes him a bitter—not to say pathetic—man. Bill is a dangerous character, but a fallible, aging one, his face emaciated under his tired cowboy appearance. A far cry from resolutely misogynistic characters like Stuntman Mike and Ordell Robbie,

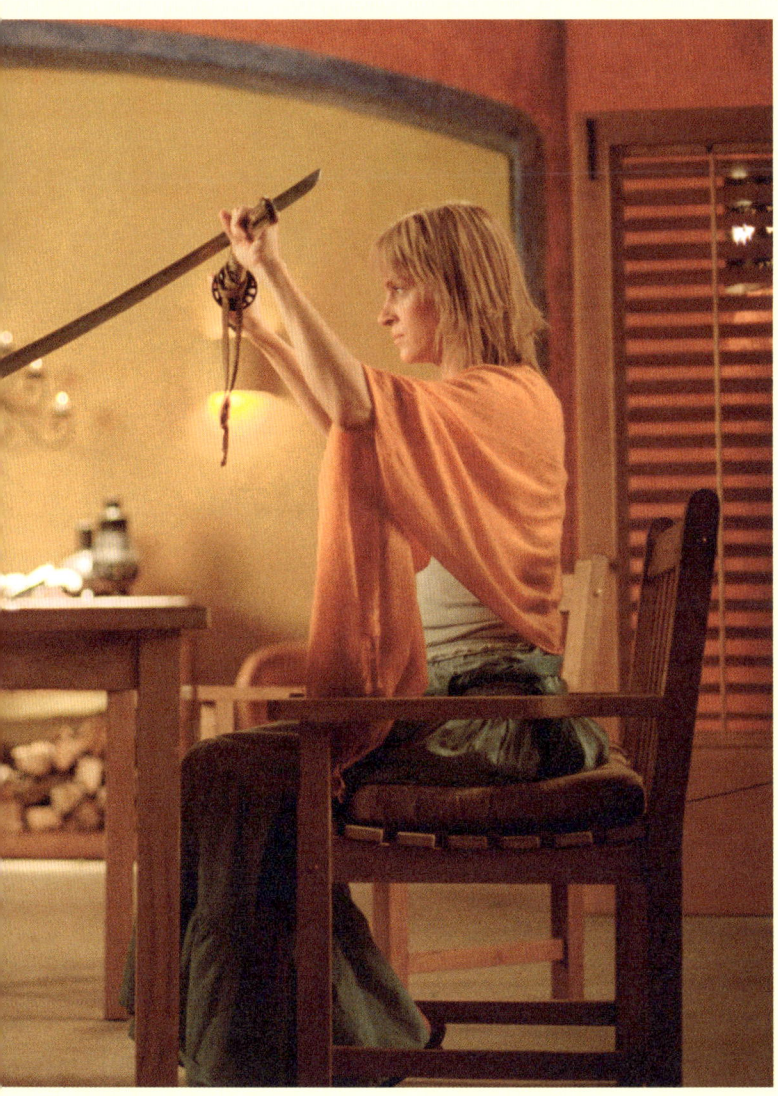

1- Ian Nathan, *Quentin Tarantino: The Iconic Filmmaker and His Work* (White Lion, 2019).
2- Mary Kaye Schilling, "From *Kill Bill* to Kids: A Q&A with Quentin Tarantino," *Entertainment Weekly*, April 9, 2004.

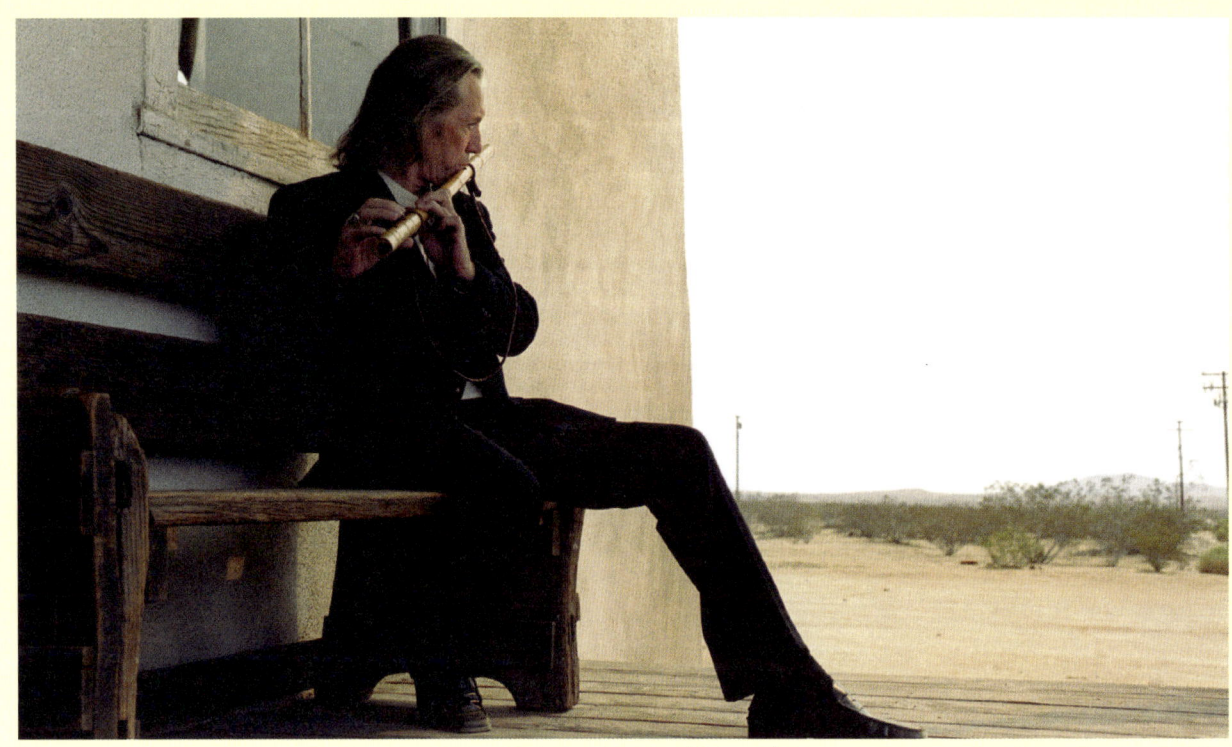

for Beatrix he is a mentor, a lover, and a father figure, as well as her tormentor. Tarantino himself grew up without a father, and Bill in *Kill Bill* has all the smoldering ambiguity of the director's portrayal of father figures in his other movies, glaringly absent or unreliable. When he appears on the threshold of the Two Pines Chapel, Bill conveys a disturbing Oedipus-like ambivalence, at once protective like a parent and tender like a lover as he speaks to his protégée in a dangerously caressing voice. She introduces him to her future husband as her father and, like a father, he offers her his blessing. "*If he's the man you want, then go stand by him,*" he whispers. Beatrix kisses him goodbye, and her fate is sealed. As she walks toward the altar, Bill's team of assassins enters the chapel.

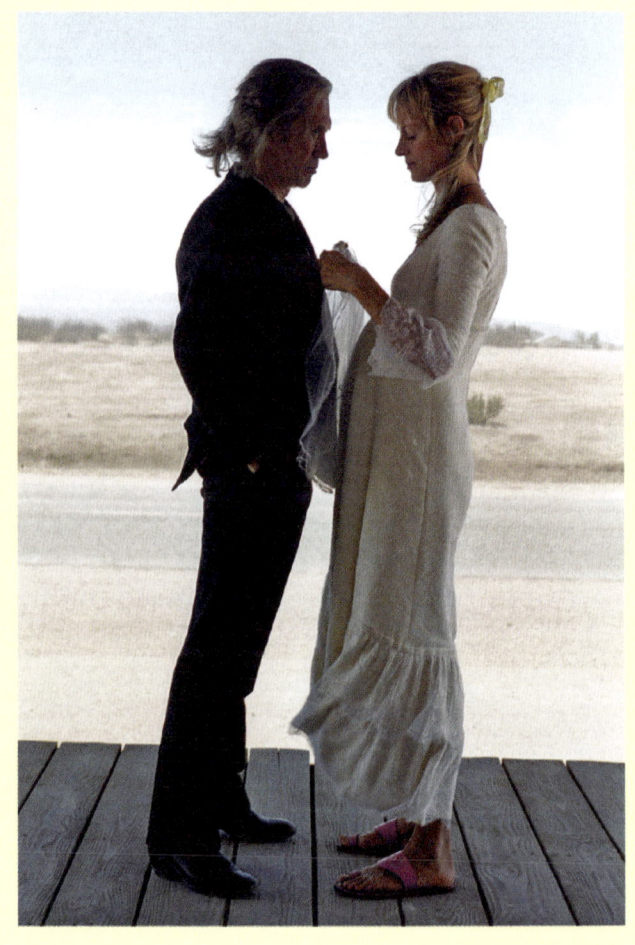

When they meet again years later, instead of being a bloodbath as we might expect, the scene plays out in one of the director's favorite arenas, speech. In his hacienda, lacing wisdom with references to pop culture, killer

Bill discourses on the subject of Superman: In contrast to most other superheroes, in his red cape the last son of Krypton is his true self, and it is as his alter ego Clark Kent that he is in disguise. Through this theory—worthy of the heady days of Video Archives, the video store where Tarantino earned his stripes—Bill reminds the Bride that she is a killer bee by nature and that it is useless to fight it. As for the massacre at Two Pines, he simply says: "*I'm a killer. I'm a murdering bastard. You know that. And there are consequences to breaking the heart of a murdering bastard.*"

Having reached the last name on her death list, Beatrix finishes off her erstwhile mentor thanks to a piece of ancestral knowledge with a ludicrously long name, the famous "Five Point Palm Exploding Heart Technique" taught to her by Pai Mei, who always refused to divulge the secret of it to Bill. Far from the cold-blooded executions which marked her journey of revenge, the Bride offers Bill a dignified death. With the tragic grace of a wounded cowboy, of a samurai ready to fall, he gets up, advances a few steps, barefooted, and collapses. The murdering bastard Bill finally succumbs, literally this time, to a broken heart. •

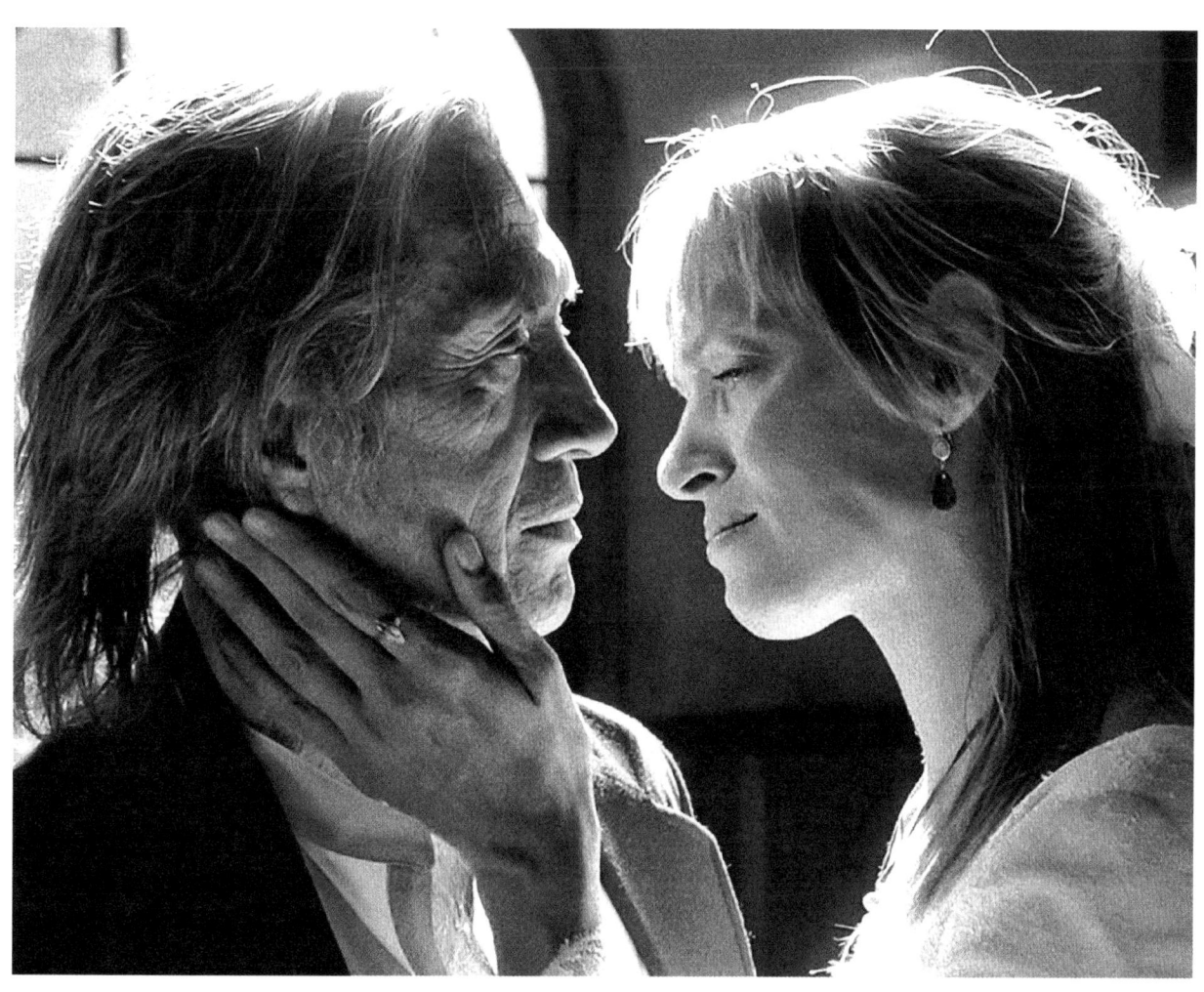

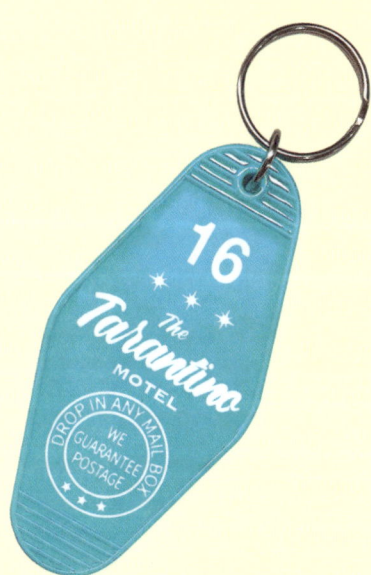

BUTCH & FABIENNE

The Boxer in Love

Could Quentin Tarantino be a big softie? It would be nice to think that there's always a sweet heart or two pumping away at the center of the chaos in the director's movies. In *Pulp Fiction*, Butch and Fabienne obviously provide this nub of sweetness, in the intimacy of an anonymous motel that isn't so different in the end from the one we welcomed you to today.

Butch Coolidge, an aging boxer, is offered a tidy sum by crime boss Marsellus Wallace to lose his next match. Butch takes the money and cheats the crime lord, because his pride won't let him go down in the fight. In a fit of fury, he beats his opponent to death before fleeing in the direction of the River Glen Motel, where his French girlfriend is already waiting for him. "*That had to be the bloodiest and, hands down, the most brutal fight this city has ever seen,*" a radio commentator shouts. Unpremeditated though it was, this murder doesn't unduly affect our boxer on the run. "*Hey, fuck him… If he was a better boxer, he'd still be alive,*" he spits into the receiver in a phone booth. Perhaps a taste for blood is in

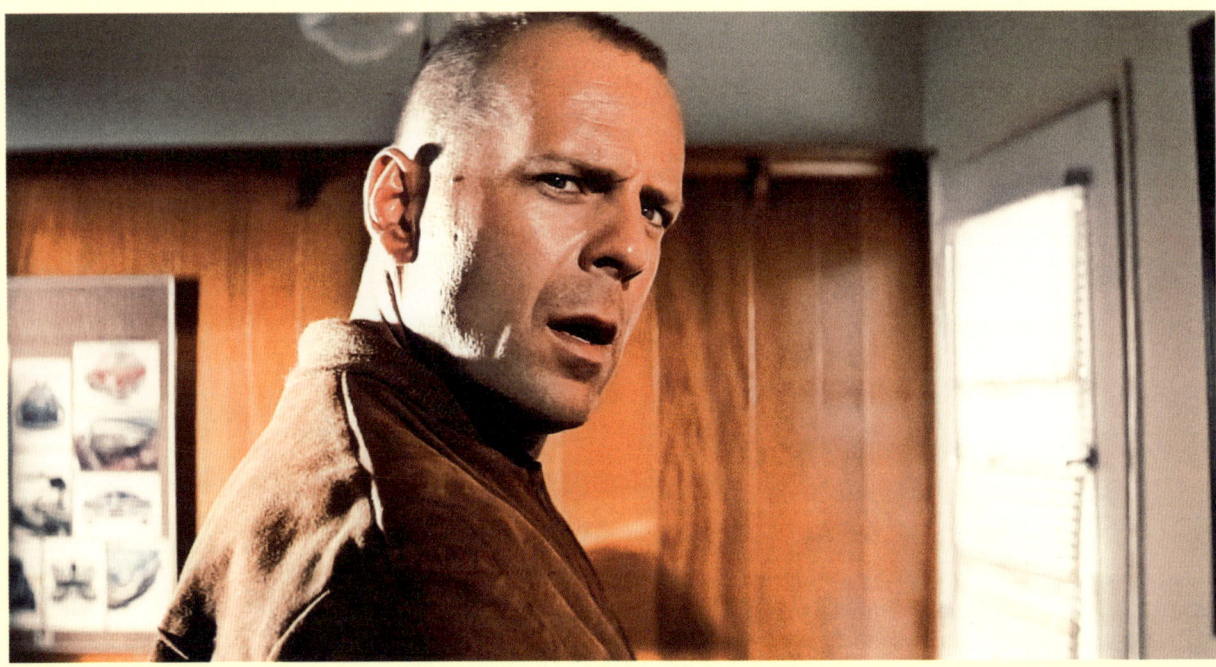

Butch's genes. Descended from a long line of soldiers, he has no war to fight, no way of venting his violence apart from in the ring or in daily life. Even his first name conjures up the idea of brute maleness fueled by an excess of testosterone.

Later, when he decides to fly to the rescue and save Marsellus from the clutches of a dangerous bunch of depraved thugs, Butch chooses his weapon with care, lingering over the possible alternatives in the pawnshop as you might over the options in a video game. While Marsellus is being subjected to the worst possible kinds of violence in the back of the store, Butch hesitates, dithers about what to go for—a hammer, a chain saw, a baseball bat? Finally, and very solemnly, he picks up a Japanese sword, prefiguring the bloodshed in *Kill Bill* (the hammer and baseball bat, meanwhile, will find their way into *Django Unchained* and *Inglourious Basterds* respectively). Does the violence the soldier's son metes out to the two abominable criminals perhaps finally demonstrate a measure of moral rigor which he had previously lacked, the integrity that separates a man of brute force from a hero? The fact that his chosen weapon is a samurai sword, steeped in a strict code of honor, could certainly signal such a transformation… But that would only be plausible if you ignored the mad light that flickers in his eyes as he toys with his prey. Is Butch perhaps, in fact, a genuine sociopath?

Our silent boxer could, however, very well be a sentimental type. After his bloody fight, he takes refuge in the arms of Fabienne, revealing a very different side of his character. "*I wanted Butch to be a complete fucking asshole. I wanted him to be basically like Ralph Meeker as Mike Hammer in Aldrich's* Kiss Me Deadly. *I wanted him to be a bully and a jerk, except that when he's with his girlfriend, Fabienne, he's a sweetheart,*" declared Tarantino.[1]

Their relationship is one hundred percent sugar, as evidenced in the sickly sweet nicknames Butch bestows on his sweetheart: "Lemon Pie," "Sugar Pop." With these two, everything comes back to their mouths: They give each other tender kisses and Fabienne asks

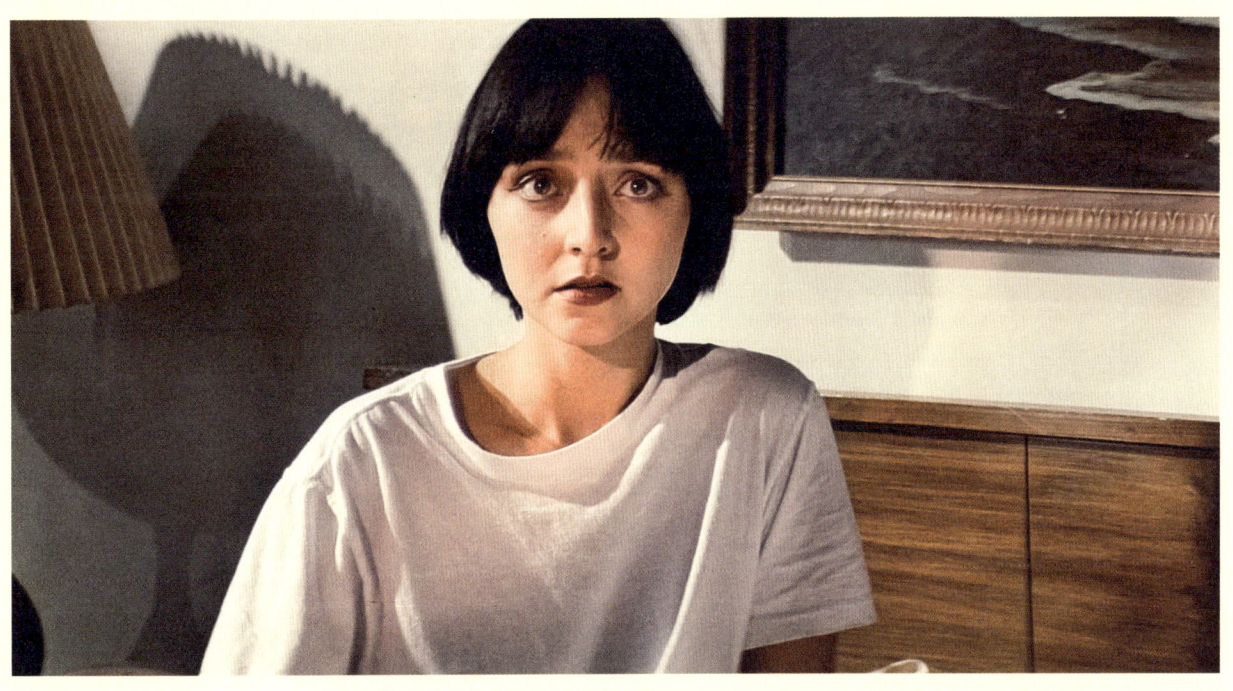

1- Manohla Dargis, "Quentin Tarantino on *Pulp Fiction*," *Sight & Sound*, May 1994, reprinted in Gerald Peary, ed., *Quentin Tarantino: Interviews* (University Press of Mississippi, 1998).

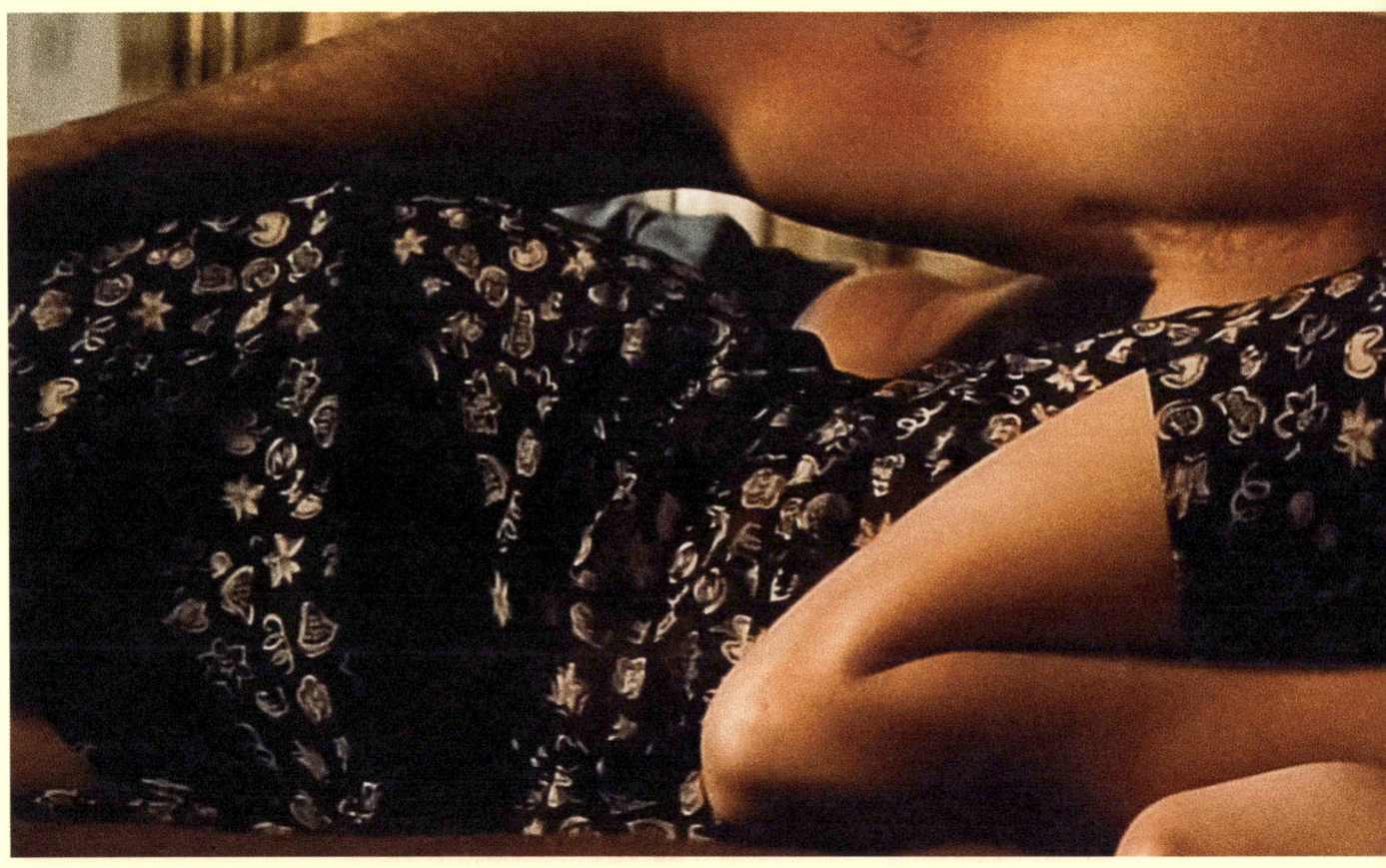

Butch to give her "*oral pleasure*." A little later, she envisions a gigantic breakfast for herself: a great stack of blueberry pancakes with maple syrup, eggs, five sausages, a cup of coffee, a large glass of orange juice, and, to cap it off, a big slice of pie. Butch is incredulous: "*Pie for breakfast?*" "*Any time of the day is a good time for pie,*" she retorts. And while he abandons his love and leaves her to her breakfast, it's once again out of excessive sentimentality, as he goes off to retrieve the watch which his father bequeathed him and Fabienne left behind. "*I'll be back before you can say* blueberry pie," Butch tells her. "*Blueberry pie!*" she cries in a voice full of emotion. Only a love interest as syrupy as this could soften the likes of a man like Butch.

They make an odd couple, the angry boxer and the irritating little French girl who is like something out of a Jean-Luc Godard movie. Whether you're a fan or not, whether you find her charming or cringeworthy, Fabienne is the only person who is capable of disarming Butch. With her infantile ways of talking and behaving, she is no Bonnie Parker, but veers rather toward one of the French New Wave movie heroines played by Anna Karina, such as Marianne in *Pierrot le Fou*, who goes off on the run with her lover (Jean-Paul Belmondo) to the Mediterranean. Between the sheets, Butch and Fabienne murmur sweet nothings to each about their own crazy escapade in a kind of foreplay. The danger that stalks them is nothing more than a lovers' game: "*Butch, my love,*" Fabienne whispers to him in French, "*the adventure begins.*"

Quentin Tarantino is a filmmaker who enjoys couples in his own way, as Jules and Vincent, Django and Schultz, Ordell and Louis, Rick and Cliff all attest. It's rather

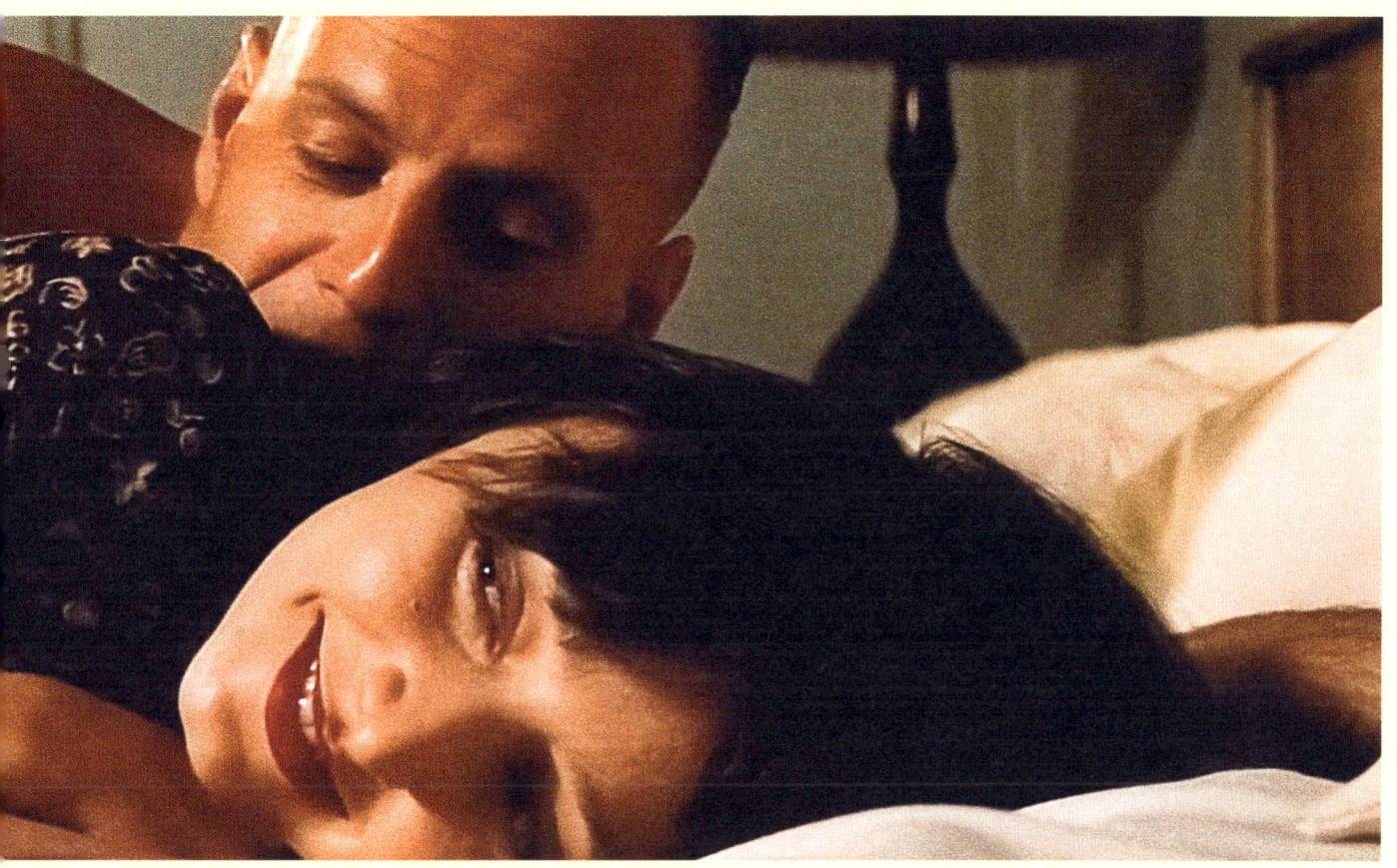

surprising, however, to hear him say that he's a great fan of romantic comedies (which he loves watching on planes). There's nothing ironic about the title of *True Romance*, he tells us. When a drifter like Clarence meets a call girl like Alabama, it's love at first sight. A suitcase full of cocaine later, and the romance turns into a frenetic road trip. But the destructive force Tony Scott injects into Tarantino's screenplay is only convincing because of the unshakable faith the viewer has in the couple's love. A similar blend of R-rated sentimentalism characterizes the criminal lovers in *Natural Born Killers*. Tarantino has since brought countless lovebirds to our screens, most of whom flourish on the wrong side of the law. In *Pulp Fiction*, Pumpkin and Honey Bunny—a pair of nicknames every bit as silly as the ones Butch gives his ladylove—clearly embody a comic version of this type of romance,

hijacking a whole tradition of lovers on the run and descending into vaudeville. "*I'm not gonna kill anybody,*" Honey Bunny simpers before yelling at the crowd like a madwoman, gun in hand. Of all Tarantino's pairs of outlaw lovers, this redneck Bonnie and Clyde, who discuss the relative merits of different sorts of robberies over the remains of their breakfast, are the pettiest.

What the lovers in Tarantino's movies have in common is that they are oddballs—outsiders and rejects adrift in the world who find in each other the one buoy they can cling to. When the world turns its back on them, our heroes turn their backs on the world, climb into a bright pink Cadillac or jump onto an Easy Rider–style chopper, and drive off down the highways of America, headed for Cancun or the South Pacific. For the lovers in Tarantino's films, the adventure—the real adventure—begins when the movie ends. •

THE RED APPLE VENDING MACHINE

Forbidden Fruit

"That's the Red Apple way!"

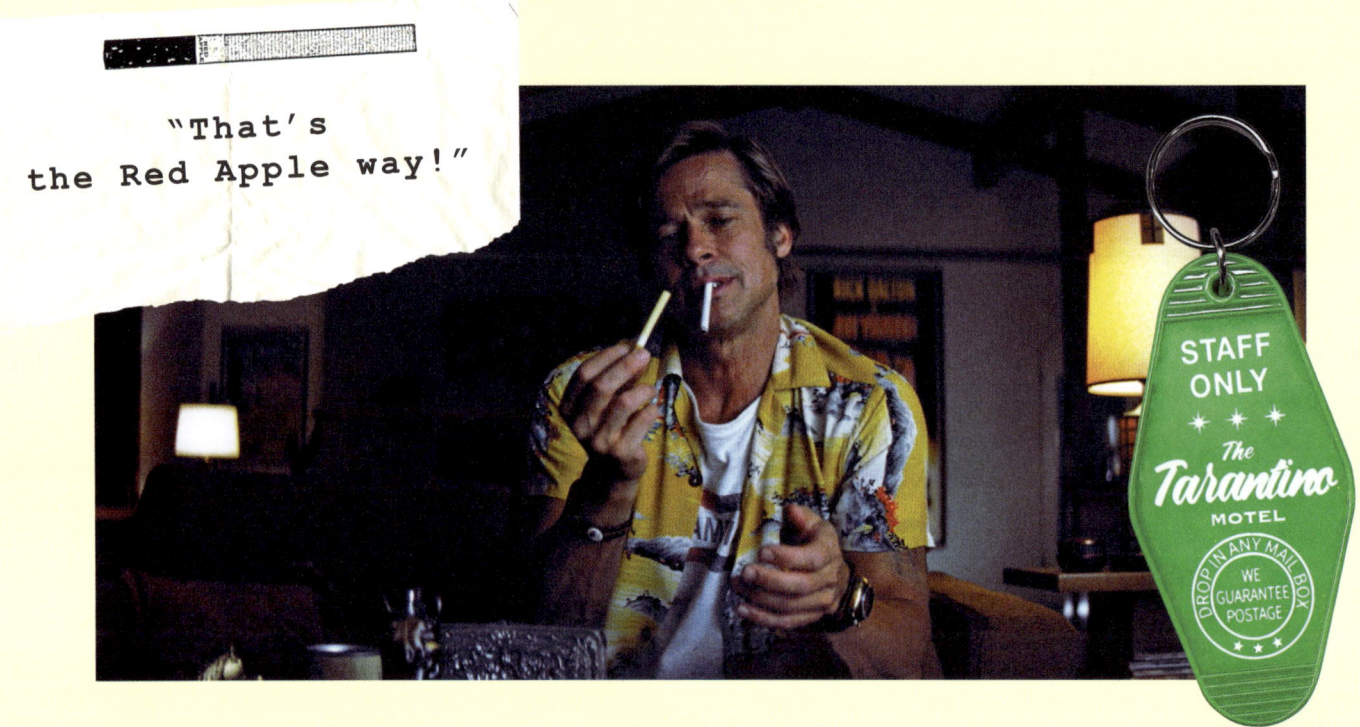

At the back of the motel, close to a machine full of cans of Big Red and G.O. Juice, is an old vending machine which is almost a collector's item… On its side is a logo in faded colors: a red apple with a worm coming out of it, a cigarette clamped to its lips, its mouth fixed in a depraved smile. Inside, you've got it, are rows of nice little carcinogenic orange cylinders. This vending machine, kindly provided to our humble town by the Red Apple company, is here to replenish our guests' nicotine supplies at any time of day or night. Of course some people prefer other brands (Arlene in *Death Proof*, for instance, has a weakness for

Capitol W Lights), but nothing is more popular than the famous Red Apple cigarettes.

This is because they go way back: According to our researchers, the Red Apple Cigarette Company was founded in 1862. It's not surprising, therefore, to catch sight of the apple logo on a packet of rolling tobacco on a table in *The Hateful Eight*, immediately after the American Civil War. Red Apple cigarettes pop up regularly in Tarantino's movies, from *Pulp Fiction* to the four-segment *Four Rooms*, through *Inglourious Basterds* and *Kill Bill*, in a parody of product placement. Their presence in

Tarantino's universe (and indeed in his extended universe, in the movies *A Night in Hell* and *Planet Terror,* directed by his friend and collaborator Robert Rodriguez) has certainly not gone unnoticed. But it is in *Once Upon a Time… in Hollywood* that the brand really has its finest hour, in a commercial in which Rick Dalton plays the face of Red Apple, singing the cigarettes' praises to his television viewers. On the strength of this endorsement, the QT brand may well topple another, equally fictitious one: the famous Morley cigarettes, which made a solid name for themselves in Hollywood through their appearances in pop culture movies and series including *Psycho*, *The Fourth Dimension*, and *The X-Files*.

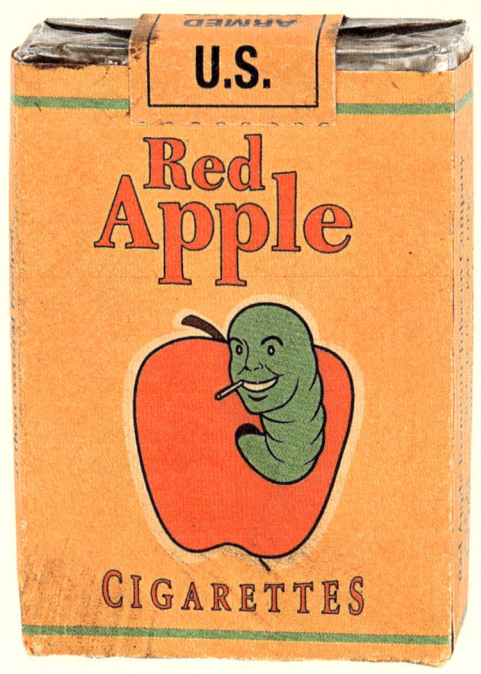

Not only have Red Apple cigarettes traveled through time, but the American brand has also spread across the globe, as evidenced by the billboard which greets Beatrix Kiddo when she arrives in the Japanese archipelago. From one film to another, QT fills out the story. All that's missing now is for one of the little orange cylinders to find its way out into the world and become a material reality… And where better than Japan to host a Red Apple vending machine? The country has over four million vending machines—that's one for every thirty inhabitants—generating a colossal annual turnover of some forty billion dollars. Over there, they're called *jidō hanbaiki*, often abbreviated to *jihanki*. These mini convenience stores, or *konbini*, are scattered all over Tokyo and in the remotest parts of the country as well, ready to supply the most pressing of needs (ah, an iced bubble tea in the middle of summer…). A good half of them are dedicated to drinks: fruit juices, sodas, hot coffee, beer, sake, and even freeze-dried ramen or soup. Need a snack? No problem: You can get hamburgers, Hokkaido cream cakes with mascarpone or genoise sponge compressed into

aluminum cans, fried oysters covered in golden breadcrumbs, and, perhaps rather less enticingly, whale meat. Yes, these machines are unlike any you might encounter elsewhere in the world. And to bring it back to where we started, it's worth noting that the very first of these machines, made by Takashichi Tawaraya, appeared in the year 1888 and was, of course, none other than a cigarette vending machine.

Today, rumor has it that our Red Apple vending machine has a twin—the only one in existence, perhaps—discreetly nestled on a little street somewhere in Japan. This legendary vending machine must surely be one of Tokyo's best-kept secrets—and don't expect us to tell you where to find it, because we don't know. A little club of inveterate smokers doubtless guards its treasure fiercely: One can imagine a figure slipping three hundred yen into the slot, quickly pocketing the iconic little packet, and then tiptoeing silently away. So if by any chance you come across a *jihanki* decorated with a beautiful red apple, don't say anything about it. Just count yourself lucky to be in on the secret, because in the real world, legends are becoming scarce… •

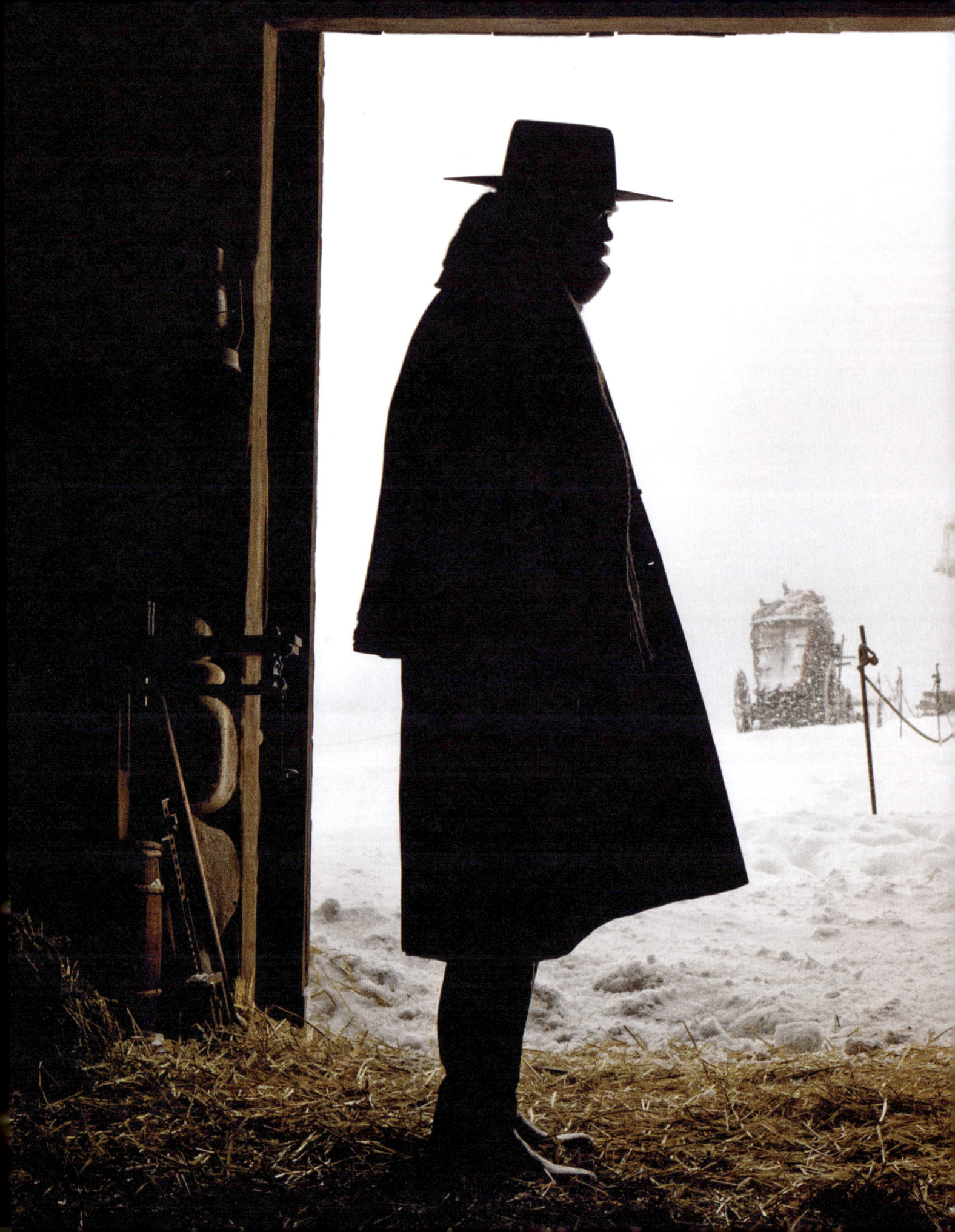

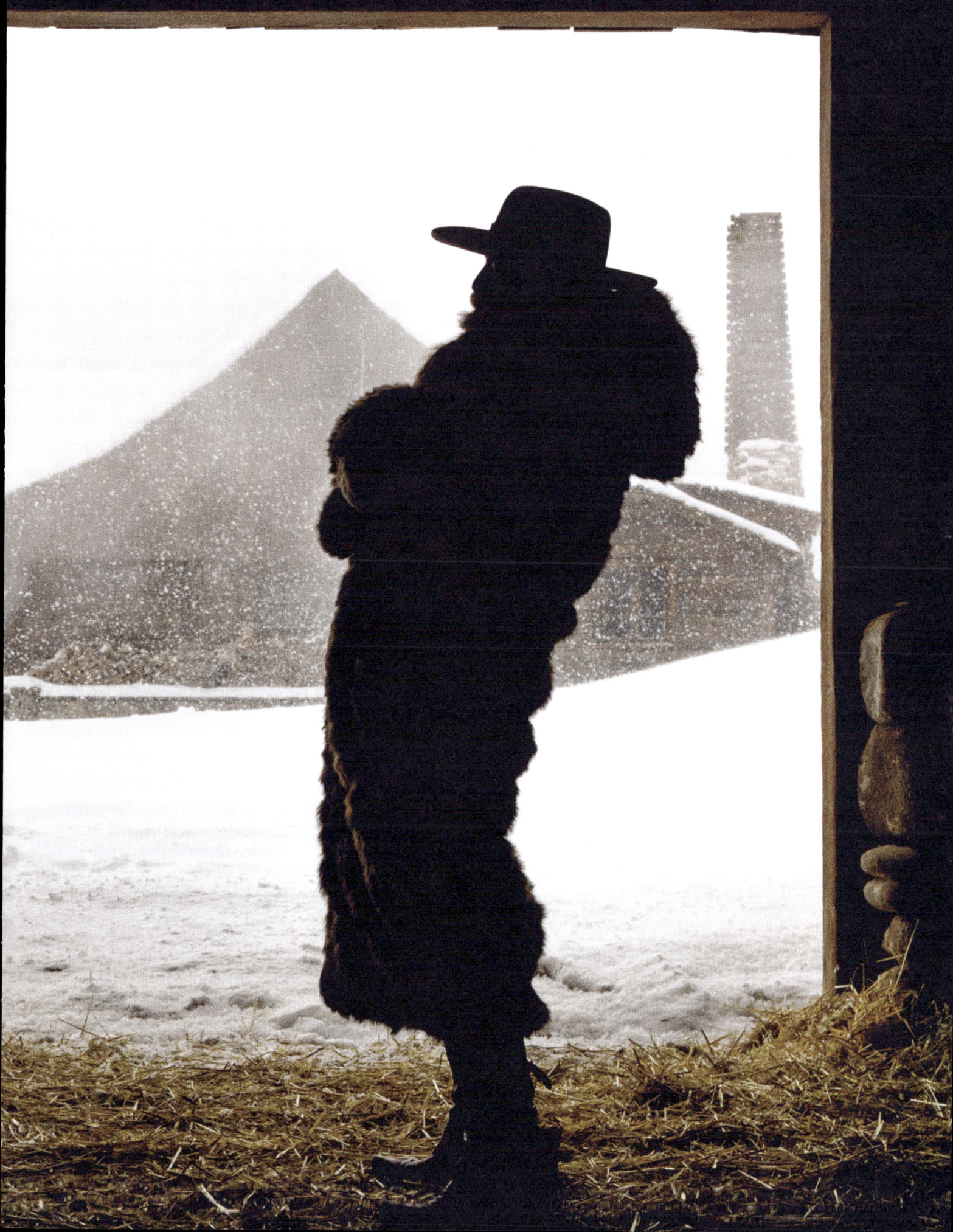

III

The Bookstore

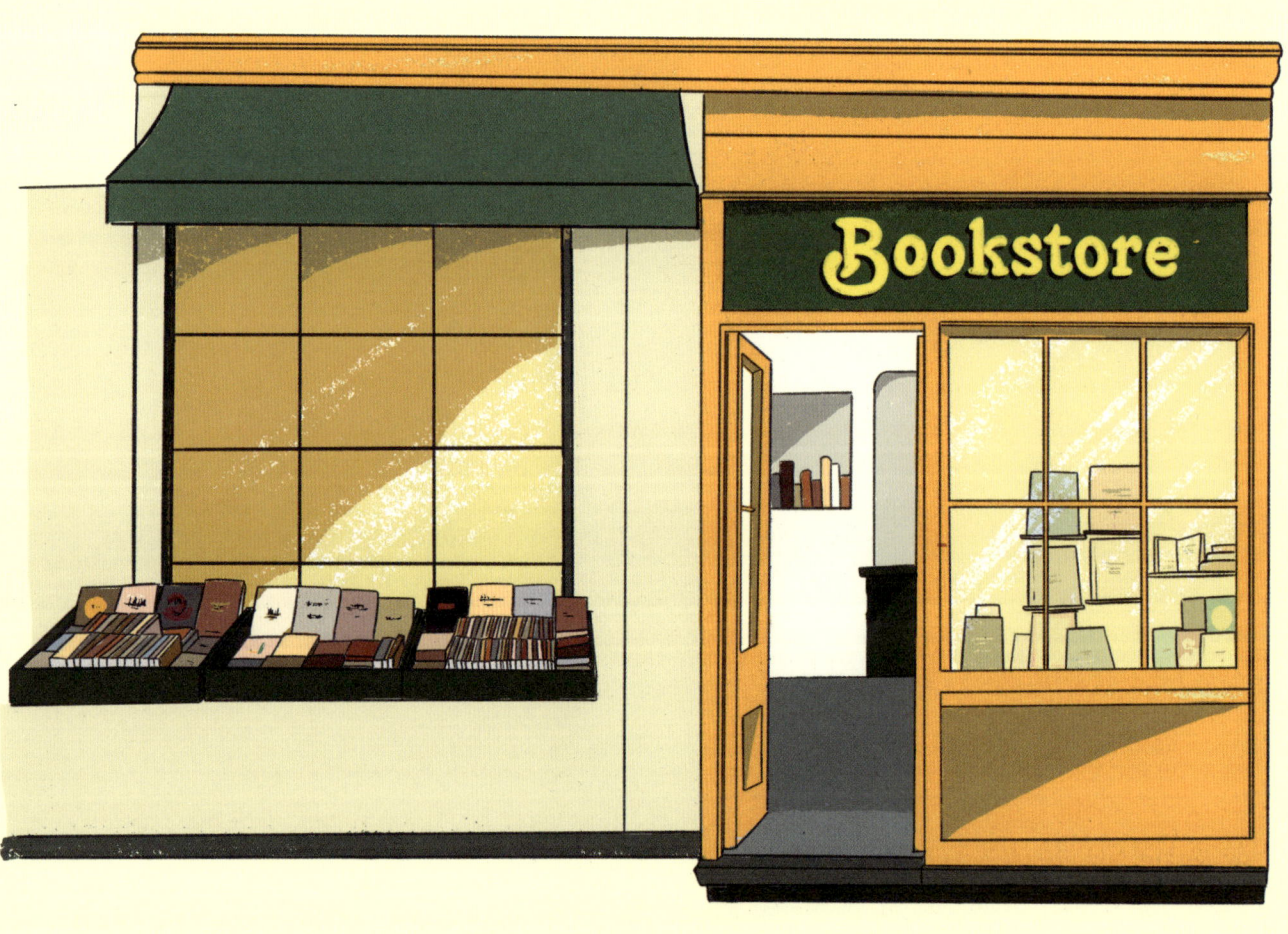

The Bookstore Reviews

THE BOOKSTORE
453 S Spring St Ground Floor
Phone 555-0123

Outside there's a stand overflowing with dog-eared old books the store will let you have for just a dollar each. In the window is a display of books with covers faded yellow by the California sun. People say you can tell the quality of a town by the quality of its bookstores, and Tarantino Town is no exception in that regard. You'll find our bookstore on a street corner. Inside, the organization defies all logic, forcing customers to ferret around through stacks of pulp fiction, magazines, novelizations, thrillers, and great classics to land on their next adventure. And while Tarantino definitely acquired his movie education sitting in obscure theaters or on a couch surrounded by thousands of VHS tapes, he also crammed his shelves with books, feeding his already fertile imagination still further and developing his screenwriting technique. Even at this early stage, QT clearly anticipated spending the next years of his career writing in various forms. Both a filmmaker with a zest for words and a brilliant dialogue writer capable of filling entire pages with black ink, whether by hand or armed with his perennial Smith Corona typewriter, Tarantino of course knows perfectly well what he owes to all those books he devoured lying in bed or in the local diner, in between mouthfuls of a Big Kahuna Burger. In a recess at the back of the store, your humble bookseller has carefully compiled a selection of well-considered reference works for you, a handful of volumes to help you immerse yourself in Quentin Tarantino's library. It's true, reading takes time and requires a certain amount of discipline, but trust your bookseller: The few hours you spend engrossed in a book will be repaid a hundredfold. So come on in, settle down in one of our reading corners, and leaf through anything and everything you can lay your hands on. We open when we can, and we close when we feel like it.

Printed in U.S.A

PULP

Pulp Fiction

pulp / ˈpəlp / n.

1. A soft, moist, shapeless mass of matter.
2. A magazine or book containing lurid subject matter and being characteristically printed on rough, unfinished paper.

American Heritage Dictionary
New College Edition

Girls and revolvers, the colors red and yellow, killers in the night and corpses at dawn, eye-catching titles, and thrilling detective stories. From the 1920s onward, dime magazines, printed on poor quality paper machine-made from wood pulp, flooded the American market. What exactly was Quentin Tarantino celebrating, however, when he deliberately made reference to all that pulp fiction which piled up in heaps in American drugstores in the first half of the twentieth century? A kind of lowbrow culture, an underestimated genre which was to literature what B movies were to the cinema—B movies being, of course, something for which Tarantino constantly declares his fondness. A second-rate genre which took literature firmly out of polite society, where it had been stuck and bored, and let it out to rub shoulders a little with the nefarious and vulgar underclasses. When he opened his second movie with the literal and figurative definition of the word *pulp*, Tarantino was effectively outlining its scope.

Pulp magazines were not limited to crime stories, of course: Science fiction, Westerns, and politely erotic romances all did very well too, and the cheap serialized stories became real testing grounds for different genres, each with their own standardized, easily recognizable worlds, reproduced ad infinitum with an emphasis on mass production. In 1939, Robert de Graff initiated something of a minor revolution in America when he brought out his "Pocket Books." The die was cast, and paperbacks took over. Determined to swamp the market, de Graff did not just focus on the 2,800-odd bookstores dotted about the country. Instead, he realized that there were plenty of cigarette vendors and newspaper kiosks, drugstores and bus stations which were only too happy to relieve all and sundry of their small change. And for roughly an extra twenty-five cents, a whole new market opened up. Paperbacks poured onto the market: As well as reprints of the classics, there was an inexhaustible supply of books with dubious titles and enticing illustrations. Very soon, it was all-out war, with every title trying to outdo the competition: Even the classics were tricked out with suggestive covers, complete with pictures of scantily clad women and the words "complete and unabridged"

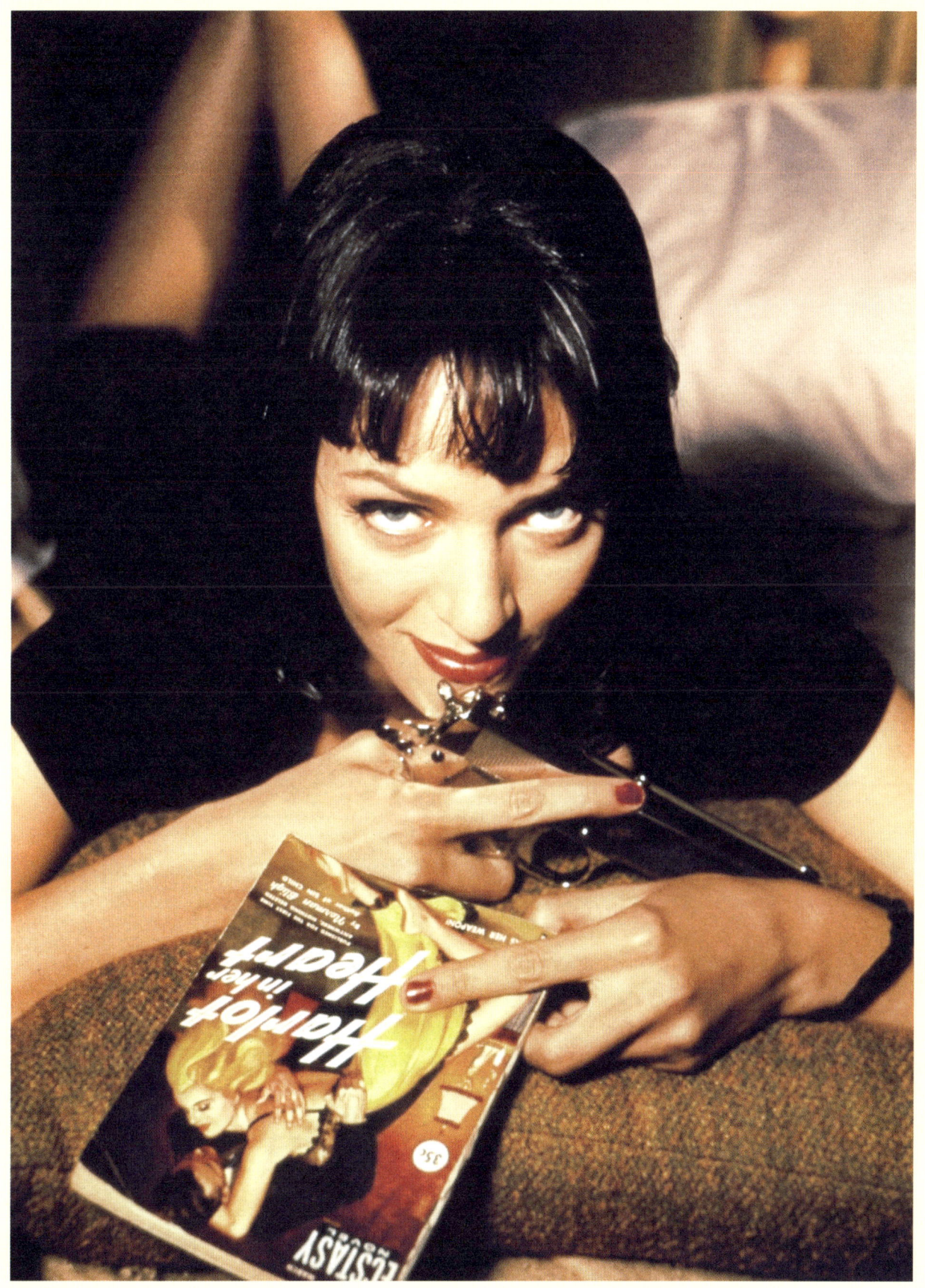

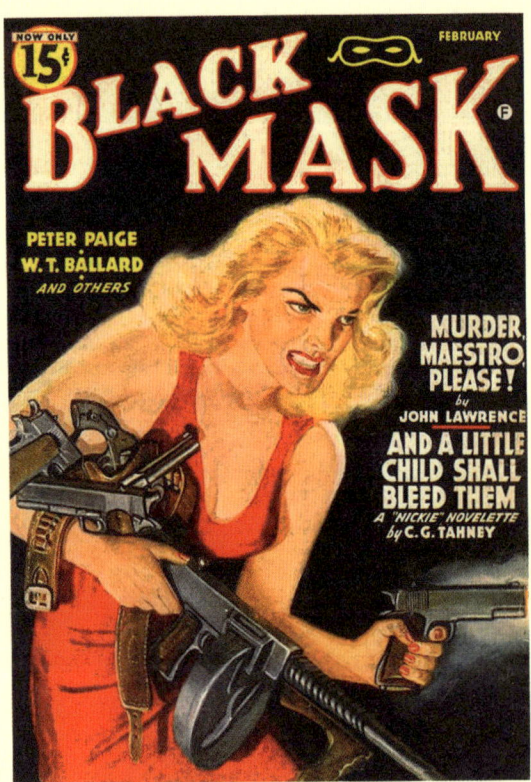

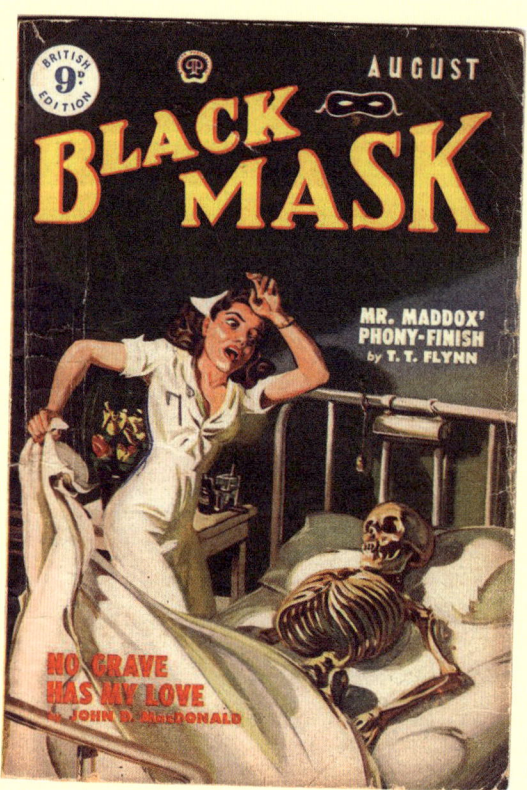

to lend them a subversive air, even
when they had never been censored.
Respectable book publishers watched
the phenomenon with a suspicious eye,
while small religious factions and
citizens' groups attacked it head-
on. These good people, for whom
books still embodied a sense of
virtue, accused pulp fiction books of
being lowbrow, politically incorrect
entertainment. Which of course they
were—and proudly so.

If pulp fiction is sometimes confused
with thrillers, it is because the two
genres intersect. Having themselves
succeeded dime novels, pulp magazines
welcomed to their pages young up-
and-coming writers who would in turn
usher in a new era in crime fiction—
authors such as Dashiell Hammett and
Raymond Chandler, among others. With
its tales of hard-boiled detectives
and their suitably hard shells, pulp
contributed significantly to the
development of the crime novel as we
know it. Of course, thrillers already
enjoyed a decidedly bad reputation.
They were considered, in many ways,

to be the lowest form of literature,
a prejudice which the inherent
shoddiness of pulp fiction books and
their ridiculously low prices did
nothing but reinforce.

The new brand of crime novel was not
a proper form of literature, and
decent society infinitely preferred
Anglo-Saxon mystery novels and the
pompous mechanics of "whodunits" in
which armchair detectives—of whom
Miss Marple is one of the greatest
representatives—manage to unmask
the culprits from a distance without
leaving the comfort of their living
room. But the new breed of writers
sprung from pulp was determined to
take crime fiction out of the living
room, where it was in danger of being
lulled to sleep by all the polite
arrests and fine pieces of deduction.
Instead, they took their hard-boiled
detectives out onto the streets and
into a world touched by squalor,
the better to show the hardships,
injustices, and shortcomings of an
unhealthy society. Needless to say,
these thrillers, with their tough

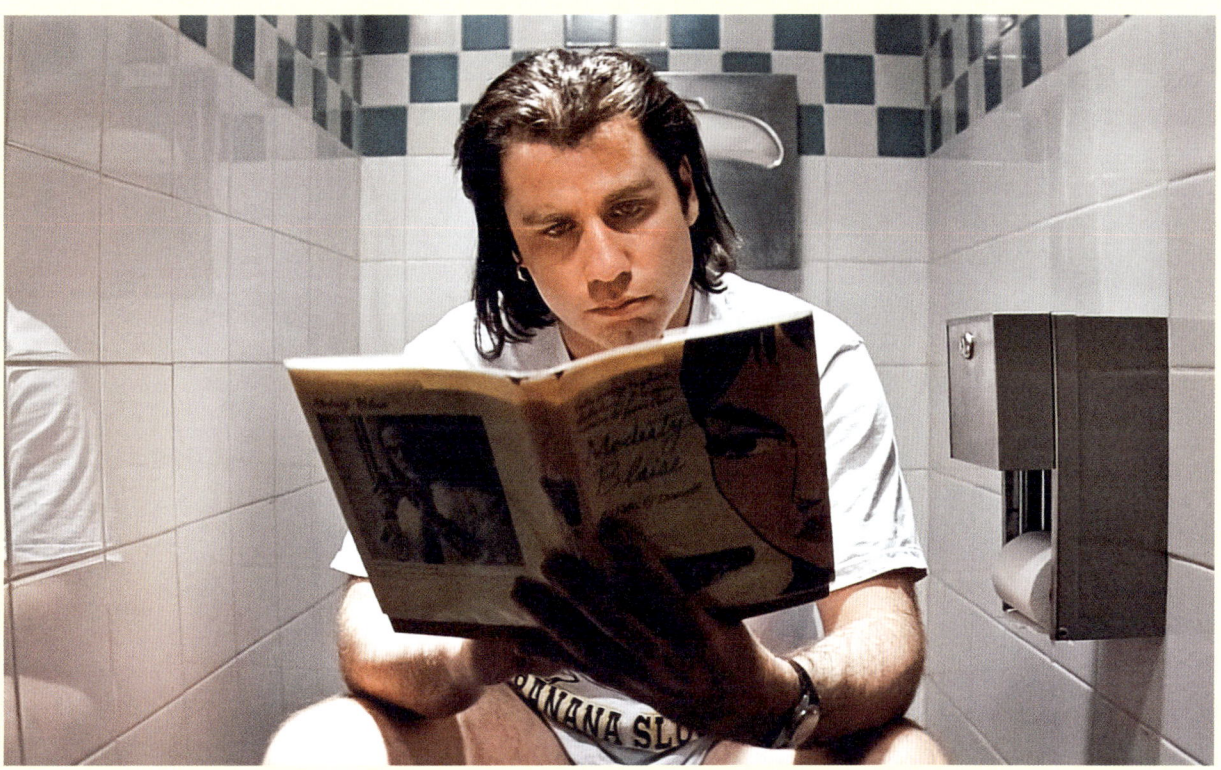

detectives chasing criminals gun in hand through the urban jungle, spawned countless progeny, both in literature and in film.

Quentin Tarantino, who likes to think of *Reservoir Dogs* as "*the pulp fiction [he] will never write,*"[1] pays clear homage to the genre with *Pulp Fiction*, from the poster for the movie to its narrative structure. He may not, by his own admission, be an avid reader of pulp magazines himself, but he nevertheless finds in them a limitless source of genre stories, full of tropes which are simply asking to be distorted. While in full promotion mode for his first movie, while he was getting the first part of *Pulp Fiction* down on paper, he explained his new project in the columns of *Positif*: "*It's a crime film anthology. Three crime stories like the old* Black Mask *magazine. The stories are completely separate, and they're the same stories you've heard a zillion times. You know, the staples of the genre, but hopefully taken where you've never seen them taken before.*"[2]

There's also a little thrill of outrageousness, of course, since Tarantino is known for being a master provocateur. Just like exploitation movies, by flirting openly with pornography while never succumbing to it, pulp fiction books and magazines knew how to avoid censorship while moving in the dodgiest of circles, playing with transgressive subject matter not just in terms of sex but of violence too, without quite crossing the line. Quentin Tarantino's self-confessed love of pulp could also reflect a commitment to a kind of democratic ideal, one which rejects any notion of hierarchy among genres and challenges bourgeois boundaries of propriety and good taste. The director might quite possibly have preferred his movie to remain undervalued, to achieve pop culture status rather than success as a mainstream favorite—who knows? But being able to rock up at the very earnest Cannes Festival and snatch the Palme d'Or with a pulp movie… that is certainly not lacking in style. •

1- Jean-Pierre Deloux, *Quentin Tarantino… fils de pulp* (FeniXX, 1998).
2- Michel Ciment and Hubert Niogret, *Positif*, no. 379, September 1992, reprinted in Gerald Peary, ed., *Quentin Tarantino: Interviews* (University Press of Mississippi, 2013).

ELMORE LEONARD

A Criminal Legacy

Quentin Tarantino can certainly be said to have prompted accusations of being something of a thieving magpie in his movies, ever since *Reservoir Dogs*. As it happens, he also has personal experience of actual stealing: At the age of fourteen, he was caught red-handed trying to pinch a novel in the aisles of a K-Mart. "*I got in huge trouble,*" he recalls. "*I was grounded all summer long. But I was so p---ed off that I didn't manage to get the book that two days later I went back and stole it proper.*"[1] Rather than presaging a career in crime or the misappropriation of books, this petty larceny introduced the young Tarantino to something that would later prove a key influence on his work: the writings of Elmore Leonard. The book he "borrowed," from the local store, *The Switch* (1978), follows a pair of criminals embroiled in a messy kidnapping. Their names? Ordell Robbie and Louis Gara. This duo turns up again in the pages of *Rum Punch* (1992), the only novel Quentin Tarantino has adapted to date, under the title *Jackie Brown*.

Elmore Leonard was a major American writer, an old hand at thriller-writing. Many of his books have been adapted for the screen (*3:10 to Yuma*, *Hombre*, *Out of Sight*, *Get Shorty*…). As he himself put it, "*I [was] what you call an overnight success, after writing almost anonymously for*

30 years."[2] From the 1950s onward Elmore Leonard threw himself into genre-writing, joining a small industry dedicated to producing Westerns which found a home in pulp publications of the kind that line the racks in the Tarantino Town bookstore. "*Westerns were big in the '50s,*" he explained. "*All the big*

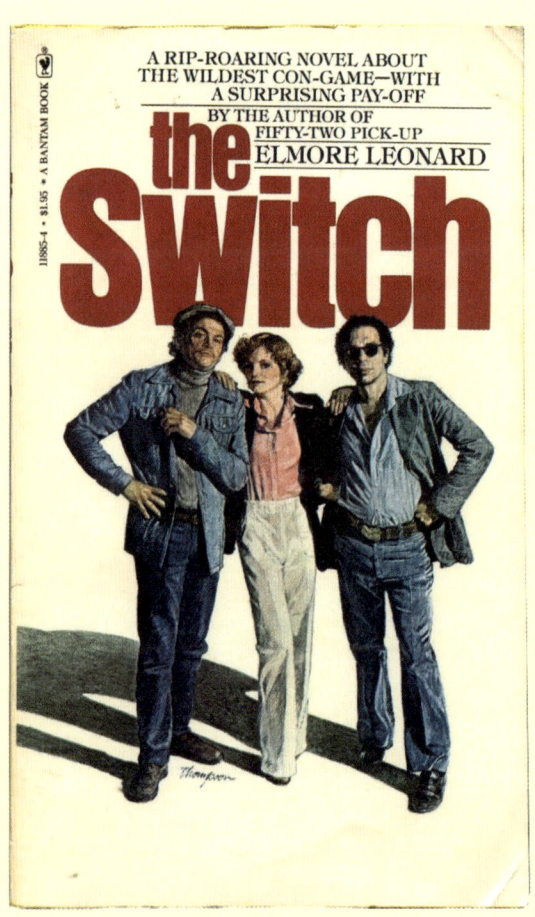

1- Benjamin Secher, "Quentin Tarantino Interview: 'All My Movies Are Achingly Personal,'" *The Telegraph*, February 8, 2010.
2- Frank J. Prial, "At Home With: Elmore Leonard; It's No Crime To Talk Softly," *The New York Times*, February 15, 1996.

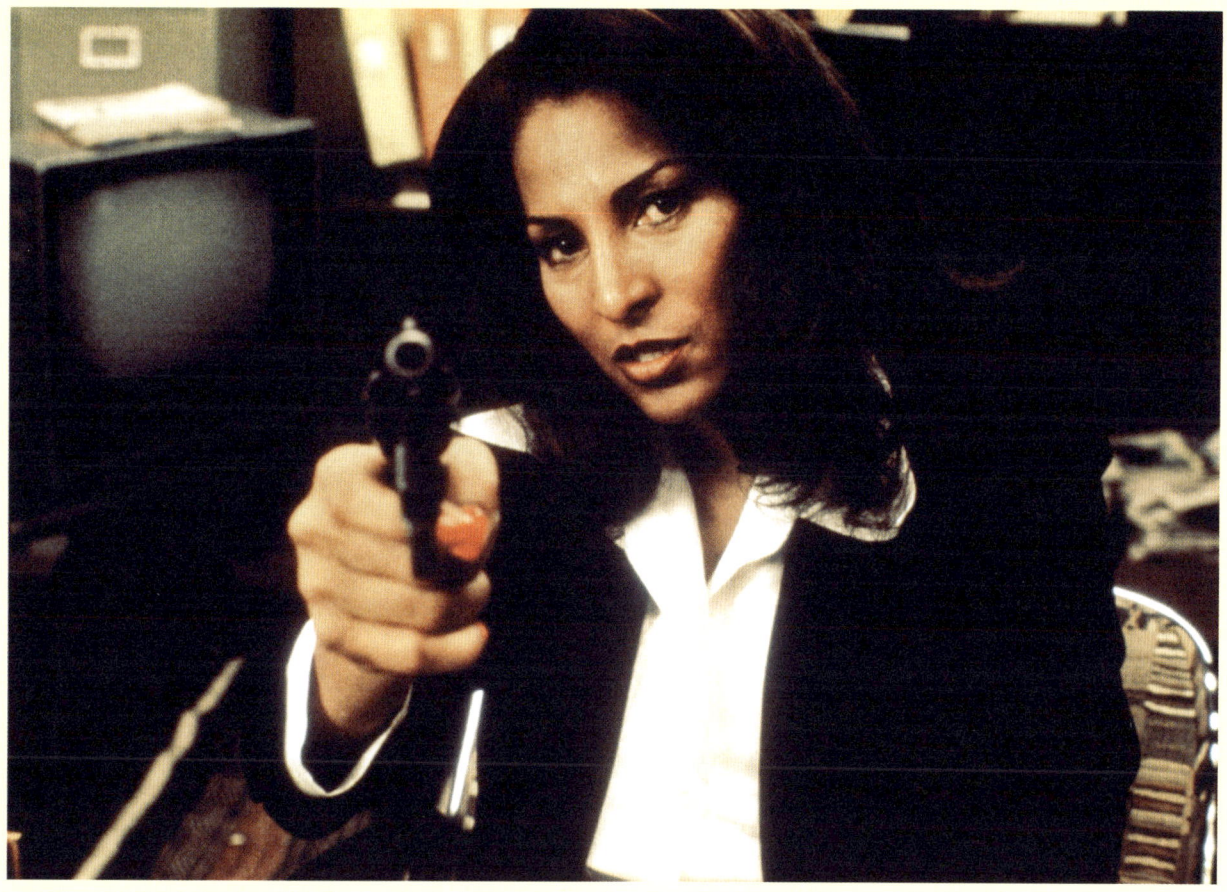

magazines published westerns. If you didn't make it there, you went to books like Argosy. Then came the pulps—Dime Western, Zane Grey, Ten-Story Western— at 2 cents a word."[3] In the early 1970s, sensing that the genre had been bled dry, he hung up his spurs and turned toward crime fiction. Far removed from his hard-boiled characters, the narrow streets of the Detroit underworld, and the petty trafficking that yielded such high returns, Elmore Leonard lived the quiet, practical life of a man who gets up early to do what good writers do: Sit at their desk and type. When he died in 2013, at the age of eighty-seven, he left behind a sizable body of work running to forty-five novels, with a forty-sixth unfinished on his desk.

His books are populated by crooks who possess excessive confidence and limited intelligence, because for Leonard, baddies always make the best characters. Even the dimmest among them. Hell, especially the dimmest among them. He himself had nothing of the bad boy about him and preferred to describe himself as a hardworking type who never did anything dangerous and always paid his bills on time. He admired Steinbeck and Hemingway, and there was nothing esoteric in the way he expressed himself. He spoke plainly. When faced with a group of students asking him to tell them the secret of how to write, he batted the question away with the back of his hand, saying, *"There isn't any secret. You sit down and you start and that's it."*[4] The rules of writing which he tossed off good-naturedly for *The New York Times* were elementary: Avoid prologues, exercise caution with description, keep your exclamation points under control. His golden rule, which he never failed to follow: *"If it sounds like writing, I rewrite it."*[5]

3- Ibid. • 4- Ibid.
5- Elmore Leonard, "Easy on the Adverbs, Exclamation Points and Especially Hooptedoodle," *The New York Times*, July 16, 2001.

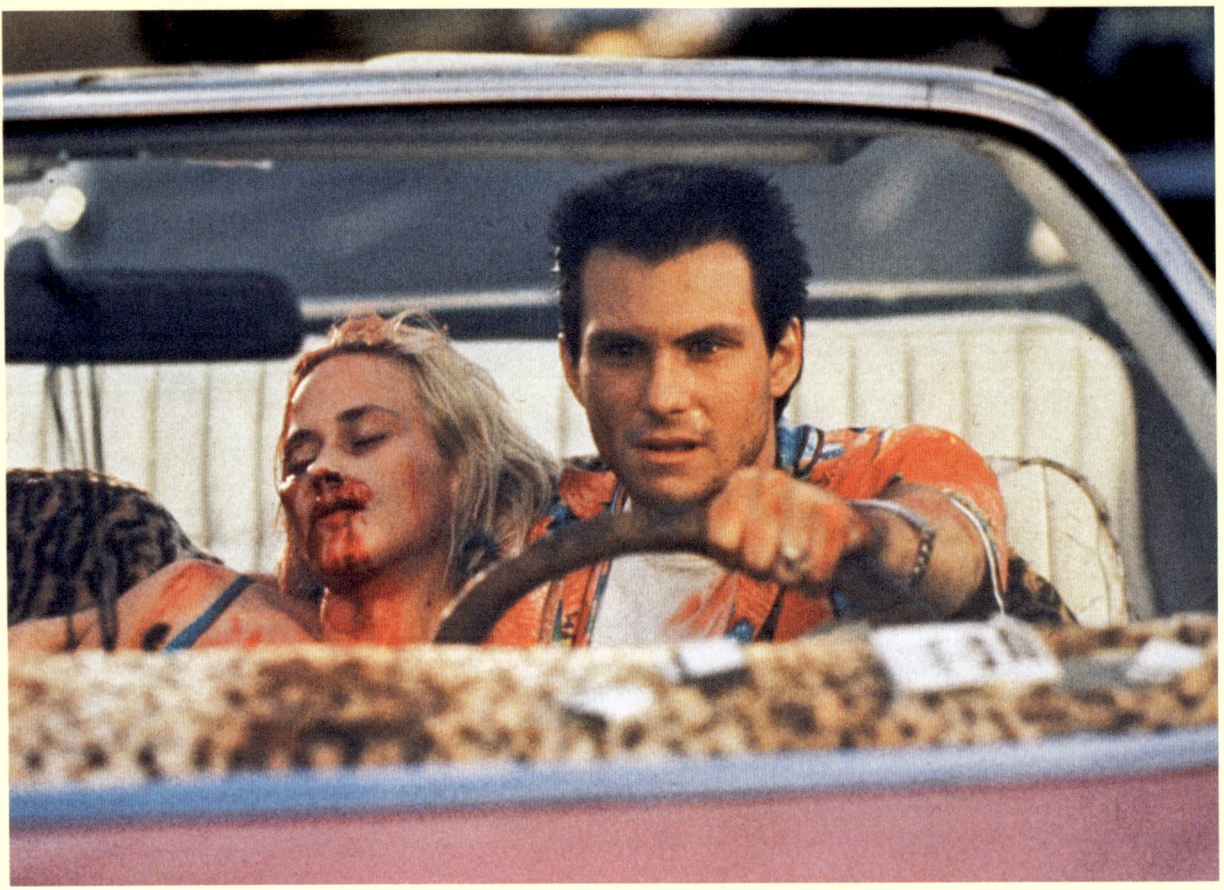

Like all good dialogue writers, Elmore Leonard had a keen ear; whether on the street or watching television, he was always tuned in to how people spoke, keeping an ear open for a new phrase or expression which he would carefully record. He let his characters emerge through dialogue, presenting them to readers through tiny touches, a thousand responses and attitudes, rather than lengthy descriptions. Tarantino's work and Elmore Leonard's have definite aspects in common—not least a particular sense of humor and a fondness for third-rate gangsters—but it is Tarantino's dialogue that most clearly shows Leonard's influence. He acknowledged this influence in *True Romance*: "*True Romance is basically like an Elmore Leonard movie… that he didn't write, you know… I actually owe a big debt to, like, kind of figuring out my style from Elmore Leonard because, you know, he was the first writer I'd ever read… that just let mundane conversations actually inform the characters.*"[6]

With their tendency to engage in idle chat, Tarantino's characters follow a pattern—one set by Leonard with his talkative characters—which deconstructs the silent, ruthless, professional killer archetype and dents their hard-boiled fictional image as a result. This is exemplified by Jules and Vincent in *Pulp Fiction*, with their endless digressions about burgers and foot massages. "*It's commonplace things that we all talk about, why wouldn't the bad guys be talking that way too? Because I think of them that way,*" Elmore Leonard explained. "*I think about the guy who is going to rob a bank getting up in the morning and he's wondering, what am I going to wear to rob this bank?*'"[7]

6- "Quentin Tarantino: Interview," *Charlie Rose*, October 14, 1994.
7- "Elmore Leonard: Interview," *Charlie Rose*, May 22, 1995.

Elmore Leonard's command of dialogue, tight prose, and formidable sense of comedy won him considerable attention in the movies. Hollywood adored Leonard, but the feeling was often not mutual. Asked about his response to previous movie adaptations of his work in a live interview with Charlie Rose in 1995, the writer replied: "*I'm not happy, because I don't think they were good movies. Not because they didn't stay with the book—that's not a concern of mine. I know that… it's got to be adapted to the screen. A lot of things have to change, but I would like to see a good movie made, that's the main thing.*"[8] Leonard was not one to hide his discontent, showing no hesitation, for instance, in walking out of the premiere of *The Big Bounce* (1969), which he deemed the second-worst film ever made (the worst being the 2004 remake), or in writing a long letter of recrimination to Burt Reynolds after the release of *Stick* (1985). When he got hold of the rights to *Rum Punch*, then, Tarantino was understandably nervous about offending his favorite author. As Leonard related, "*He called me up and said I've been afraid to call you for the last year. And I said why, because you're changing the title and you're making the lead a Black woman? And he said yeah. I said, well, I like Pam Grier and I like your movies. So go ahead. Do whatever you want.*"[9] Tarantino did whatever he wanted, and his movie, along with *Get Shorty* (Barry Sonnenfeld) and *Out of Sight* (Steven Soderbergh), constituted a kind of mid-1990s trilogy in Leonard's honor, with all three movies meeting with a favorable reception from the writer. A few years later, in 1999, when asked once again by Charlie Rose about his response to movie adaptations of his novels, he delivered a typically plain Leonard-style compliment—quick and direct, without any unnecessary emphasis or exclamation points: "*And then Quentin Tarantino did* Jackie Brown. *I thought that was very good, close. Yeah.*"[10] •

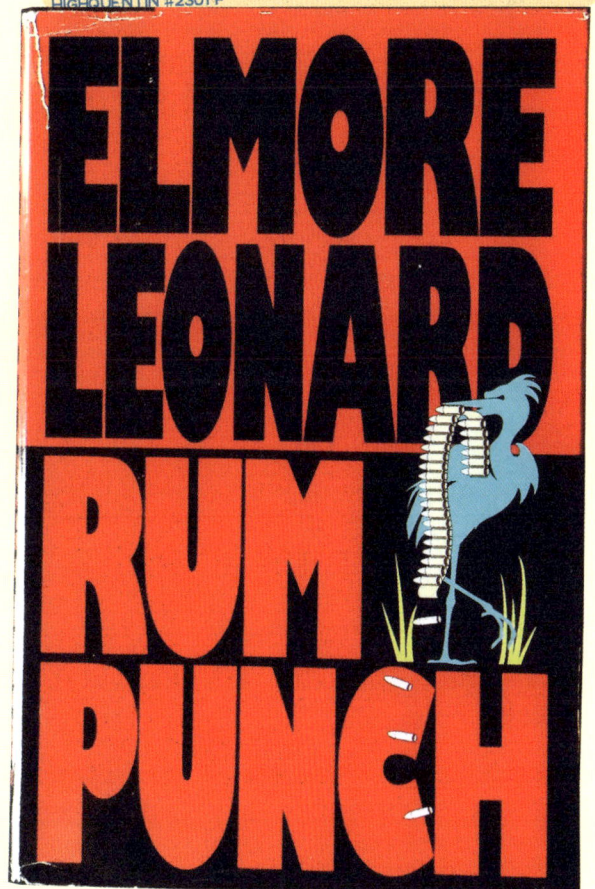

THE LIBRARY CARD

HOLDER	QUENTIN TARANTINO	
DATE DUE		**TITLE / AUTHOR**
MAR 1 2	The Switch Elmore Leonard	
SEP 2 6	Rum Punch Elmore Leonard	
APR 2 3	3:10 to Yuma Elmore Leonard	
NOV 1 9	Hombre Elmore Leonard	
FEB 2 8	Get Shorty Elmore Leonard	
OCT 1 1	Out of Sight Elmore Leonard	

HIGHQUENTIN #2301 F   PRINTED IN U.S.A

ELMORE LEONARD RUM PUNCH

8- Ibid.
9- Terry Gross, "*Fresh Air Remembers Crime Novelist Elmore Leonard*," *Fresh Air*, 2013.
10- "Elmore Leonard: Interview," *Charlie Rose*, 1999.

ROBERT FROST'S POEM

The Last Miles

Deep in a windswept forest, a traveler lingers in the dark, seized by the cold beauty of the place. Conscious that he still has a long way to go before he can stop and rest, he continues on his way. The last miles to go feature in American poet Robert Frost's poem "Stopping by Woods on a Snowy Evening," published in his 1923 *New Hampshire* collection. As always, there is space to read between the lines in Frost's poem: It can be understood as an invitation to stop and contemplate, but it could equally well suggest the pull of death, alluding to a rest deeper than sleep, the big sleep of death, which seems to tempt the traveler, momentarily seduced by the idea of cutting short his journey. But his hour has not yet come and, overtaken by his sense of duty, he continues on his way.

In *Death Proof*, the last stanza of Frost's poem is quoted twice to Arlene, on two separate occasions, inviting viewers to track the changes from one scene to the other in a movie which is entirely constructed to create a mirror effect.[1] The first time, the lines are spoken in a lascivious woman's voice by Jungle Julia, who has used them, stripped of all context, to send a distinctly sexual message over the airwaves: During her radio show that morning she announced that whoever recites the words to Arlene—nicknamed Butterfly on air, foreshadowing the ephemeral nature of

> The woods are lovely, dark and deep,
> But I have promises to keep,
> And miles to go before I sleep,
> And miles to go before I sleep.

her existence—will be the recipient of a torrid lap dance. Here, the miles separating the traveler from sleep suggest long sleepless nights and the promise of adventure. The second time the lines are spoken, they work a snake-like spell on Arlene. This time it is Stuntman Mike, who has followed his prey, who delivers them in a different, more disturbing way: "*Did you hear me, Butterfly? Miles to go before you sleep…*" Like the traveler in the poem, Arlene finds herself at a crossroads, caught between the pull of life and the pull of death, which could not be better symbolized than by Stuntman Mike's racing car which terrifies her so much.

But *Death Proof* is a movie which hankers after intertextuality—if the pile-up of references is anything to go by, anyway—and not only is the poem quoted twice, it is in itself a double quotation. This is because

1- The movie is split into two parts: It begins with Stuntman Mike pursuing the girls in Austin, Texas, before shifting to his pursuit of the girls in Lebanon, Tennessee. Following a similar pattern of repetition, the poem scene is first acted out in fun by Julia and Marcy before becoming real with Stuntman Mike.

Frost's poem had already served as an "activation signal" in a 1977 movie directed by Don Siegel called *Telefon*, starring Charles Bronson. At the height of the Cold War, the Soviet Union plants sleeper agents near military sites all over the United States. Years later, these "inactive" Soviet agents are living quietly as respectable Americans, without any idea who they are. Until the day, that is, that they receive a strange phone call. When they pick up the receiver, they hear a distant voice recite a few lines from Frost, enough to activate them as agents and trigger them to carry out suicide missions in a state of near-hypnosis. Tarantino introduces this reference into *Death Proof* not because he particularly cares for Siegel's movie—in fact, he accused him of sabotaging a perfectly delightful plot—but because he was struck by the performance of one of the actors in it: "*Donald Pleasence, as he is in all of his pictures for Siegel, is a theatrical beast. Not to mention his reading of the Robert Frost trigger poem, once heard, is never forgotten.*"[2]

Anchored in Tarantino's memory, the poem resurfaces on Stuntman Mike's lips. Shifting from one state to another, Arlene listens transfixed to the stuntman's voice. Vacillating between fear and fascination, she decides to honor the promise made in her name and performs a memorable lap dance. Here, as in Siegel's movie, the poem acts as a signal, but instead of being the sexual prompt we thought, it triggers a tragic turn of events. Could Arlene have avoided her fate had she declined the stranger's challenge? No one knows. Believing, as the traveler in Frost's poem does, that she can make her way out of the forest and back onto her road, Arlene fails to realize that something has been accompanying her since even before she entered the forest… The chase is on. There are only a few miles to go before the big sleep. •

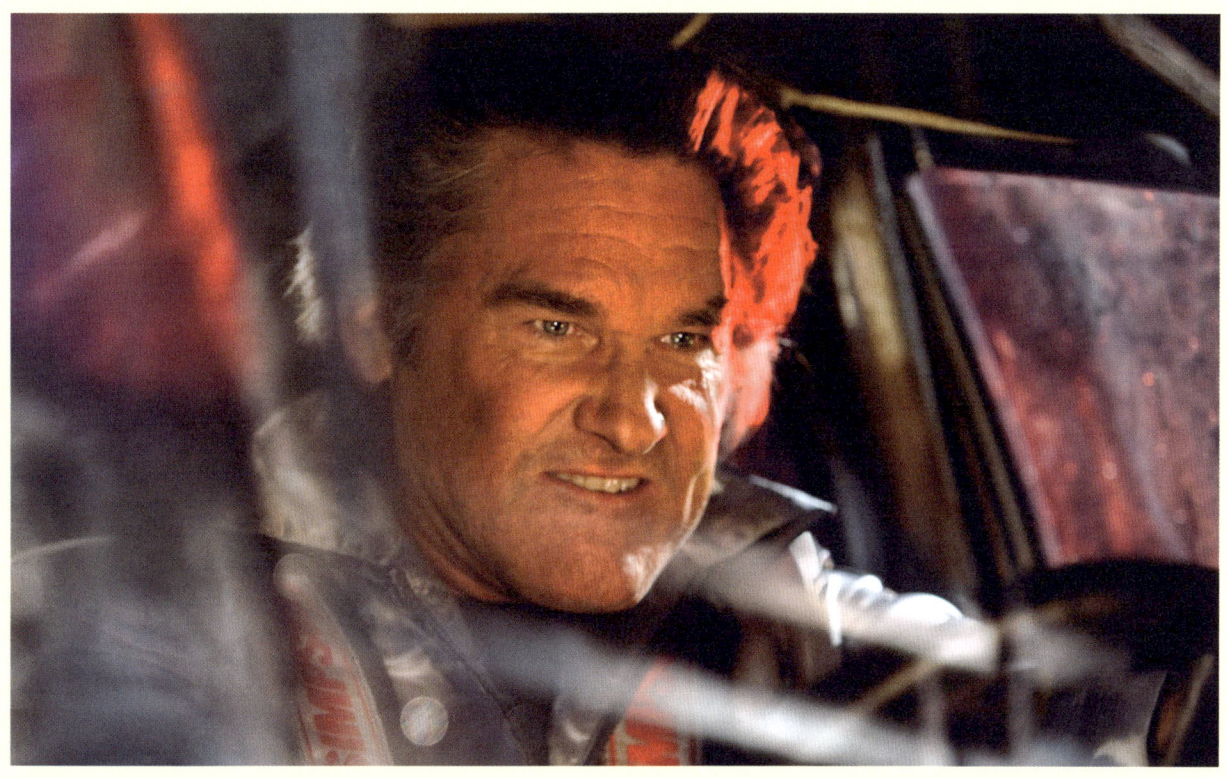

2- Quentin Tarantino, *Cinema Speculation* (Harper, 2022).

NOVELIZATIONS

Back to Front

*A*lien, *2001: A Space Odyssey*, *Close Encounters of the Third Kind*, *Taxi Driver*, *King Kong*, *E.T. The Extra-Terrestrial*, *Star Wars*, *Basic Instinct*, *Les 400 Coups*, *Jaws*… No, you haven't got the address wrong, as that great smell of old paper and fresh ink will tell you. You're still wandering around among the stacks of the Tarantino Town bookstore. These well-known titles, which are scattered among the other books throughout the store, from the metal stands by the door to the chaotic bookshelves that line the walls, make up a kind of paper video store waiting to be leafed through. But what are these books? Are they little-known novels, eclipsed by their more famous movie adaptations? Quite the opposite: They are "novelizations," a largely underrated genre, often confused with screenplays, which Tarantino may have helped bring back into the spotlitght with his own novel, *Once Upon a Time… in Hollywood*, published in 2021.

The relationship between film and literature is what one might call a pretty unequal one: While the former borrows shamelessly from the latter, boning up on the classics and resurrecting some of its most obscure productions, the reverse remains a distinctly marginal activity. Like their distant cousins, pulp fiction books, novelizations belong to a somewhat suppressed branch ot literature that is little or poorly regarded. Perhaps this is because,

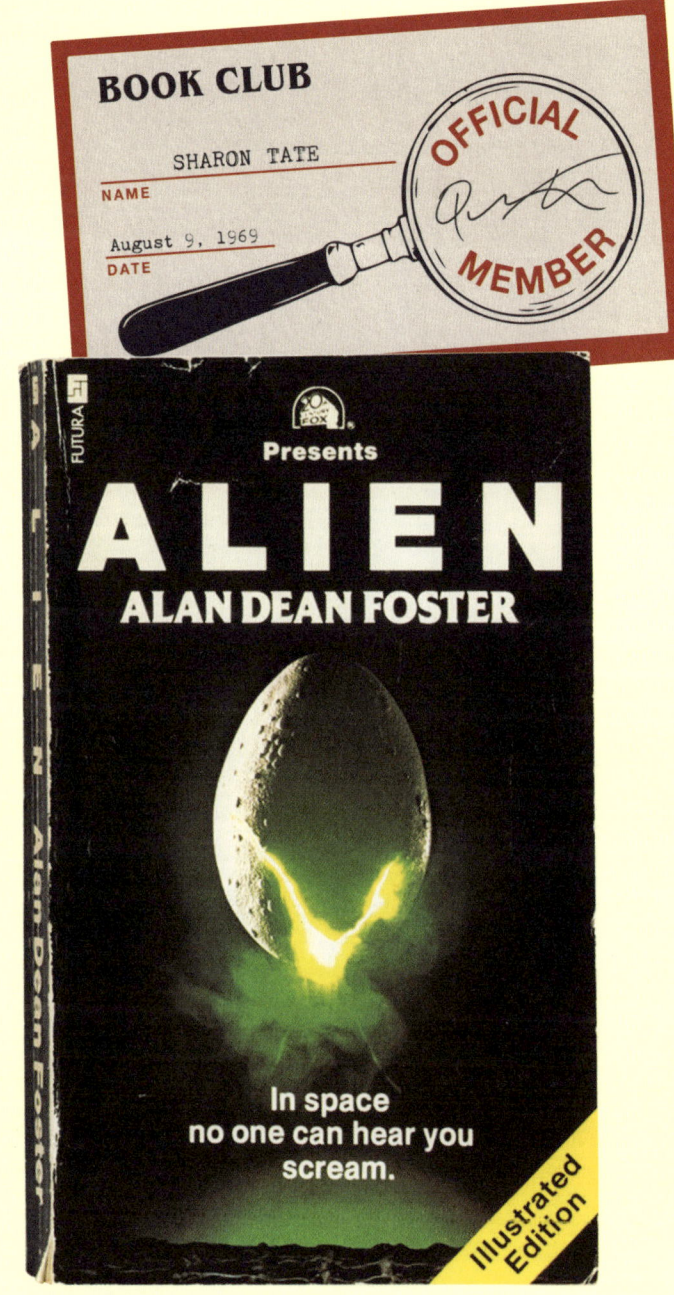

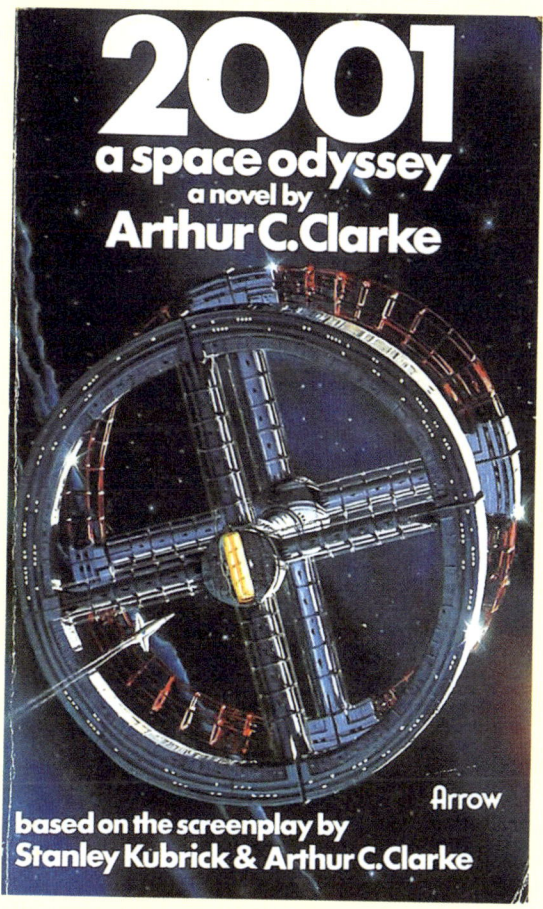

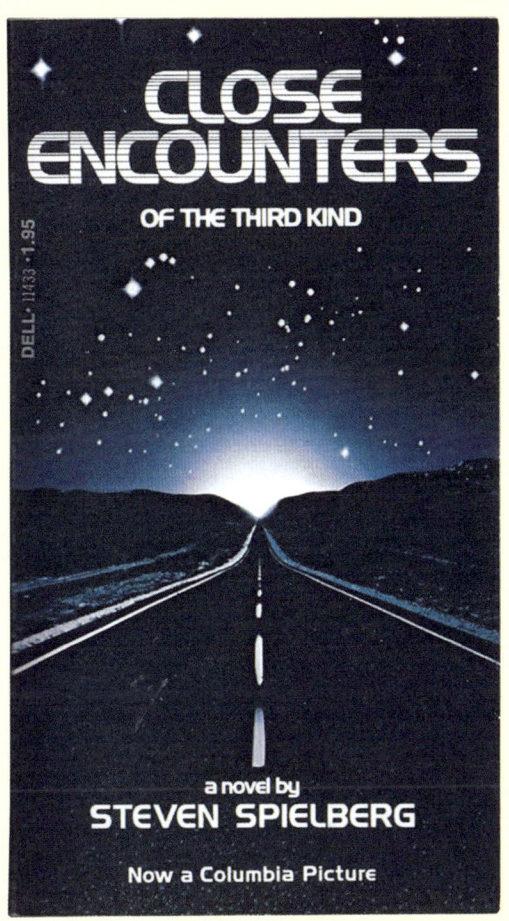

like pulp fiction, they make no attempt to hide their commercial nature: They do their best to capitalize on a movie's success, looking like yet another piece of merchandise churned out by the great Hollywood marketing machine. Then again, perhaps it is because they are seen as lesser, lacking in inspiration, essentially plagiaristic in nature. Or it could be that they are put in the same category as the work of ghostwriters, hired hands who get paid to tell a story and are typically thought of as artisans rather than artists. Finally, it may be that good taste is somehow offended by literature getting a little too mixed up with the movies, too eager to adopt their language and conventions, and becoming compromised as a result. Perhaps there is a good and a bad direction to go from one medium to another: Could it be that novelizations are simply adaptations

which are effectively reversed, moving from back to front?

"*The scorn attached to such byproducts of the cultural industry is so massive and lasting that any involvement at all in novelization, whether as a reader or (even worse) an author, is a losing proposition, even if there may be some redeeming qualities,*" notes specialist Jan Baetens.[1] Yet these novelizations—which are sometimes published entirely anonymously, giving the director sole credit—can be the work of very able writers. Big names in this small genre include the likes of Max Allan Collins (*Waterworld*, *Saving Private Ryan*, *The Mummy*…) and Alan Dean Foster (*Alien*, *The Thing*, *Star Trek*…). Sometimes novelizations are the product of an extended process, full of repeated back-and-forth between one medium and another: *Total Recall*

1- Jan Baetens, *Novelization: From Film to Novel* (Ohio State University Press, 2018).

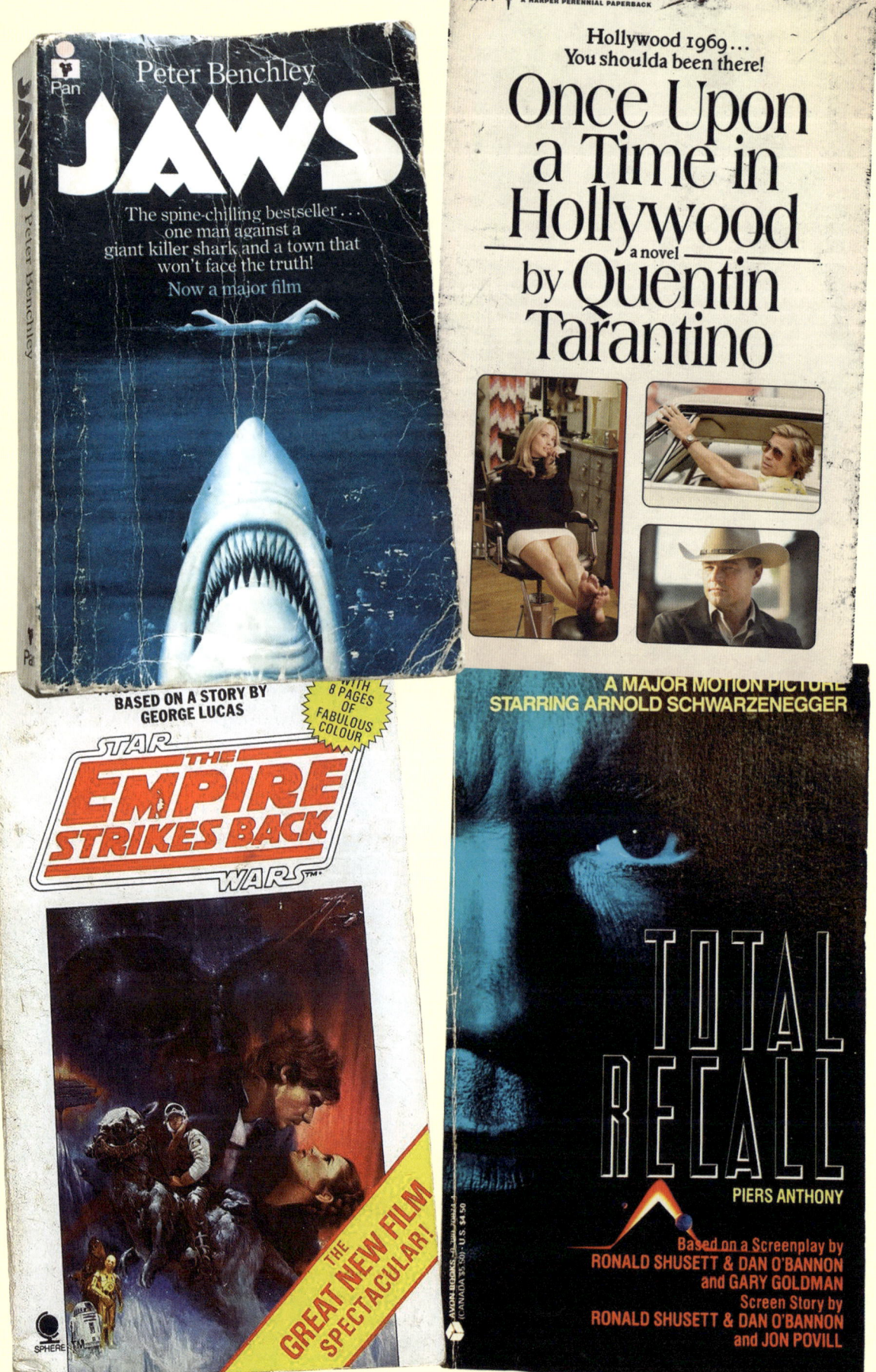

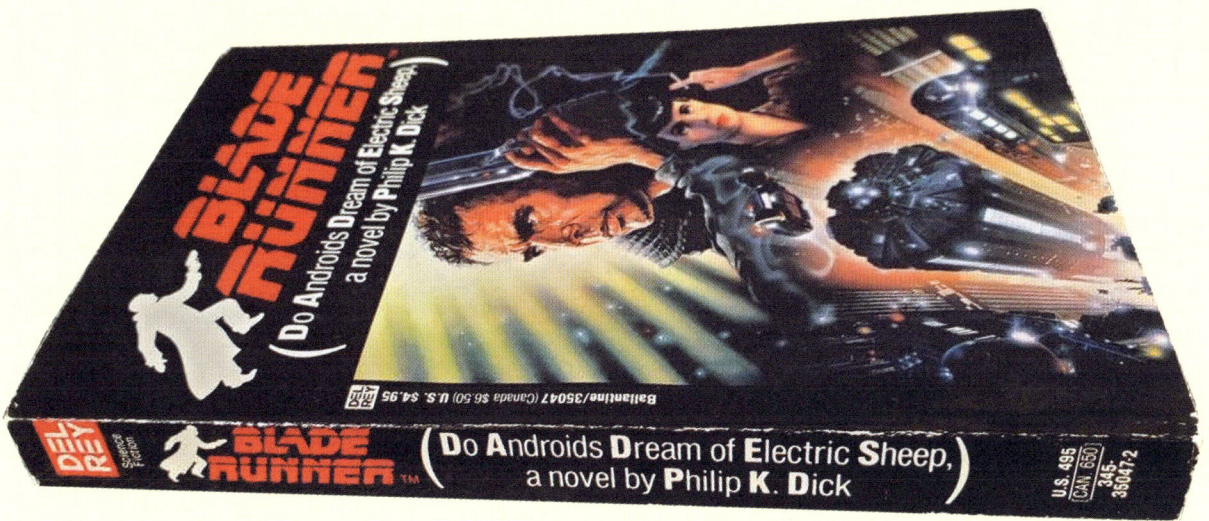

by Piers Anthony and *Blade Runner* by Les Martin, for instance, are novelizations of movies which are themselves adapted from short stories by Philip K. Dick. But they can also be written while the movie is being made, based on exactly the same screenplay, making it impossible to tell which came first, movie or novel.

Residing as they do at a point where two worlds intersect, somewhere in that great undefined space between film and literature, novelizations were bound to speak to Quentin Tarantino and be dear to his heart. The idea of hierarchy—that literature might be so superior to film that it could be corrupted by having anything to do with it—is not one the director espouses: He likes nothing better than to mix up the sacred and profane. A total movie buff, Tarantino adores every genre imaginable, down to the very basest hybrid, and has become a great champion of pop culture, to which novelizations undoubtedly belong. In his youth, he paid regular visits to his local drugstore to sift through the wire racks bulging with books costing a few dimes each: "*I think the first time I actually bought one of those paperbacks from the spinner rack, it was a movie novelisation,*" he recalled.[2] Many years later, at the age of fifty-

eight, Tarantino published his first novel. His novelization of *Once Upon a Time… in Hollywood* is pure pulp, right down to its original cover, which looks as though it's just fallen off a train station bookstand. When asked how he copes with the stress of the blank page, he replies that he loves writing, seeing the mountains of "*ridiculously overwritten*"[3] pages, covered in an illegible scrawl, pile up every day on his worktable. For once, the man who catches himself adapting novels in his head as he reads them had to do the reverse. He threw himself into the venture, guided by his sense of the actors who play his characters: "*When I wrote the book I saw Brad Pitt doing everything,*" he said. "*I saw Leonardo DiCaprio doing everything.*"[4] His movie already had its own voice, and he listened to it carefully. Among the many possible projects the director has mentioned in interviews over the years have been novelizations of *True Romance* and *Reservoir Dogs*. A few chapters of an adaptation of *Reservoir Dogs* are apparently lurking in a cardboard box somewhere: "*Reservoir Dogs would make a great little paperback. It's a crime story, there's a crime section in every bookstore, it's got a place all ready to go.*"[5] It certainly does in our store, anyway. •

2- John Phipps, "Quentin Tarantino: 'There's a Lot of Feet in a Lot of Good Directors' Movies,'" *GQ*, September 3, 2021. • 3- Ibid. • 4- Ibid. 5- "Quentin Tarantino: Interview Special," *The Empire Film Podcast*, December 32, 2021.

PAULINE KAEL

The Movie Critic

When Quentin Tarantino is not making movies, he's watching them. In his youth, he kept detailed records of the astronomical number of movies he devoured every year. Brian De Palma, Jean-Luc Godard, and Sergio Leone were among his heroes and mentors. "*Those were my cinema teachers*," he explained. "*And the other one was Pauline Kael.*"[1]

Born on June 19, 1919, in California, Pauline Kael was without a doubt the most feared and fearsome of all movie critics. In 1967, having honed her skills in San Francisco in a few editorials and radio programs, she made her debut at the prestigious *New Yorker* with a memorable piece praising *Bonnie and Clyde*. She went on to publish hundreds of articles and pieces of criticism in the magazine, writing for it for over twenty years, until Parkinson's disease forced her to lay down her pen in 1991. Pauline Kael's pen was always sharp, whether she used it to carry out a complete assassination or praise a movie to the skies, to enthuse or chastise. Her writings were characterized as ferocious, opinionated, if not downright wrong, and earned her both admirers and detractors in at least equal measure. If a person's influence is judged by the number of enemies they have, it has to be said that Pauline Kael had no shortage of enemies, as much among directors as moviegoers, as well as

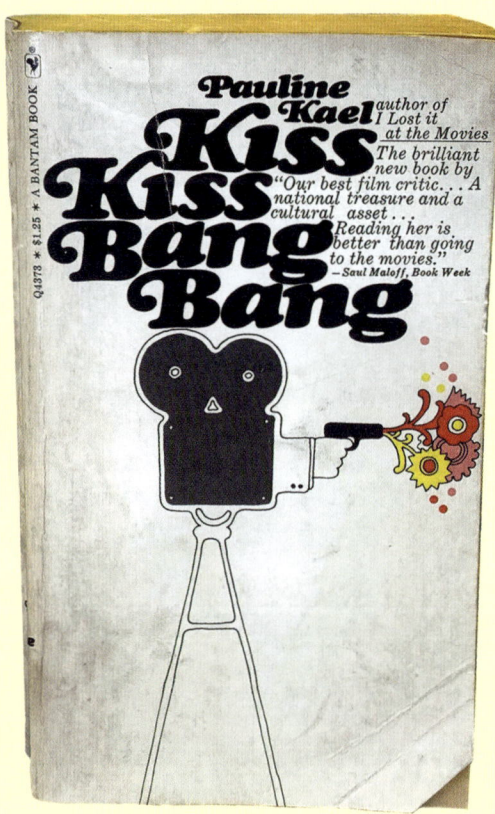

among her own peers and even her fellow writers in *The New Yorker*. Andrew Sarris, her enduring rival at *The Village Voice*, scornfully claimed: "*Pauline is loved by people who don't know about movies.*"[2] Kael's influence was such, however, that a wave of aspiring young critics followed in her steps, nicknamed "Paulettes" without a hint of affection by her opponents.

Her acerbic character and writing style made Kael one of the most

1- Michel Ciment and Hubert Niogret, *Positif*, no. 379, September 1992, reprinted in Gerald Peary, ed., *Quentin Tarantino: Interviews* (University Press of Mississippi, 2013).
2- Quoted in André Lavoie, "Faut-il relire… Pauline Kael?," *Le Devoir*, December 30, 2023.

conspicuous women working in a resolutely male industry. Not everyone approved, as letters from readers never ceased to remind her, often in a far from elegant manner. Speaking into the microphone at KPFA Radio in 1963, she poked fun at some letters pulled from her mailbag, one of which read: "*Dear Miss Kael, since you know so much about the art of the film, why don't you spend your time making it? But first, you will need a pair of b----.*" Deploying to the full the irony for which she was famous and to which so many had fallen victim, she replied: "*Mr. Doe Doe—I use the repetition in honor of your two attributes—movies are made and criticism is written by the use of intelligence, talent, taste, emotion, education, and discrimination. I suggest it is time you and your cohorts stopped thinking with your genital jewels. There is a standard answer to this old idiocy of 'If you know so much about film, why don't you make movies?': You don't have to lay an egg to know if it tastes good.*"[3]

Never one to shy away from even the slightest provocation, Pauline Kael was not afraid to incur the wrath of radio stations any more than that of her editor in chief, William Shawn, with whom she had several battles behind the scenes. There was nothing cynical about Kael, however. Passionate and true to herself, she entered into the business of criticism with gusto, practicing it with a contagious, unrestrained enthusiasm that was matched only by her devotion to film. Actor Jerry Lewis vented his annoyance at her but recognized her ability: "*Pauline Kael. She's never said a good thing about me yet. That dirty old broad. But she's probably the most qualified critic in the world. 'Cause she cares about film and those that are involved in it.*"[4] Far from peering down from the lofty perches of the New York intelligentsia, Pauline Kael wrote at viewers' level. She sat alongside them in darkened theaters, experiencing the movie with them and watching their reactions, which she sometimes recorded in her

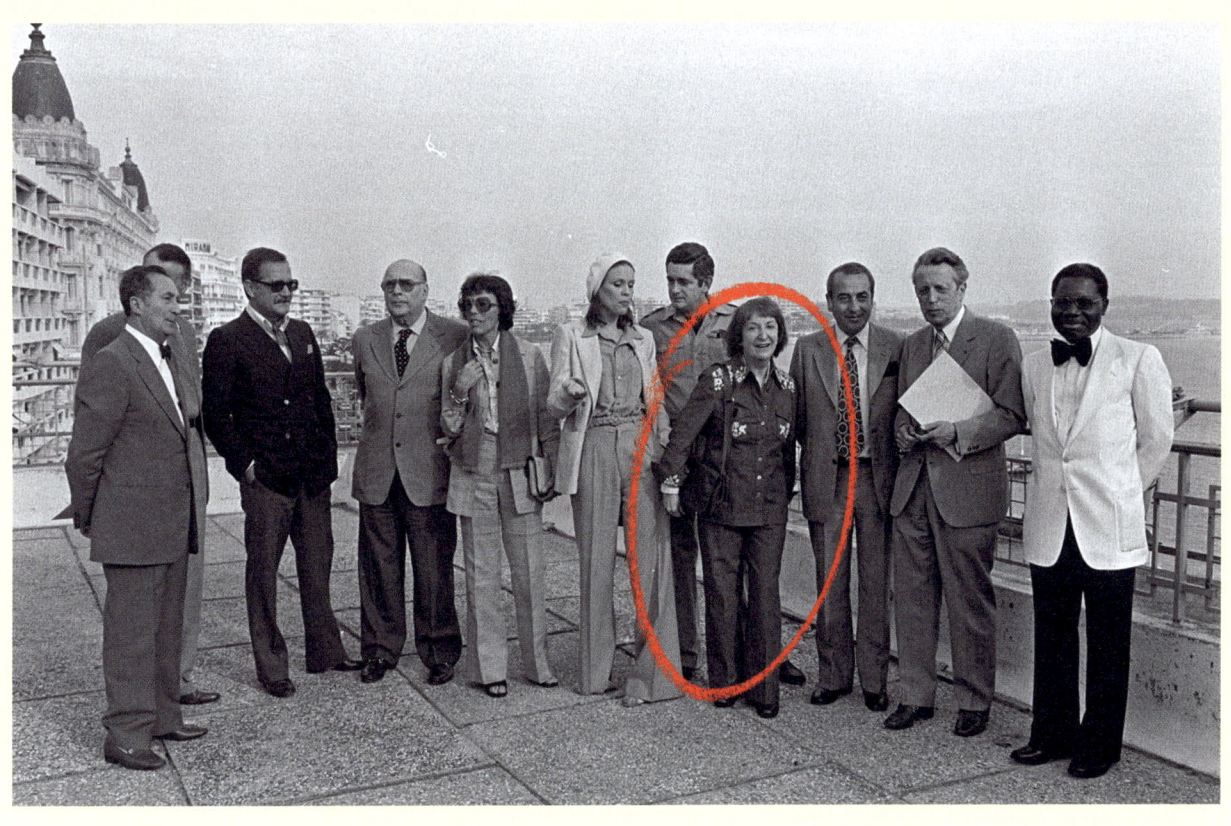

3– *What She Said: The Art of Pauline Kael*, directed by Rob Garver, 2019. • 4– Ibid.

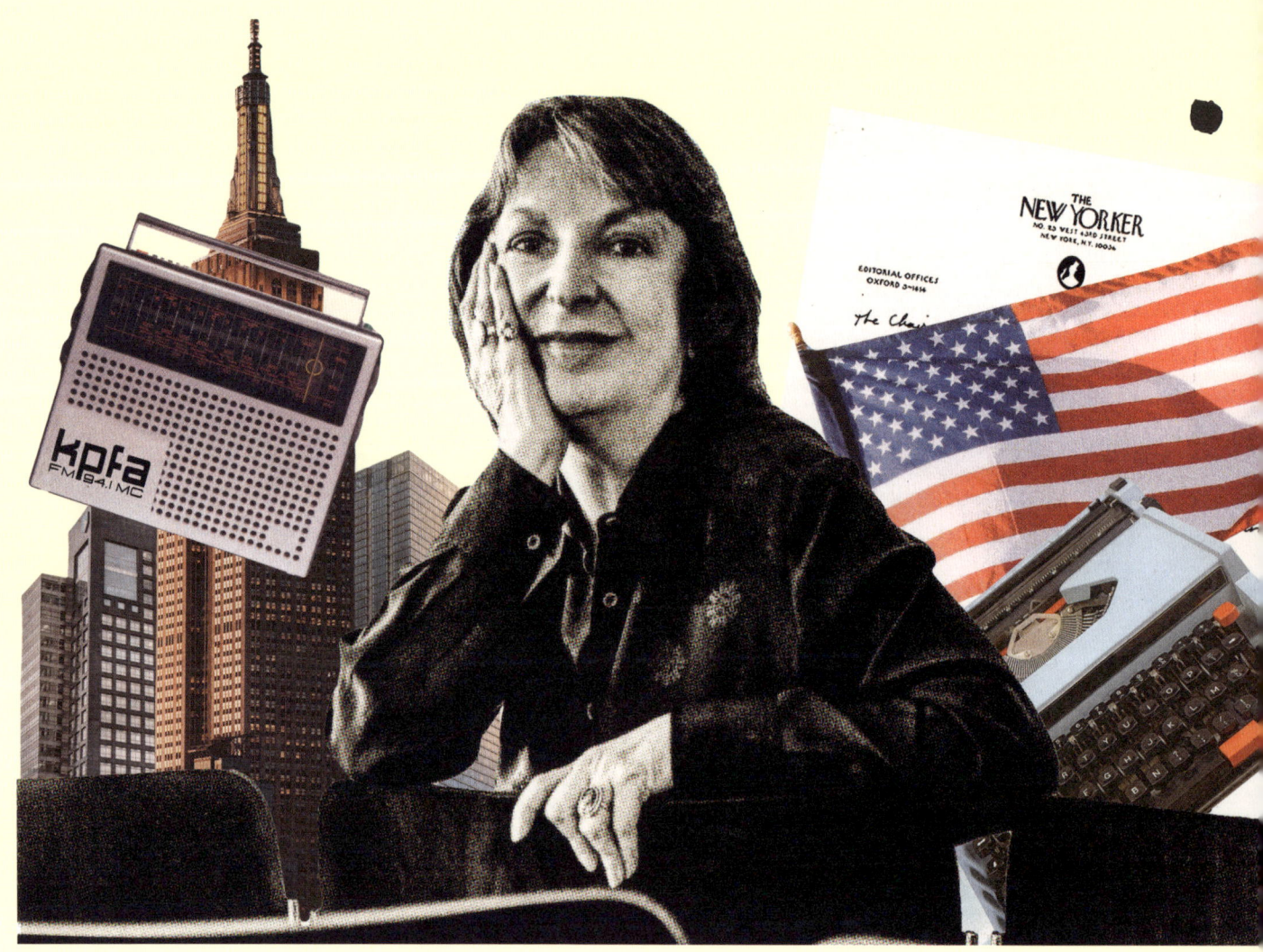

articles, which were often couched in a broad, inclusive first-person plural, as if she were the voice of a whole community of movie buffs. This sense of a shared movie experience could not but speak closely to Quentin Tarantino, who interweaves criticism of movies with memories of particular film screenings in his book *Cinema Speculation*. It is perhaps the idea of kinship with the audience that ultimately connects the two of them. As Pauline Kael put it, "*The romance of movies is not just in those stories and those people on the screen but in the adolescent dream of meeting others who feel as you do about what you've seen. You do meet them, of course, and you know each other at once.*"[5]

Pauline Kael was not afraid of offending good taste, and she loved nothing better than a little dose of amorality in a movie. This is reflected in the deliberately eye-catching titles of her collections of essays, with their barely concealed sexual innuendos (*Deeper into Movies*, *When the Lights Go Down*, *I Lost It at the Movies*…). In one of her most famous essays, "Trash, Art, and the Movies," she states the importance of a little subversion in film, writing: "*I don't trust anyone who doesn't admit having at some time in his life enjoyed trashy American movies.*"[6] She rejected wholesale the ideal of objectivity which some critics felt bound to uphold. On the contrary, she didn't hesitate to inject a good dose of subjectivity and autobiographical detail into her writing, gradually creating a persona for herself in the process. Her tastes in film were divisive, unpredictable, and her passions were

5- Pauline Kael, "Trash, Art, and the Movies," *Harper's*, February 1969. • 6- Ibid.

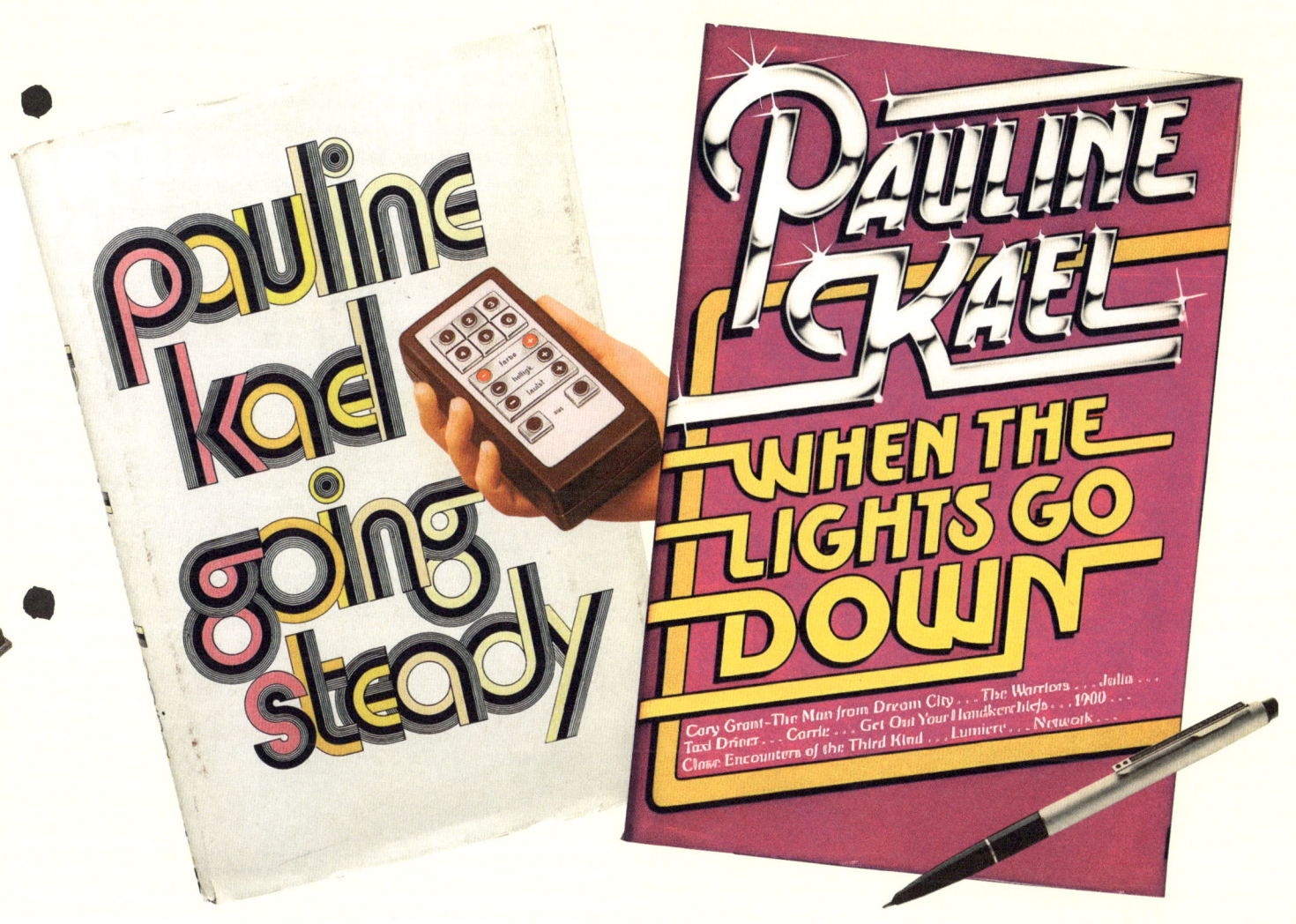

as famous as her pet peeves. She applauded Peckinpah, sang De Palma's praises, and defended Coppola while lambasting Stanley Kubrick, David Lean, and Federico Fellini (not to mention Clint Eastwood, to whom she had an abiding and loudly proclaimed aversion). *"She may be in error, but she is never in doubt,"* Andrew Sarris sarcastically wrote.[7] But as the adage goes, *"Without the freedom to criticize, there is no true praise."*

Pauline Kael was not bothered, finally, about swimming against the tide: *"If they like you, I think you should start getting worried,"* she declared.[8] Nobody was obliged to share her opinions, but her admirers applauded her for the strength of her convictions, her fierceness of character, and her devastating force, all of which combined to

set her critical essays in a league of their own. The young Tarantino was enthralled by her resounding voice and rebellious spirit from the moment he first discovered her book *When the Lights Go Down,* when he was sixteen: *"I read it and thought, 'Someday maybe I'll be able to understand a movie like she does.' I've read everything she's ever written for* The New Yorker *and got all her books, and I've learned as much from her as I have from filmmakers. She taught me a sense of how to be dramatically engaging, how to make a connection with the audience. She was my professor. In the film school of my own making…"*[9] •

7- Andrew Sarris, "The Queen Bee of Film Criticism," *The Village Voice,* July 28, 1980.
8- *What She Said: The Art of Pauline Kael,* directed by Rob Garver, 2019.
9- Michel Ciment and Hubert Niogret, *Positif,* no. 379, September 1992, reprinted in Gerald Peary, ed., *Quentin Tarantino: Interviews* (University Press of Mississippi, 2013)

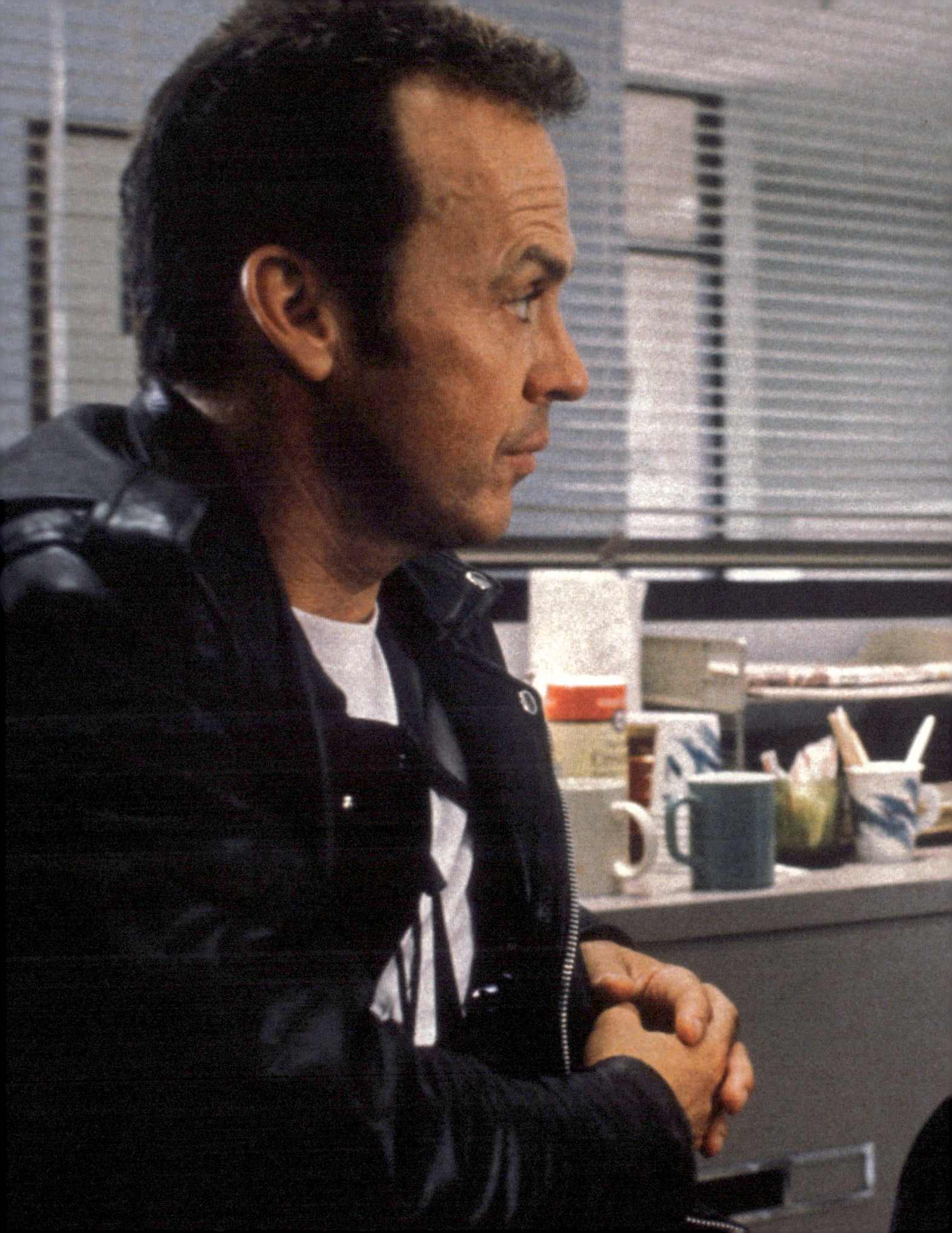

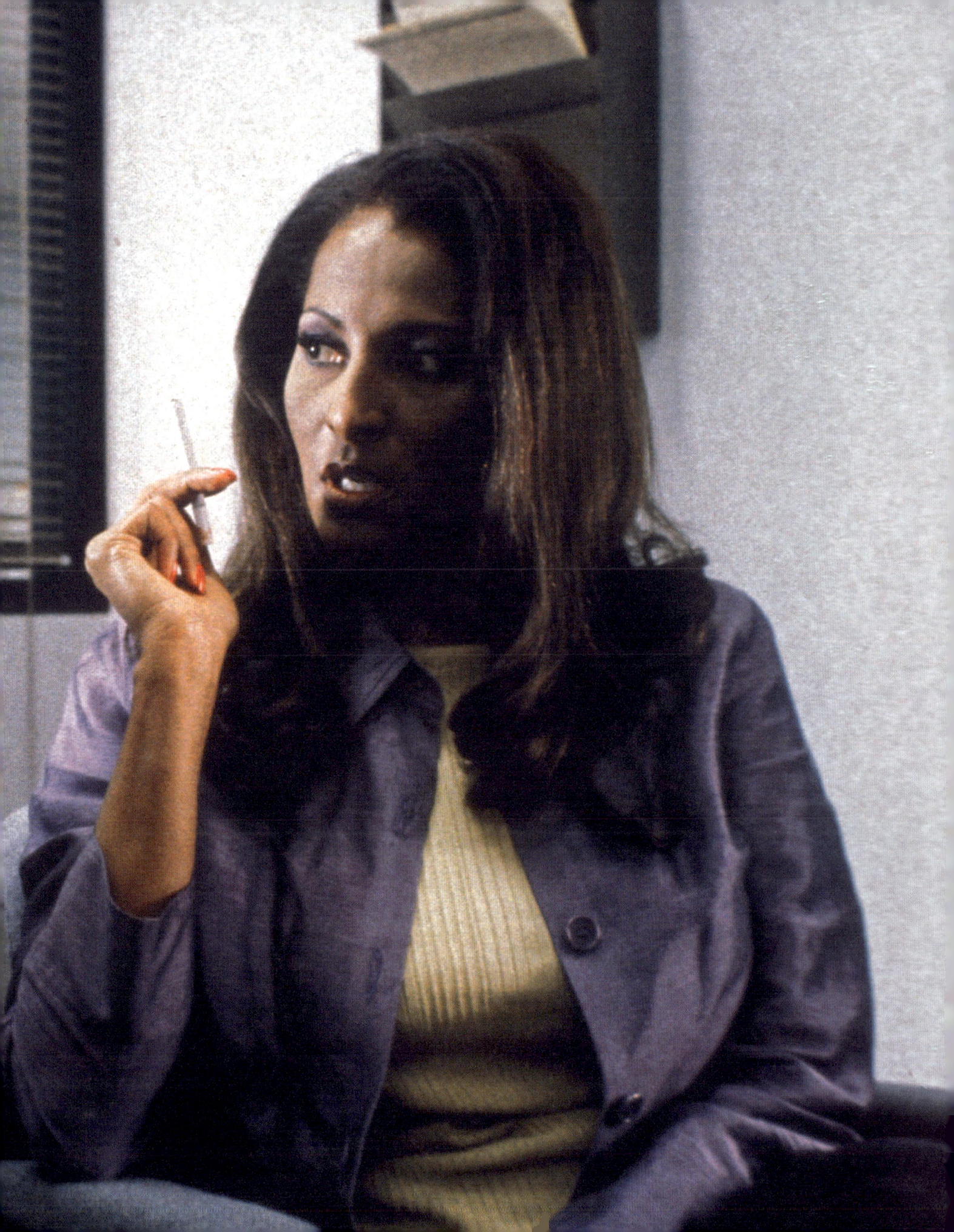

IV
THE RESTAURANT

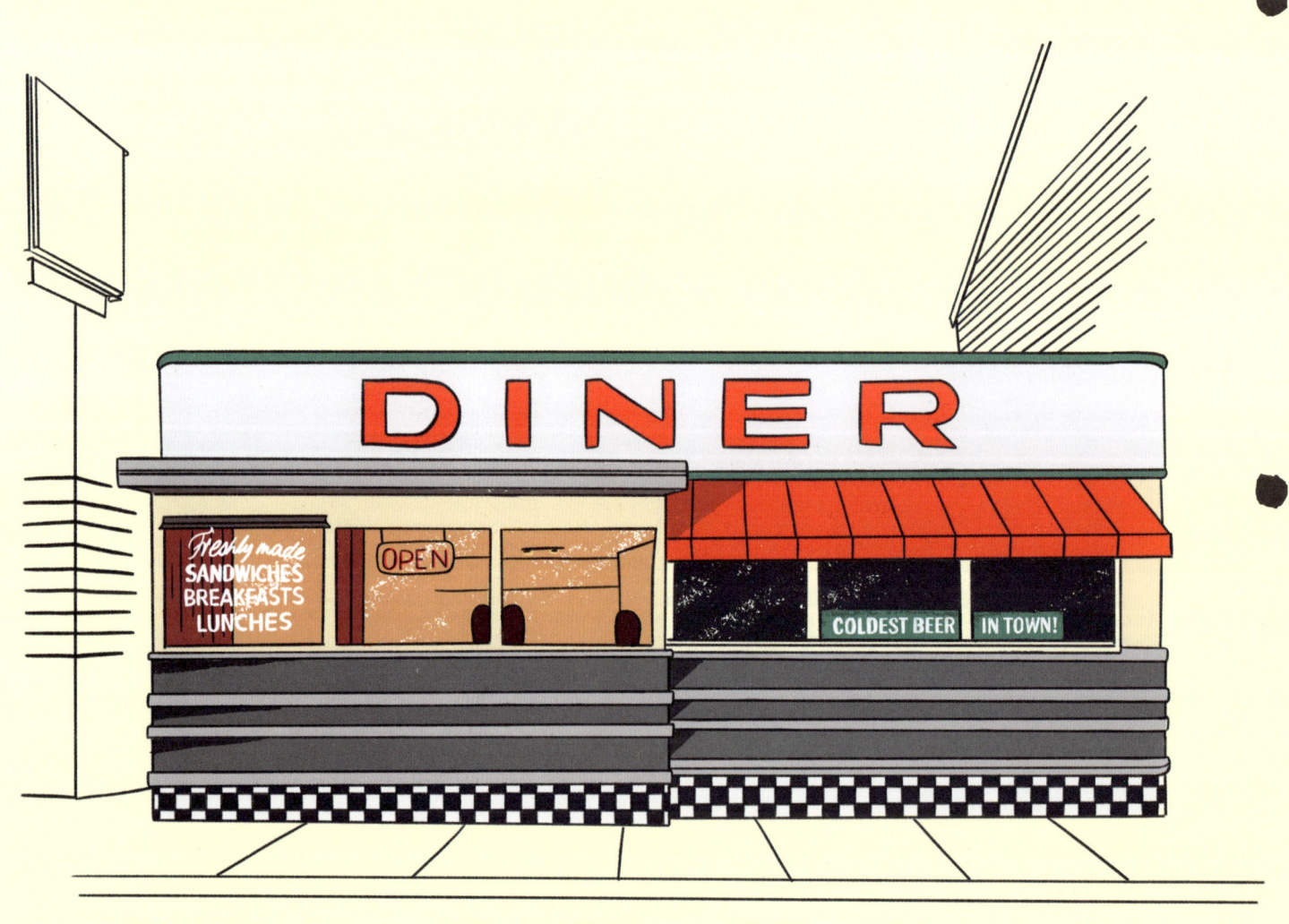

Hawthorne GRILL

Welcome, you must be hungry! After your long stroll around the streets of Tarantino Town, it's time to stop for a well-earned break. The menu in the town's best (and only) diner features all sorts of comforting retro specialties: smooth five-dollar milkshakes, succulent Hawaiian-style burgers, generous servings of straight-from-the-oven *Apfelstrudel*, and greasy nachos that will ooze cheese all over your fingers. Although Tarantino is certainly a filmmaker who can conjure up magic with dialogue, he is not content with stuffing his characters' mouths with words alone. In movie after movie, he gives us some of the juiciest tidbit-filled scenes of recent decades. But what, you might ask, is the point of all the classic snacks that QT treats us to? Well, aside from having an obvious mouthwatering appeal, they are powerful narrative devices, capable of conjuring up a character in a matter of mouthfuls, controlling the power dynamics in a scene, or ratcheting the tension up to a dangerous level… They are key ingredients, in short, for piling on the suspense, Tarantino-style. So visiting our humble town and not stopping in at its excellent diner is out of the question. Slide into one of the vinyl booths and grab a menu. As Butch would say, you'll be served before you can say *blueberry pie*. Enjoy your meal!

APFELSTRUDEL

The Crème de la Crème

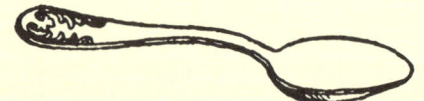

The thin dough these pastries are made from, called *Strudelteig*, is baked until it is golden as the summer sun, crisp to perfection, and melting in the middle. Pierce one of the pastries with a dessert fork, and you will be rewarded by the sight of delicious sugary liquid trickling from its insides, which are jammed full of delectable, slightly tart apple chunks. The famous *Apfelstrudel*, like Colonel Hans Landa, comes to us from the Austrian Alps. It has become a classic dessert in Ashkenazi Jewish communities. This distant cousin of baklava pastries—which date back to the ancient Ottoman and Persian empires—has traveled across continents, from the East to Europe, to make it onto our plates so that we can join other food lovers from all over the world in gorging ourselves on it. But what does *Apfelstrudel* mean? Well, *Strudel* is the German word for *whirlpool*, and *Apfel* is German for *apple*. *Apfel* and *Strudel*, how delightful the words sound! It wouldn't be surprising to discover that they were the names of two children in an old Bavarian fairy tale.

Apfelstrudel is a poem in itself: Just listen to its crisp crackle, telling you all about the chopped walnuts, almonds, cinnamon (not too much, or the flavor would overwhelm everything else) and raisins inside it… In German-occupied France, however,

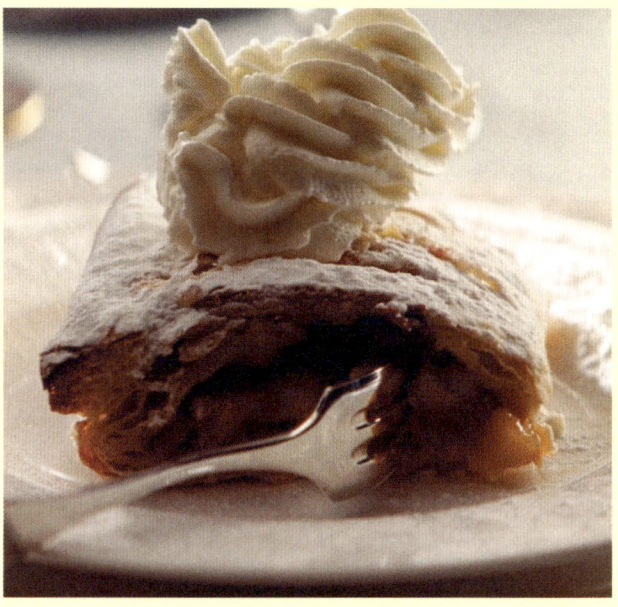

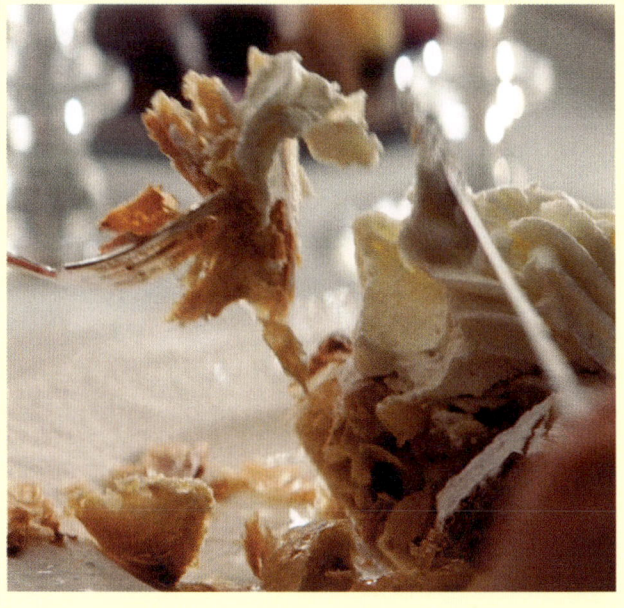

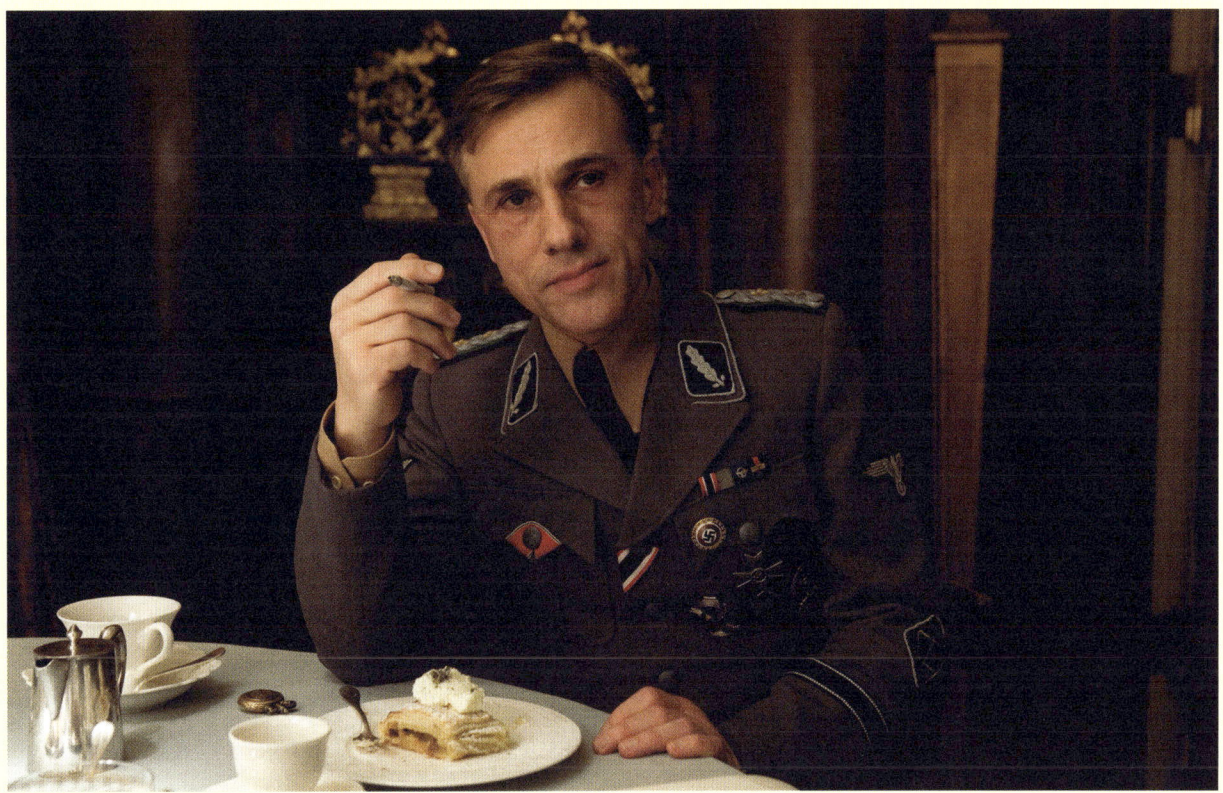

far away from glamorous restaurants and fine dining, the people of Paris are faced with hunger, fear, and a lack of everything. Food ration cards dictate what goes onto their plates, compelling them to count every gram of sugar and fat. "*Paris is cold, Paris is hungry,*" poet Paul Éluard wrote in 1942.[1] But it is not surprising to find *Apfelstrudel* on the menu in the capital's finest restaurants—as here, at Chez Maurice—which are obliged to cater to a clientele of German officers and dignitaries who've come to enjoy the relaxed Parisian way of life. Chez Maurice is a fictional version of the hallowed Maxim's, which found itself commandeered by occupation forces, its cloakroom lined with officer's caps.

Throughout a long film career in which food features heavily, Quentin Tarantino has linked food and language closely together. Tarantino's characters are all mouth—everything is conveyed though their voracious

and voluble lips: the issues at stake; the tension, which can be lowered or raised by a witty remark; or even the stab of a fork, which can swing the movie one way or another. This idea definitely reaches a peak here, in *Inglourious Basterds*, when Shosanna once again encounters Colonel Landa, not at the end of a gun barrel this time, but over a tasty strudel. When Tarantino's characters are not talking, they're eating. Sometimes they do both at once. When he was getting ready to shoot the scene, Tarantino told Christoph Waltz, who played Landa, to "*eat the strudel. Eat the strudel all the time. Just do your scene, talk, you can talk with your mouth full, but just concentrate on that strudel, you eat it and you love every raisin.*"[2]

Between mouthfuls, the colonel conducts a polite interrogation, sending shivers down the spine of his young guest, who recognizes her tormentor but doesn't know if he recognizes her in turn. His

1- Paul Éluard, "Courage," in *Au Rendez-vous allemand* (Les Éditions de Minuit, 1945).
2- Jeremy Kagan, *Directors Close Up 2: Interviews with Directors Nominated for Best Film by The Directors Guild of America* (Scarecrow Press, 2013).

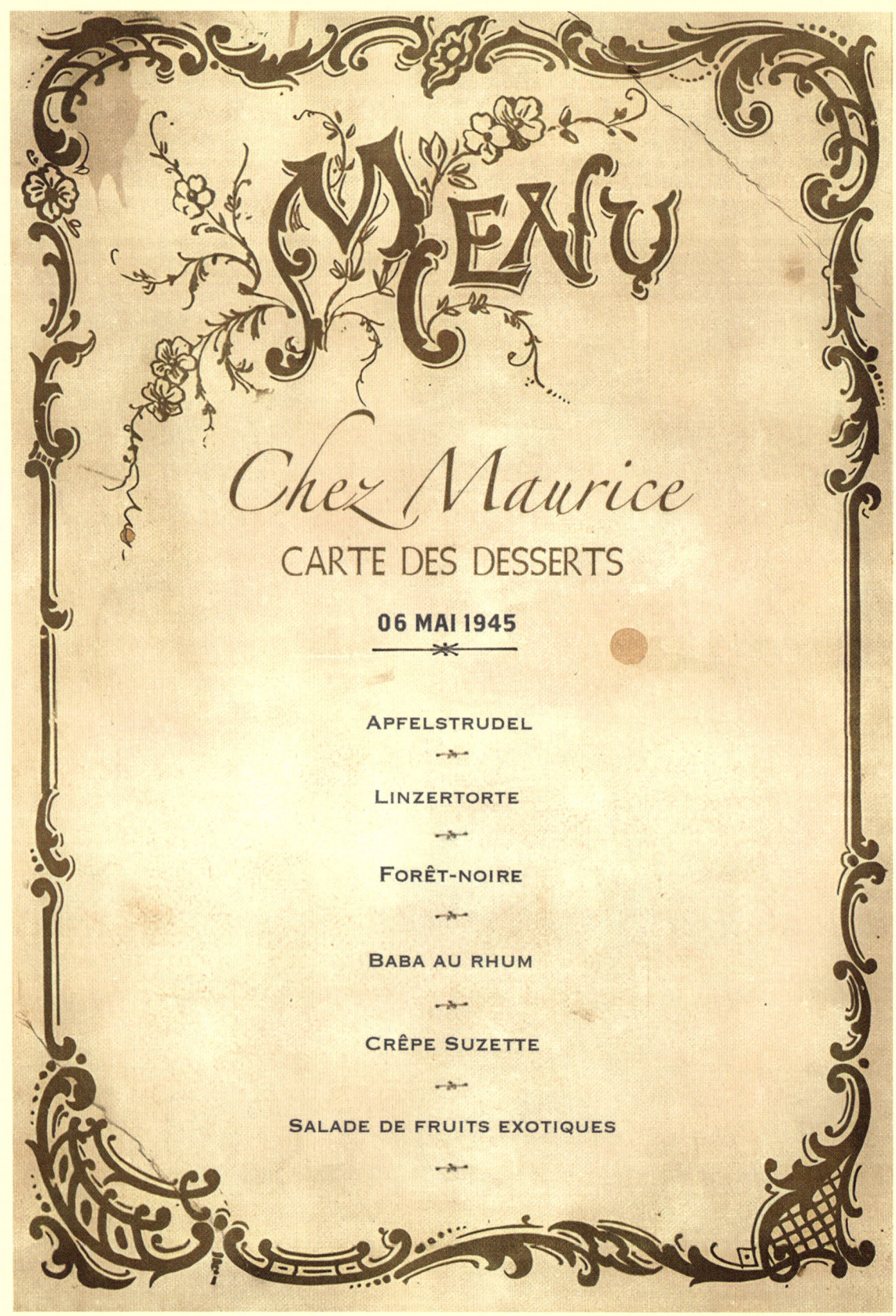

Menu

Chez Maurice
CARTE DES DESSERTS

06 MAI 1945

Apfelstrudel

Linzertorte

Forêt-noire

Baba au rhum

Crêpe Suzette

Salade de fruits exotiques

questions are interrupted by the balletic business of restaurant eating: ordering, the comings and goings of the waiter, the first mouthful Shosanna has to swallow under a pair of searching eyes. But beneath this veneer of civilization lurks something monstrous. When the affable colonel orders a glass of milk for the young woman in a fatherly tone of voice, this could be construed as comforting. However, it is already imbued with a sense of the sinister, because it sparks a memory of an image previously lodged in viewers' minds, of the glass of milk Landa demanded in a little French farmhouse from the humble farmer whose cows produced it, presenting his compliments to the Frenchman before ordering his men to gun down Shosanna's family.

Milk is also rich in symbolic meaning. It is, after all, what you might call the "original food," associated in our minds with scenes of nurturing, mothers and babies. In the Old Testament, along with honey, it symbolizes the plenty of the Promised Land, where it will flow in rivers. But this symbol of innocence is sometimes hijacked and distorted in the most disturbing of ways: from the gleaming white, possibly poisoned, milk in *Suspicion* (Alfred Hitchcock, 1941) to the feast suggested by the preacher in *The Night of the Hunter* (Charles Laughton, 1955) and the menu prepared by Norman Bates in *Psycho* (Alfred Hitchcock, 1960), not to mention the milk laced with psychotropic drugs in *A Clockwork Orange* (Stanley Kubrick, 1971) or the bottle of milk Anton Chigurh picks up in *No Country for Old Men* (Joel and Ethan Coen, 2008). In the wrong hands, milk can signify a distortion, a corruption of something we otherwise associate with an ideal of purity. Philosopher Gaston Bachelard had previously discussed the idea of "*the secret blackness of milk,*"[3] an expression he borrowed from poet Jacques Audiberti. There is another side to this wholesome, reassuring

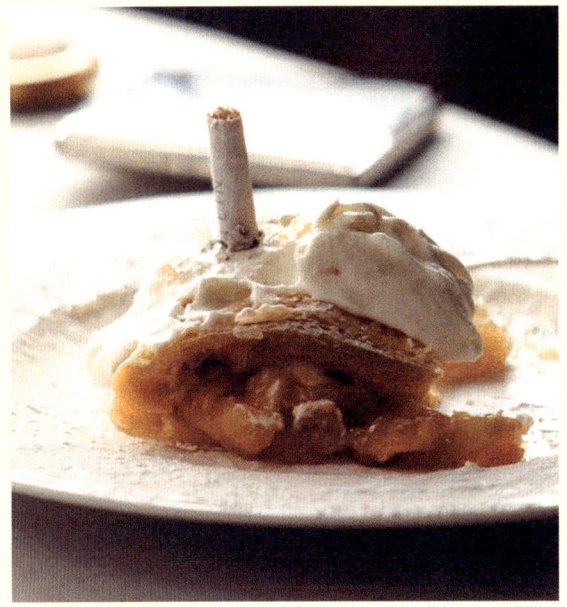

milky whiteness, a disturbing contradiction that Tarantino is quick to exploit when he chooses to make milk the colonel's favorite drink, as if all the more clearly to illustrate the duplicity and viciousness which underlie the character's apparent bonhomie.

Depraved he may be, but Colonel Landa is a fine connoisseur when it comes to food and makes no mistake when he commands Shosanna to wait for the cream before laying into her dessert. *Apfelstrudel* is normally served hot with cream, sometimes even a scoop of ice cream. In *Inglourious Basterds*, the dessert is delicately covered in delicious whipped cream. It's enough to make you salivate: "*I actually think that if you're doing a scene like that,… if the audience isn't hungry for strudel, you have not done your scene right,*"[4] the director declared. So when that bastard Hans Landa shows his utter vulgarity and contempt by stubbing out his German cigarette in the middle of the *Apfelstrudel*, we would happily go back in time and teach him some manners! Motherfucking Nazis. •

3- Gaston Bachelard, *Earth and Reveries of Repose: An Essay on Images of Interiority*, trans. Mary McAllester Jones (Dallas Institute Publications, 2011). • 4- Jeremy Kagan, *Directors Close Up 2: Interviews with Directors Nominated for Best Film by The Directors Guild of America* (Scarecrow Press, 2013).

THE BIG KAHUNA BURGER

The Patron Saint of Burgers

While our first memory of a Big Kahuna Burger may be rooted in *Pulp Fiction*, we need to go back to *Reservoir Dogs* to find the first appearance of the brand in Quentin Tarantino's movies. Yes, there it is: Mr. Blonde casually sipping a soda in a Big Kahuna Burger paper cup. Almost all of Tarantino's films feature the brand's pseudo-Hawaiian logo somewhere, gradually building up a culinary legend succulent enough to make any lover of comfort food drool.

For many of us, it all starts with a crinkled paper bag stamped with a picture of a surfer staring toward the horizon. In front of him is not the Pacific Ocean, but a huge burger bathed in light. "*Hamburgers! The cornerstone of any nutritious breakfast! What kinda hamburgers?*" inquires Jules, interrupting Brett's breakfast. This isn't any old kind of hamburger—it's the iconic, classic fast food brand's star sandwich: the Big Kahuna Burger. "*I hear they got some tasty burgers. I ain't never had one myself, how are they?… Mind if I try one of yours?*" We can picture it: juicy, creamy, enormous, too big to bite into, overflowing with ingredients. But what actually goes into this legendary concoction? Obviously there's the bun—that's a must—two halves of soft bread resembling memory-foam cushions. On top of this, there's lettuce, tomato, cheese (see the two lightly molten orange squares?), a hearty ground beef patty, and—this is where the distinctive flavor comes from—pineapple slices. The jury may still be out for some people when it comes to pineapple on pizza, but the tropical fruit has definitely won over the hearts of burger lovers of every kind. A delightful juxtaposition of sweet and savory is in full swing here, ready to satisfy the greediest of customers.

Quentin Tarantino likes nothing so much as devising brands and logos, and for our part, as viewers, we like nothing more than dissecting them. What does his Big Kahuna brand communicate to us? In cultivating its fantasy Hawaiian image, the junk food brand is falling back on the "tiki" iconography which became so popular in America in the fifties and sixties as a result of the sudden surge of interest in all things Polynesian. This postwar consumerist fad interpreted the term widely, including everything from Hawaiian shirts (a selection of which you'll find when you step into our modest thrift store) to Elvis Presley's extravagant concert in Honolulu, *Aloha from Hawaii*, which was broadcast live by satellite. But the Polynesian myth had already lost some of its luster by the time Tarantino took hold of it, and here it is looking as tawdry and cheap as a plastic hula girl on a car dashboard. Somewhere en route from the Pacific Ocean to the wrappers of second-rate burgers, the vision seems to have become well and

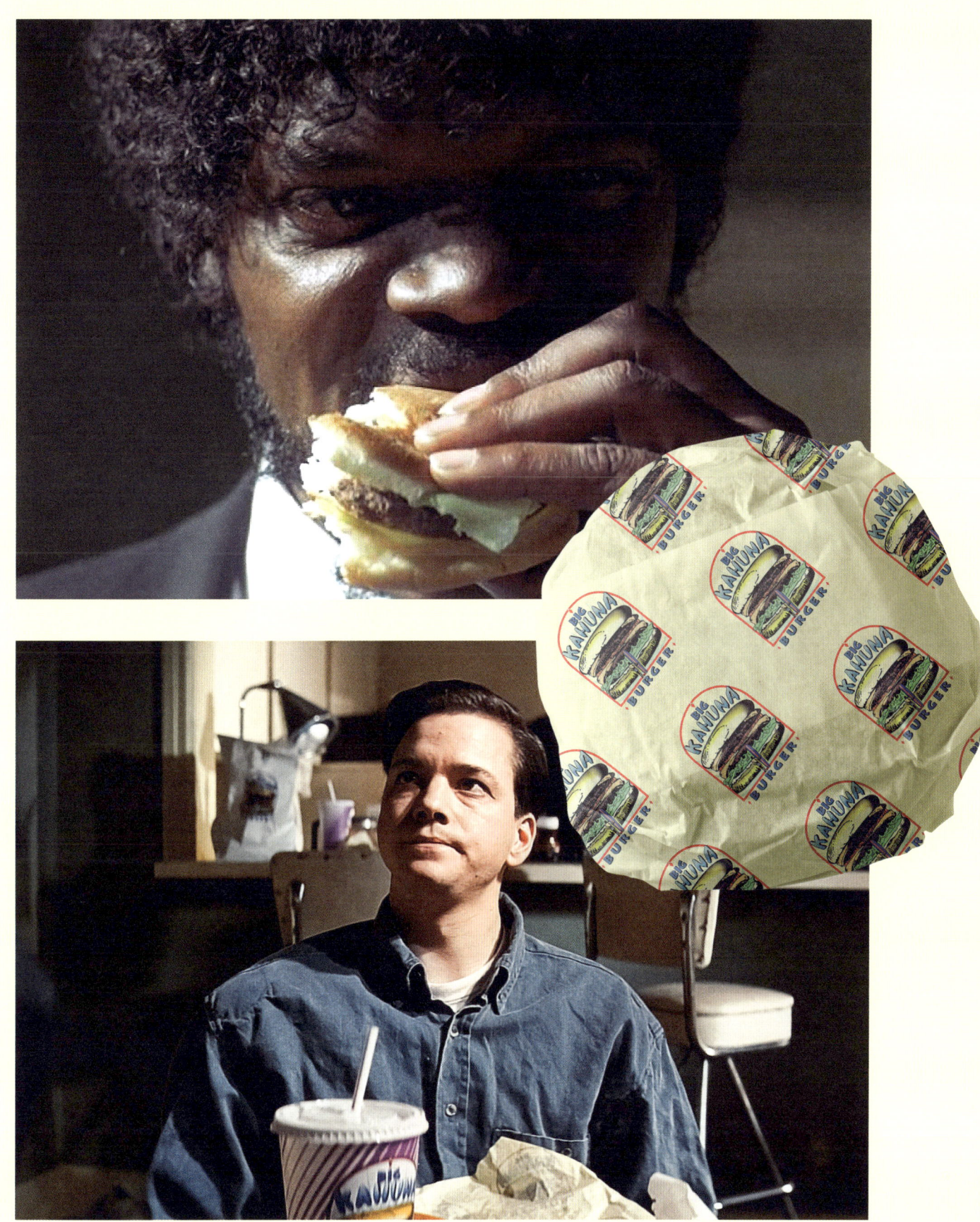

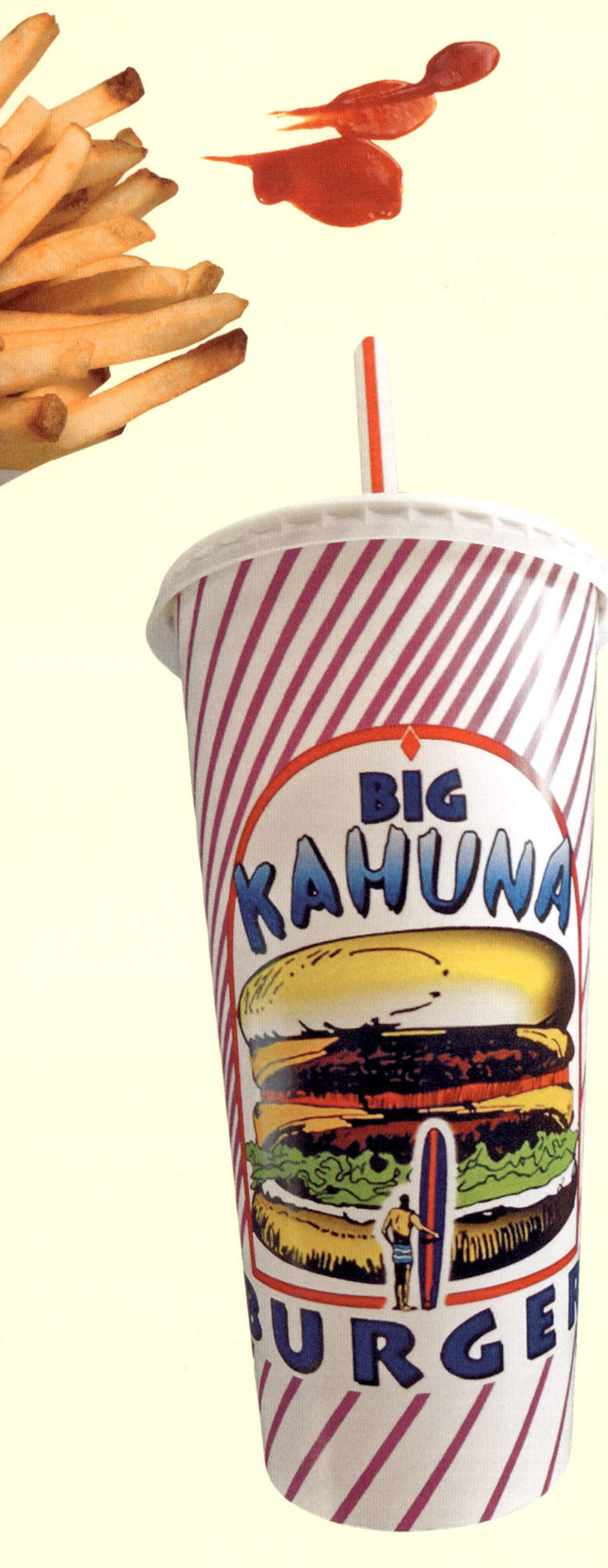

truly tarnished. Even the Hawaiian term *kahuna*, originally used to refer to a bearer of ancestral wisdom, has ended up melting like those cheese slices and merging into American slang as a word for an important man, a big boss, and even by extension, perhaps, a master crook. Big Kahuna Burger may no longer be quite the place to hang out.

"*Mmmm, this is a tasty burger!*" raves Jules, who then launches into an earnest digression on topics ranging from his vegetarian girlfriend to the metric system before downing Brett's huge cup of Sprite in one go, a hint of a challenge in his eyes. But what is the point of this gastronomic interlude in the middle of what is indisputably a gangster scene? The answer is that our Big Kahuna Burger doesn't just have nutritional properties, but narrative ones too: Its very presence is enough to cruelly delay the inevitable hour of retribution. Will the imperious Jules spare Brett from his doom once his stomach is full? Nothing is less likely, but his sadistic approach keeps both the miserable Brett and the audience in suspense. It reminds us, of course, of another choice Tarantino interlude: the legendary "Sicilian scene" in *True Romance*, masterfully directed by Tony Scott, in which a warm moment of shared laughter leaves us hoping for a more favorable outcome for the characters… But Tarantino's killers are not the kind of men to get emotional on the strength of a moment's bonding or a shared meal, even if a flash of humanity runs through the scene like a glimmer of hope. Death and burgers, the gospel and blasphemy, the sacred and profane, the existential and trivial, all set off with a good streak of blood-red ketchup: These are the key ingredients of a Big Kahuna Burger.

It's easy, then, to imagine Vincent and Jules stopping by one of the countless fast food joints dotted all over Los Angeles to get a bite to eat and tucking into one of these calorie-laden monsters, then wiping their lips with a white napkin which won't stay that way for long. They'd follow this with a few swigs of soda pop to wash it all down, in true Jules Winnfield style, before lighting up a Red Apple and settling down to watch time and the cars go by on Cahuenga Avenue. Anyone who's spent any time strolling down the sidewalks of Los Angeles knows that there's no shortage of fast food restaurants ready to cater to passersby, but none has yet acquired anything like the legendary status which Big Kahuna Burger has in the collective unconscious. We envy Quentin Tarantino's characters their ability to sample the fare on this delicious menu—we too would really like to have our fingers dripping with grease and our stomachs rebelling at the indigestible food. So all together, let's go and order our own dose of junk food, raise our Big Kahuna cups high, and cap off our afternoon on the couch watching *Rolling Thunder* or the latest episode of *Columbo*. •

The Big Kahuna Burger

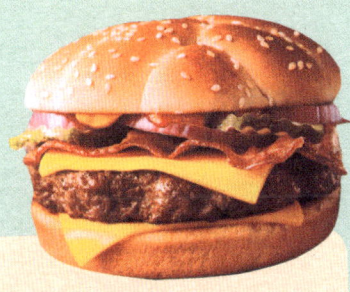

INGREDIENTS

Ground beef	1 lb. (500 g)
Burger buns	4
Lettuce	4 leaves
Tomato	1
Pineapple	1
Onion	1
Cheddar cheese	8 slices

TO PREPARE

Wash the lettuce leaves, making sure they are nice and fresh. Cut the tomato into slices. Peel the pineapple and cut into thick or thin slices, depending on how adventurous you feel. Peel the onion, cut into rounds, and sauté in a pan until caramelized, then set aside. Toss the pineapple slices in the hot pan and cook until lightly browned, then set aside. Shape the ground beef into four patties, flatten, and sauté until cooked as you like. Lay the slices of cheddar on the bottom halves of the burger buns and put them in the oven. Watch until the cheese melts gently into the bun. Take them out of the oven without burning yourself, and then layer the meat, caramelized onion, pineapple, tomato, remaining cheese, and lettuce leaves on each bun. Coat liberally with ketchup, barbecue sauce, mustard, or even teriyaki sauce before capping with the top half of the bun. Eat with your hands!

Certified by Big Kahuna Burger

STUNTMAN MIKE'S NACHOS

Food Porn

A big plate lands on the bar, joining a couple of piña coladas (a virgin one for our man, believe it or not) and the margaritas which the girls in *Death Proof* adore. The dish is greasy, calorie-laden, and overflowing with chips… sorry, nachos. Greed knows no bounds, which is just as well: These fried corn chips from Mexico have conquered the whole of the United States. They have long been a feature on Tex-Mex menus, and the Texas Chili Parlor is hardly going to be the one to depart from the rule. In other words, nachos have found their place in Quentin Tarantino's world, and he regales us here with a classic food-porn scene.

Sitting on his own at the bar, Stuntman Mike stuffs them into his mouth as if he were half-starved, his chin dripping with grease, stopping only to lick his glistening fingers. All it takes is a few shots of him masticating in quite the unappetizing way, and we've got a picture of him. Tarantino had already grasped the gently erotic potential of mouths as they sip, chew, and talk, tapping into this as he did in the shared milkshake scene in *Pulp Fiction*. Here the scene has a distinctly salacious, almost pornographic feel which projects a great deal about the stuntman's dangerously libidinous character. Stuntman Mike devours his nachos with an appetite that verges on the obscene, and yet… A close-up shot of

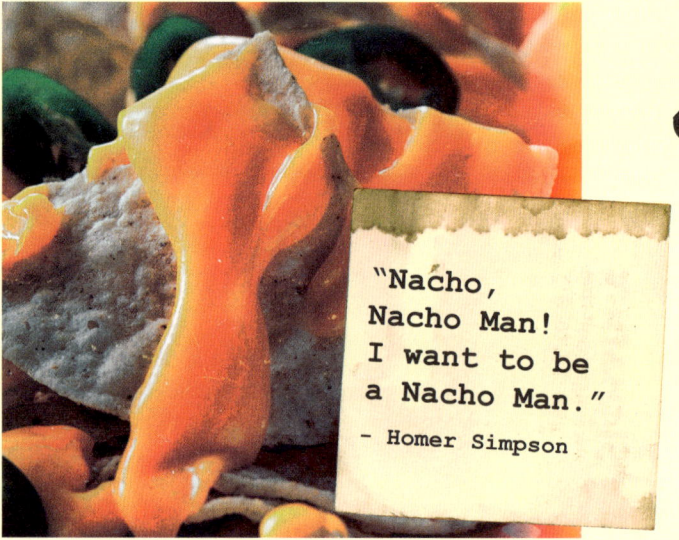

"Nacho, Nacho Man! I want to be a Nacho Man."
- Homer Simpson

the dish of nachos leaves us somewhere between wanting to be sick and wanting to tuck in. We have to bow to the facts: We would happily stick our own fingers in.

Who wouldn't set their culinary principles aside for a night and let themselves indulge in this orgy of cheese and salsa? Because nachos never come alone. They come with backup—in this case, a coating of melted cheese covering them like an avalanche of grease, as if all they've been waiting for is to be bathed in pools of fat. A handful of olives and a few bits of yellow and red pepper add a dash of color to the mix. But don't start getting any funny ideas: There's not enough here to qualify as even a token vegetable ("See? I'm eating vegetables too!"). No, we have to accept the

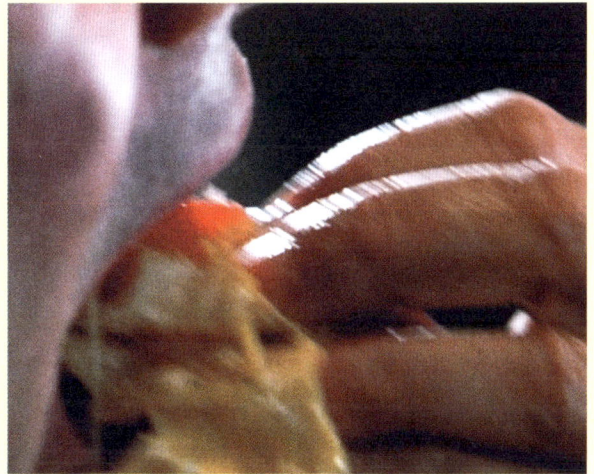
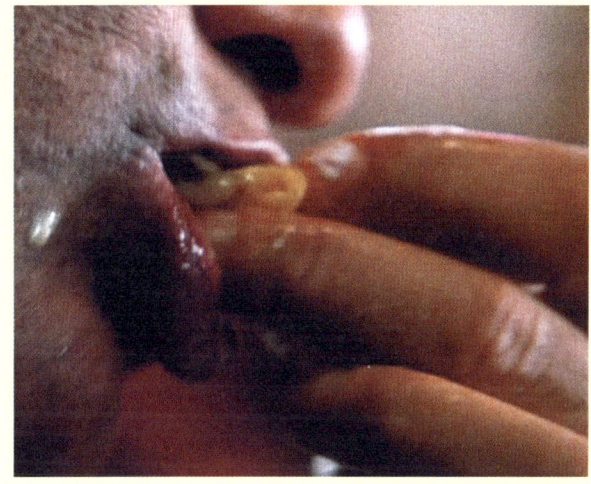
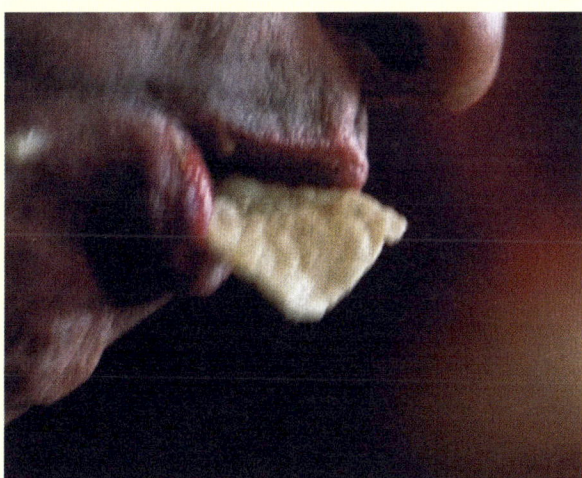
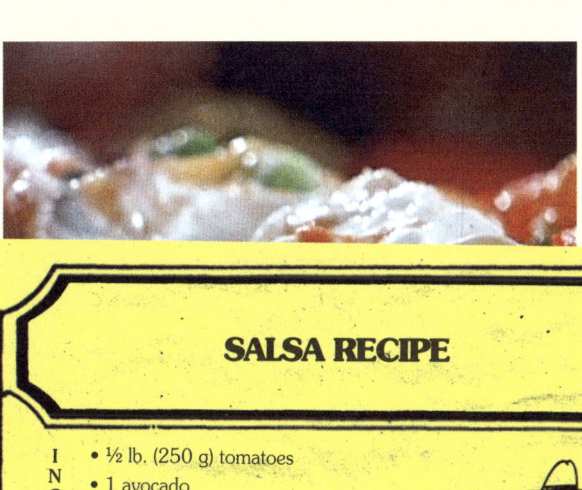

fact that we've lost the fight after the first bite, and we certainly do not feel guilty about it. We'll go back to eating healthy on Monday, as we always do. Right now, it's all about wallowing in excess until we make ourselves sick. A slave to his depraved impulses, Stuntman Mike has made a specialty of this. We would love to have a wild, opulent feast, with "Down in Mexico" by the Coasters playing in the background. With a bit of luck, you too might win a devilish lap dance one torrid summer night, somewhere in a corner of Austin, Texas. If by any chance someone offers you a lift, though, don't take them up on it. The road isn't safe and surely there are a few nachos left to scoff down. Take it from us, you're better off fat than dead. •

SALSA RECIPE

INGREDIENTS

- ½ lb. (250 g) tomatoes
- 1 avocado
- 1 lime
- 3½ oz. (100 ml) olive oil
- A pinch of chili flakes
- A few stalks of fresh cilantro (optional)
- Salt, pepper

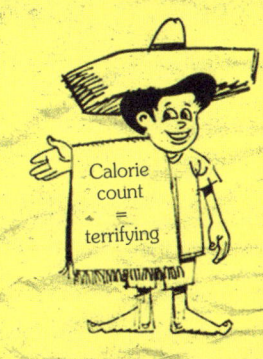

Calorie count = terrifying

STEPS

1.
Dice the tomatoes and avocado.

2.
Throw everything into a bowl and dress with freshly squeezed lime juice, olive oil, chili flakes, and salt and pepper.

3.
Add the finely chopped cilantro (you don't have to, we told you, didn't we?), mix well, and serve with nachos covered in an indecent amount of melted cheese.

CLIFF BOOTH'S MAC AND CHEESE

TV Dinner

This is perhaps the most famous pasta dish not to come out of Italy. From a distance, one might describe it as… yellow. Up close, the same. The packaging of the many different brands and varieties, however, shows an alluring array of colors ranging from luminous orange to golden brown. Mac and cheese, that famous dish of macaroni blanketed in cheese—lots of cheese— is the ultimate comfort food, and that's the image it conjures up first and foremost, with its breadcrumb topping sizzling crisply as it comes out of the oven and its lashings of melted cheddar, to which a real cheese buff might even add a healthy grating of gruyère for good measure. It's unmistakable, whatever form it comes in—whether served with bacon or jalapeños, garnished with herbs or a drizzle of Tabasco, or even accompanied with truffles or lobster for the poshest among us. As a pairing, pasta and cheese goes way back, of course: It can be traced back to medieval cookbooks in both England and Italy. Macaroni and cheese has traveled a long way over the years, recipe by recipe, from Victorian England all the way to Thomas Jefferson's table. It first appeared in boxed form in America in 1937, offering the promise of a nutritious meal which could be ready in minutes at an unbeatable price. Boxed mac and cheese quickly became a firm favorite with young and old, and it carried on its way from table to couch, where it established itself in the sixties as a TV dinner, eaten in front of the hallowed family set.

Quentin Tarantino got it completely right when, in *Once Upon a Time… in Hollywood*, he had Cliff Booth decide to make himself a good shovelful of mac and cheese in his trailer in the heart of the valley, on the other side of Los Angeles, in 1969. You start to salivate at the mere thought of that golden, steaming macaroni, which you would happily eat with the plate propped on your knees and your feet crossed on a low table in front of you, a napkin over your shoulder and an old movie crackling on the TV. When you'd eaten the whole plate, you'd set it down on the floor next to the couch, telling yourself you'd do the dishes in the morning. At any rate, that's how we picture Cliff Booth's evening playing out, and yet… With Tarantino, food scenes are never as innocent as we might expect. Fittingly for the man himself, a confirmed bachelor since his wife's (suspicious) death, Cliff Booth's mac and cheese betrays a degree of neglect. From the inevitable blue mac and cheese box to the cans of beer to the (rat or raccoon flavored?) dog food for his guard dog, his cupboards are full of processed, one hundred percent factory-made food. Mac and cheese is definitely a doable option for a single underpaid stuntman after a long day's work. He prepares it with one hand on the corner of a filthy stove, doling out Brandy's glutinous dog food into a dirty bowl with the other. He then garnishes the lot in Cliff Booth fashion, tipping the sachet of orange powder which does duty for cheese into the pot neat, without any butter or milk, before going over to the TV and casually wolfing down the mix straight from the pan, without a second thought. Here, then, the unfathomable Cliff Booth, perpetual right-hand man, is presented as more human, more accessible through the simple device of a dish as unreformed as it is badly prepared. And we are treated to another classic gastronomic interlude from Tarantino—who knows that there's nothing people want more badly to see on screen than Brad Pitt eating. •

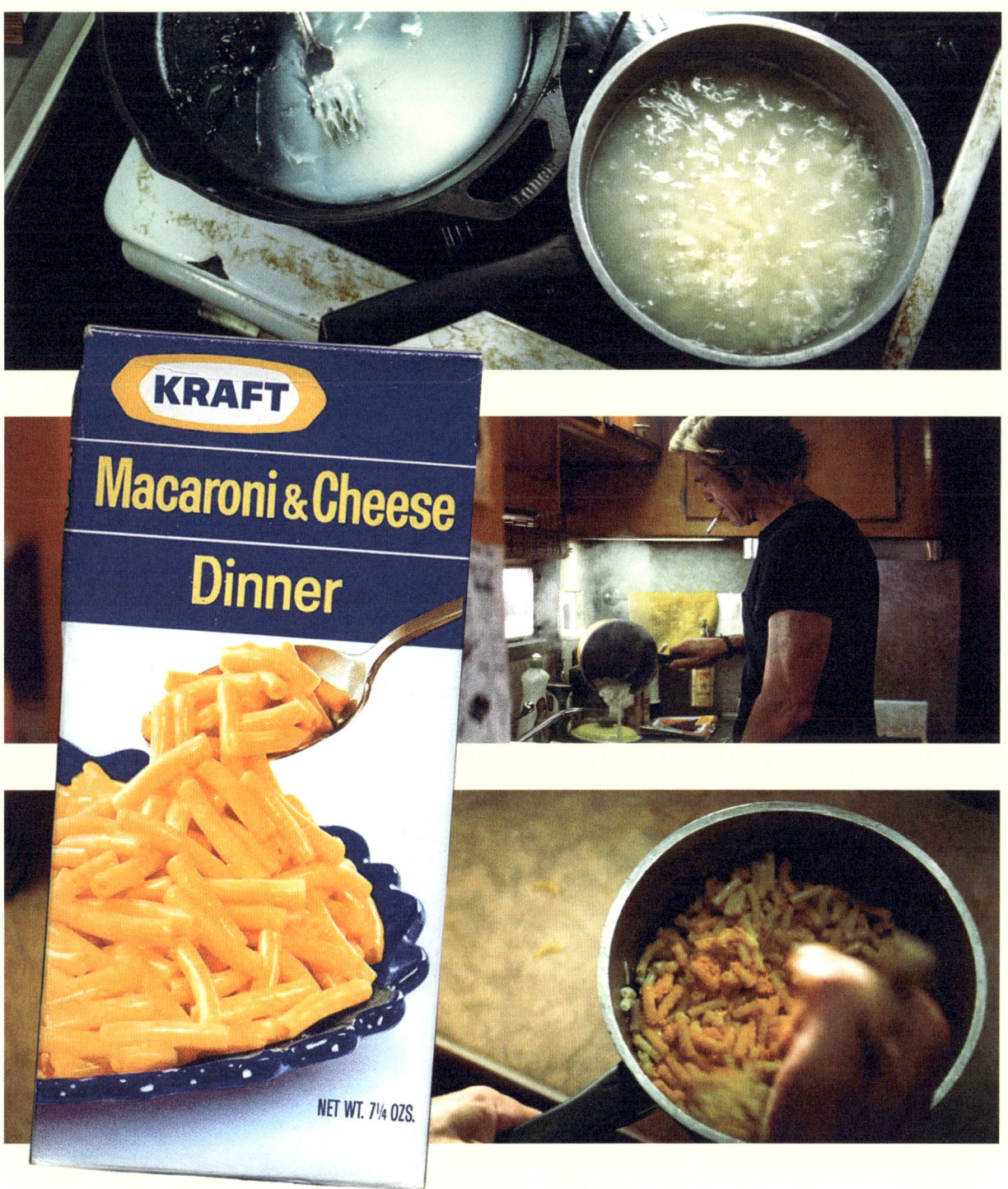

THE FIVE-DOLLAR SHAKE

"It Costs Five Dollars?"

It's a beautiful affair, as if airbrushed to perfection to look cool, sexy, and unmistakenly Californian. It stands proud, neatly encased in a tall, slim-fitting glass, dressed with a smooth topping of whipped cream and crowned with a soft red cherry which verges on pink. Getting back to the beautiful New World creation itself, its history goes back to at least 1885, when the word *milkshake* first appeared in a newspaper. It referred then to a creamy concoction of whiskey, eggs, and eggnog, mixed together in a shaker and served with ice cubes—the start of a wonderfully sweet adventure which led to the milkshake as we know it.

In Tarantino's world, the obvious place to drink one is at Jack Rabbit Slim's, where it will be served up to you by Jayne Mansfield (unless it's her day off), Buddy Holly, or another faded star brought back from the American Hall of Fame. The atmosphere is entirely artificial, unadulterated fifties: You ease yourself into a leatherette seat in an old Cadillac which has been turned into a dining booth. It's here, right in the middle of this beautiful, phony American fantasy of a place, that Mia orders her aptly named Jerry Lewis and Dean Martin vanilla milkshake. When she asks the waiter for the famous "five-dollar shake," Vincent Vega is incredulous. He repeats the price after her, clearly seeing it as exorbitant. *"You don't put bourbon in it or anything?"* he continues ironically. At five dollars a hit, our friend Vincent is keen to set his lips on Mia's straw and sample the iced treasure for himself to find out whether it's worth the handful of bills they'll leave on the Formica table.

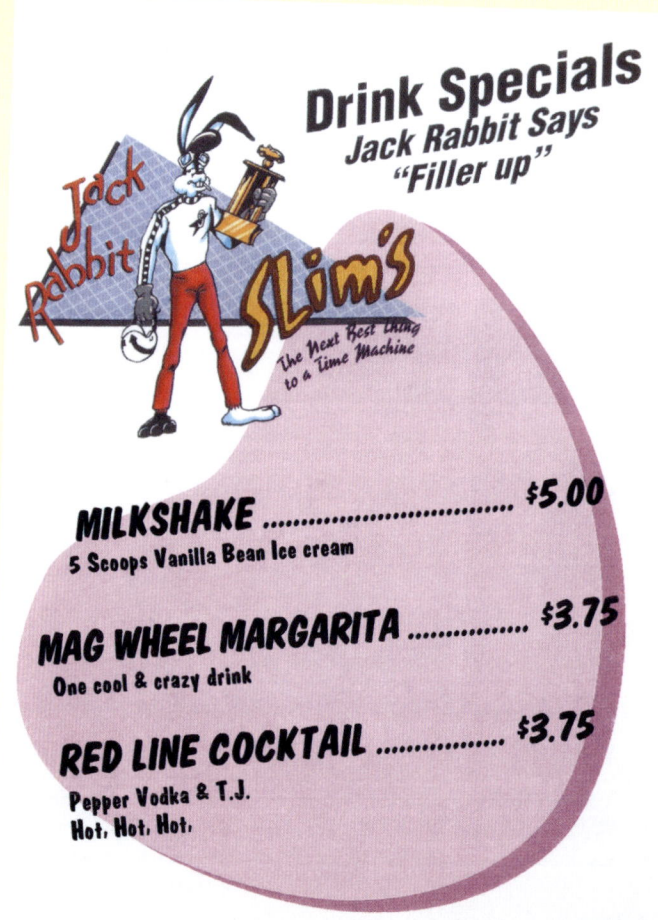

Drink Specials
Jack Rabbit Says "Filler up"

Jack Rabbit Slim's
The Next Best Thing to a Time Machine

MILKSHAKE **$5.00**
5 Scoops Vanilla Bean Ice cream

MAG WHEEL MARGARITA **$3.75**
One cool & crazy drink

RED LINE COCKTAIL **$3.75**
Pepper Vodka & T.J. Hot. Hot. Hot.

Mia and Vincent share the shake like a couple of teenagers—a helluva risk to take when you know what Mia's husband, Marsellus Wallace, is like… The milkshake is like a modern-day Proustian madeleine, with that familiar vanilla taste of nostalgia and innocence. Mia and Vincent are no angels, but they indulge for a moment in a chaste love ritual, looking into each other's eyes as they share both the milkshake and the straw. One straw, two pairs of lips: It's a virtual kiss, the only kind, perhaps, they are allowed.

Vincent lets out a stream of swear words in praise of Mia's choice of beverage: "*Goddamn! That's a pretty fuckin' good milkshake.*" It proves, in the end, to be well worth those five green bills. Tarantino doesn't miss a trick with this cult scene: Sipping a milkshake through a straw is a way of embracing the great American adventure of life, diving headfirst into an iced pop culture legend. This leaves us with just one question: Do you need to take a break to go powder your nose, as Mia does, while you wait to be served? Make sure nobody pinches your cherry! •

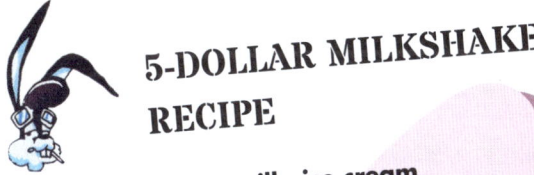

5-DOLLAR MILKSHAKE RECIPE

- 5 scoops of vanilla ice cream
- ½ cup cold milk
- ½ cup fresh cream
- A few drops of vanilla extract
- Whipped cream and a Maraschino cherry

1. Blend all the ingredients (except the whipped cream and the cherry!) together to a smooth, creamy liquid.

2. Pour into a tall retro glass and top with a good serving of whipped cream. Place a cherry on the very top, and that's a wrap!

3. Drink very cold, through a straw, at a table in the local diner, on your own or with a friend…

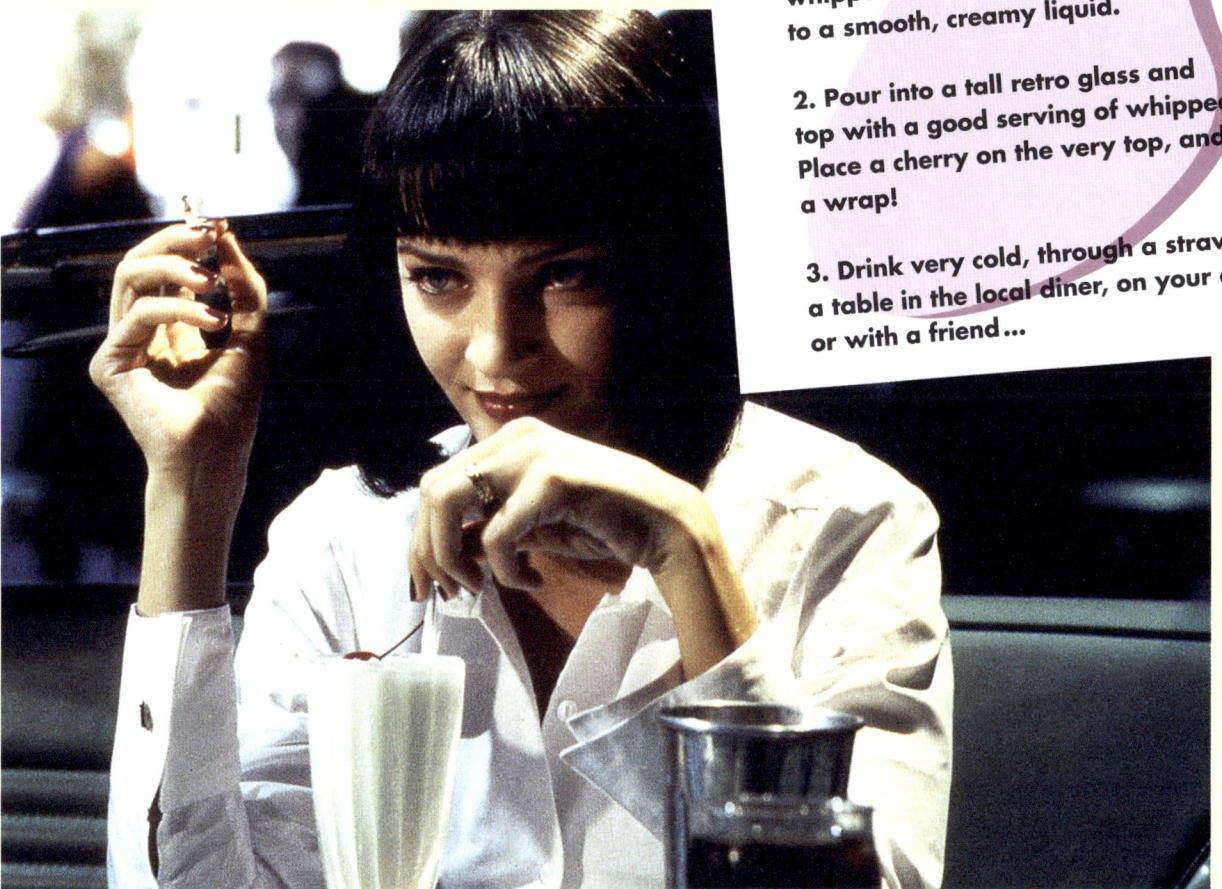

TERIYAKI DONUT

Sweet and Savory

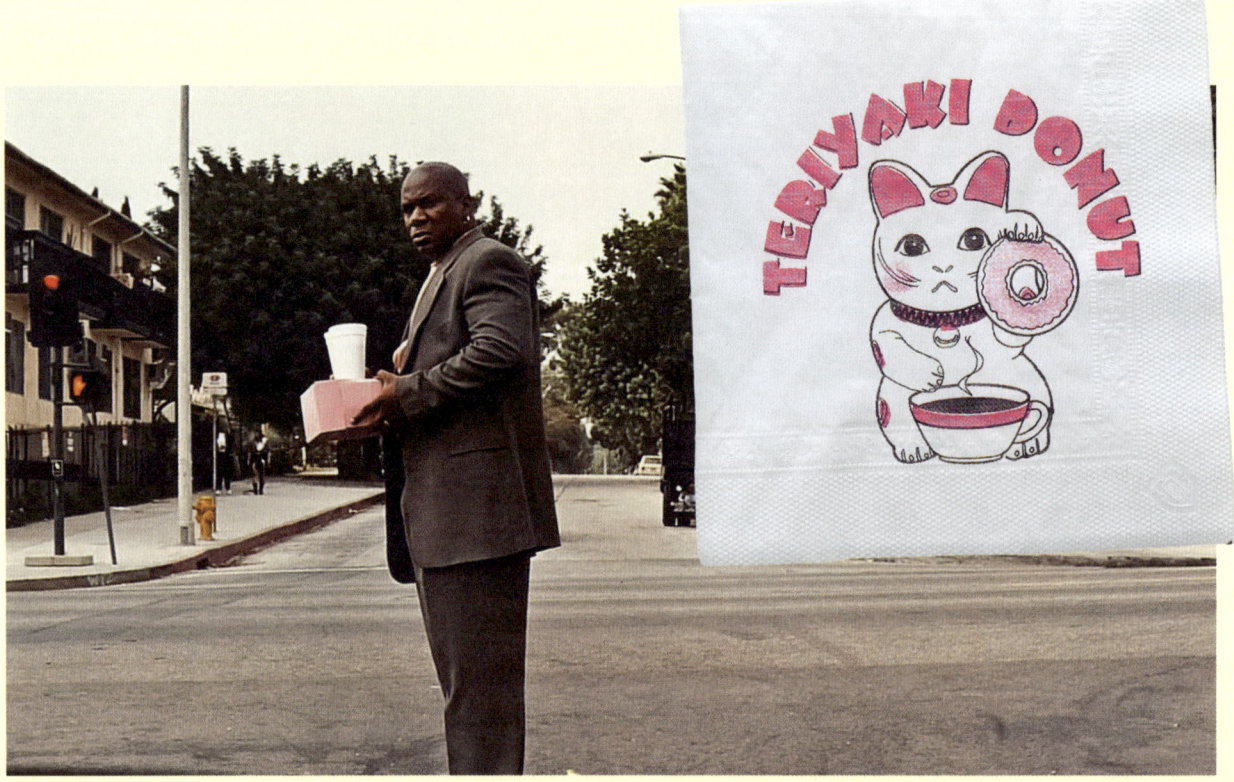

First, let's go back to the basics. In Japanese cooking, *teriyaki* is used to describe a piece of meat, fish, or any other substitute which is glazed with a marinade of soy sauce and other ingredients and then grilled. Donuts, of course, are sweet ring-shaped fritters, generally iced and sometimes with a filling. So when Quentin Tarantino adds yet another fictitious logo to his world, this time for a brand called Teriyaki Donut, we don't know what to make of it. How can we possibly imagine the big, soft, sweet treat we know and love as the donut being cooked teriyaki-style? By the same token, how could the three pillars of Japanese cooking, sake, mirin, and soy sauce, possibly get tangled up with the famous American donut? An unholy, unnatural marriage, surely? Perhaps not.

The logo makes its first discreet appearance in *Pulp Fiction*, in a carbon copy of a scene in *Psycho* in which Marion Crane sees her boss, whom she has just robbed, crossing the road at a crosswalk in front of her as she is driving along in her car. In QT's replay of the famous

Hitchcock scene it's Butch who is at the wheel (of Fabienne's Civic Honda), and Marsellus Wallace crossing the road. Marsellus stops in the middle of the crosswalk, furious, clutching a box of nice fresh donuts and two large styrofoam cups of coffee, which he's just picked up from the local Teriyaki Donut, as the script tells us. The Japanese-American brand finds its way into a more prominent role in *Jackie Brown*, in the food court of the Del Amo Mall, in the heart of suburban Los Angeles. On two separate occasions, Jackie sits down to enjoy the chain's specialties: Gracing her tray is a bowl with two chopsticks and a tall white styrofoam cup with the familiar logo. Teriyaki Donut's mascot is a *maneki-neko*, one of those Japanese lucky cat charms which now turn up all over the world but have their very own temple in their home country: the temple of Gotoku-ji, in the Setagaya area of Tokyo. In its traditionally lifted paw, this lucky cat holds a beautiful pink donut, ready to dip it into a steaming hot cup of coffee.

The menu on offer at Teriyaki Donut no doubt has all the hallmarks of Quentin Tarantino's films: sweet and savory, reflecting opposing influences, capable of combining, without any apparent hint of contradiction, quiet moments and gentle chitchat with flashes of uncompromising violence. The combination the director dreams up here is an impossible mix of Japanese gastronomy and American greed. The mishmash of food available at Teriyaki Donut may very well be similar to the sort of fusion cuisine the director likes to cook up in his postmodern oven: a wild mix of references of every sort and kind, from the noblest to the most base, all blended to excess. Certainly this kind of bastardized cuisine perfectly sums up what we find in Tarantino's movies.

As for the specific creation itself, with its almost criminal combination of American pastry and Japanese sauce— for of course the donut with teriyaki sauce features on the menu of our humble diner—we can't promise that it will be a gustatory delight, but we can assure you that it will be pure Tarantino. Neither good nor bad taste prevails in Tarantino's world, giving the imagination free rein to come up with the wildest notions possible, like this improbable teriyaki donut. Something to think about and give a try. •

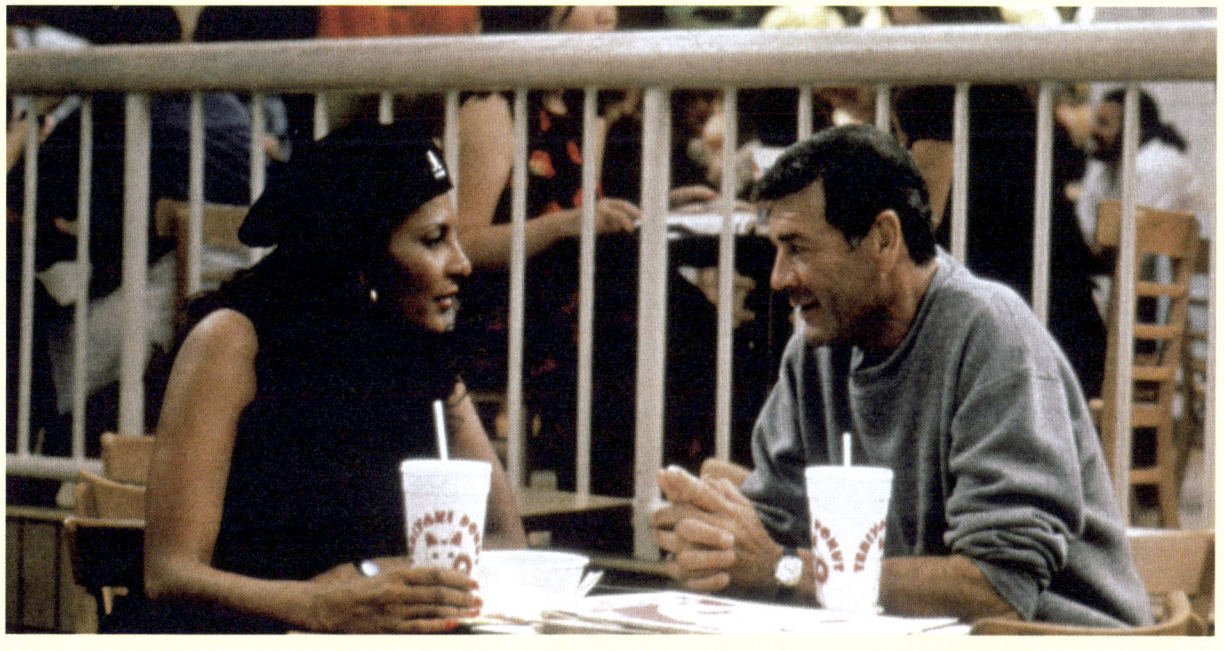

WHITE CAKE

Too Much Sugar

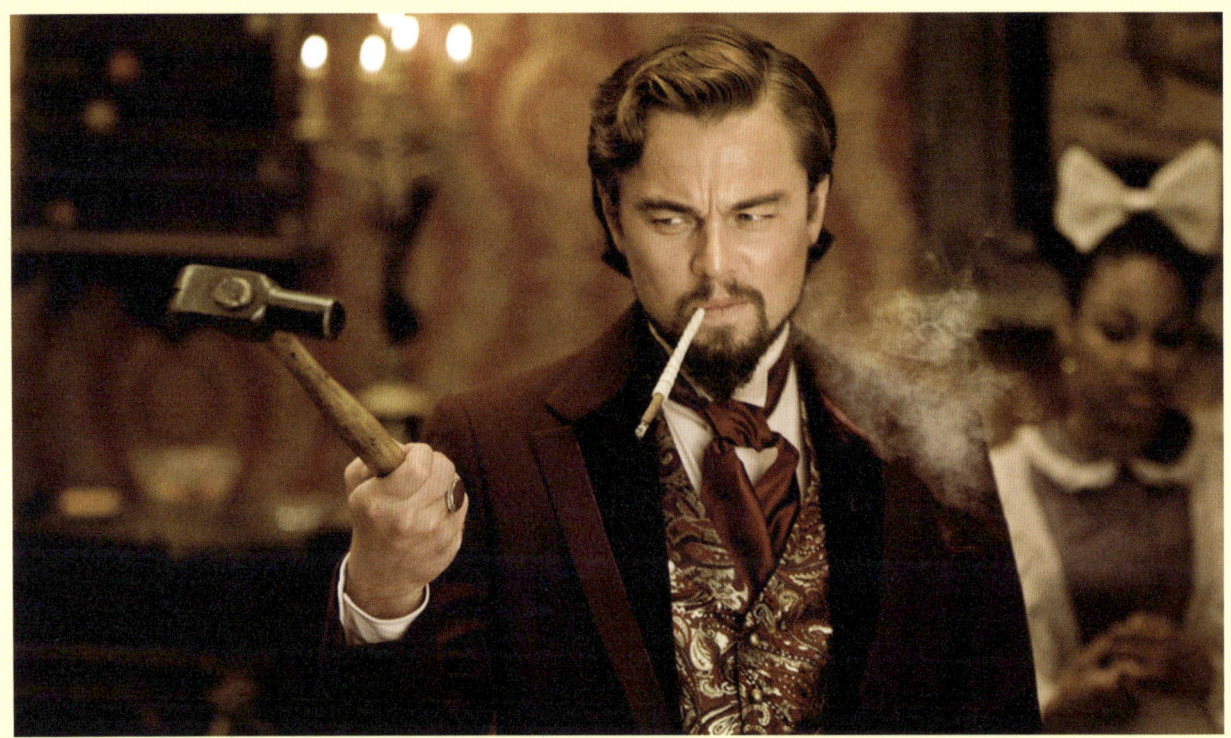

This big cake is made up of generous layers of sponge cake spread with butter cream and coated in virginal white icing. "Monsieur" Candie, as the Francophile likes to be called, is not one to ever pass up dessert. He's got a sweet tooth, as his surname would suggest. In scene after scene, we see him reaching for a piece of candy, tucking into a sugary treat, or sipping sickly sweet cocktails until finally we get to an explosion of sugar in the form of this beautiful white cake which he serves up to his guests.

White cake graced the most prestigious of tables in its time; it was even served at Queen Victoria and Prince Albert's wedding in 1840. Here, it is offered to King Schultz to mark the completion of a commercial transaction, the sale of a young enslaved woman. Can a cake be considered racist? It's a strange question, one which you have probably never asked yourself. That's entirely understandable—and the answer is, of course, no. But perhaps it could unwittingly become a symbol of racism... In *Django Unchained*, this is what

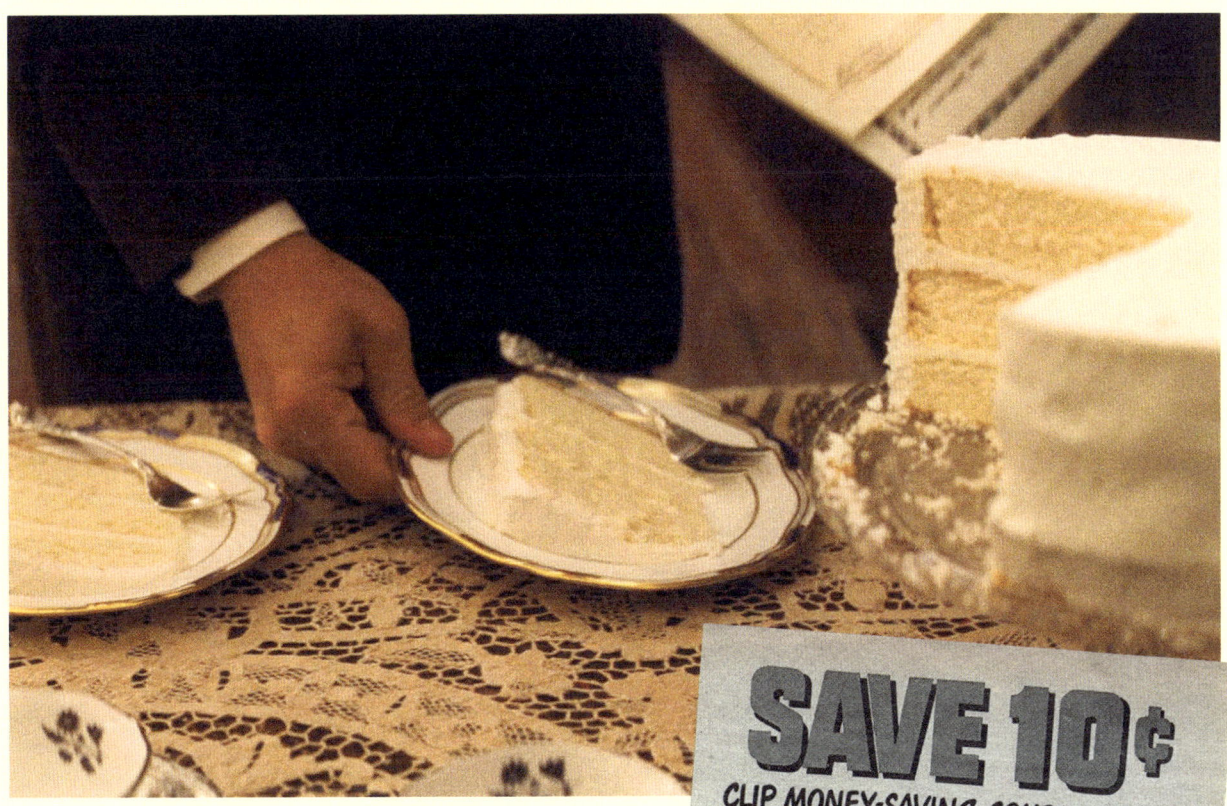

happens to the poor white cake, which
hasn't asked for anything from anyone,
least of all these white supremacists
of every hue. It's all because of that
immaculate white coat, which lends it
the regrettable look of a Grand Dragon
in the Ku Klux Klan, whose sinister
rituals Tarantino takes delight in
mocking. Apart from a blazing torch
and a horse, the white cake has
everything it needs to blend in among
the members of this evil brotherhood—
it absolutely looks the part. And yet
if you think back to that famous scene
with the makeshift hoods cut out of
sacks, the members of the Klan seem
to be a ridiculous bunch of bumbling
bumpkins. In contrast, the white cake
is infinitely more elegant, a true
gentleman among cakes, with its smooth
layers and tiers of delectable sponge.

Landowner and slaver Calvin J. Candie
prides himself above all on being
a man of the world, and this refined
cake flatters his ego. In his great
colonial plantation house, our
host insists on being addressed

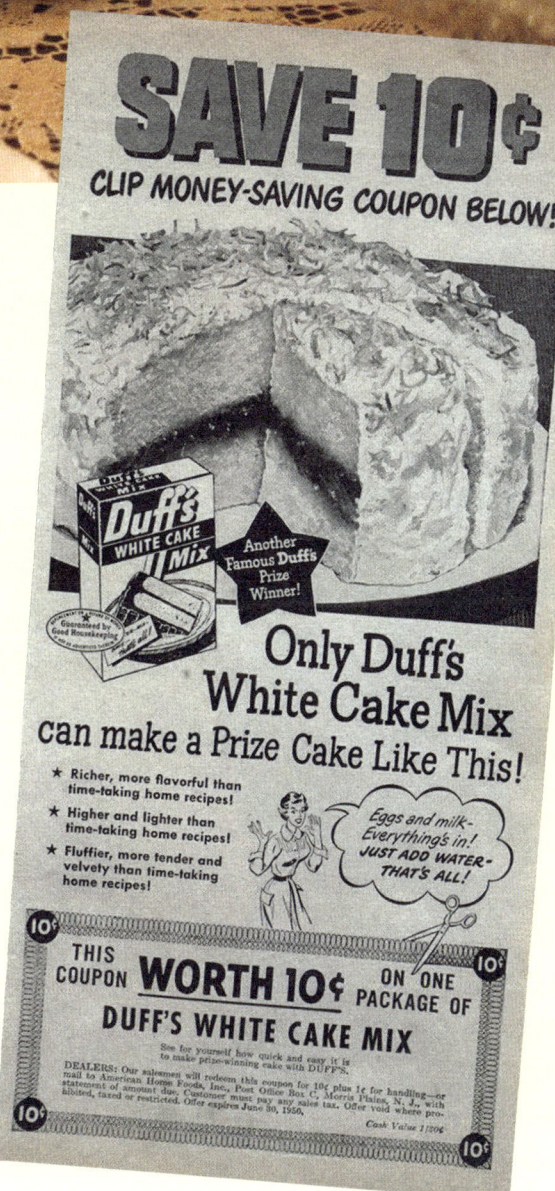

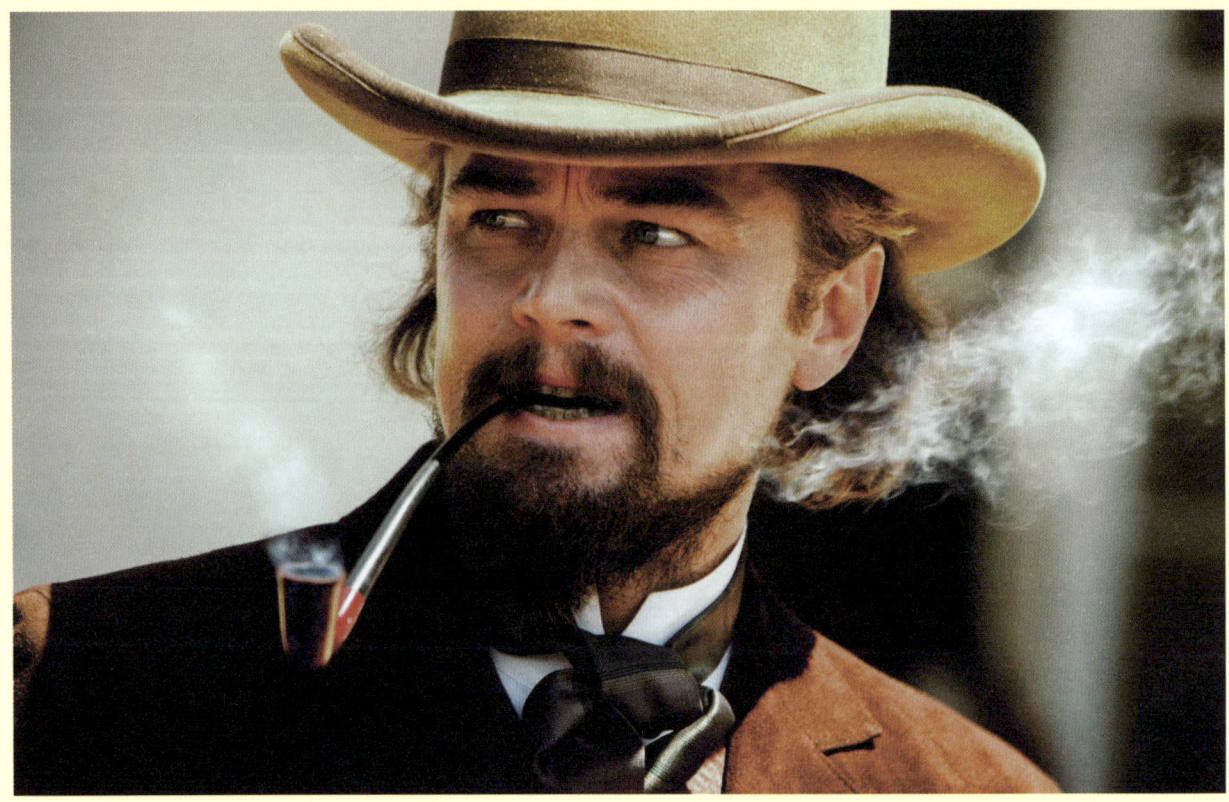

as *Monsieur* (despite not speaking a word of French himself), refers to Alexandre Dumas (whose books he hasn't read), and takes great pains to play the gentleman in front of his guests. But under this polite-society veneer, Candie is a boor and a bastard of the worst kind, a loafer whose only pleasure is watching cruel *mandingo* matches—a term inspired by the title of the melodrama directed by Richard Fleischer—in which slaves are pitted against each other in a fight to the death. The white cake isn't an innocent addition to the party: Served to Django, it's a reminder of the supposed racial superiority Candie drones on about to his guests. Schultz knows it full well—there is something rotten in the kingdom of Candie. When he smiles, the master of the house reveals his unfortunate teeth, ruined by too much sugar, which in turn speak volumes about his corrupt nature. A former dentist turned humanist, Schultz refuses to sink his own teeth into the offending cake. "*I don't go in for sweets, thank you*," he says

coldly. Might Tarantino be spinning us a little dentistry-inspired moral tale here?

From Hans Landa's *Apfelstrudel* to Jules Winnfield's Big Kahuna Burger, Tarantino often uses food in a scene to give visual and material form to the power relations and power dynamics unfolding between his characters. Calvin Candie's white cake, of course, represents the position of authority this immoral and depraved character adopts and the domination he exercises. And yet in the world of Tarantino, white frequently attracts red… and it's often the greediest who end up savoring it. So if someone offers you a piece of this delicious cake, take a moment to think about Calvin Candie's disgusting smile before you hand over your plate. Too much sugar is bad for your health. •

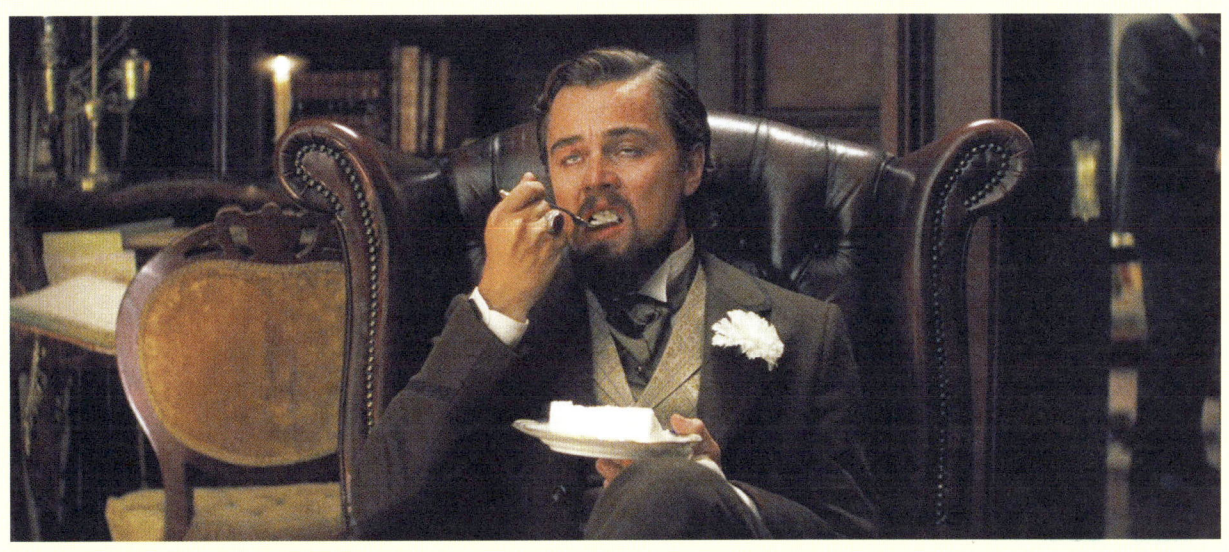

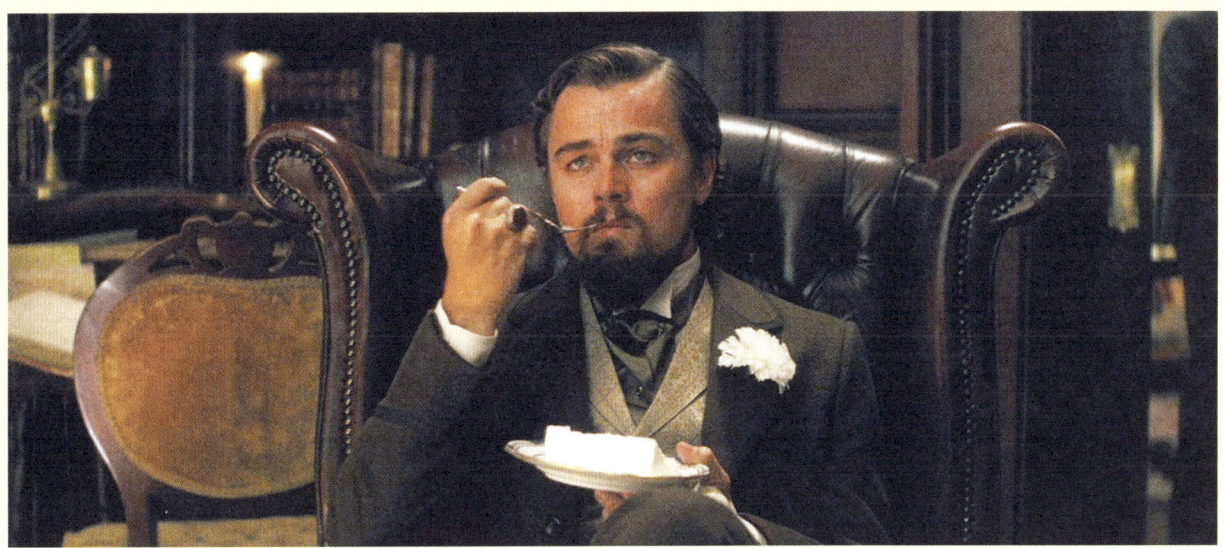

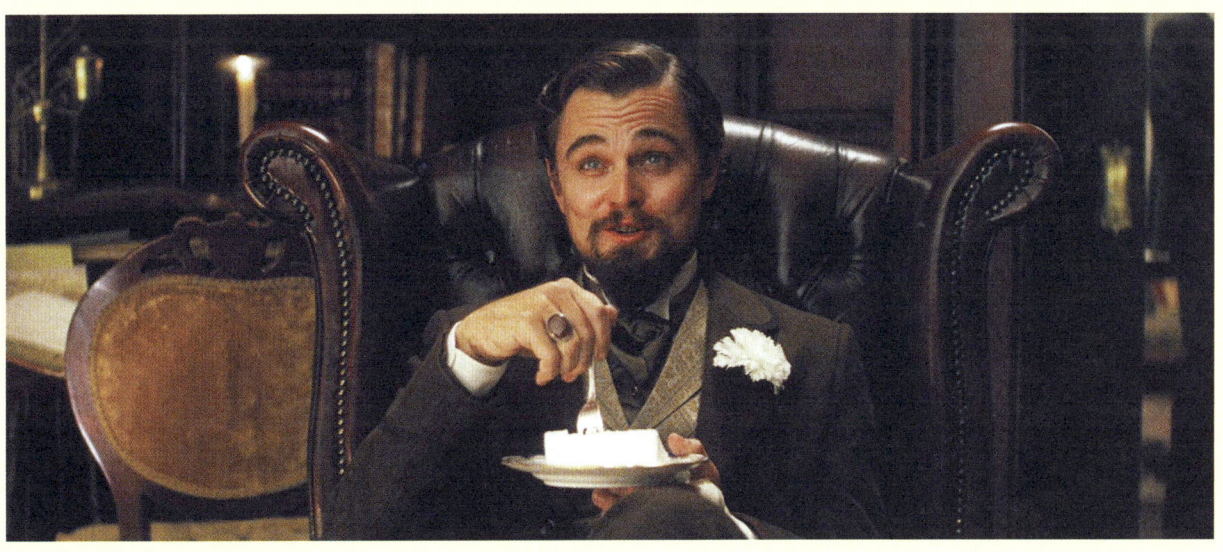

MINNIE'S STEW

The Taste of Betrayal

This signature dish is a thick, reddish mixture which has been bubbling on the hearth since the morning. Ladled out in great glopfuls into crude wooden bowls, Minnie's stew is not exactly an appetizing prospect. Floating in the pot is a questionable mixture of meat and boiled vegetables which we won't attempt to identify. Luckily, there's no need to: The primary purpose of this authentic American stew is to warm you up and keep your body and soul together, and that it does, even if it weighs a little heavy on the stomach.

As a violent blizzard engulfs the mountain, Minnie's Haberdashery provides a refuge for an assortment of travelers who are tired and freezing cold after their long journeys. Our hostess may not be there to tend to our hateful eight in person, but her stew is simmering away. Time for supper! Without a second thought, the characters sit down to eat, setting their differences aside to concentrate on what they have in common: the hunger tugging at their entrails. No point in any more dithering, no need to keep fanning the flames with endless debate or to divide the room in two in a reenactment of the Civil War, with Georgia by the fire and Philadelphia by the bar. The coffee is hot in its little tin pot, and Minnie's stew is still steaming. Swapping their rifles for wooden spoons, our characters lay into Minnie's honest mush with gusto.

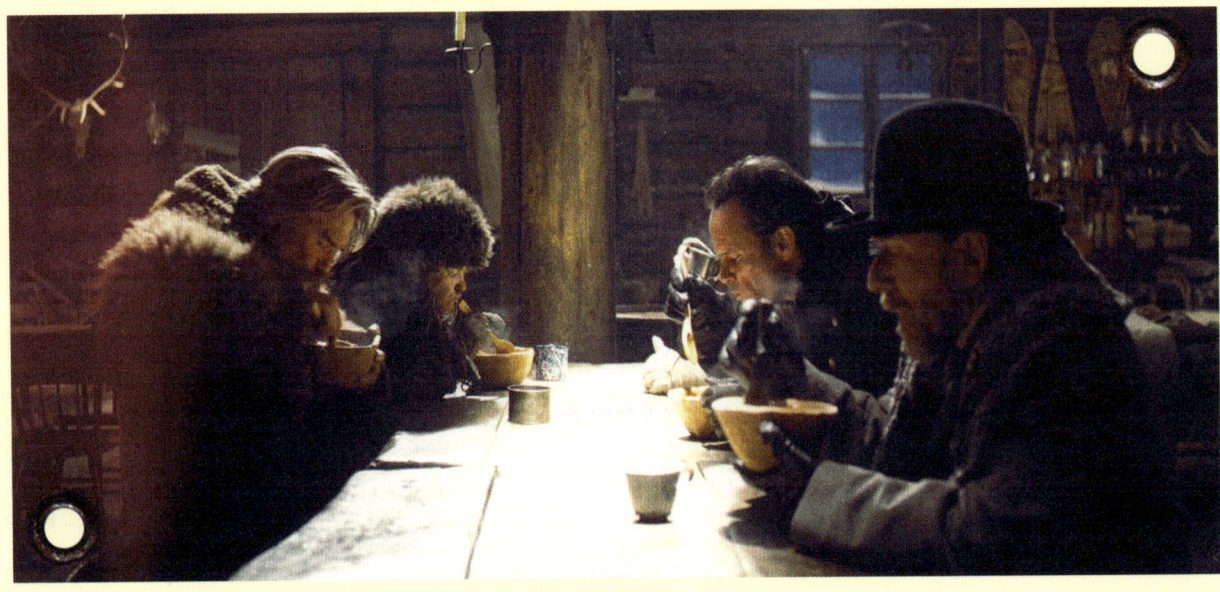

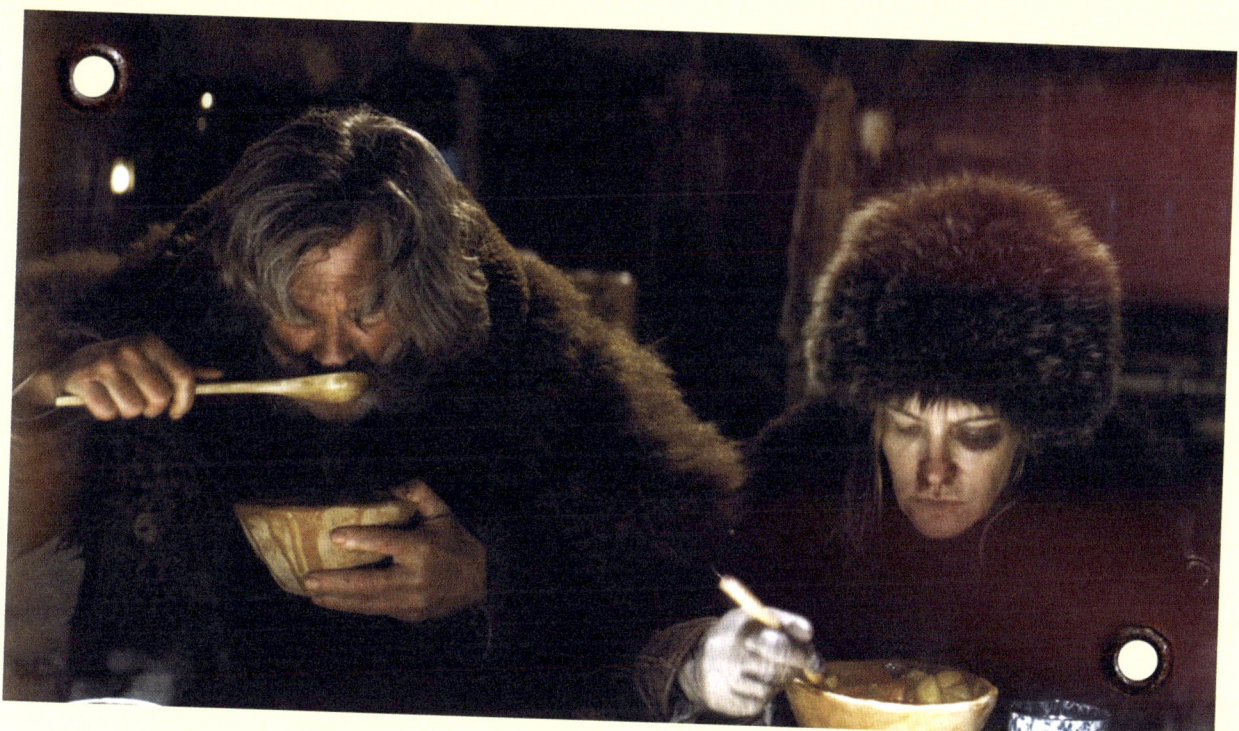

There is a lull while they eat. Sitting down with their bowls, Yankees and Southerners, Black and White people, those who are sentenced to death and those who will mete that horrible punishment out, sheriffs and criminals, break bread together and do so wholeheartedly. In honor of the occasion, the merciless bounty hunter John Ruth even unchains his prisoner, Daisy Domergue. Major Marquis Warren, meanwhile, who fought on the side of the Union, goes over to his old enemy, the Southern general Sanford Smithers, commonly known as "the Confederate," with a conciliatory mess tin. Minnie's stew may not be tasty, but perhaps it has a pacifying property or two. Could it be that these people who were ready to kill each other not an hour ago have finally found peace around a hot meal and a good crackling fire? Are you kidding? These guys? Not a chance.

Quentin Tarantino is a master not only of the theatrical twist, but of what we might call the theatrical twist of the fork: In his world, the most insignificant bite of food can serve as a catalyst for action. His carefully concocted culinary interludes are unbeatable narrative devices, capable of escalating or de-escalating suspense, ratcheting up the tension like a pressure cooker until viewers are on the edge of their seats, waiting for it all to explode. While the director sometimes uses food and drink to establish a bond of trust between characters—in the brief moment it takes to share a milkshake, as in *Pulp Fiction*, for example, or to have a coffee together, as in *Jackie Brown*—here he does exactly the opposite. The hearty meal upsets the delicate equilibrium between the different forces and sets off a spiral of mistrust which infects the rest of the movie. Some of the characters are treated to a swig of poisoned coffee, while the most cunning of our hateful eight recognizes the stew for what it really is: a damning piece of evidence that will allow him to unmask any impostors who might be sitting at the table. While the storm rages outside, the stew, which initially seemed so comforting, turns out to have a rancid aftertaste of betrayal. In such questionable company, it's better to go to bed on an empty stomach. •

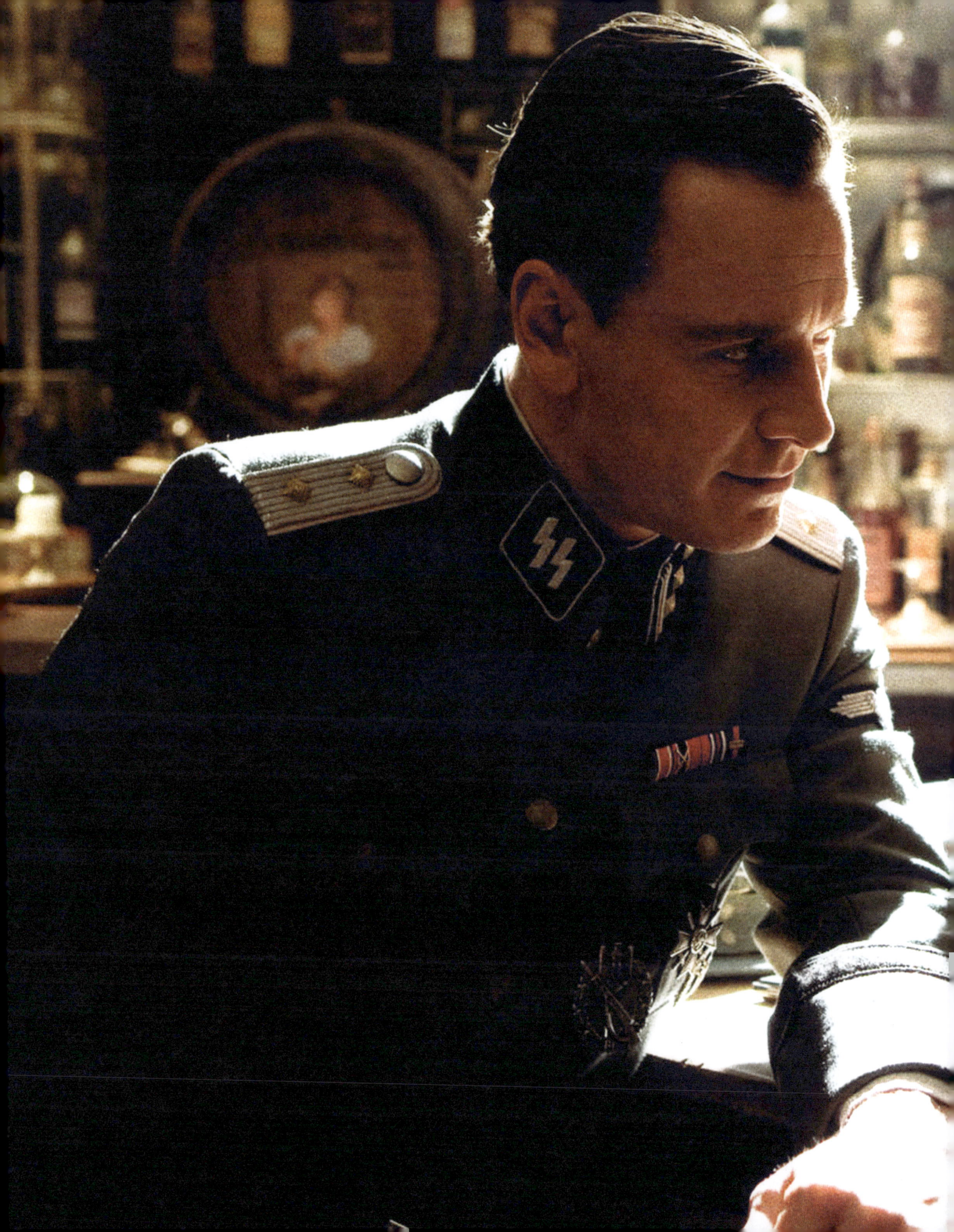

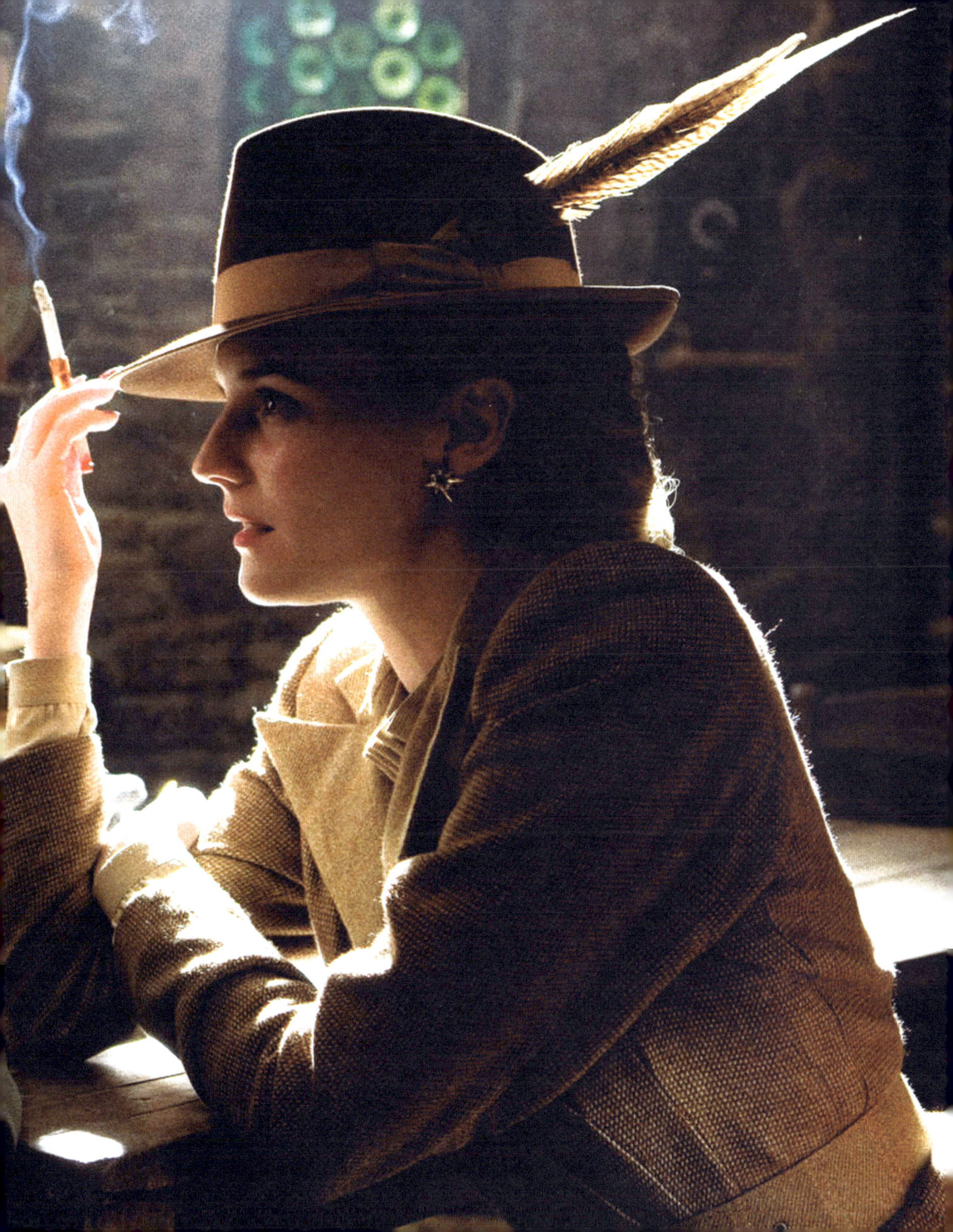

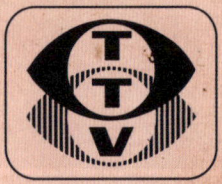

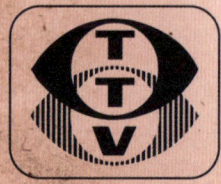

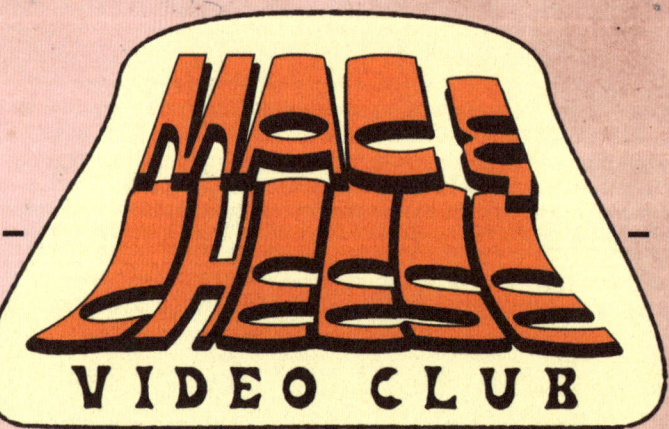

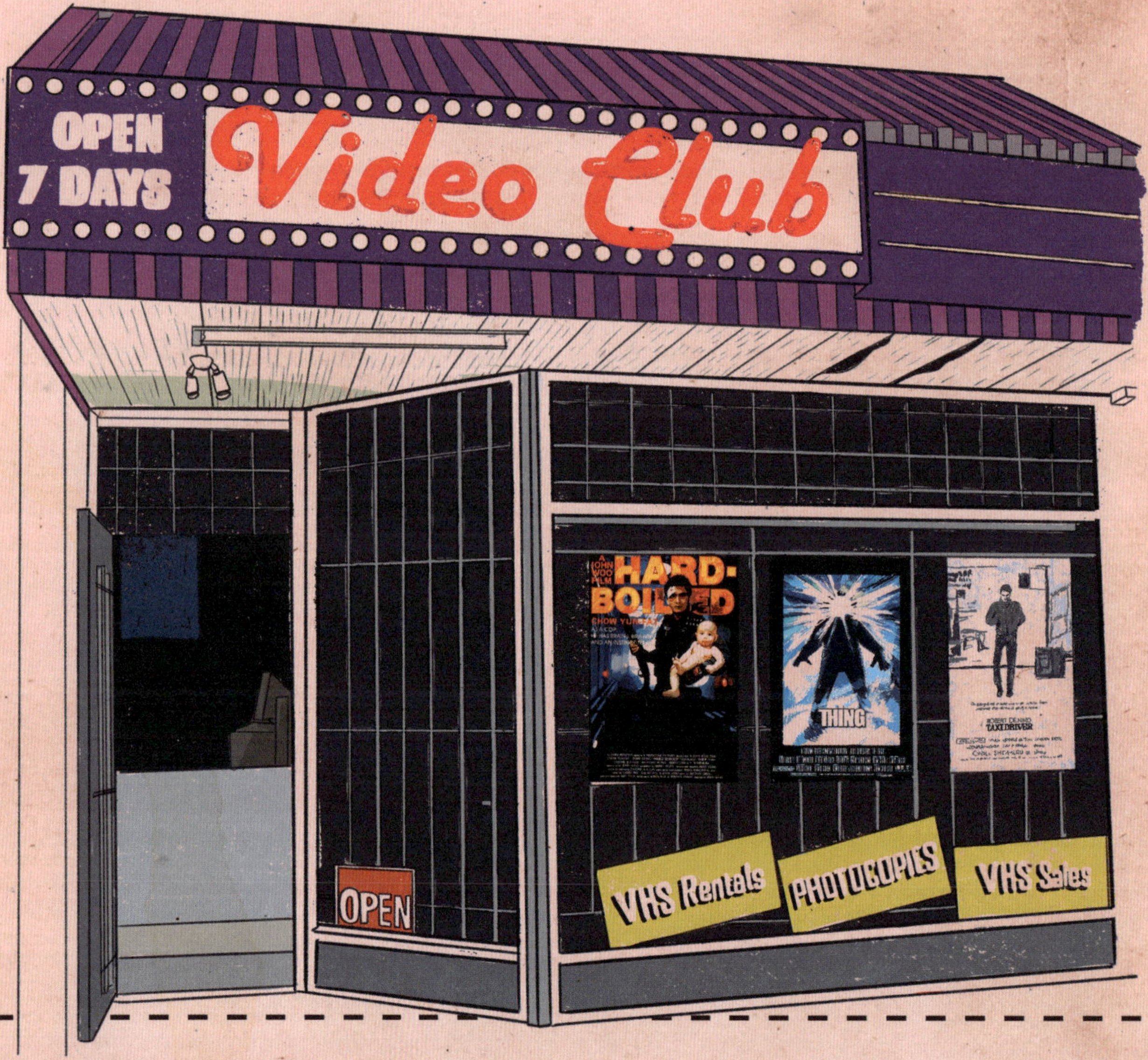

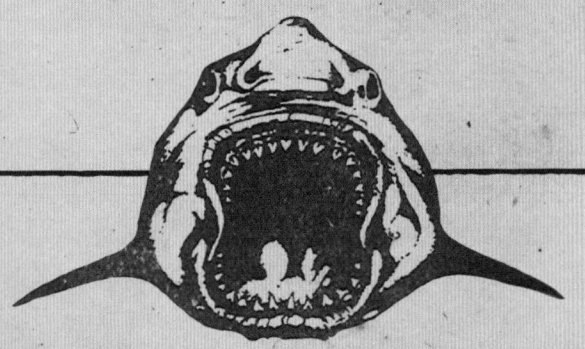

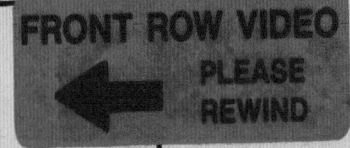

FRONT ROW VIDEO
PLEASE
REWIND

The Mac & Cheese Video Club is a well-known local haunt,
a place where the inhabitants of Tarantino Town meet up and
exchange ideas, a sanctuary whose details are spread by word
of mouth among connoisseurs. When she finishes a job, Alabama's
first thought is to head to the diner and grab a nice slice
of pie—and when he takes off to catch a movie, QT is pursuing
a similar kind of greedy pleasure. Naturally, then, our local
video store takes its name from the comforting dish Cliff Booth
loves so much. If you find yourself in sudden need of a movie,
head to the front desk. A member of staff, if you can find one,
will be happy to offer you a membership, even if you're only
passing through. Once properly inside this temple to film,
you'll find knots of regulars holding forth loudly and clogging
up the carpet-covered aisles. Among the colorful covers packed
onto the shelves, you'll discover a mini-selection of VHS tapes
that are close to our favorite director's heart. With a
little ferreting around, you'll be able to lay your hands on
everything you need—from Westerns to Hong Kong movies, pure
thrillers to movies about friendship—to create your very own
portable video collection to take with you when the time comes,
sooner or later, to abandon everything and live on a desert
island alone with your VHS tapes and your full-screen TV
(if, like us, you still live in 1993). So get your reheated
mac and cheese out of the microwave and take that peanut
butter pretzel-flavored ice cream out of the freezer well
in advance (so it becomes a thick cream you can swallow by
the spoonful). Settle yourself down, insert a video cassette
into a suitable player, call your friends, and get ready
for the best Saturday evening of your life!

BLOW OUT
PURE CINEMA

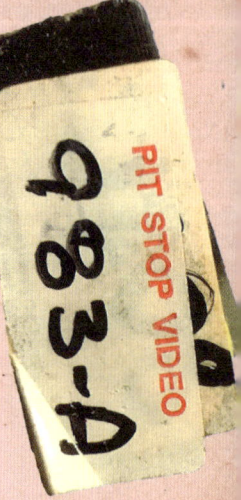

"It's one of the greatest films ever made, because it's Brian De Palma's finest film... As we all know, Brian De Palma is the greatest director of his generation."[1]
— Quentin Tarantino

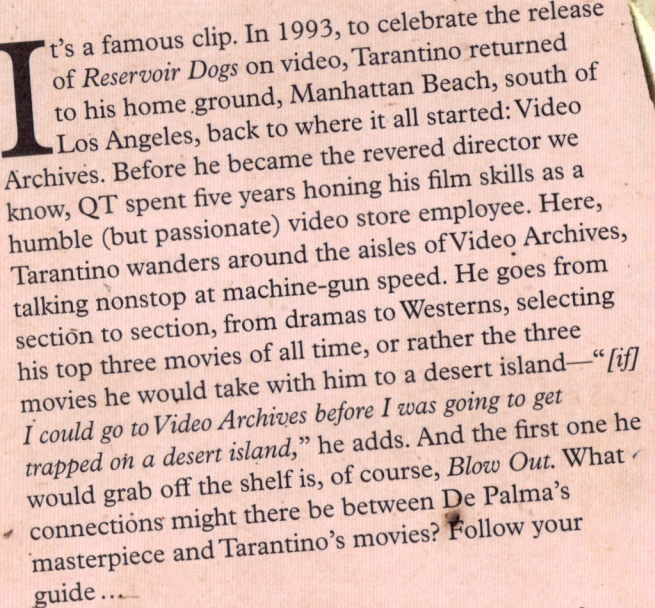

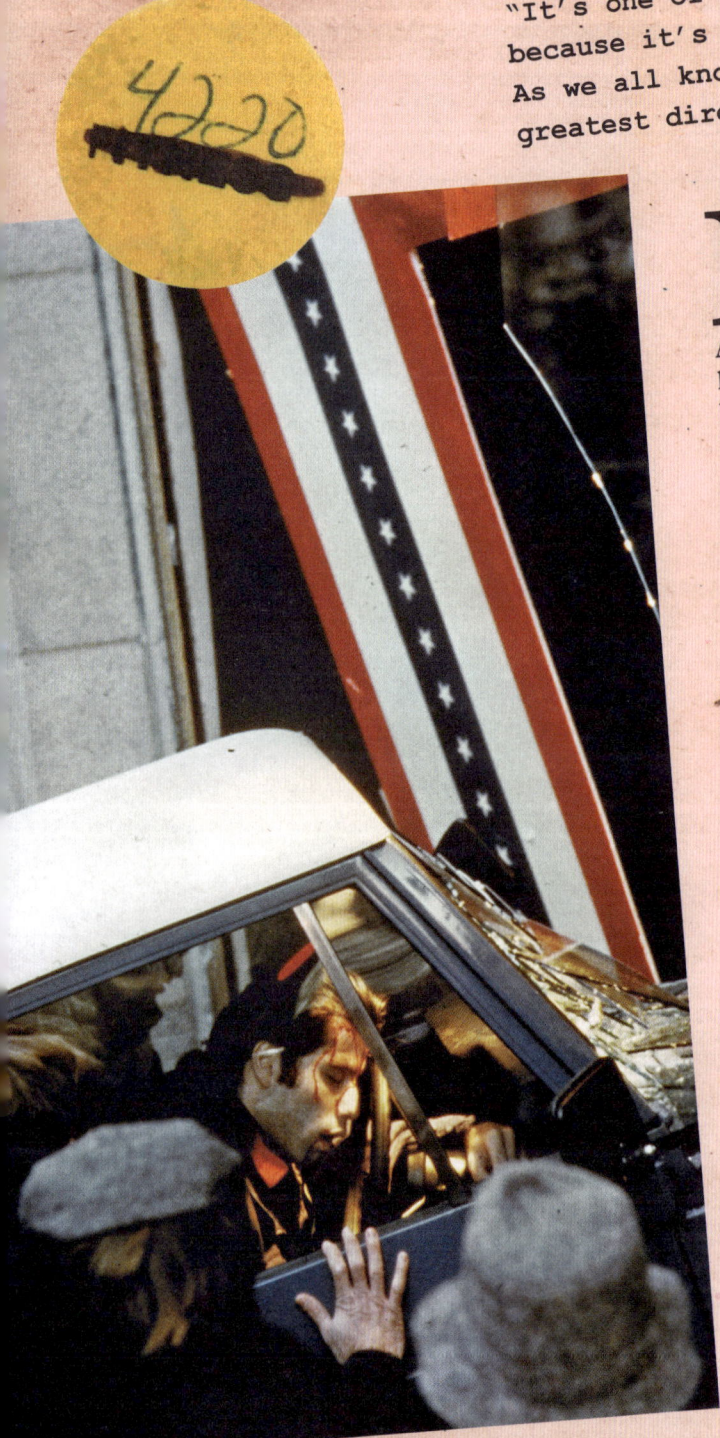

It's a famous clip. In 1993, to celebrate the release of *Reservoir Dogs* on video, Tarantino returned to his home ground, Manhattan Beach, south of Los Angeles, back to where it all started: Video Archives. Before he became the revered director we know, QT spent five years honing his film skills as a humble (but passionate) video store employee. Here, Tarantino wanders around the aisles of Video Archives, talking nonstop at machine-gun speed. He goes from section to section, from dramas to Westerns, selecting his top three movies of all time, or rather the three movies he would take with him to a desert island—"*[if] I could go to Video Archives before I was going to get trapped on a desert island,*" he adds. And the first one he would grab off the shelf is, of course, *Blow Out*. What connections might there be between De Palma's masterpiece and Tarantino's movies? Follow your guide…

What does *Blow Out* have to tell us on this score? The movie was released in 1981 and capitalized on John Travolta's recent rise to fame following his appearance in John Badham's highly successful *Saturday Night Fever*, a major box-office hit which catapulted him to international stardom. For his part, De Palma, who was obsessed with Francis Ford Coppola's *The Conversation* (interestingly, the only interview he ever undertook in his career as a "journalist" was with Coppola about this movie), wanted to try his hand at a political thriller and be on par with the godfather of New Hollywood. He also wanted to make one of those movies heavy with the dark shadow of American scandals and conspiracies, from Watergate to the assassination of John F. Kennedy. *Blow Out* is based on the shadowy Chappaquiddick incident in which Senator Ted Kennedy nearly lost his life in a car accident that his passenger, Mary Jo Kopechne, did not survive. Paranoia, which was already clearly evident in

1- Taken from archival material dated April 1993, in *Tarantino, le cinéma dans la peau*, directed by Didier Allouch, 2004.

De Palma's earlier movies, here operates on an unprecedented scale. Travolta's character, Jack Terry, witnesses a strange accident involving a presidential hopeful. A simple sound technician who works on B (not to say Z) movies, Jack quickly finds himself caught up in a storm which overtakes him. Together with Sally (Nancy Allen), the young woman he rescued from the "accident," Jack painstakingly and methodically retraces every step of the incident, piecing together evidence from sound and video recordings.

De Palma then sets about reconstructing the "missing image," taking the construction apart and putting it back together in minute detail in what is a sequence of pure cinema. The director takes us into the micro-mechanics of sound and video editing, most notably in a classic scene in which we follow Jack, hard at work, around his editing room. The scene is filmed in a long, apparently infinitely recurring shot which goes around and around him—a stunning mise en abyme of a man caught in the eye of a cyclone. We can imagine a young Tarantino leaning forward in his seat, remote control for the VCR player in hand, going over and studying every point, every detail of *Blow Out* as he immerses himself in the secret mechanisms of the movie itself.

Tarantino's obsession with De Palma's films was such that in his youth he meticulously collected in a folder every interview the director gave to the press, perhaps in a bid to glean a secret or two about filmmaking. Finding himself face to face with the older man when the two of them were brought together in a filmed interview, Tarantino visibly became once more that young movie buff whose infectious enthusiasm lit up Video Archives in its heyday. Even Tarantino's choice of John Travolta to play the role of Vincent Vega in *Pulp Fiction* was not entirely unconnected to Travolta's performance in *Blow Out*, for which QT was full of admiration: "*John Travolta, by the way, gives one of the greatest performances of all time in this movie,*" he says in the middle of his guided tour of the video store. Brian De Palma's influence is also detectable in Tarantino's use of one of his distinctive split screens. "*When Daryl Hannah walks down the hall of*

the hospital in Kill Bill: Volume 1, *whistling Bernard Herrmann, then it slides into a split screen, it's almost as if Brian De Palma has seized control of the movie for a moment,*" recounts Tarantino.[2] In *Death Proof*, finally, Tarantino appropriates the theme composed by Pino Donaggio to accompany the tragic finale of *Blow Out*, which he declared contained "*one of the most heartbreaking shots in the history of the cinema.*"[3] And here we are, back where we started. While at first sight there may not be many tangible traces of De Palma's masterpiece in Tarantino's movies beyond a musical nod, this is perhaps because we need to look further, at what ties them so closely together— cinema, no more and no less—and understand that it is Tarantino's entire oeuvre that can be recognized as a tribute to De Palma's masterpieces. •

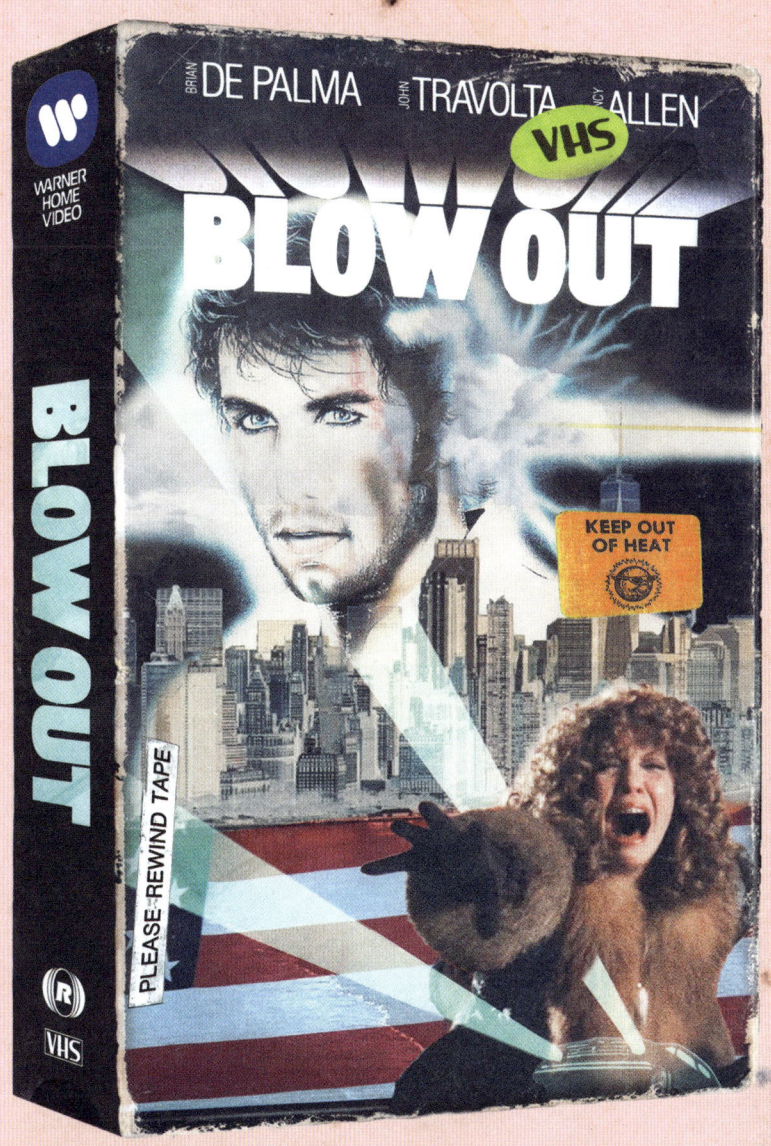

111

2- Quentin Tarantino, *Cinema Speculation* (Harper, 2022).
3- Michael Sragow, "*Blow Out*: American Scream," *Criterion*, April 5, 2011.

TAXI DRIVER

GOING THROUGH HELL

"Listen, you fuckers, you
screwheads. Here is a man who
would not take it anymore. A man
who stood up against the scum, the
cunts, the dogs, the filth, the
shit. Here is a man who stood up!"

— Travis Bickle

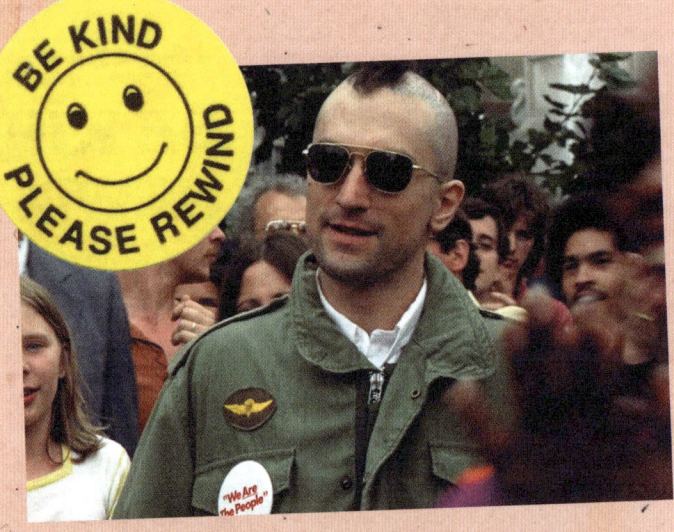

*T*axi Driver opens like a dream. Not the kind
we have at night, but the kind our brains
concoct during the day, with our eyes wide
open, as the sounds of reality percolate into
our thoughts and warp our imagination. This lends the
movie a sweet and sour taste, a strange torpor that is
both dreamy and violent at the same time. This is the
territory *Taxi Driver* carves out for itself, somewhere
between day and night, reality and feverish imagination.
And this, then, is the setting in which Scorsese unfolds
his urban tale of the streets of a doomed New York.

Taxi Driver is the story of a man who can find no
way into the society which surrounds him, stifles him.
At the wheel of his taxi, Travis Bickle is ready to go
anywhere. He isn't bothered by the mid-seventies hell
of New York—he has just come back from another
hell, Vietnam. Travis doesn't sleep, not anymore,
and he can carry on just staring haggardly at that
effervescent tablet as it slowly dissolves in a glass of
water. As Martin Scorsese has admitted, interestingly,
this scene is a New York companion to a scene in Jean-
Luc Godard's movie *Two or Three Things I Know About
Her.* Travis Bickle's nighttime wanderings took shape
in Paul Schrader's screenplay. Schrader's own story is
well-known: He sank into depression and eked out an
existence living in his car, spending his days and nights
roaming the city. Suffering from insomnia, he got to
know the people who took over central Manhattan after
nightfall, long before the city's future mayor, Rudy
Giuliani, came in and sold up whole districts to Disney
as part of a vast operation designed to make New York
a safer place and, in Travis Bickle's words, to *"wash all
this scum off the streets."* It's worth remembering here
that Schrader was raised in a strict Calvinist family and
didn't see a single movie until he was seventeen…

In a way, Travis Bickle was something of an alter
ego for Schrader: a man who got *"headaches … so
bad, you know. It's like—they just never go away."*
The screenwriter set down on paper all the dark
thoughts that ran through his mind, with little
inkling at this stage that he was about to bring
into the world one of the greatest classics in the
history of film. In this urban hell, Travis seeks
a path to redemption: He thinks initially that
he has found it with Betsy (Cybill Shepherd),
a nice young woman in every way who sends
him packing after he takes her to see a 25-cent
porno flick. Next, he seeks salvation with Iris,
a twelve- (*"and-a-half"*) year-old prostitute
played by Jodie Foster, freshly escaped from the
Disney stable. But Travis has a furious, almost
biblical hatred toward New York, a hatred
which can only be sated by blood. Originally,
the young man was going to kill only African
Americans, but Schrader and Scorsese quickly
changed their minds about this. *Taxi Driver*
seems to have captured the (fetid) feel of
the time, the peculiarly New York zeitgeist of
the day, in the steamy stench that emanates
from each shot. And yet, as the movie's chief
cameraman Michael Chapman admits, you find
yourself lamenting the disappearance of this
part of the city, perhaps because of the sense

of total, dangerous freedom blowing through it, or perhaps because it was a place where for just a few dollars even the most down-at-heel could take refuge in a movie theater or in a bar around the corner. So you let yourself glide along the sidewalks of this ruthless metropolis, accompanied by the soundtrack by Bernard Herrmann. It's a composition which is both disturbing and strangely sensual at the same time, with brass giving way to jazzy saxophones that sound like something you would find in the subdued atmosphere of a club. Herrmann was never to see his work transposed to the screen, dying the day after he completed the score.

Scorsese maintains that *Taxi Driver* is a horror movie. It certainly borrows extensively from Mario Bava's movie staging, from the lighting in Giallo movies, and from the freedom of approach of France's very own chief cameraman and darling of New Hollywood, Raoul Coutard, "*the best chief cameraman of all time*" according to Chapman. And what about Robert De Niro? Fresh from winning an Oscar for his performance as Vito Corleone in *The Godfather Part II*, Bob navigates

his way through the movie with a terrifying naturalness. Even the cult line "*You talkin' to me?*" is something he came up with himself in an improvised monologue. Before shooting began, De Niro spent months driving a taxi at night to gain a better understanding of his character, his frustration, and his damaging loneliness. Clearly, he got it all down pat: His performance seems to exude the corruption of the city. Travis is New York, and New York is Travis: a sick mind in a sick city.

If the VHS tape of *Taxi Driver* has pride of place in our aisles, this is not least because it's a movie which should feature prominently in the catalog of any self-respecting video store. It's also because this film regularly makes it into Tarantino's top three favorite movies. The director first saw it when he was barely fifteen, in a double feature at the Carson Twin Cinema, where it was shown with *The Farmer* by David Berlatsky. He devotes an entire chapter to the screening in his book *Cinema Speculation*, commenting that "*the violence, the despair, the grotesquery, and the absurd comedy had never been depicted with such verve and accuracy in a Hollywood picture before.*"[1] Elsewhere, he states: "*You can't quite boil* Taxi Driver's *power down to one or two sentences. I will say it is probably the most novelistic, complex character study for my money in the history of cinema.*"[2] Indeed, the director described the central character of what was supposed to be his final film, *The Movie Critic*, as a sort of Travis Bickle who has given up his taxi and become a writer for a porno magazine. This was to be Tarantino's tribute to *Taxi Driver*, but the project has been shelved, to our great disappointment, and we may never see the movie. Luckily, Martin Scorsese did make *Taxi Driver*, and it will be with us forever. •

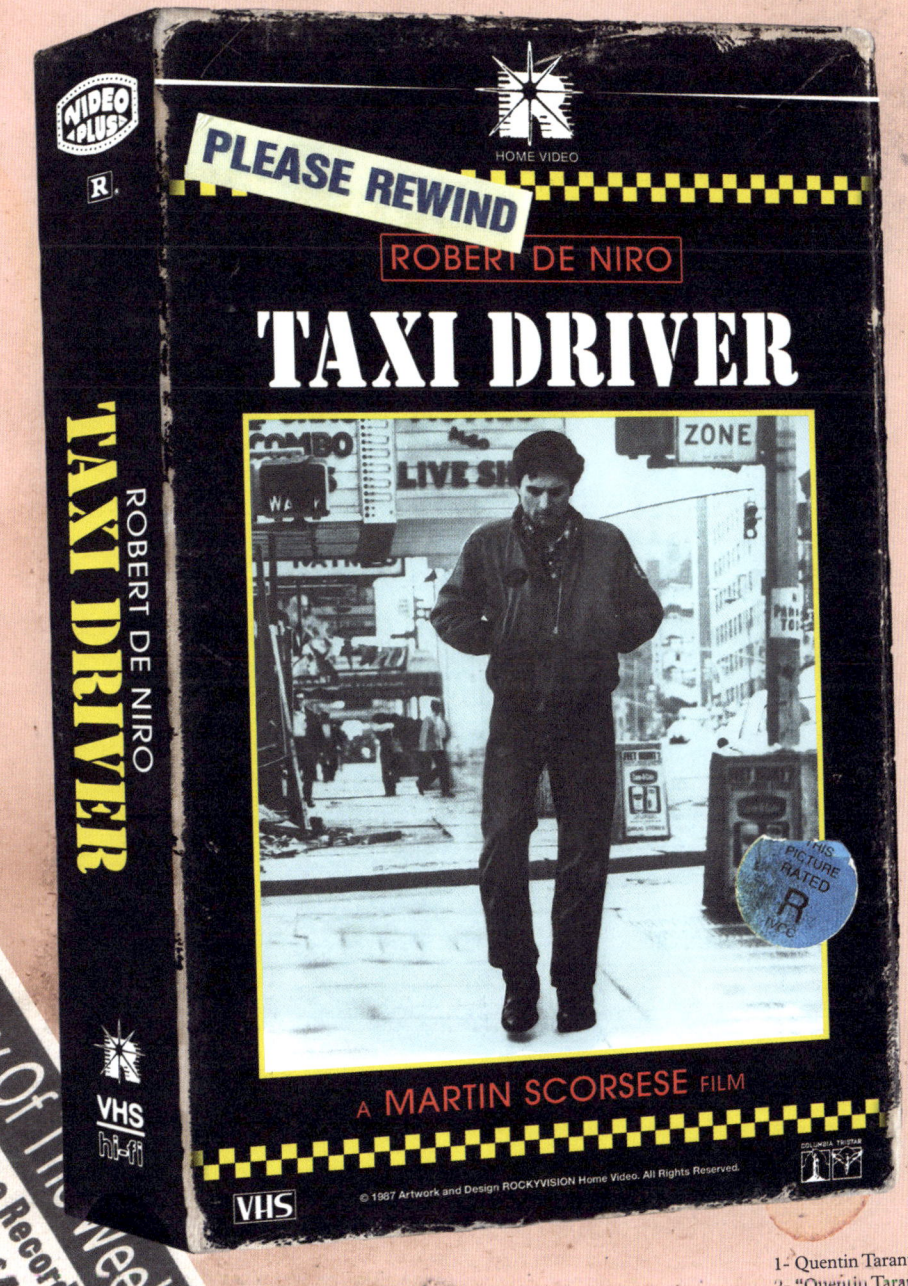

VIDEO PLUS
R
HOME VIDEO
PLEASE REWIND
ROBERT DE NIRO
TAXI DRIVER
ROBERT DE NIRO
TAXI DRIVER
THIS PICTURE RATED R MPAA
A MARTIN SCORSESE FILM
VHS hi-fi
VHS
© 1987 Artwork and Design ROCKYVISION Home Video. All Rights Reserved.

1- Quentin Tarantino, *Cinema Speculation* (Harper, 2022).
2- "Quentin Tarantino: 'It's A Corrupted Cinema,'" *The Talks*.

BOUNTY LAW

DEAD OR ALIVE

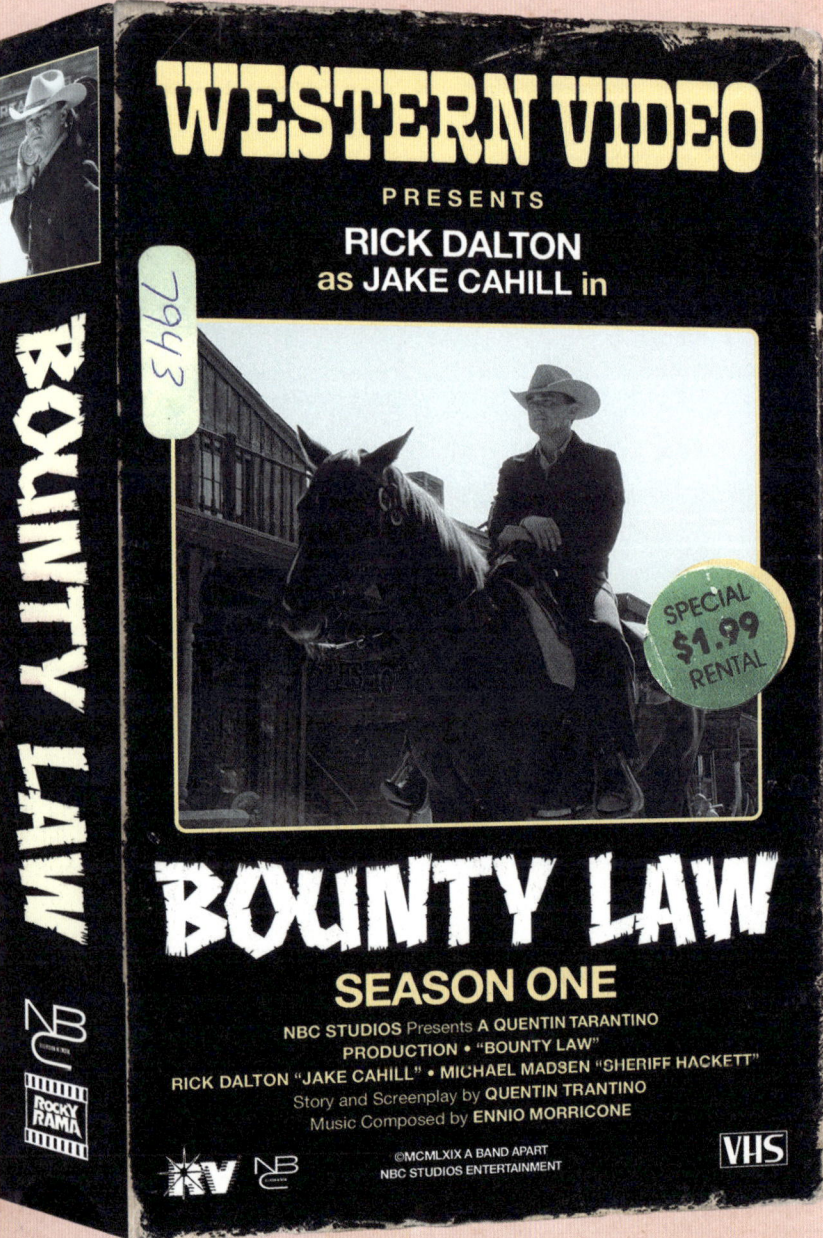

This is really something we've got here. A hunk of a piece, big enough to be divided into twenty-four helpings, twenty-four good thick slabs, just the way we like them. This enormous box set certainly stands out on the cluttered shelves of our local video store. You've got twenty-four VHS tapes here, which take up a lot of space—try holding that in two hands! Together they contain no fewer than forty-eight episodes—two per cassette tape—of the legendary (in both the literal and the figurative sense of the term) series *Bounty Law*, which was modeled on some of the most popular shows of the small screen in America in the early sixties—more specifically, from 1958 to 1963. Creating *Bounty Law* for *Once Upon a Time… in Hollywood* allowed Quentin Tarantino to tell a parallel story of American television in his film. While Hollywood may seem entirely focused on the big screen, television still has something of a presence on the fringes of the film industry.

Bounty Law is of course directly linked to the Western series *Wanted: Dead or Alive*, broadcast from 1958 to 1961, in which Steve McQueen plays a bounty hunter who travels the great American West with his Winchester under his arm. The series is also a close cousin of *Gunsmoke*, which stormed the airwaves first as a radio serial and then, from 1955 to 1975, as a television series. It was from watching *Gunsmoke* that a certain Connie Tarantino became infatuated with the young Burt Reynolds, who was cast as Quint Asper, giving her the idea of calling her future son Quentin. But getting back to our cowboys… Some episodes of *Bounty Law* stand out as having proved particularly striking to TV viewers, who used to set their watches and clocks by the program's weekly broadcast at 8:30 p.m. on Thursdays, exclusively on NBC. These include "*Incident in Inez*," "*Incident in Beaver Falls*," "*Incident at Henry Minks Homested*," "*Incident on a Stage Bound for Tuscon*," "*Incident in Janicetown*," "*Incident in Perrytown pt. 1*," and "*Incident in Perrytown pt. 2*"… incident after incident, great TV moment after great TV moment, shared, more often than not, with the family on the living room couch.

First and foremost, *Bounty Law* is about one character: bounty hunter Jake Cahill, who is quick on the draw and no slower with a scathing reply. Played by the inimitable Rick Dalton, Cahill is the quintessential lonesome cowboy, always spoiling for a fight, who is set on delivering to the sheriff the most dangerous troublemakers around—dead or alive, but more often dead. "*This man is worth $500, and this man's going to collect. He's Jake Cahill, and he lives by… 'Bounty Law,'*" runs the trailer. Nothing will ever be the same again for the highway bandits and other outlaws when Jake Cahill rides up on his black horse in the very first episode, titled "*The Restless Gun*"—from the name of another Western series, broadcast from 1957 to 1959 under the NBC banner. Of course the series owes a great deal to its lead actor, Rick Dalton, memorable for his appearances in movies such as *Operazione Dyn-O-Mite!*, *Comanche Uprising*, and *Nebraska Jim*, directed by Sergio Corbucci and made in Italy, where Dalton "got back in the game," as the saying goes, after something of a rough patch in Hollywood. After returning to America with his new wife, Francesca, on his arm, Rick Dalton enjoyed a second wind playing villains, baddies, and other hateful characters so sorely missing from the screen in so many worthy B movies. Between movie shoots, Dalton was also the charming face of the highly popular Red Apple cigarette brand in what became a cult TV commercial.

But Rick Dalton's blue eyes closed forever on May 20, 2023, in Hawaii, where he had spent his well-deserved retirement far from the hustle and bustle of film sets and the hubbub of modern life. Countless tributes were paid to the star of *Bounty Law*, forever synonymous with Jake Cahill for TV viewers, with many testimonials lauding the actor for maintaining a solid course and retaining his integrity even when America wobbled. Nor did Quentin Tarantino neglect to pay his respects to Rick Dalton on that sad day, and through him to Jake Cahill and the host of other characters the actor played. Once, Tarantino let slip to the media that he was thinking of making five or six episodes of *Bounty Law*, perhaps signaling a foray into television… Consummate professional that he was, Rick Dalton made no distinction between the big and the small screen: Some may dismiss him as a hard-working, second-rate actor, the kind who could never win an Oscar, but he certainly won a place in the hearts of Americans. •

Western Adventure

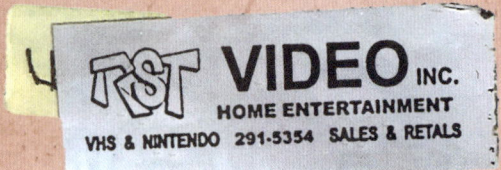

CLERKS

WASTING AWAY IN THE VIDEO STORE

At first sight, there's no obvious connection between Kurt Cobain and Quentin Tarantino. None of the American director's movies seems to have any hint of the grunge disenchantment of the nineties running through it. But if you think about it, hanging around the local supermarket in sneakers might be some of Tarantino's characters' idea of an Olympic sport. It's an image which also brings to mind the late eighties literary movement known as "K-Mart realism," with its naturalist portrayal of the commonplace world of laundromats and Diet Cokes picked up at the local mini-mart. From *Jackie Brown* to *Pulp Fiction*, Tarantino's movies have their share of antiheroes who wander from fast food joints to shopping malls. It's not difficult to imagine the likes of Jules Winnfield and Vincent Vega, cups of soda in hand, talking endlessly about what was on TV last night while hanging out in the most average shopping mall in suburban Los Angeles, like true mall rats.

One movie in particular encapsulates the desultory mood of this post-adolescent state, with its interminable afternoons spent putting the world to rights in the most mundane of settings, its endless hanging around on the never-ending highway of life: *Clerks*. Kevin Smith brought out his depressive masterpiece in 1994, the same year *Pulp Fiction* was released. Critics hailed Smith as one of the great new writers in America, one of the independent moviemakers who made the nineties interesting, along with Steven Soderbergh, Larry Clark, Paul Thomas Anderson, Harmony Korine, Todd Solondz, Richard Linklater, Sofia Coppola, and … Quentin Tarantino. In the space of just this one movie, Smith managed to nail a very particular time in the nineties when America rocked to the dark strains of Nine Inch Nails, the depressing tones of Nirvana, and the decidedly punk sounds of Hole. Generation X likes its idols, and Kevin Smith entered its galaxy of greats on the strength of this little black-and-white movie, shot pretty much in secret, featuring a bunch of losers whose only thought is to do zilch (and, paradoxically, to sleep with as many girls as possible), who while away the time asking each other the occasional existential question: Would a plumber working on the Death Star in *Return of the Jedi*, for instance, be a victim of collateral damage, or would he deserve to share his employer's fate? All of this in the far recesses of a godforsaken grocery store and a video store in the darkest depths of an America bored out of its mind. Its ludicrously low budget ($27,575) made the movie one of the most profitable in history, bringing in receipts of three million. *Clerks* was a success from all points of view, securing a place in the highly select club of cult and generational movies.

Clerks is nothing short of a flagship "hangout movie," a genre coined by Tarantino himself which covers the kind of movies you watch in the way you would hang out with a bunch of old friends. In the end, there's scarcely a rolling paper's thickness between Tarantino and Smith, between *Pulp Fiction* and *Clerks*, between Jules Winnfield and Jay, or between Vincent Vega and Silent Bob, and our gut instinct is that the two directors could have sat down and shared a joint in front of one those movies made for this very purpose, with a Pineapple Express on the side for the hell of it, a stack of comic books to hand, and the BBQ still sizzling hot. Tarantino, a grunge hero? Well, now you know. •

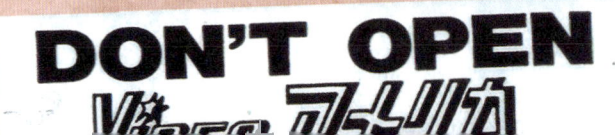

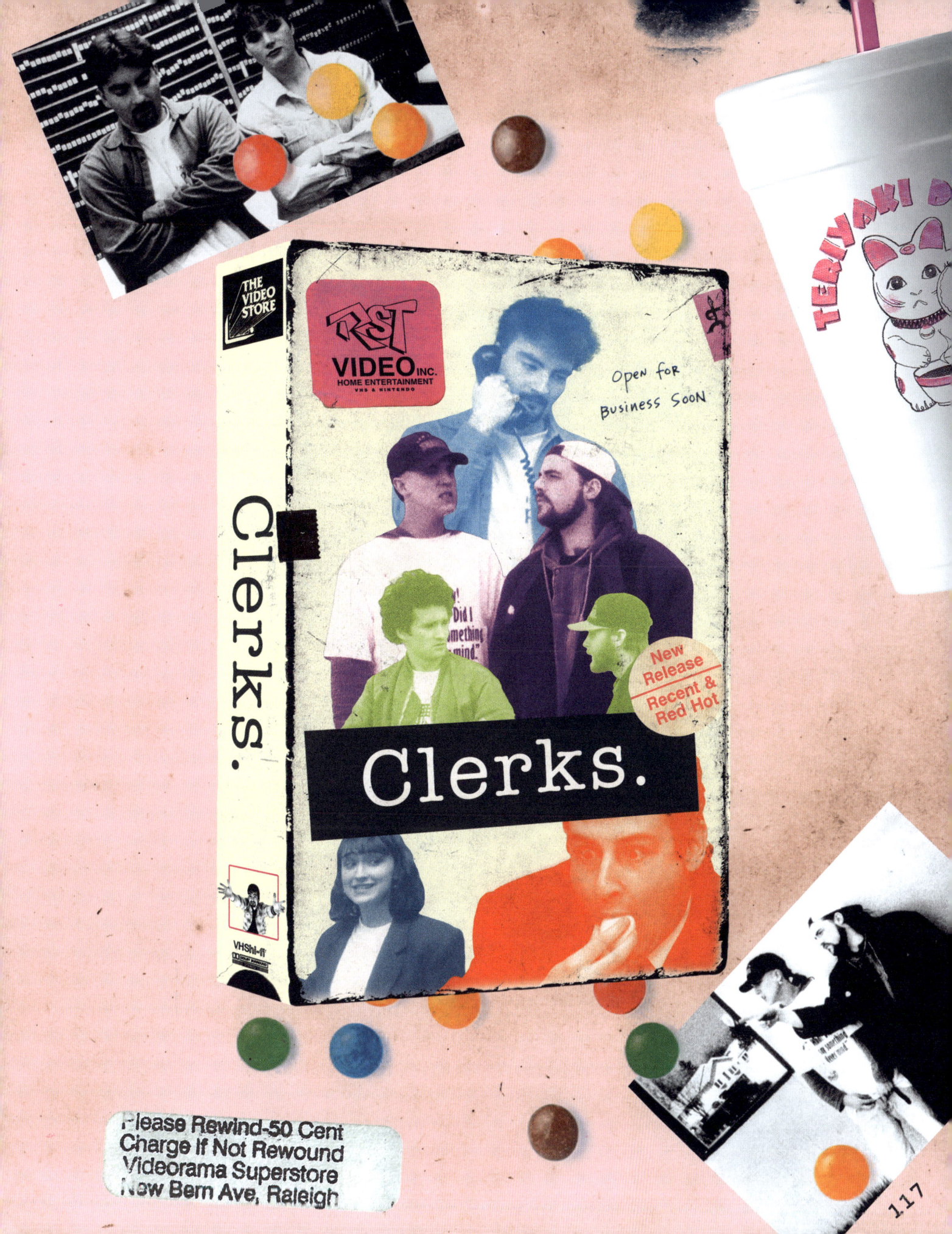

THE THING

THE THRILL OF YOUR LIFE

Did you know that Rick Dalton turned down the part of Gerry in *The Thing*? Quentin Tarantino says so in his *Video Archives* podcast. The actor Donald Moffat eventually landed the role. Even the film's producer, Stuart Cohen, remembers the story: Rick hated the snow and certainly had no intention of playing second fiddle in a monster movie…

What can possibly tie Quentin Tarantino more closely to John Carpenter than this astonishing story, and the incredible sense of setting and staging? Nothing, on the face of it, and yet… When it came out, everyone agreed that *The Hateful Eight* was one of the finest homages to "Big John." It had it all: the cold, the snow, the confined setting and brewing poison, a sense of the looming end of the world, and a good dose of paranoia to cap it all off. If this description reminds you of *The Thing*, read on. If not, the store has a VHS tape of it to rent out. So we urge you to grab hold of it, insert it into the nearest video player as quickly as possible, and then reread the last few lines once the closing credits have finished rolling. *The Thing* is a masterpiece, we know that now. But in 1982, the public largely shunned John Carpenter's movie in favor of another extraterrestrial movie which came out the same year, featuring the likeable, family-friendly E. T., more in line with viewers' expectations and more in tune with an America which had had a bellyful of gloom in the seventies. Time to say goodbye to Watergate, Vietnam, and all the other awful memories of the last ten years! It was the dawn of the Reagan era, American soft power was in full swing, and optimism, ice-cold Coca-Cola, popcorn, and rollerblades were the order of the day.

Although it was subsequently largely rehabilitated, *The Thing* was the movie that brought John Carpenter's career to an abrupt stop and forced him off the highway, onto an enormous (and unwarranted) detour across the desert. The director never quite got over it, and these days he seems to be happiest playing video games and watching the NBA on his huge TV

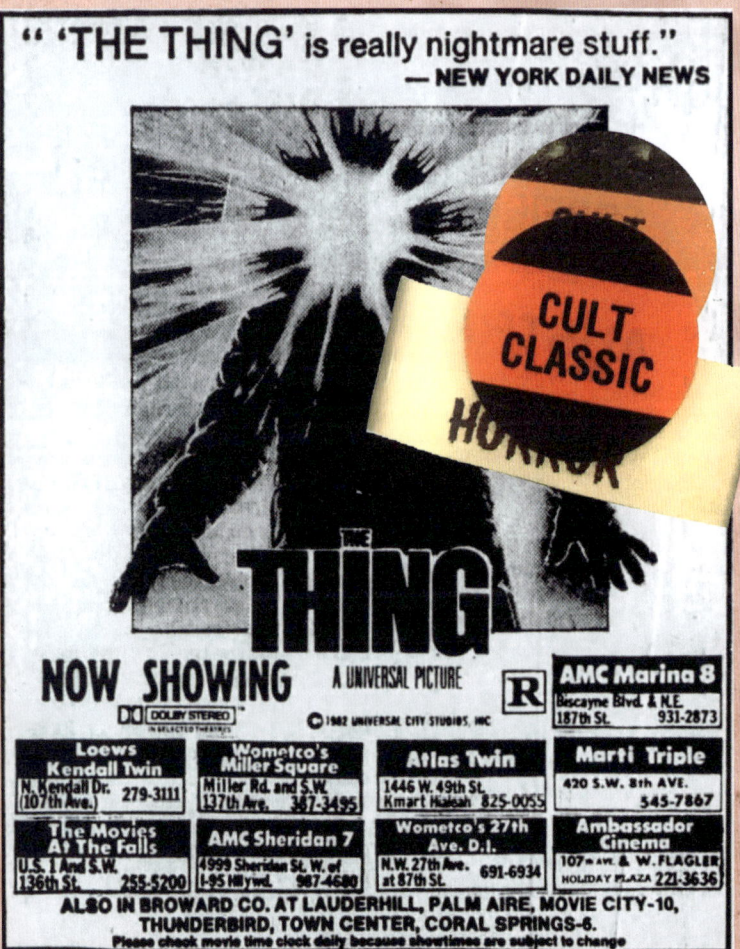

screen in his slippers. We can only thank Quentin Tarantino for jogging our memories and reminding us of a man who was one of the greatest proponents of the CinemaScope system and an exceptional director to boot, capable of conjuring up the most extraordinary worlds and atmospheres. Hanging over *The Thing* is a glacial atmosphere which Tarantino manages to transcribe brilliantly in his somber Western, complemented by music by Ennio Morricone, who also worked on … *The Thing*, of course.

Tarantino had long mulled over the nihilistic mood and oppressive sense of a dead end which Carpenter's movie exudes, and this found form in his own films, starting with the claustrophobic, highly paranoid *Reservoir Dogs* and culminating almost as poison coursing through the veins of *The Hateful Eight*. Just as the virus in *The Thing* spreads through the research station trapped in the snowy isolation of the Antarctic, in Tarantino's movie a shot of poison tipped into a pot of coffee spreads of its own accord, setting off a wave of fatal suspicion. John Ruth—played by Kurt Russell, who also starred in *The Thing*—paid the price, vomiting up his guts in a scene every bit on par with the nightmare images dreamed up for Carpenter's movie by Rob Bottin, who was then only twenty-two years old. "*Rob Bottin's special effects in that movie are some of the greatest practical special effects ever put on a movie theater screen … I think it's one of the greatest horror movies ever made, if not one of the greatest movies ever made.*"[1] For Tarantino, who is a big fan of horror movies and is not easily scared, what makes *The Thing* so terrifyingly effective is the paranoid fear which grips the movie: "The Thing *I got scared in … and it made me want to put it under a microscope about why I was actually frightened during that movie. And I think the reason is this … the movie makes the paranoia of that so palpable, so real, it's like, it's almost like another character in the movie, just the sheer paranoia of it. But they're trapped in the Antarctic. They're trapped in this shelter. And so the paranoia is bouncing off of the four walls, bouncing, bouncing, bouncing: the fear, the paranoia, bouncing, bouncing, bouncing, until it has nowhere to go except through the fourth wall into the audience, and I started feeling exactly like they felt.*" *The Thing* was adapted from a novella by John W. Campbell and also owes a great deal to the genius of a certain H.P. Lovecraft. As well as a being a huge homage to John Carpenter, could *The Hateful Eight* also be a movie bow on Quentin Tarantino's part to the master of cosmic horror? It's surely a question worth asking … •

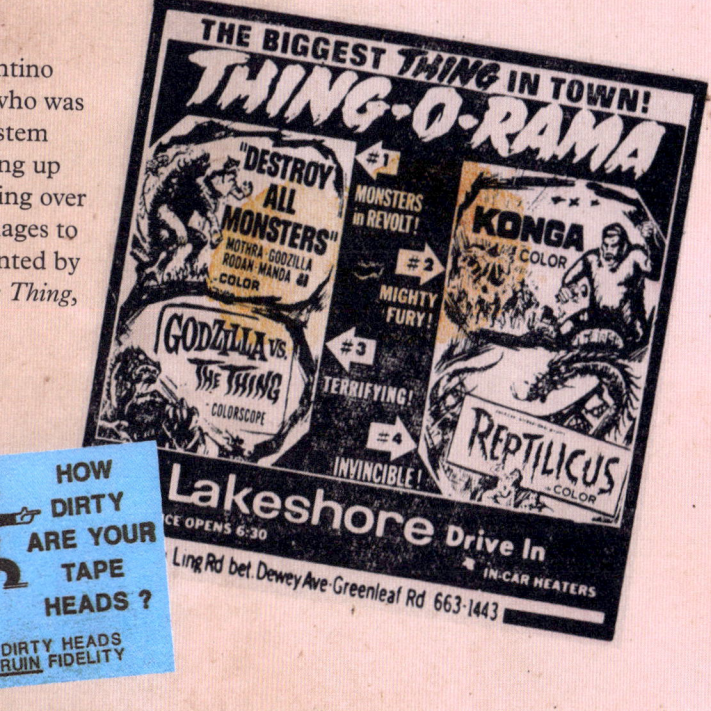

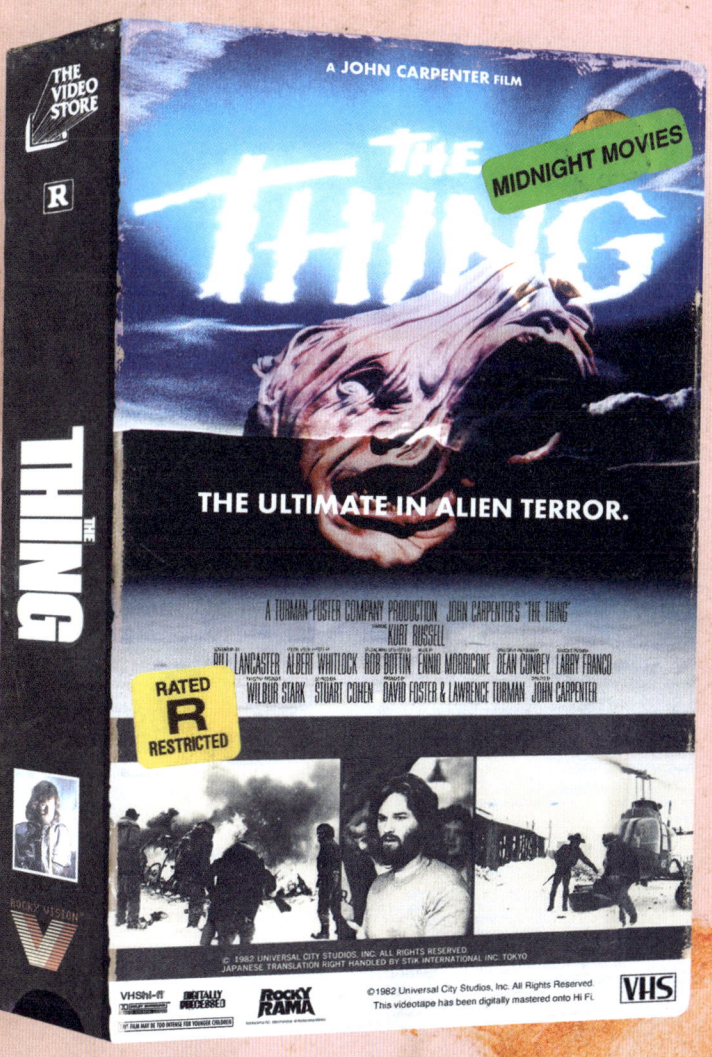

1- Quentin Tarantino, *The Late Show with Stephen Colbert*, CBS, November 9, 2021.

119

HARD BOILED

LAST STAND

1992, Hong Kong. John Woo was getting ready to effect a complete reset of the action movie with his latest ultra-violent "stinky tofu" flavor symphony. But did he know, at this point, that this was the last thriller he would make in HK before taking off for Hollywood? As yet, the film world knew nothing about him, but it was about to experience what amounted to an unaffiliated follow-up to *The Wild Bunch* (1969), another nihilistic requiem of the kind you encounter once every thirty years at best. The sheer energy of the movie, transmitted via video cassettes originating from Hong Kong, was about to create a huge stir and give birth to a whole generation of HK movie fans across the world—including, of course, Quentin Tarantino. "*I often went to Chinatown to watch Hong Kong movies, and that's how I discovered John Woo's early films like* A Better Tomorrow I *and* II. *I'd even say that it's a little bit thanks to me that John Woo became known among movie buffs in Los Angeles,*" Tarantino confided while promoting *Pulp Fiction*.[1] While he doesn't seek to emulate the intensity of the action in John Woo's movies in either *Reservoir Dogs* or *Pulp Fiction*, he is clearly aware of the nonchalance and elegance that Woo's heroes exude in their suits—which were themselves largely inspired by Alain Delon in Jean-Pierre Melville's movies—and bases his characters' killer uniforms on these. "*I was really taken with Chow Yun-fat a lot at that time, I thought he was one of the cooler actors to come out in movies. He kind of had this Chinese Alain Delon quality. When I saw not even* The Killer *but* Better Tomorrow, *part two in particular, I got a big long coat like him, I got a pair of glasses like him and walked around for like three months dressing exactly like Chow Yun-fat.*"[2]

With *Hard Boiled*, John Woo took his filmmaking to a new level, creating in Inspector Tequila (Chow Yun-fat) a worthy successor to Dirty Harry: hard, ruthless, but always immaculate behind his shades, without a spot of ketchup or splash of coffee on his shirt. John Woo likes to imbue his characters with an almost absurd sense of sacrifice, loyalty, and uncompromising honor—they have the mindset of a modern-day knight and deep respect for rules and conventions. QT, by contrast, endows his, with a touch of irony, with the baseness of traitors and petty crooks. His characters are would-be thieves and humble gunmen who end up riddled with bullets sitting on the john. Where John Woo goes in for what is often referred to as a form of ballet, cleverly orchestrating set pieces of gruesome choreography, Tarantino prefers to hang on to his characters. In *Pulp Fiction* and *Reservoir Dogs*, the violence comes in fits and starts, in a sporadic and messy way—when it isn't carefully sidestepped altogether and left off-screen for viewers to imagine for themselves. And finally,

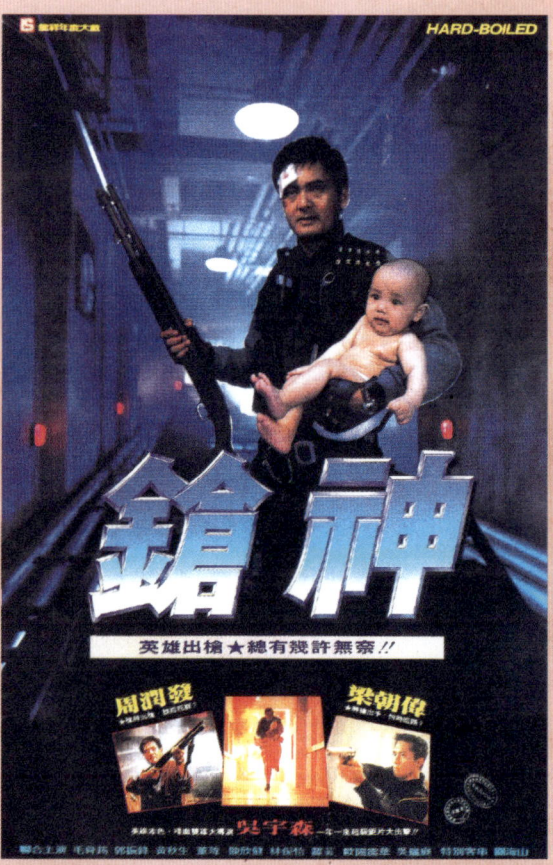

1- Serge Kaganski and Samuel Blumenfeld, "Quand Quentin Tarantino nous parlait de 10 films essentiels," *Les Inrocks*, May 12, 2020.
2- Scott Campbell, "The Director Quentin Tarantino Calls 'a Major Hero,'" *Far Out Magazine*, February 17, 2024.

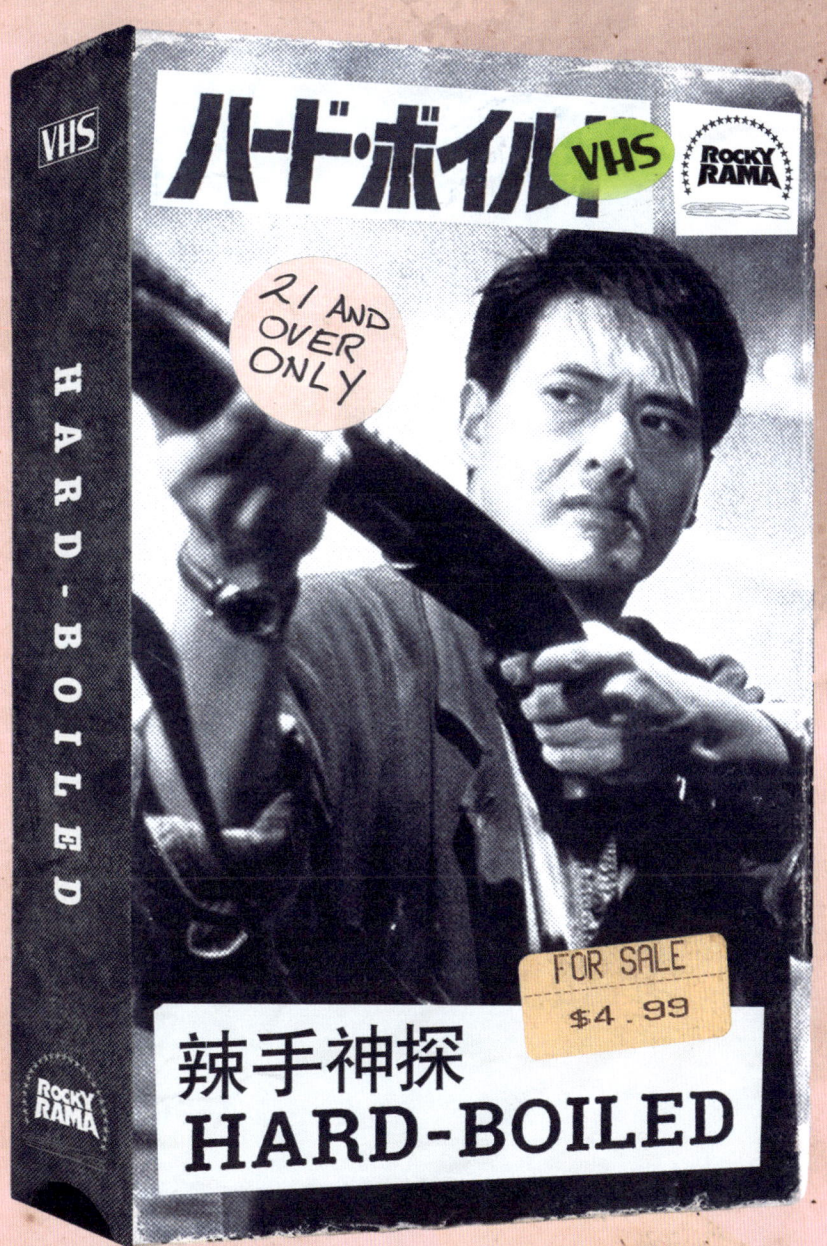

VHS

ハード・ボイル VHS

ROCKY RAMA

21 AND OVER ONLY

H A R D - B O I L E D

FOR SALE $4.99

ROCKY RAMA

辣手神探
HARD-BOILED

while the Hong Kong director makes his heroes into iconic figures who are as silent as a stone, our American filmmaker crams whole encyclopedias into the mouths of his characters, who are always happy to digress and talk about trivial topics, philosophizing about foot massages or the meaning of life, a burger in one hand and a gun in the other.

Everything about them seems to set them apart from each other, and yet each recognized something of himself in the other's work, in much the same way that Stanley Kubrick and Steven Spielberg each admired particular qualities in the other which they thought they themselves lacked. John Woo is high up there in the galaxy of influences Quentin Tarantino recognizes on his filmmaking: "*John Woo was a major hero to me at the time, I was just so influenced by Hong Kong cinema. To this day, I still think it's the most invigorating cinema that's made in the world … there had not been a Sergio Leone to come out and show us what we'd seen before but with new eyes until John Woo.*"[3] As for *Hard Boiled*, it remains fiercely cherished as a cult movie. Getting hold of this precious gem, however, in these days of platforms and lukewarm running water, is not so easy. So if you would like another dose of *Hard Boiled*, stop by the Mac & Cheese Video Club and treat yourself to a burst of ocean spray from the Bay of Hong Kong, some fried pig's intestines from Mong Kok, and an array of gray and beige suits from Kowloon, all yours to enjoy for the modest rental price of two dollars. For a trip to holy ground, it's well worth it! •

3- Ibid.

ROLLING THUNDER

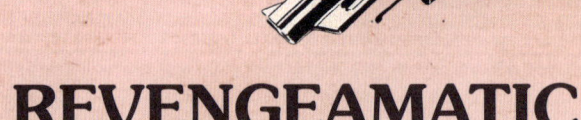

REVENGEAMATIC

*K*ill Bill belongs to an ultra well-defined class within the great family of genre movies: the revenge movie. Revenge movies generally follow a tried and tested formula: A character suffers some form of injustice, disappears for part of the movie, and returns stronger, ready to exact revenge, generally following a plan developed while out of the picture. *Kill Bill* is no exception to the rule: Beatrix Kiddo takes her time eliminating all those who made the mistake of leaving her for dead, since it takes her no less than two movies to get to the final boss. As we know, Tarantino has all the classics at his fingertips, but to find a really good revenge film you may need to venture a little further and root around in the far recesses of the video store, which are home to some of the most radical B movies ever made—movies that chose to push the cathartic concept which gave rise to them to its very limits. Of all of these, there is one for which QT has a particular fondness…

Made in 1977 by John Flynn, who could be described as an honest and efficient workman, *Rolling Thunder* carved out such a place for itself among Tarantino's favorite movies that the director even named his short-lived distribution company after it. But what is the revenge in *Rolling Thunder* all about? Major Charles Rane (William Devane), a soldier in the US Air Force, comes back from the Vietnam War with Sergeant Johnny Vohden (Tommy Lee Jones). When he gets home, he finds his family suffering and shattered, and the commemorative coins he receives are a meager recompense for the service he has given. But news of them is enough to excite the local vermin, and a bunch of Texan bastards who go by the name of the Acuña Boys (whose name Tarantino later

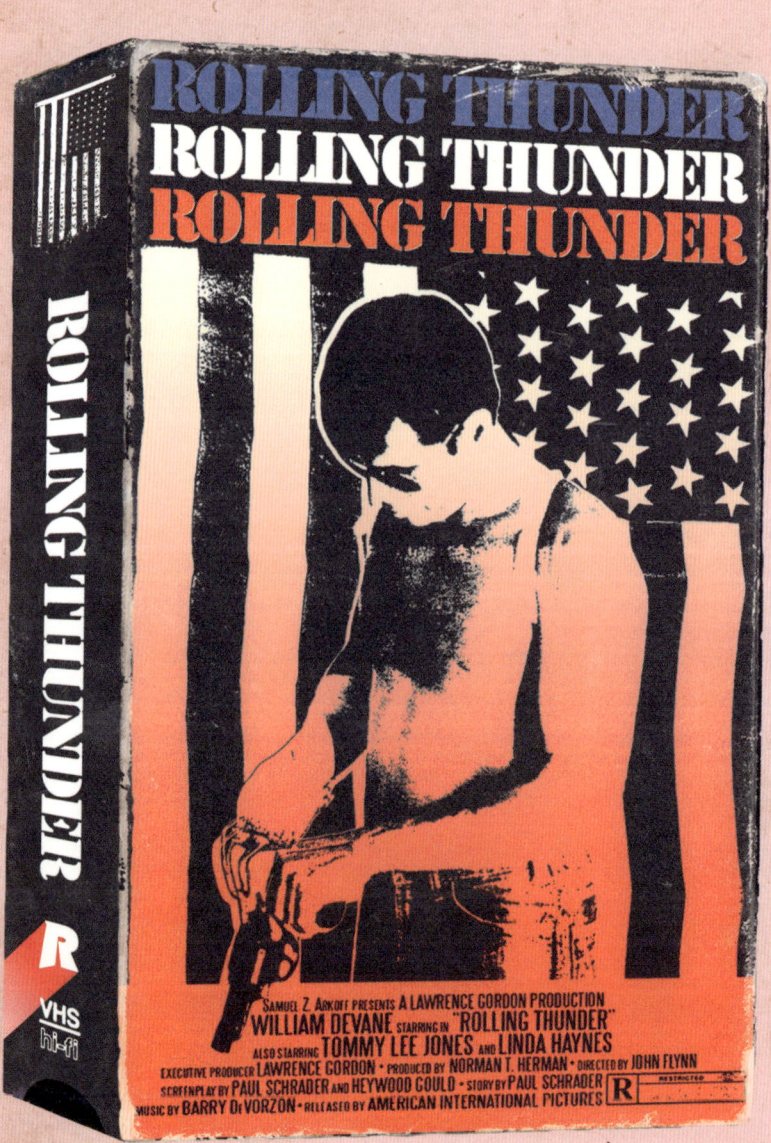

borrows for his fictional brand of Tex-Mex food) figure there is definitely something worth stealing tucked up the decorated soldier's woolen stocking. The mission has a tragic outcome and Major Rane, aided by Vohden, has only one thing on his mind: revenge. Despite it being a fairly classic tale—done in a terrifically effectively way—Tarantino is right to rate and recognize the qualities of the movie: Flynn's crisp direction, Devane's performance, and Paul Schrader's uncompromising screenplay make *Rolling Thunder* a model of the genre. "*To me*," Tarantino declared, "*it's the greatest combo of action film and character study ever made. If you like revenge movies, this is the best revenge movie to see.*"[1]

Coming as it did at a point when post-Nixon America seemed to be teetering on the brink of collapse, *Rolling Thunder* hit the spot with its small-town Texas setting, lowbrow baddies, and countless guns, all tied up in an incendiary screenplay by Schrader, who, fresh from his triumph on *Taxi Driver*, had just been handed the screenplay for Brian De Palma's *Obsession* by Scorsese. When all was said and done, all Flynn had to do at the end of the movie was let the final credits roll, leaving the audience mesmerized, the young Quentin Tarantino included. "*Well, at that age*," he remembers, "*Revengeamatic films—with dynamic blood-all-over-the-walls climaxes—were my idea of a good time at the movies.*"[2] The future director went back again and again to watch this particular example in the movie theater, studying the audience's reactions and dissecting the tiniest of scenes. By his own admission, *Rolling Thunder* is the movie which allowed him to think of himself seriously as a critic. At the age of nineteen, he

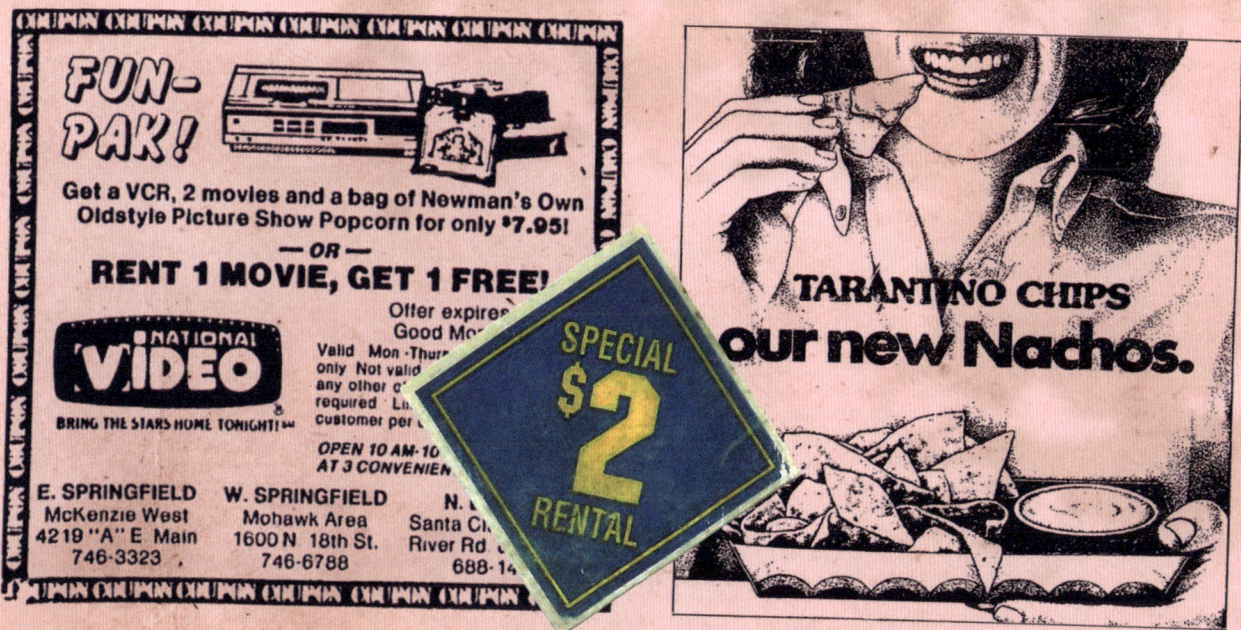

decided to interview the director: He sifted through the telephone directory, ferreting out all the John Flynns in Los Angeles, and then called them one after another until he hit on the right one.

Rolling Thunder was greeted with far from universal acclaim when it first came out. Paul Schrader was one of the first to criticize it: He felt betrayed by the way his screenplay had been rewritten, watering down the final great bloodbath and the message of protest, and he went so far as to describe the movie as "fascist." Perhaps, Tarantino granted in *Cinema Speculation*, "*yet … the greatest savage, fascist, Revengeamatic flick ever made.*"

Many years later, when Tarantino was working on what was planned to be his next film, *The Movie Critic*, Paul Schrader revealed in an interview with *Le Monde*: "*Quentin will insert extracts from films from the 1970s. And he will also make his own versions of films from that era. He asked my permission to shoot the ending of* [Rolling Thunder], *by John Flynn, as I had written it in the original screenplay.*"[3] … A movie buff's treat if ever there was one, and something to see … •

1- Jason Bailey, *Pulp Fiction: The Complete Story of Quentin Tarantino's Masterpiece* (Voyageur Press, 2013).
2- Quentin Tarantino, *Cinema Speculation* (Harper, 2022).
3- Aureliano Tonet, "Paul Schrader, cinéaste: 'La mort, voilà mon sujet. Et mieux vaut ne pas traîner!," *Le Monde*, December 28, 2023. English translation in Rodrigo Perez, "Paul Schrader Reveals Quentin Tarantino's 'The Movie Critic' Will Recreate & Reimagine '70s Films Like 'Rolling Thunder,'" *The Playlist*, December 29, 2023.

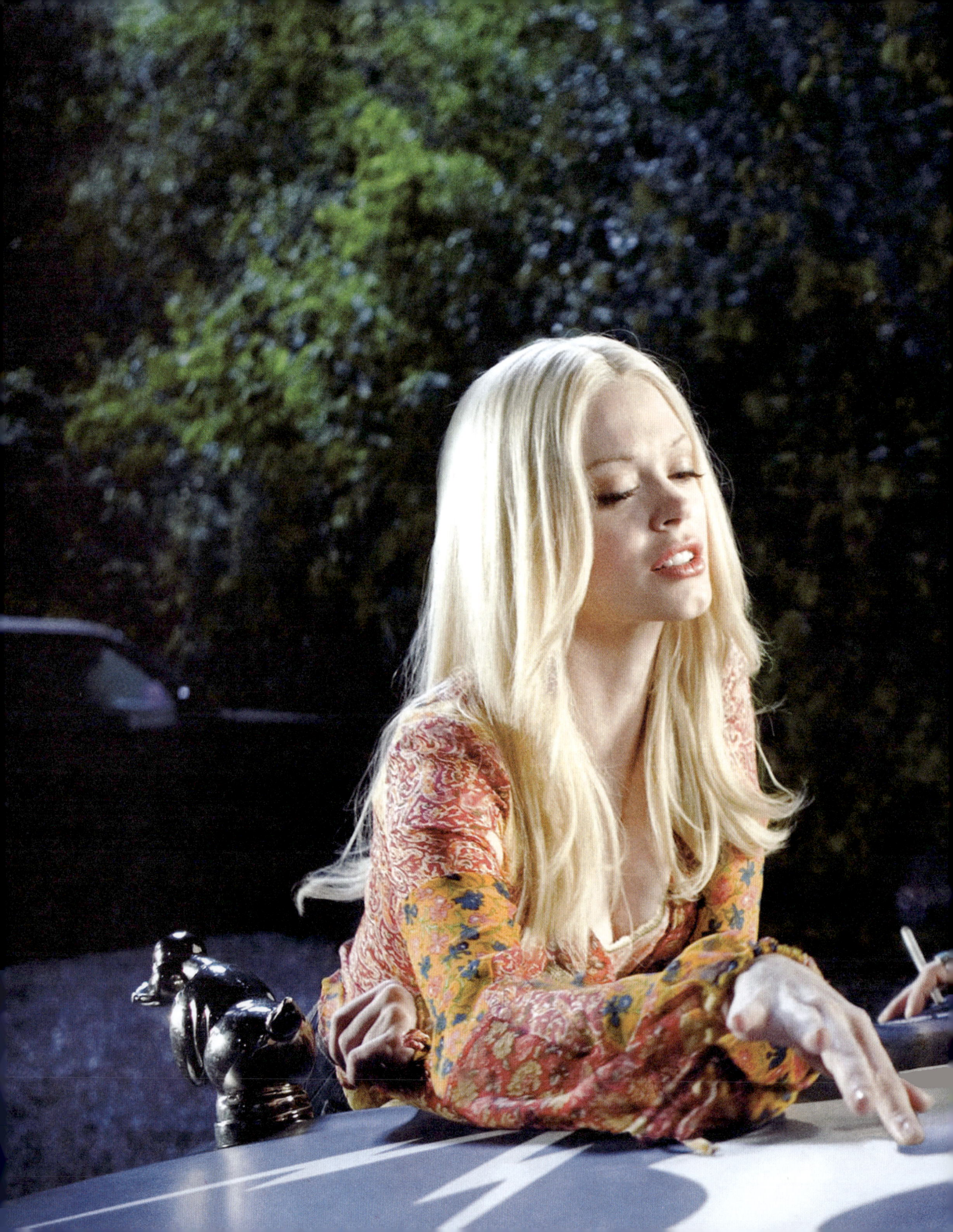

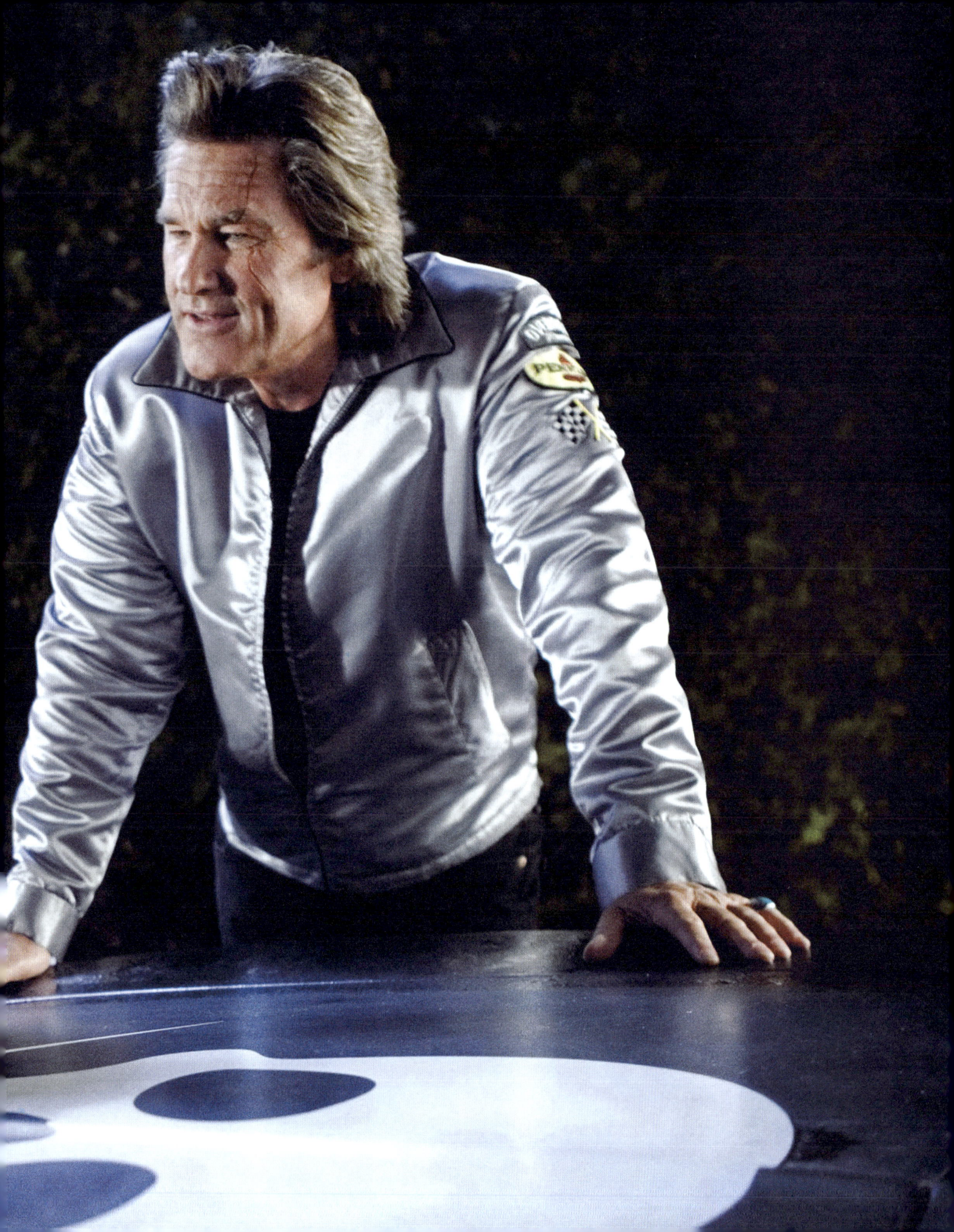

VI
THE TRAVEL AGENCY

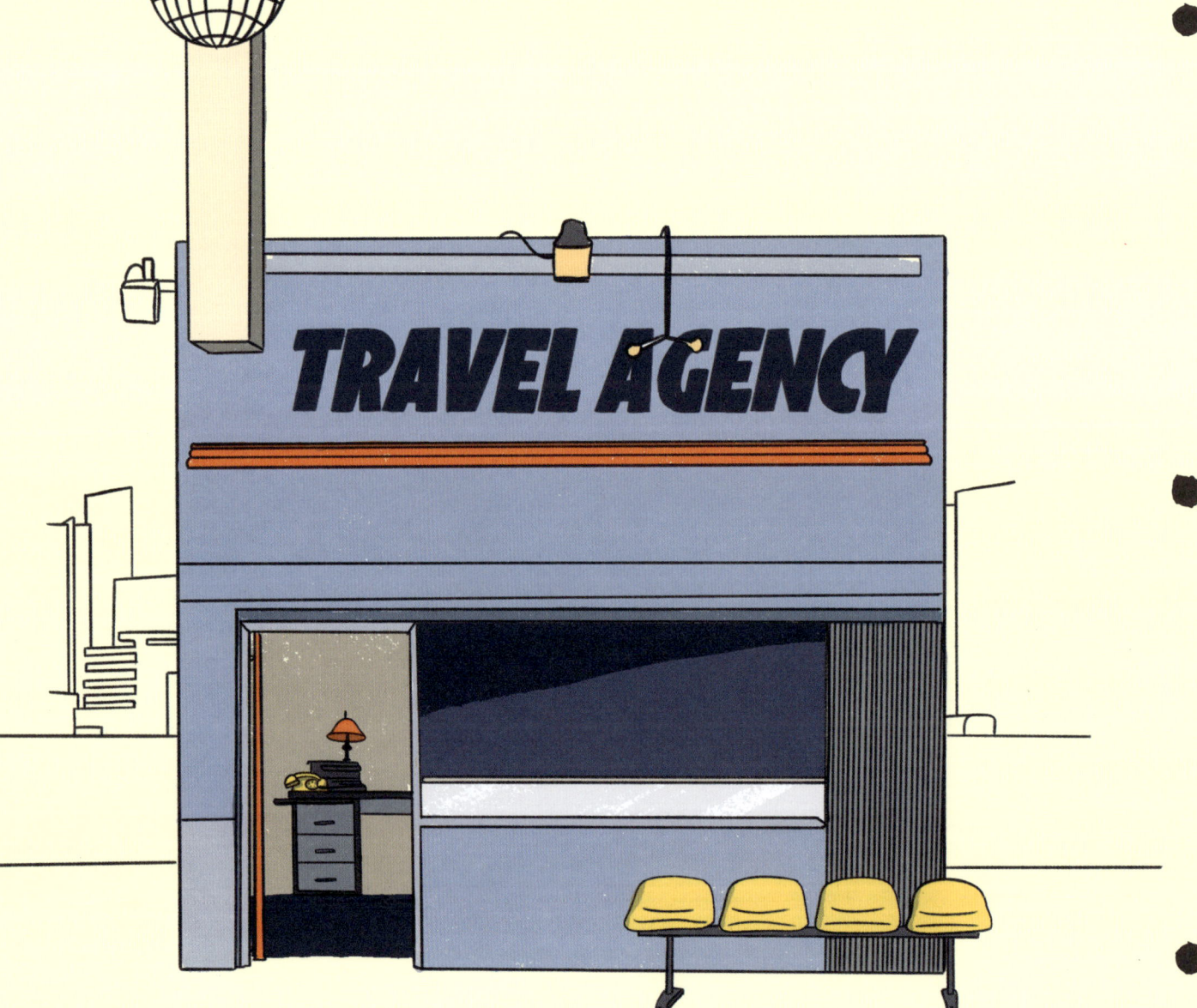

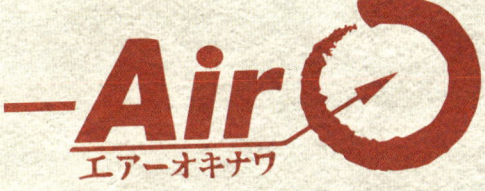
Beyond Tarantino Town, of course, lies Los Angeles,
which has long had a special place in Tarantino's
heart. The city is a big part of his world—almost
a character in its own right. *Reservoir Dogs*,
Pulp Fiction, *Jackie Brown*, and *Once Upon a Time…
in Hollywood* all pay tribute to the beloved City of
Angels. QT was raised in this city, and he explored
its different districts, getting to know it from
all angles: from the most glamorous avenues to its
working-class neighborhoods. Tarantino may have
been born in Tennessee, but he's a true Angeleno
at heart, no doubt about it. Of course the director
would also be happy to take us somewhere else, like
Paris or Okinawa, but it was in Los Angeles that his
real passion for film was born. For visitors staying
in Tarantino Town, our travel agency has drawn up
a list of places in L.A. which every QT fan should
visit. It includes a movie theater, a record store,
a video store, a diner… In short, all of Tarantino's
familiar haunts are here. Trust your new favorite
travel agents—all the places on the list not only come
highly recommended by Quentin Tarantino, but they've
been tested by your hosts. So get back in your car and
head straight out to the Californian desert—it's the
only thing between you and the City of Angels. Go get
a taste of real life, as lived by Tarantino!

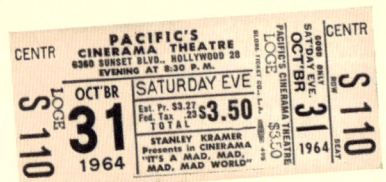

CINERAMA DOME

The Temple of the West Coast

The crowds gathered that night at 6360 Sunset Boulevard. The men were dressed up in their finest suits and the women wore their most elegant attire, and huge projectors lit up the sky. It was one of those moments the city of Los Angeles is so good at producing, for which it seems to have the exclusive rights. This was not just any night: It was New York director Stanley Kubrick's major movie event, the preview of *2001: A Space Odyssey*. The movie itself was a mega-production which pushed every technical boundary, and MGM pulled out all the stops for the preview.

A movie of this scale and scope—to infinity, and beyond—called for the biggest and best screen in the world. The science fiction masterpiece was screened in 1968 at the Cinerama Dome, a unique architectural masterpiece that would later be classified by the city as a Historic-Cultural Monument. This building has played host to innumerable premieres, and countless stars have congregated under its legendary dome. Its influence on the city remains as powerful today as it was when it opened on November 7, 1963. So if you're going anywhere near the City of Angels, don't miss visiting this masterpiece of Googie architecture, the movement which was all the rage in southern California in the early sixties. Even if the preview of *2001: A Space Odyssey* now seems to be light years ago, the Cinerama Dome is very much still alive and kicking. Quentin Tarantino was not wrong to include it in *Once Upon a Time… in Hollywood*, looking its absolute best, covered in lights and neon, enchanting both filmgoers and anyone who happens to pass by… •

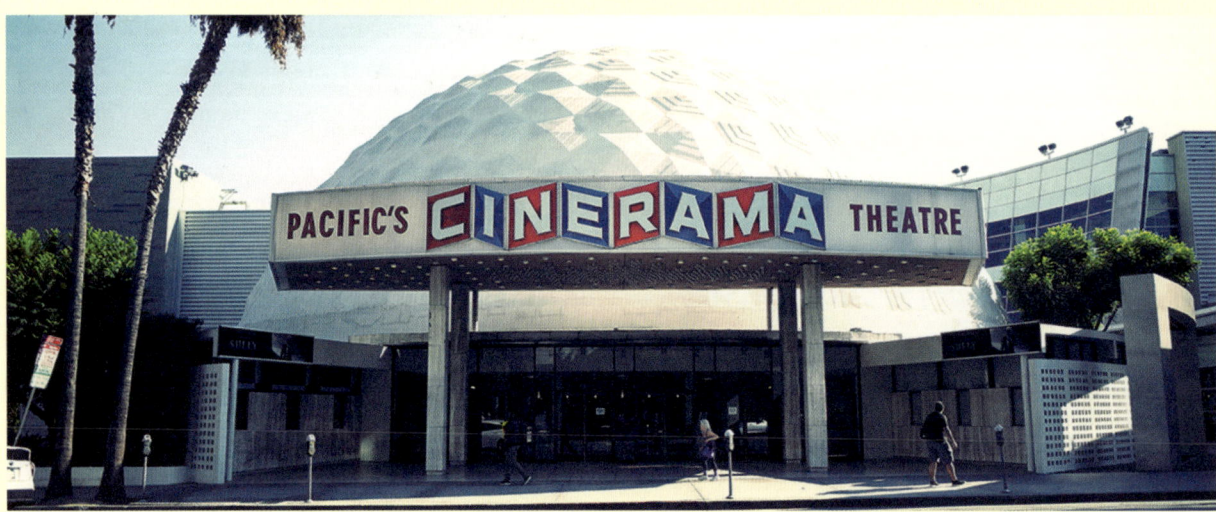

BARNEY'S BEANERY

What's a Few More Pounds?

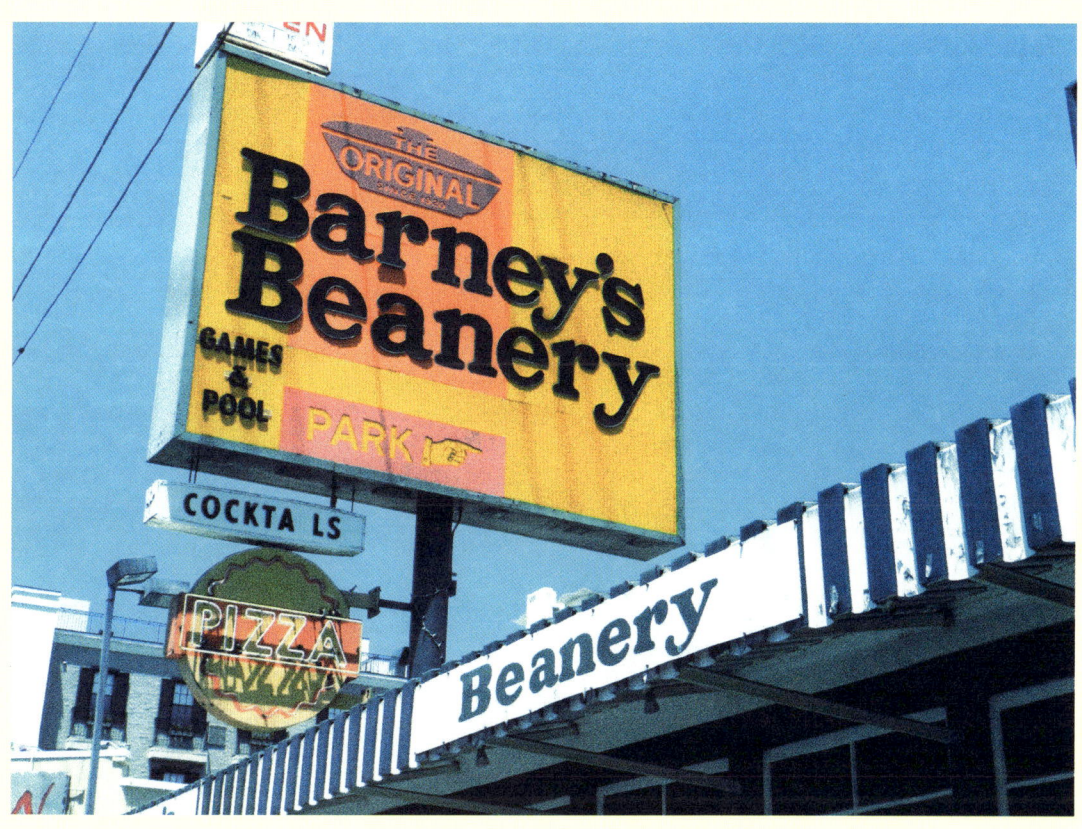

You're driving toward Santa Monica, it's 11:30, and the sun is telling you to get yourself down to the Pacific Ocean. You find yourself near 8447 Santa Monica Boulevard, in West Hollywood. It's still early, but you remember reading in the Japanese magazine *Brutus* that Quentin Tarantino is a regular at a diner not far from here. A turn of the wheel, and here you are, parked outside said restaurant. You take a seat at the bar and they bring you a large printed sheet of paper listing dozens of culinary options, a full-on American menu: burgers, Mexican omelets, sundaes, mac and cheese, sodas, french fries with bacon, with pepper, plain… It's hard to know what to choose, and judging from the size of the plates on the surrounding tables, the servings are generous to say the least! You're at the bar in a diner, getting ready to devour an enormous burger and fries, with a nice big cold soda to wash it all down, and it's only 11:30—but hey, that's how we do it. •

AMOEBA MUSIC

A Dying Breed

Here it was, just a stone's throw from the Cinerama Dome, on the other side of the street. The biggest independent record store in the world used to be here, in a fantastic building with a curved front topped with a small tower. Along with its close rival Tower Records, which was not far away, Amoeba Music was one of the last survivors of the days when you bought records to complete your collection. The tradition was to catch a good movie at the Cinerama, grab a patty melt at Mel's, and then head straight into Amoeba to lose yourself in the endless aisles. You rarely came out without a record or two under your arm, or perhaps even a movie: There was a huge floor overhanging the hundreds of thousands of records which served as a video store. All the various music and movie genres were mixed up together, and regulars were just as mixed, with rap connoisseurs rubbing shoulders with heavy metal fans. It became a cheerful melting pot of a place, with people giving mini-concerts under its roof and the biggest stars stepping foot in the door at least once in their lives. If we talk about it in the past tense, it's because Amoeba moved out of the area and took up residence on Hollywood Boulevard, in a characterless modern building, losing a little of its abundant soul in the process. Los Angeles found itself stripped of an iconic site, despite people writing thousands of letters in protest. And even if the selection and range of music on offer remains positively ginormous, you can't help but feel nostalgic for those amazing evenings on Sunset Boulevard which carried on until Amoeba Music closed. •

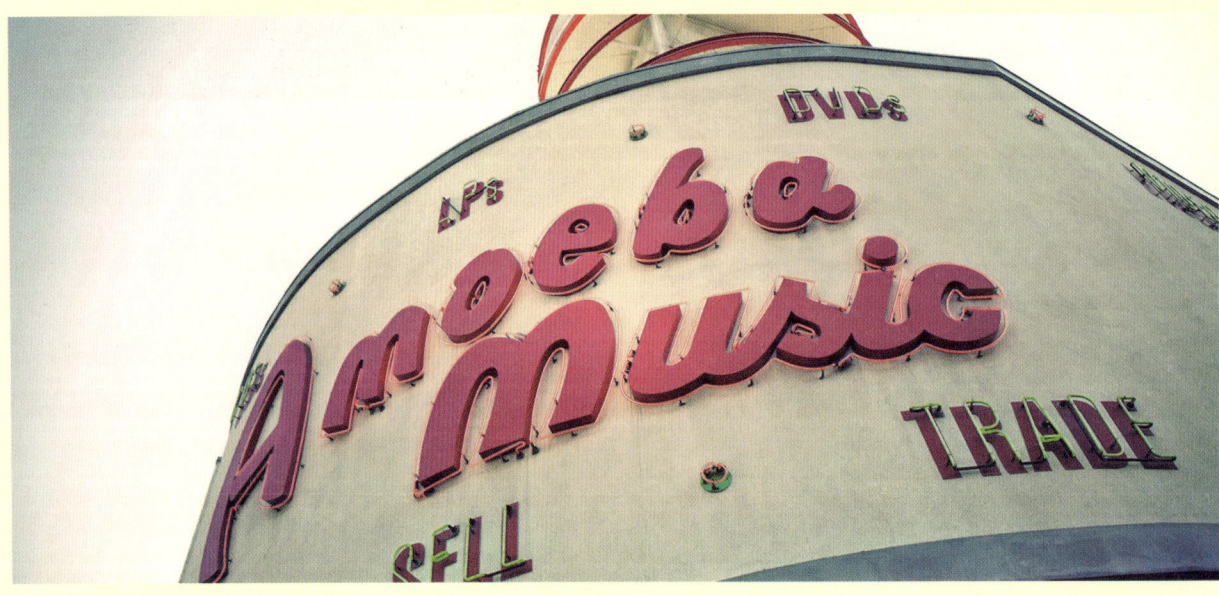

NEW BEVERLY CINEMA

The Local Movie Theater

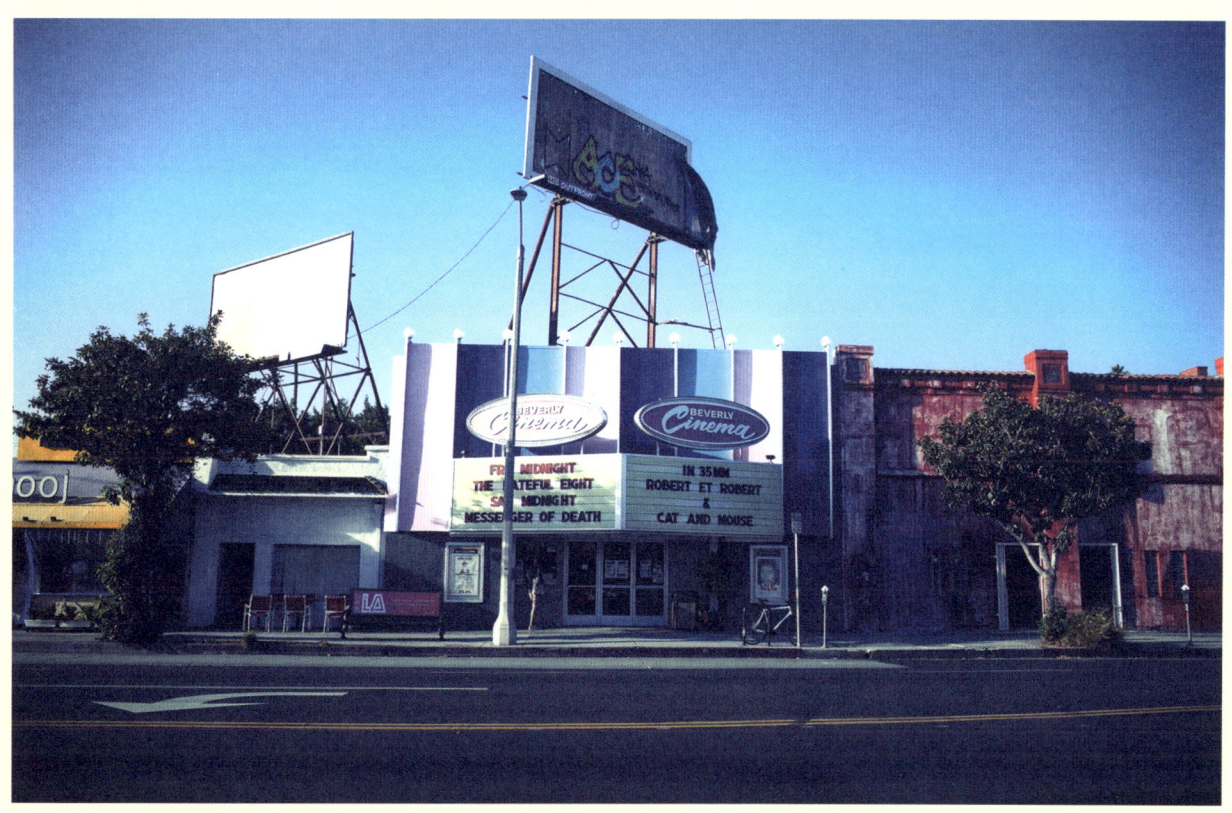

Picture the scene… You are in Los Angeles, on Beverly Boulevard to be exact. After a great day pacing the avenues of the city under a blazing sun, having scarfed down another burger, inhaled a few more french fries, and swigged a nice cold extra-large soda, you feel like catching a movie. The legendary Cinerama isn't far away, of course. But right now, what you'd really like is a small local movie theater with an unexpected program.

Well, you've found it here, at 7165 Beverly Boulevard, Los Angeles, CA 90036, USA: the New Beverly Cinema, Quentin Tarantino's movie theater. We don't mean that it's his favorite theater or the one he usually goes to—no, this is his very own movie theater, which he bought in 2007 and has been supplying with his own movie reels ever since. This superb 1920s edifice had several lives before becoming QT's temple and home to his grindhouse nights. Built in 1929, it

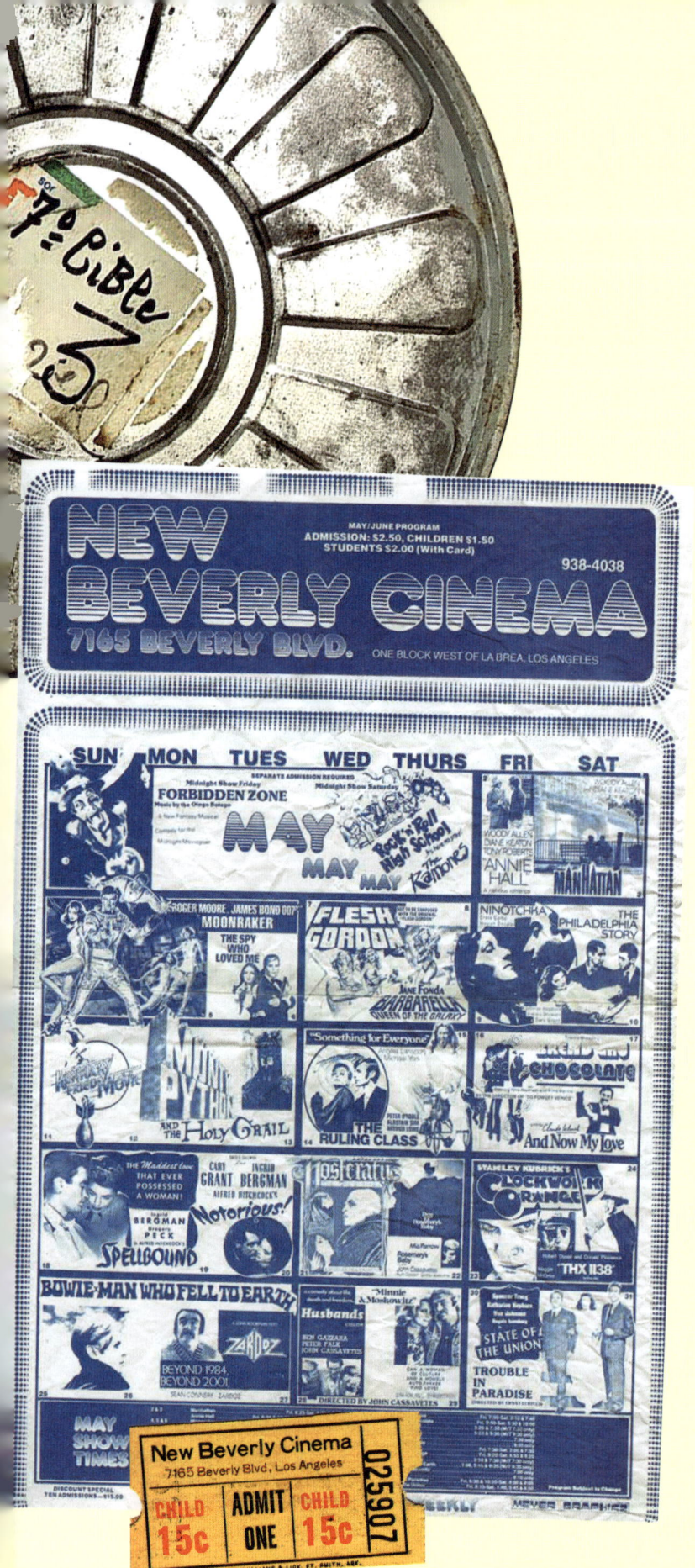

was home in turn to a candy store, a Jewish community center, and a disco frequented by celebrities before being turned into a movie theater called the Riviera-Capri in the late fifties. But the changes didn't stop there: The venue subsequently became the New Yorker Theater, then the Europa (which specialized in foreign films), and finally the Eros, which showed pornographic movies until 1977. The year 1978 saw the start of a new chapter, when Sherman Torgan reopened the theater as the New Beverly Cinema, with a double feature of *A Streetcar Named Desire* and *Last Tango in Paris*. For almost thirty years, Sherman Torgan devoted all his energy to sharing his love of film, making the New Beverly thrive. Among his faithful supporters was, of course, the young Quentin Tarantino. When Torgan died in 2007, the director bought the movie theater to save it from almost certain permanent closure. "*As long as I'm alive, and as long as I'm rich,*" he declared, "*the New Beverly will be there, showing double features in 35mm.*"[1] Amen. The director paid for some welcome renovations, restoring the theater to its former glory, and launched a program which is now famous for its screenings of double features in 35mm from his own collection— two movies a night, complete with commercial breaks featuring vintage advertising.

So head on down and take a look at the beautiful exterior. If you check out the posters, you might find yourself thinking that a good Claude Lelouch film would be just right—perhaps it's *Robert et Robert* tonight, with a bunch of old French ads. A dream for any movie buff in search of something a bit different, or for anyone who wants to get away from a world that seems to be moving a little too fast. Go ahead and take refuge in Quentin Tarantino's movie theater. Just make sure your cell phone is firmly switched off. •

1- John Scott Lewinski, "Quentin Tarantino Saves L.A. Theater," *The Hollywood Reporter*, February 18, 2010.

VIDEO ARCHIVES

On Holy Ground

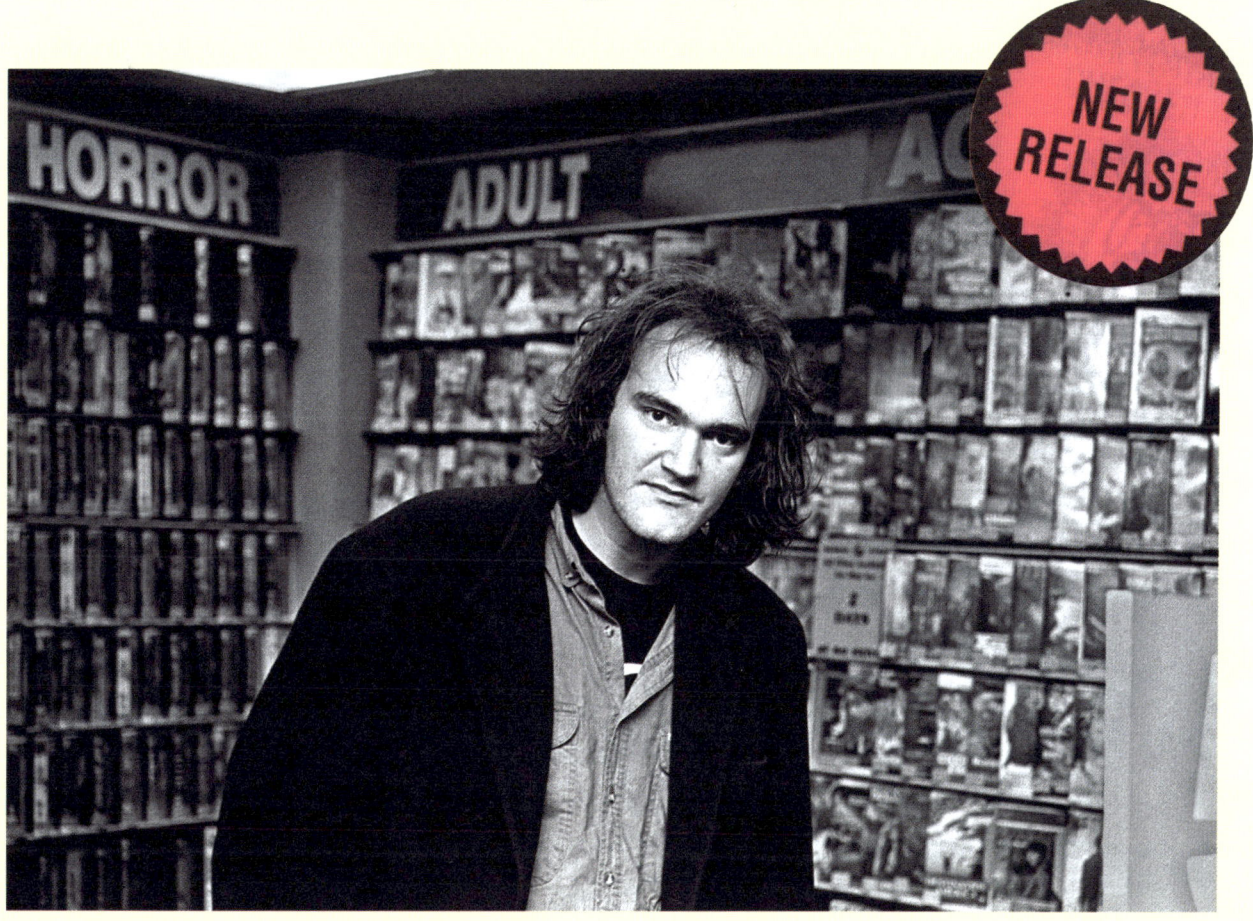

NEW RELEASE

It was a long time ago, long before Netflix, Apple, Amazon, and all the other platforms that encourage us to spend hours at a time scrolling through tens of thousands of movies, most of which we won't even watch when it comes down to it. It was a time when, without a VCR player, we were restricted to programs broadcast at set times on a handful of channels at best, without any means of replaying them. It's something you can only imagine today if you weren't

there to see it for yourself: knots of budding movie buffs swapping VHS tapes in school hallways or outside apartment blocks, taking out their felt-tip pens and designing new cassette covers in their bedrooms, in class, anywhere and everywhere. There was one place where VHS tapes could all be found together in a single venue, a veritable temple for all cassette worshippers: the video store. Everyone knows that it all started in the aisles of Video Archives for

Quentin Tarantino, at 1822 Sepulveda, in Manhattan Beach. It was here that our director acquired much of his encyclopedic knowledge of cinema, from the great classics to art house films to B movies, or even Z movies. In the aisles of what he proudly calls "*the best video store in the Los Angeles area*,"[1] he made friends with colleagues who were passionate about film, including Roger Avary, with whom he would make his debut in the industry. "*Now Video Archives is like L.A.'s answer to the* Cahiers du Cinéma,"[2] Tarantino states jokingly. It gave him access to a database of thousands of movies through which he honed his love of film, talking loudly and with infectious enthusiasm the whole time. "*I basically lived there for years*," he adds. He was surrounded by movies: On the shelves Ford sat not just next to Hawks, but alongside Ed Wood and Roger Corman. It was a place without barriers or boundaries.

There really wasn't anything in the nineties, just as there isn't today, that would make you want to drive so far south of Los Angeles, well past Venice Beach and the obvious tourist border. Tarantino, however, made the district his headquarters at the time. In South Bay, to which *Jackie Brown* pays affectionate homage, he gave his film compulsion free rein, unaffected by the snobbery of Greenwich Village New Yorkers. Fully aware that yes, *Street Trash* might not be on a par with *Twelve Angry Men*, but that the two of them have a perfect right to live alongside each other. It is not surprising that his democratic and completely nonhierarchical passion for film blossomed in a local video store like this one, where he ran into both average, ordinary customers and people who were real experts, responding to them all equally and seeking to imbue each and every one of them with something of his love of movies. This idea of film being for everyone is one which Tarantino seeks to bring to the

screen in his own movies. He takes a seriously obscure Hong Kong thriller and blends it with an equally little-known Spaghetti Western, throws in a nod to one of the classics to top it off, and concocts something which is as digestible as it accessible.

Video Archives closed its doors in 1995. Tarantino bought up a large part of its stock and incorporated it into his own already sizable personal video library. And in 2022, Video Archives was reborn in the shape of a podcast of the same name in which Tarantino and Avary offer us a selection of tapes to discover from the video store's original catalog, just as they did back in the good old days. "*We never imagined that 30 years after we worked together behind the counter at Video Archives, we would be together again doing the exact same thing we did back then: talking passionately about movies on VHS*,"[3] the two partners declared. The podcast offers us a trip into the past and invites us to sample for ourselves what it was like to be a customer at Video Archives, where it all began. •

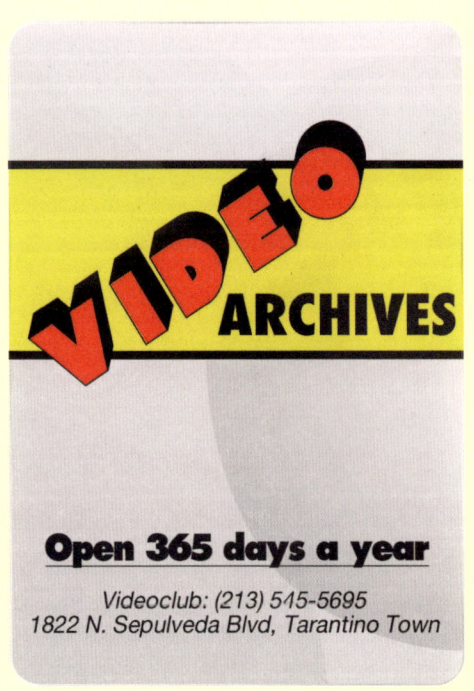

1- David Wild, "Quentin Tarantino: The Madman of Movie Mayhem," *Rolling Stone*, November 3, 1994.
2- Ibid. • 3- Kory Grow, "Ex-Video Store Clerks Quentin Tarantino, Roger Avary Launch Podcast to Talk VHS Tapes," *Rolling Stone*, June 2, 2022.

WACKO

Treasure Trove

Forget tourist Hollywood—the Boulevard, the Walk of Fame, and the showy storefronts, each more ostentatious than the last. Forget the guy dressed up as Spider-Man, the wannabe Hulk clad in green foam, the homemade superheroes who look like something out of a movie by Michel Gondry. No, if you want to walk in Quentin Tarantino's footsteps, you need to hang a right when you see the exuberant Chinese Theatre in front of you. If you're on foot, you'll need to walk for a good forty minutes—but nobody does that in Los Angeles.

The place you're heading for is at 4633 Hollywood Boulevard, Los Angeles, CA 90027, USA: That's where you'll find Wacko. The cheerful chaos which lies behind its multicolored facade is hard to describe. It's a giant bric-a-brac store, a vast bazaar of a place which draws you in with incense of every imaginable scent as you walk by. Books, badges, plastic animals, T-shirts, "smoking" paraphernalia, gadgets by the dozen, records… With its profusion of objects of all kinds, Wacko gives us a concentrated blast of Californian culture, a taste of the spirit that still pervades the West Coast, the legacy of the hippies and all those New Age religions that waged war on the Bible Belt in their time. It's no coincidence that you'll be able to find anything you might need to practice magic and conjure up spirits. And finally, if you go on the right day, you might just run into Quentin Tarantino. He loves the place. •

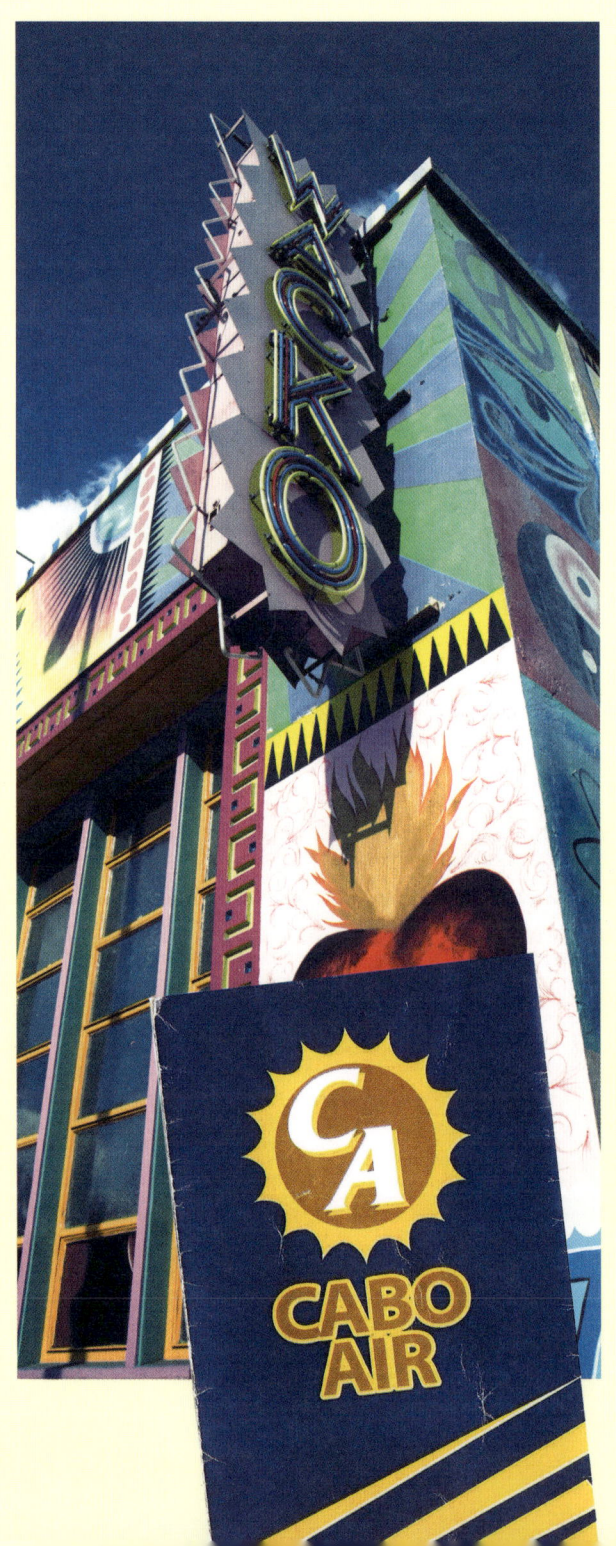

EGYPTIAN THEATRE

In the Time of the Pharaohs

You've probably never heard of Sid Grauman and Charles E. Toberman, and nobody can blame you. Yet they were the founders of one of the iconic institutions of Los Angeles, the magnificent Egyptian Theatre. The movie theater opened its doors to great fanfare on October 18, 1922, in the midst of the silent movie era, for a premiere of *Robin Hood*, with the inimitable Douglas Fairbanks, who played the leading role, in attendance. The movie showed continuously at the Egyptian Theatre for a year, in a totally exclusive run in the City of Angels. The theater itself cost $800,000 and took almost eighteen months to build, and its

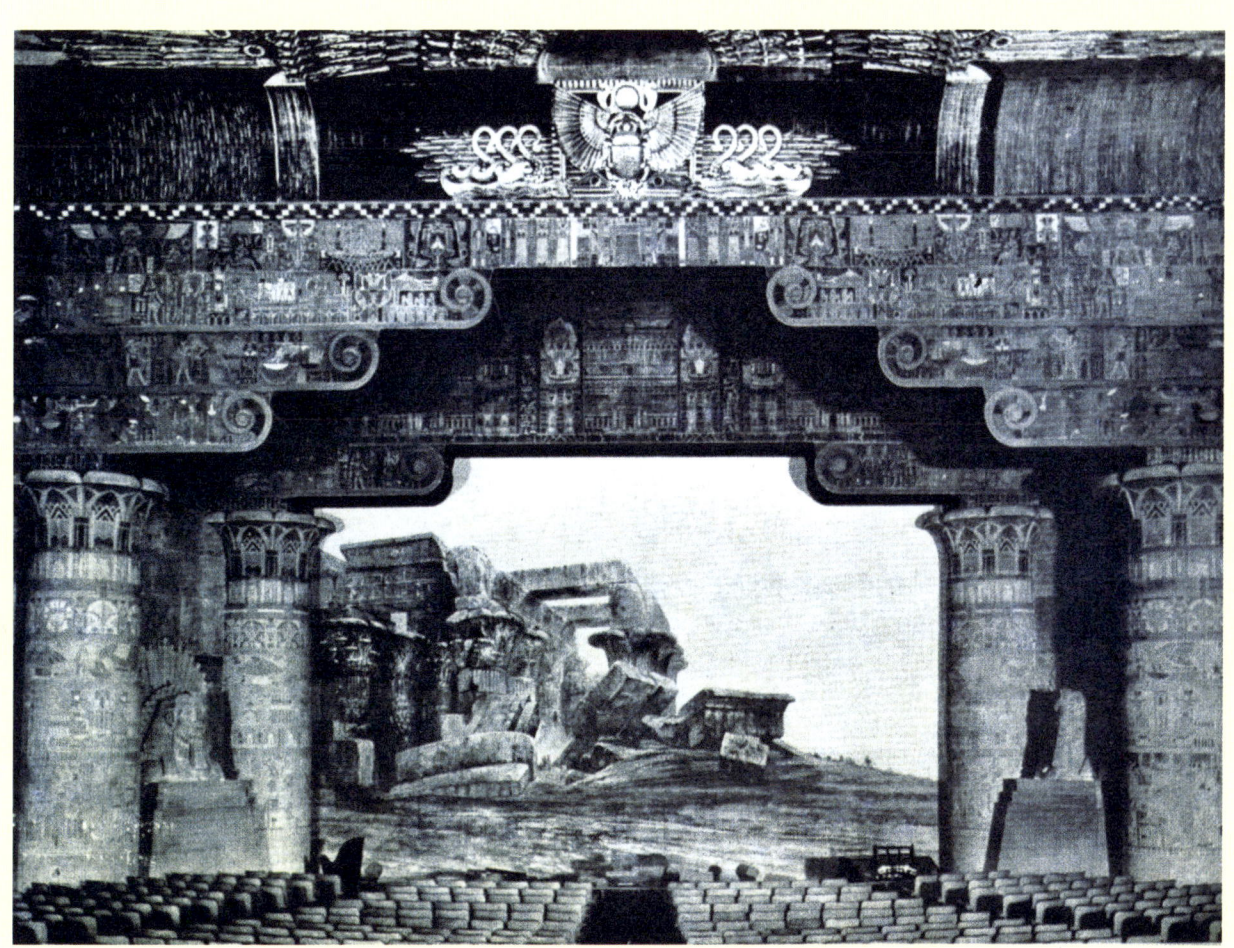

architecture was and is distinctive, to say the least… Ever fancied a trip to Egypt? Happen to be in Los Angeles? No problem then. With its endless columns, sandy colors, pharaohs' heads, hieroglyphics, and gold scarabs, the Egyptian Theatre could be a film set. Designed by the famous architects Meyer & Holler, in its day this dream palace was one of the most ambitious examples of the neo-Egyptian style which was all the rage in the nineteenth century. Today, the movie theater on Hollywood Boulevard is something of a landmark in the city of Los Angeles. With its amazing decor, it could certainly brand itself as a tourist site. And yet the Egyptian Theatre is also the Hollywood home of the American Cinematheque, which bought it for a nominal dollar in exchange for undertaking its complete restoration. As part of the renovations, the vast auditorium, built to accommodate more than 1,700 viewers, was divided to create two theaters, with the opulent main theater seating 616.

Grauman and Toberman went on to build the El Capitan Theatre and the super-famous Grauman's Chinese Theatre. If you find yourself with time on your hands on a trip to Los Angeles, go visit the Egyptian Theatre and be sure to ask to see photos of the original auditorium, which looked like something that might belong on one of the epic sets for Cecil B. DeMille's *The Ten Commandments*. Truly pharaonic, let us tell you. •

138

GOLDEN APPLE

Time for a Break

If you're looking for the best comic book store in the city, and one of the best on the whole of the West Coast, you'll find it here at 7018 Melrose Avenue. Going to Golden Apple Comics is like stepping back in time, finding yourself suddenly propelled back to that not-so-distant era when superheroes had not yet escaped from the pages of the comics where they belonged and Marvel was still a publisher, affectionately called "the house of ideas."

Golden Apple does everything it can to keep this tradition alive—a true remnant of a golden age when week after week, kids (including the very biggest kids) jumped on the new issue of their favorite comic to devour their heroes' latest exploits. It's an era which Quentin Tarantino likes to reference in his movies and screenplays, through nods and winks, as if to remind us of an age when people took time to browse, to make discoveries, to take a necessary break from the world. So if you take a stroll on Melrose, stop by Golden Apple for a moment. Wander around looking at the thousands of comics, buy one or two, and go find yourself a perch in the nearest diner where you can have a good read and a slice of pie to go with it. It's still one of the best ways to experience what could well be a scene in Quentin Tarantino's next movie… •

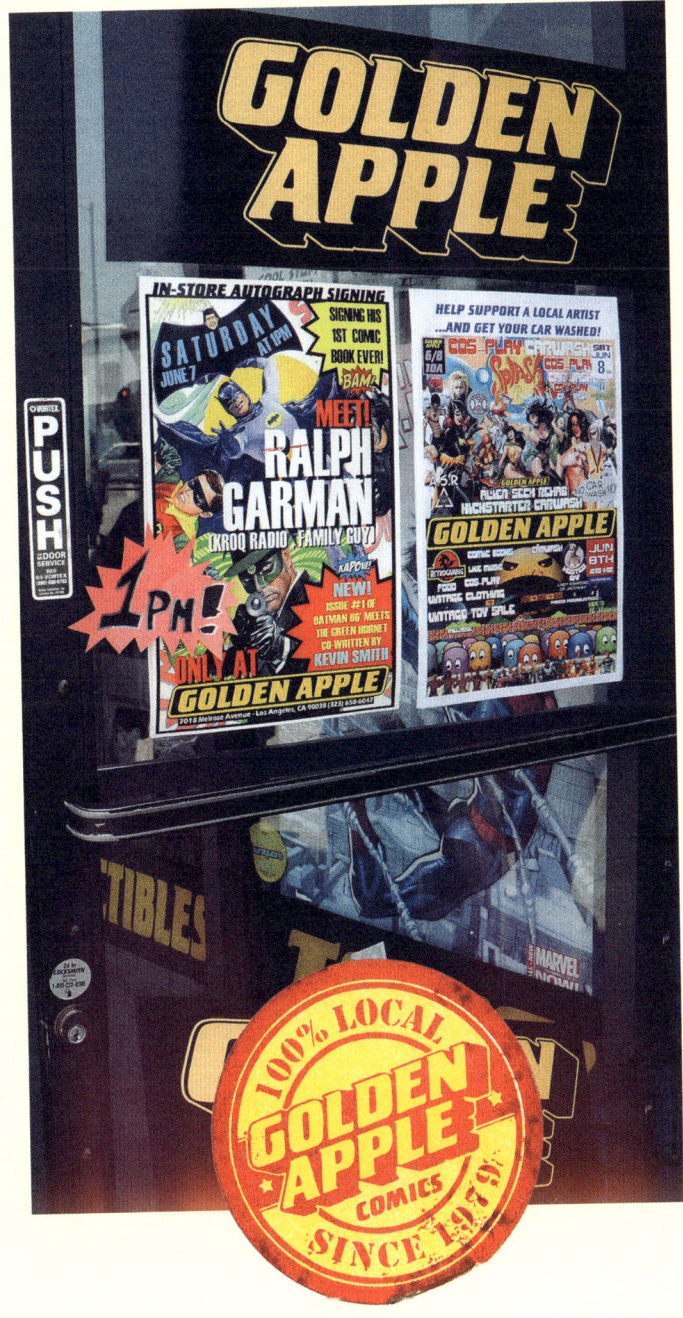

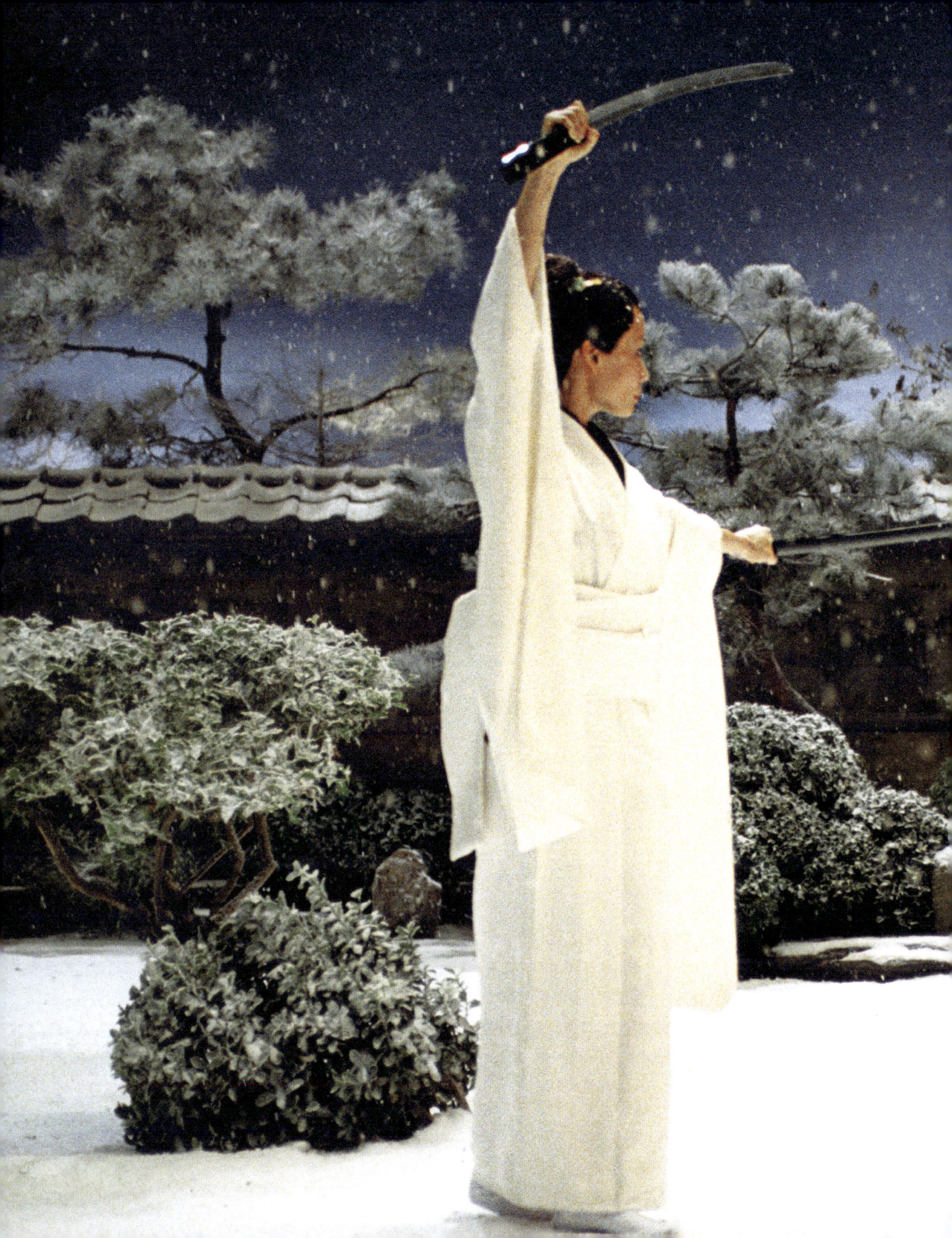

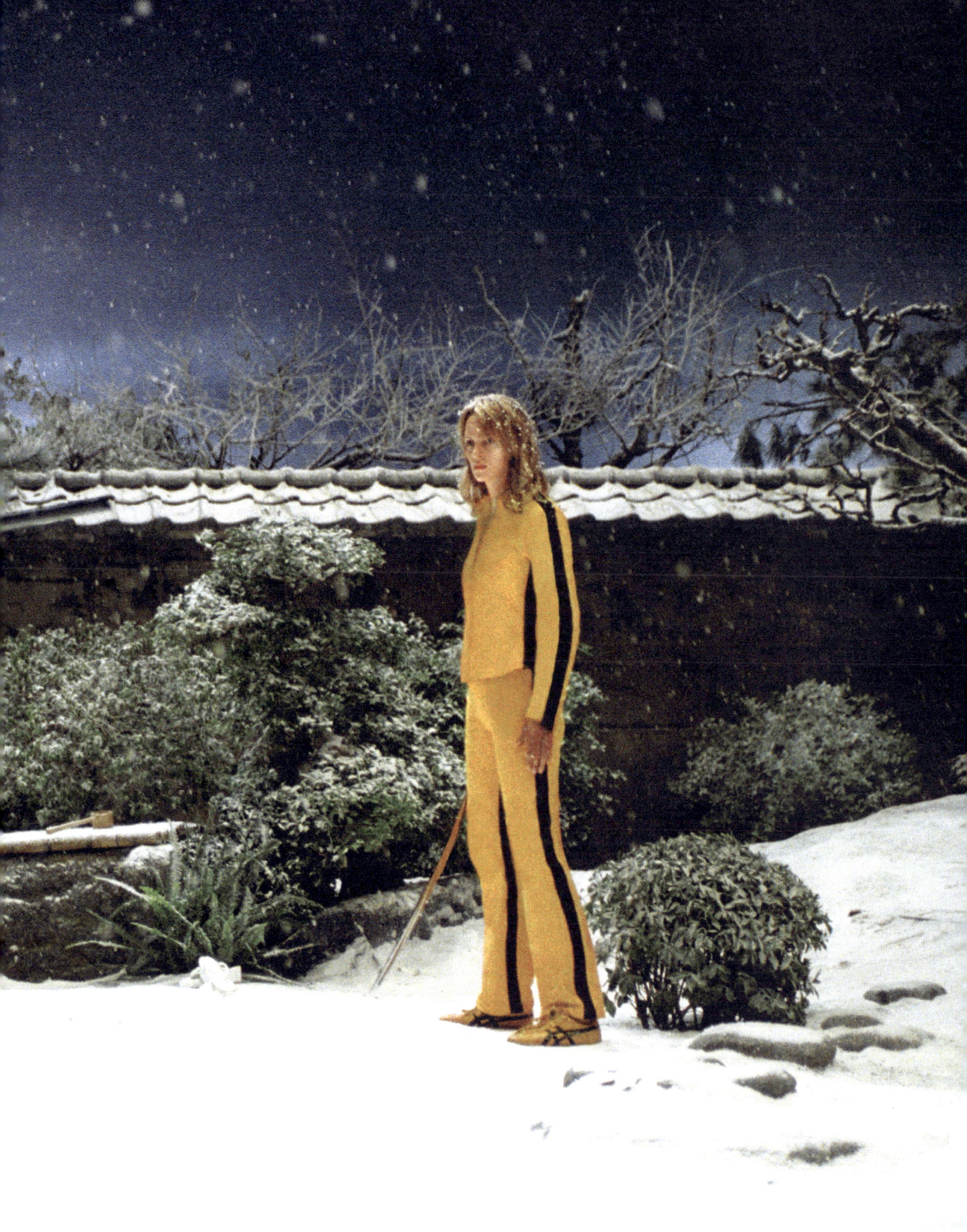

VII

THE RECORD STORE

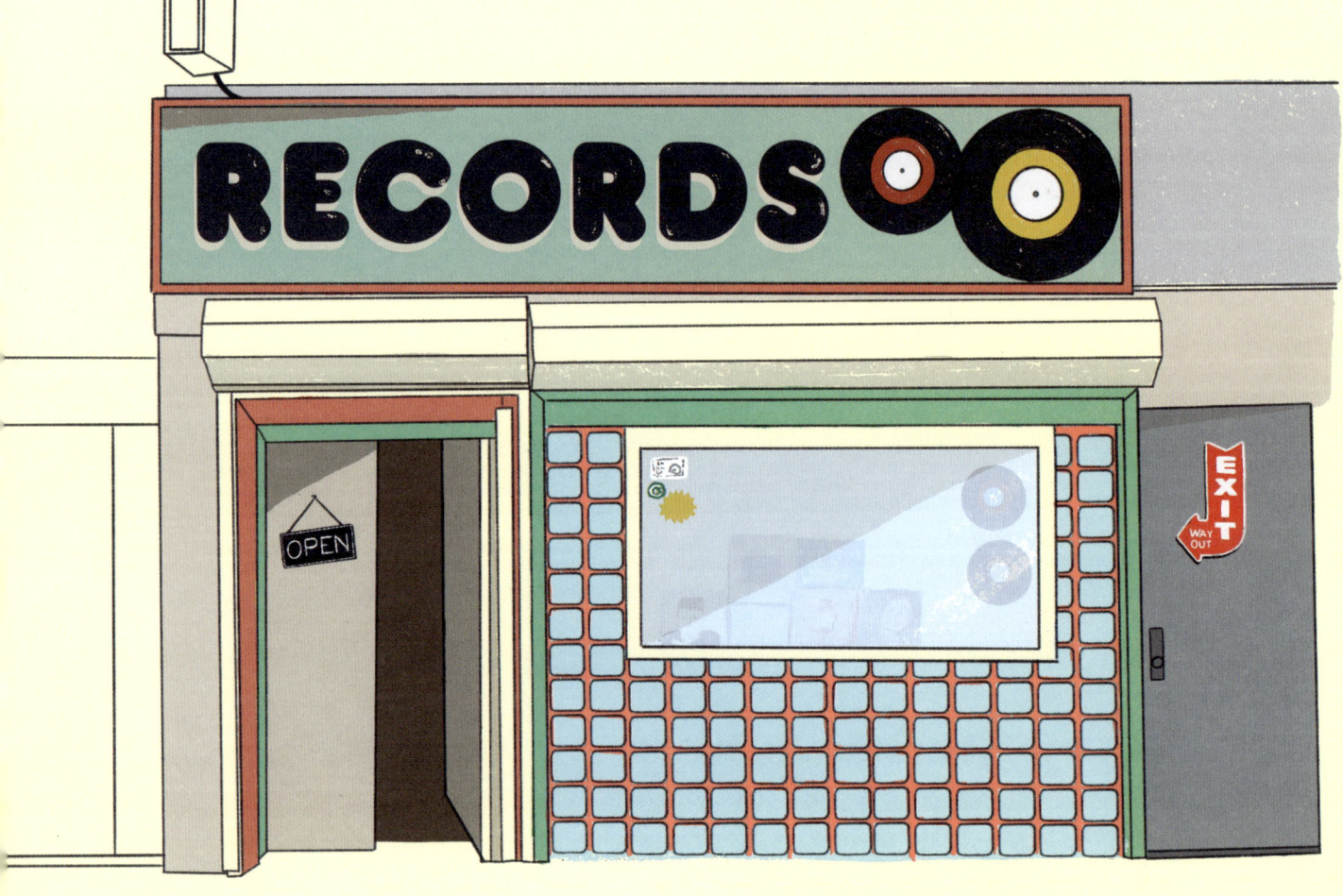

EXECUTIVE OFFICES
321 WEST 44TH STREET
TARANTINO TOWN

TELEPHONE
EXCHANGE
HOLLY 2301

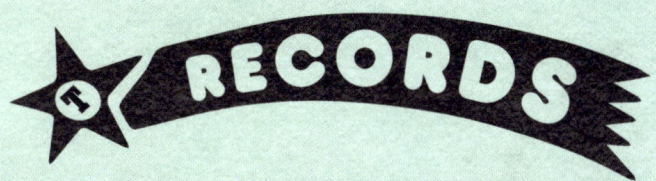

PERSONAL MANAGEMENT - STARS, INC & RECORDS SHOP, TARANTINO TOWN

Reservoir Dogs opens with one of Tarantino's characters telling the others what "*'Like a Virgin' is about.*" From the very first seconds of his very first film, back in 1992, Tarantino has his gangsters sitting around a solid breakfast table discussing the real meaning of one of Madonna's hit songs. For this pop culture maniac, music is key as a reference, inextricably bound up with his movies and his sense of narrative. In truth, music is the starting point for his writing itself: When he's looking for inspiration, he starts by trying to catch a sound, rummaging through his record collection for a sound that will anchor the movie firmly in his imagination. If Tarantino's movies "sound right," this is never by chance. What sets him apart, from *Reservoir Dogs* onward, is not just his flair as a director, but his choice of music and the effect it has, whether it's imparting an iconic quality to his men in black by having them step out to the rhythm of "Little Green Bag" or traumatizing viewers with a rush of upbeat violence played out to the sound of "Stuck in the Middle With You." His skill at compilation was confirmed once and for all with *Pulp Fiction*, for which he concocted a soundtrack which quickly became legendary and which audiences of the time flocked to go and buy at the end of the movie, as if to prolong the magic and be able to carry on living side by side with Vincent, Jules, Mia, Butch, and the rest of them. The Tarantino Town record store obviously stocks these original soundtracks, but more significantly, it also explores the huge range of music that went into them. Quentin Tarantino is a veritable machine when it comes to putting together a compilation, both in music and in film, and it would almost certainly take several lifetimes to unpack all his references. Since you're only passing through our humble town, our music aficionados have set out a small selection of records at the front of the store for you to listen to. So light up a Red Apple, lower the needle onto the first track, and turn up the volume. The rest is up to you…

MEIKO KAJI

The Flower of Carnage

Meiko Kaji has tried her hand at every kind of revolt, on screen at least: She's played gang leaders, killers thirsty for revenge, rebellious prisoners, yakuza. In the midst of the cultural upheavals of the seventies, she was the quintessence of defiance, with her surly expression, dark looks, a cigarette hanging from her lips, and jeans that people said gave the wrong impression. In 1970s Japan, she was the epitome of an emancipated woman, the embodiment of female liberation, completely in tune with the rebellious youth of the day, hell-bent on change. This allowed her to take on roles which had largely been the preserve of men: As a biker or gangster, Meiko Kaji gave as good as she got.

It comes as no surprise then, that Quentin Tarantino is among her fervent admirers. He loved the ferocious characters she played in everything from the *Female Convict Scorpion* series to *Lady Snowblood*, ready to spill her enemies' blood at the drop of a hat. The fight to the death between O-Ren Ishii and the Bride that takes place in the middle of a Japanese garden in the first volume of *Kill Bill* clearly references the final scene of *Lady Snowblood*. As O-Ren Ishii, leader of the yakuza, is killed, we hear a few notes strike up a melancholy tune, and a voice begins to sing. It's Meiko Kaji's voice, and she is singing "Shura no Hana," or "The Flower of Carnage"—none other

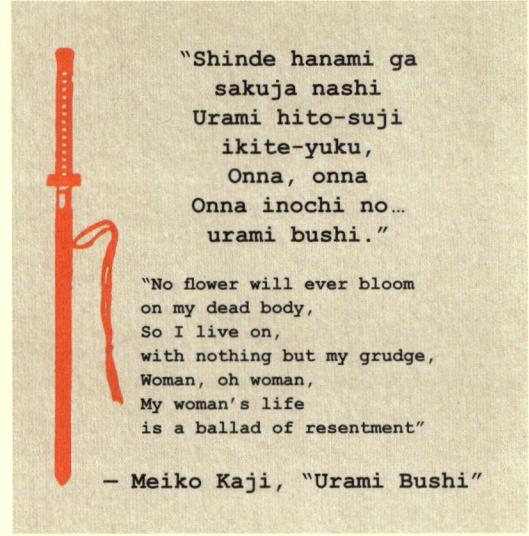

"Shinde hanami ga
   sakuja nashi
Urami hito-suji
   ikite-yuku,
Onna, onna
Onna inochi no…
urami bushi."

"No flower will ever bloom
on my dead body,
So I live on,
with nothing but my grudge,
Woman, oh woman,
My woman's life
is a ballad of resentment"

— Meiko Kaji, "Urami Bushi"

than *Lady Snowblood*'s theme song, about the absurdity and loneliness of the path of revenge. There's a trace of this, too, in the song "Urami Bushi," borrowed this time from *Female Convict Scorpion*, which with its trumpets and guitar chords would not be out of place in one of the Spaghetti Westerns the director loves so much. Throughout *Kill Bill*, Tarantino pays tribute to the actress and repays the debt he owes to a whole swathe of Japanese movies. And if he adores Japan, Japan is pretty keen on him too. When the movie came out, Tarantino secured a feature on himself in the Japanese magazine *Brutus* and threw open the doors of his house in Los Angeles for it. For his fans, the resulting special issue was worth its weight in gold.

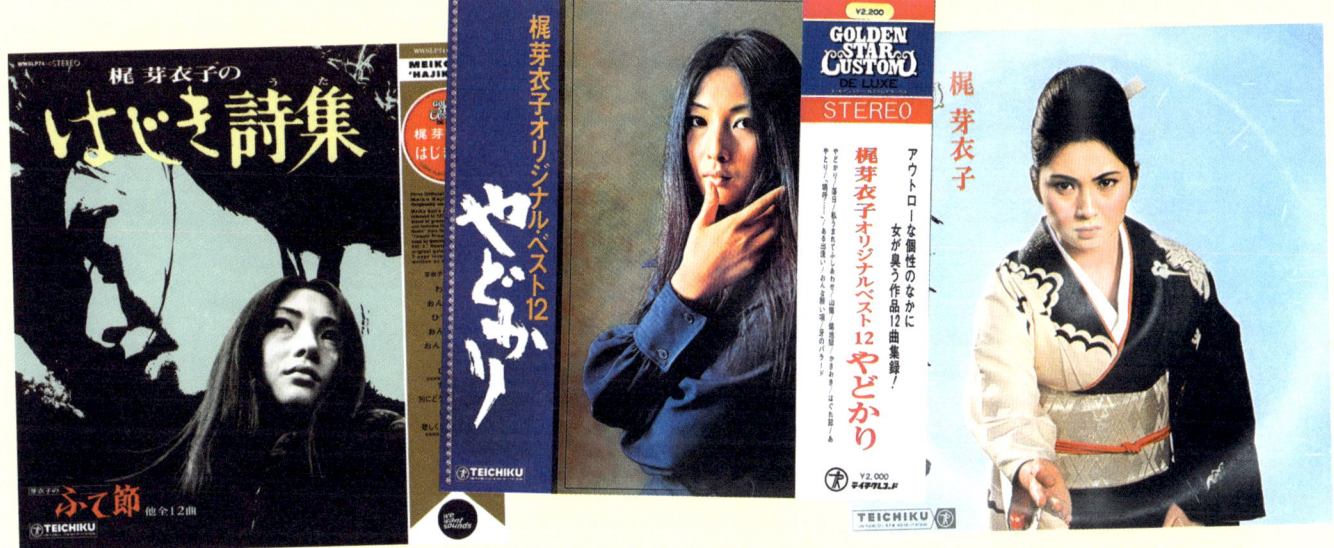

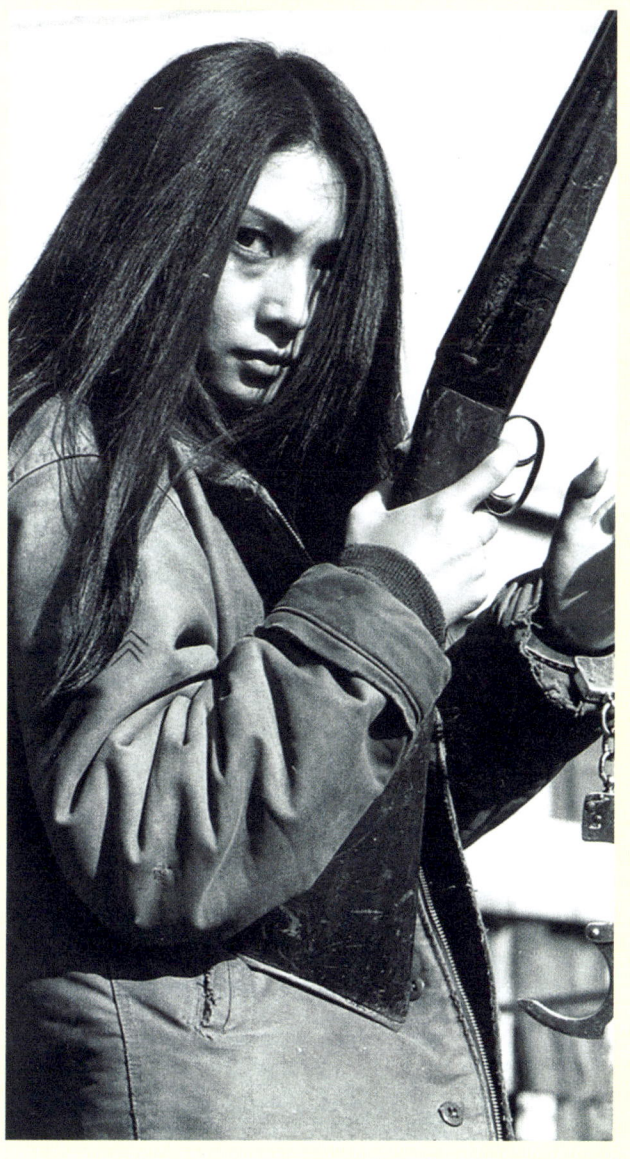

Meiko Kaji was born Masako Ota on March 24, 1947, just after World War II, in the Chiyoda district of Tokyo. Although she began her career in film as an actress, she soon added another dimension to it: At producers' behest, and as Japanese custom then demanded, Meiko Kaji lent her voice to the closing credits of her movies to help promote them. Without any pretension or training as a singer, the young actress was diffident about doing what the producers required of her, both on set and in the recording studio. These two sides of her career remained closely linked, and yet they were exquisitely and radically different. A far cry from the ruthless characters she played, there is a softness and sadness in Meiko Kaji's songs which those heroines were never allowed to exhibit. On cover after cover she looks distant, inaccessible, wearing an expression impossible to break through with a smile. Perhaps in the end it was this, and not just her iconic status as a revenge movie star, that drew Quentin Tarantino to Meiko Kaji: the mystery she exudes, the depth and tragic quality of her gaze, the sense of melancholy which could only come from Japan and which hovers constantly over the archipelago. Japan is a sad place, as the saying goes, and Meiko Kaji is the embodiment of it. •

ACROSS 110TH STREET

Getting Away

There's one record in the aisles of our local record store that deserves center stage: Bobby Womack's "Across 110th Street." This song occupies a very particular place in Tarantino's work. It is forever linked in viewers' minds with the movie *Jackie Brown.* Not only does the song open and close the movie, but it also plays a key role in the film itself. Take it out and have a listen…

It is almost a given that QT will make allusions and references in everything he does. His use of music is no exception: Underpinning *Jackie Brown* is a strong sense of compilation derived from many hours spent watching blaxploitation movies. Among the pieces he selected for the movie is the song "Across 110th Street," taken from the soundtrack for the movie of the same name, a 1972 thriller by Barry Shear about two cops investigating a case in 1970s Harlem, against a backdrop of gang wars and Mafia score-settling. Legendary soul man Bobby Womack wrote the lyrics for the original soundtrack composed by trombonist J. J. Johnson. The New York street which gives its name to both the movie and the song runs symbolically between the policed areas around Central Park and the Harlem ghetto in the north of Manhattan, mirroring the historic social divide in America.

"Across 110th Street" is an urban lament. With this piece of soul straight from the seventies, Tarantino establishes the movie's rhythm right from the start. "*I find the personality of the piece through the music that is going to be in it,*" he explains. "*Once I know I want to do something, then it is a simple matter of me diving into my record collection and finding the songs that give me the rhythm of my movie.*"[1]

The opening scene is very much a declaration of intent: Jackie is filmed in profile, letting herself be carried to the sound of Bobby Womack's lyrics along a seemingly endless moving walkway. Were it not for the airport walls flashing past behind her, you might think she's entirely stationary. It's useful to look at this opening sequence alongside that of Mike Nichols's *The Graduate*, which begins with Benjamin getting off his

1- Adrian Wootton, "Quentin Tarantino Interview (II) with Pam Grier, Robert Forster and Lawrence Bender," *The Guardian*, 1998.

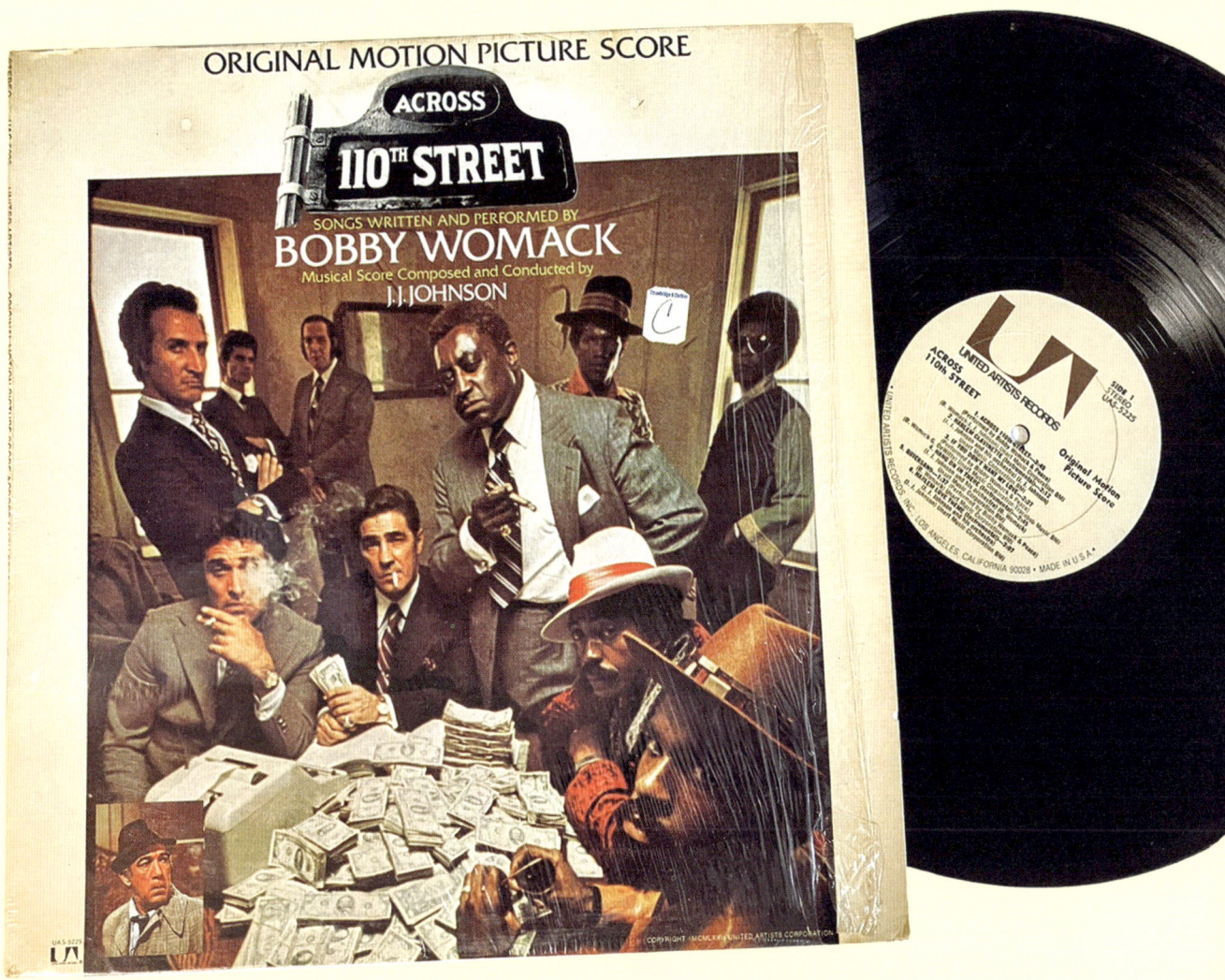

plane and being carried vacantly along a moving walkway to the melancholy strains of Simon and Garfunkel's "The Sound of Silence." But our two protagonists' paths diverge fundamentally here. The introductory scene of *The Graduate* conjures up a character on autopilot, a single static point in a moving world. Freshly graduated from one of the top schools, Benjamin is a boy with nothing to do, looking for a way out of the bourgeois life that awaits him. But while he can idle about and float lazily in a tiled pool in a fashionable L.A. suburb while he figures out what to do, Jackie doesn't have the luxury of doing nothing.

When she gets to the end of the walkway, she makes her way across the airport. Bag in hand, she picks up her pace and starts to run, smoothing her hair nervously with her hand before taking up her position at the boarding gate, wearing her most charming smile. She's got a long day ahead of her and she's not one to slack off: You have to hurry, be on time, put on a good show, make ends meet. Bobby Womack's song reinforces this: "Across 110th Street" is all about the need to get away from the ghetto—the sacrifices you have to make and the will you have to have to escape your position in society. As well as a game of cat and mouse, *Jackie Brown* is a movie about tiredness, exhaustion, and the song resonates like an anthem of courage for Jackie, who is not in a position to procrastinate like the hero of *The Graduate,* but has to keep moving to survive.

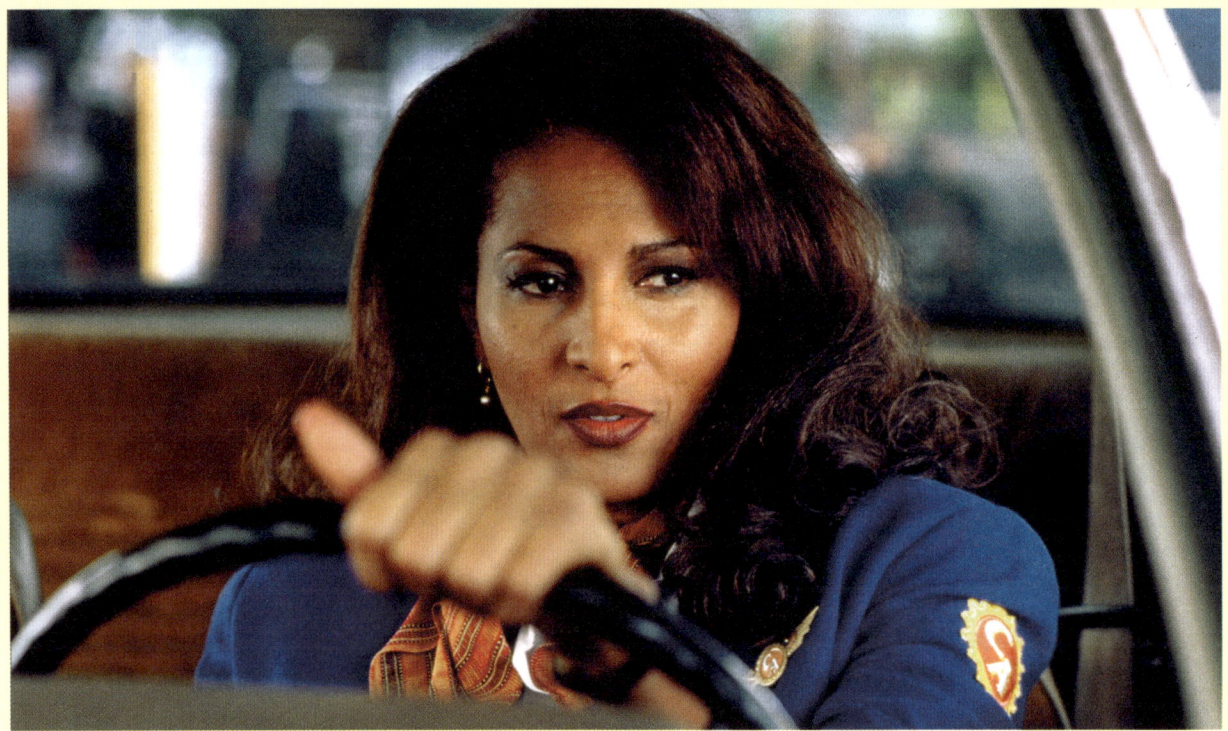

The opening songs of both *Jackie Brown* and *The Graduate* return in their final scenes, connecting the two movies once more. Both Jackie and Benjamin are on their way to a future that we hope will be a better one, seeming to have found a path to freedom through defiance. For Jackie, this means freeing herself from a game that is rigged against her—which she accomplishes by cheating a system that sets people up to lose from the start. For Benjamin, it means escaping from his parents and tearing Elaine away from her marriage—taking agency, in short, for himself. But something rings false as the heroes of *The Graduate* sit at the back of the bus that will take them far away from a life of conformism. As we look at the lovers' euphoric faces, a glimmer of doubt passes over them. Benjamin returns to silence as "The Sound of Silence" plays once again, taking us full circle. The ending of *Jackie Brown* is different, and yet it has the same indefinable touch of melancholy following Jackie and Max's tender parting.

As "Across 110th Street" plays again, this time on the radio in her car, Jackie silently mouths the words of Bobby Womack's song. Singing to herself with a faraway look in her eyes, wearing a curiously vacant expression, she seems free at last, and yet more alone than ever. She couldn't look more different than she did in that emblematic shot in profile in the opening sequence: Now she faces the camera, inviting us to examine her features more closely, in search, perhaps, of some suggestion of a happy ending. As we look at the face of the actress, Pam Grier, we see a shadow of worry, a hint of sadness in the tilt of her mouth, which suddenly breaks into a smile that fades almost as soon as it has appeared. Jackie has finally managed to get away from everything, but getting away comes at a price, and that price is, perhaps, loneliness. •

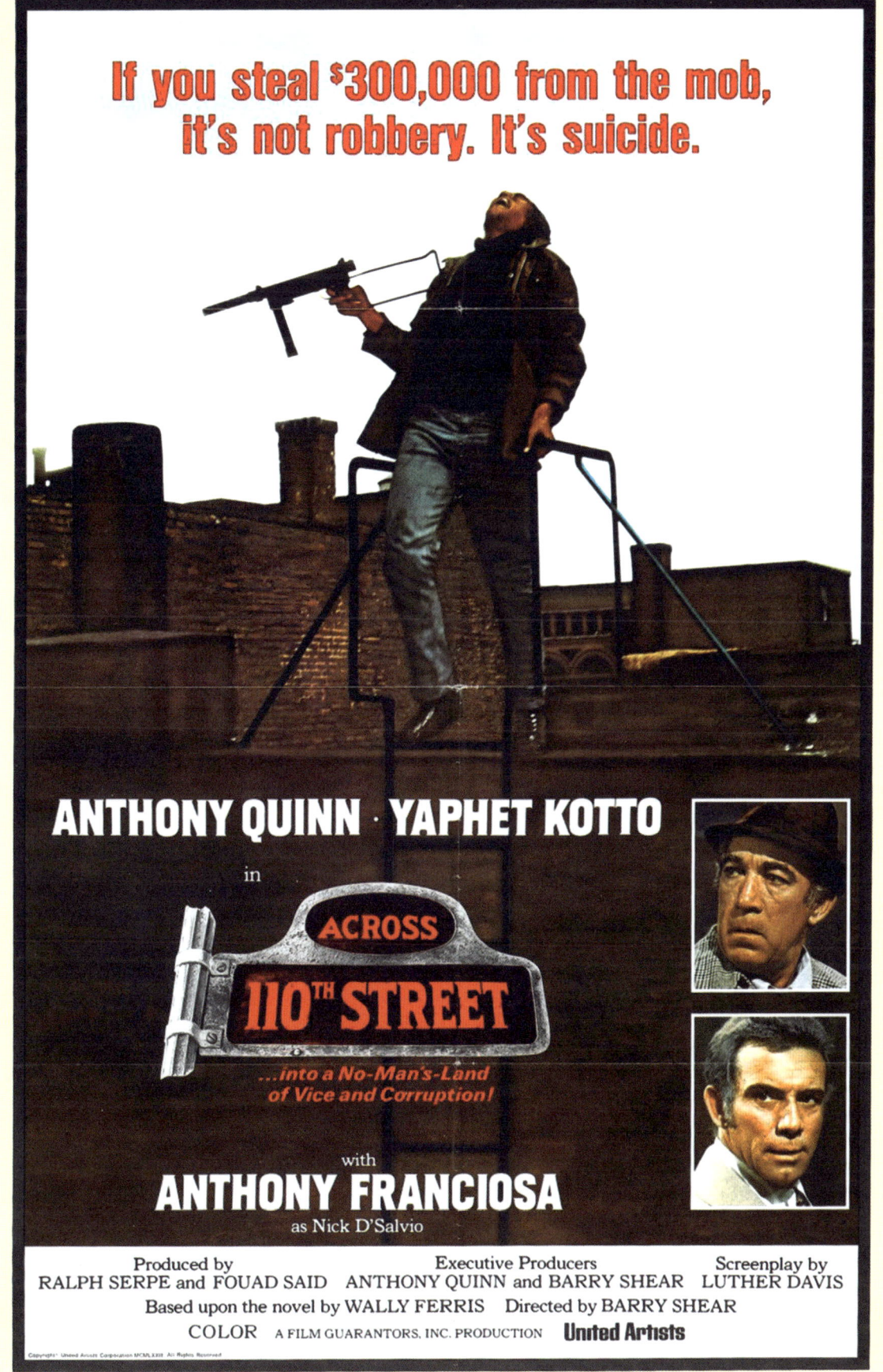

ENNIO MORRICONE

Not a Single Wrong Note

Ennio Morricone died on July 6, 2020, in Rome, where he was born and lived his whole life. Some people even maintain that Morricone was the real mayor of the city (along with AS Roma's legendary striker Francesco Totti). The Maestro, as he was called, had always seemed immortal. During his life he composed four hundred movie scores, and his death left generations of people with a profound sense of loss, because as well as being virtuoso pieces in their own right, his compositions were imbued with viewers' personal memories of great moments of cinema which they had either shared or experienced on their own. Like all great artists, Ennio Morricone took a little bit of us with him when he died, leaving us feeling bereaved. Perhaps Quentin Tarantino even felt something beyond bereavement. He had always been desperate to work with the Maestro and continually studded his own original soundtracks with plums drawn from all over the composer's colossal range of film credits. But Morricone was the only person who could compose a soundtrack capable of replacing one of

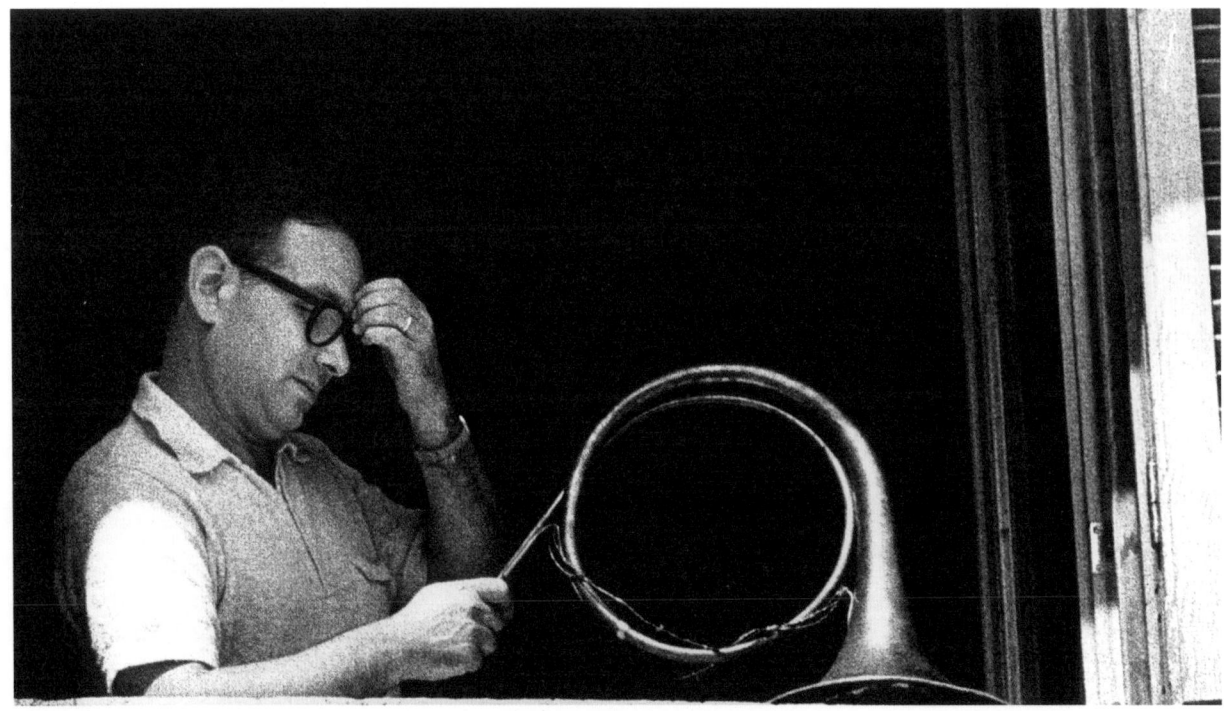

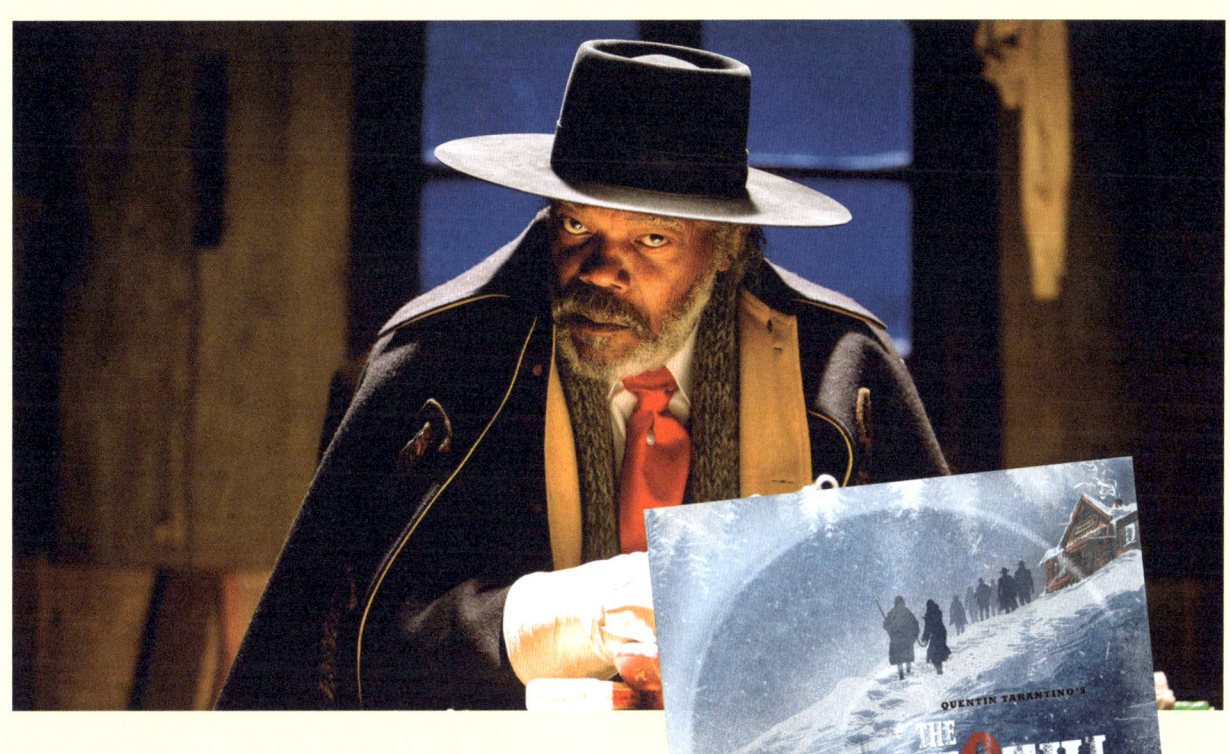

Tarantino's own meticulous, unexpected concoctions—reusing material and blending disparate influences, packed with new discoveries and old finds, incorporating pieces ranging from super-famous to totally obscure. After *Reservoir Dogs*, viewers waited eagerly for every new Tarantino movie and playlist, knowing they were in for a musical treat.

On that sad day in July, to return to Morricone, Tarantino must surely have been remembering how difficult it had been to persuade the Italian maestro to take up his baton and create the music for one of his movies. After a lengthy game of cat and mouse, the miracle finally came true in *The Hateful Eight*. For his 70mm Western, Tarantino wanted the very best: a score by the great Morricone. As well as collaborating on countless movies with Sergio Leone, the Maestro was also behind the original soundtracks for Sergio Corbucci's *The Great Silence* and John Carpenter's *The Thing*, from both of which *The Hateful Eight* is, of course, a legitimate descendant. When he was invited to visit the

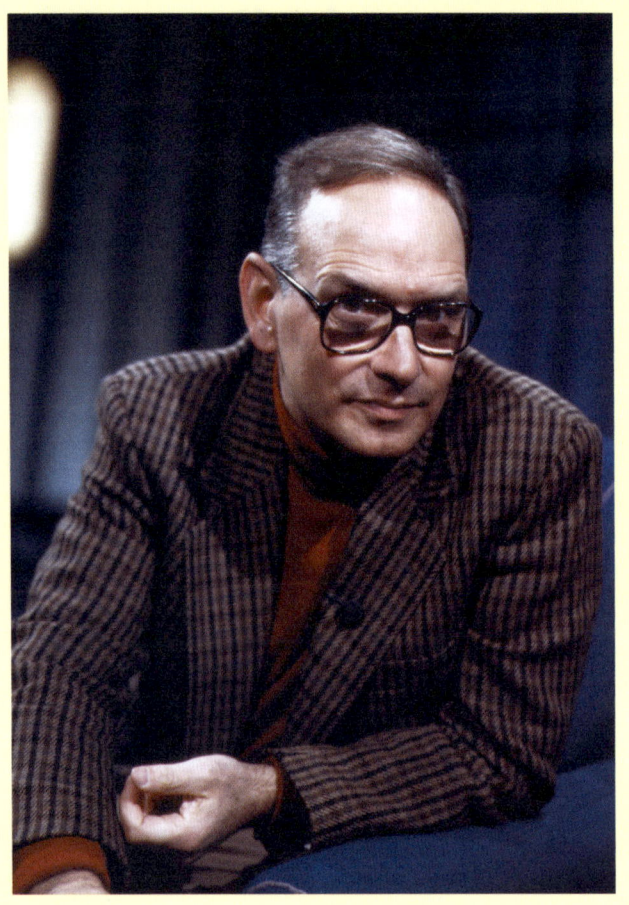

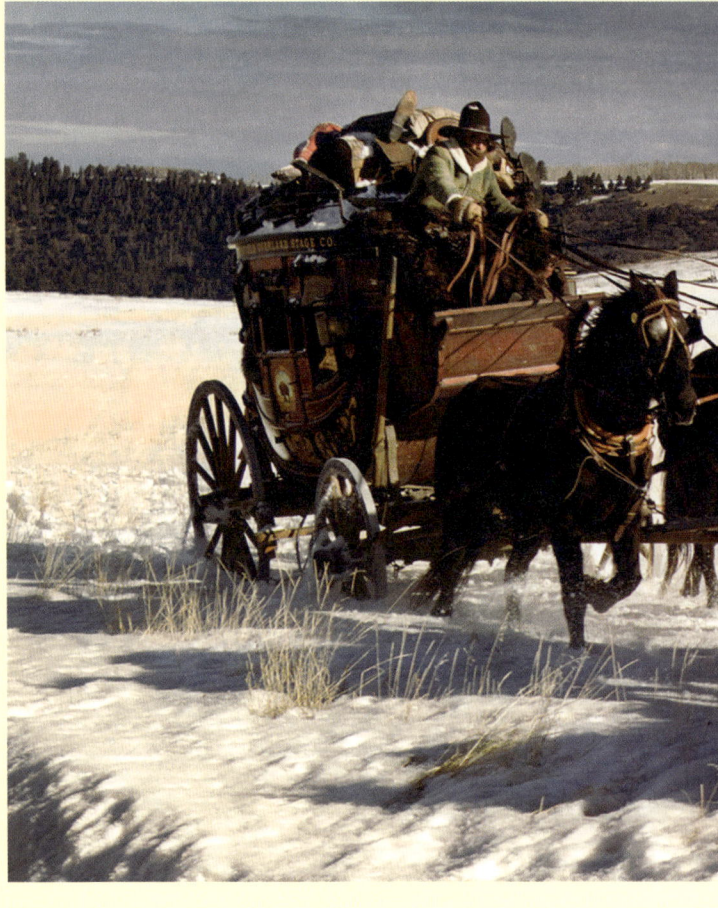

master in his apartment, Tarantino announced, typically unabashed, that he needed the score within a month. But Morricone was about to start work on another movie, the schedule was already tight, and the project QT had pinned his hopes on looked largely dead in the water. As he learned more about the sinister game of Clue that Tarantino had conjured up against the cotton-white landscape of the icy West, though, Morricone began to hear the menacing rumble of a stagecoach approaching in the snow. "*I was like, 'Oh, please, tell me more about that theme that you can't do for me.'*"[1] As the conversation went on, the composer changed his mind: He said he could create an original theme. "*I saw Ennio the very next night,*" Tarantino continues, "*and he grabbed my hand and said, 'I'm going to give you more music.' Ten minutes of music became 16 minutes of music, became 22 minutes*

of music, became 32 minutes of music. He kept getting inspired and adding more to it."[2]

Adding Morricone to the credits of his movie was a dream come true for Tarantino as a filmmaker. In 2015 he unleashed the horses of his *Hateful Eight* across the globe, and with them Morricone's latest composition. Movie fans and music lovers the world over waited with bated breath. They knew the stakes: Would the long-awaited collaboration live up to their expectations? The answer came resoundingly with the very first few notes: It was yet another masterpiece. The man who had waited decades—borrowing existing pieces in the meantime, as if to while away the time, fill a gap, summon up a dream—was finally rewarded by Morricone with one of his last great scores. "*In the past he's used music that I've*

1- Joe Utichi, "Tarantino & Morricone Settle the Score with Hateful Eight," *Deadline*, December 11, 2015.
2- Ibid.

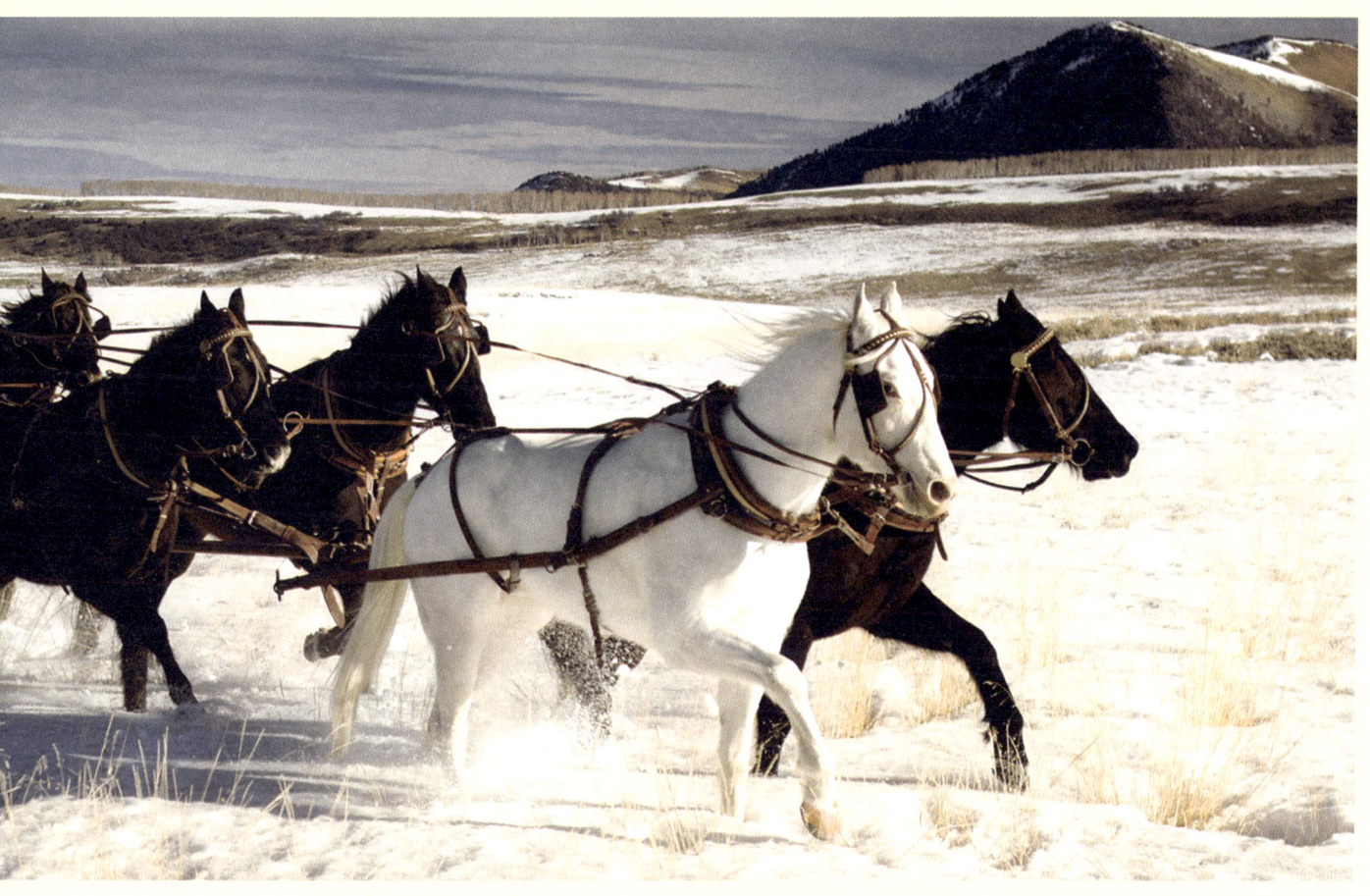

written in a masterful way… Since
he was so generous and showed so
much respect and trust, he deserved
something unique and totally different,
and this score is totally different
from all the other scores I've
composed. It's a symphony dedicated
to Quentin Tarantino,"[3] the Maestro
declared. In the studio shots of them,
Tarantino looks as if he's been given
the best Christmas gift ever as he
stands next to the greatest composer
of film music of all time. "I knew
in my heart it wouldn't be a Western
score," he explained. "I knew he'd
respond to the drama of the story and,
frankly, he gave me a horror movie
score, to some degrees a Giallo score,
complete with a diabolical music box
that comes in from time to time. It
was perfect for the movie."[4]

With this "perfect" soundtrack,
Tarantino effectively secured two

significant successes: First, he finally
fulfilled his ambition of collaborating
with the legendary Italian, and
second, he helped Morricone win his
first Oscar. However outrageous it may
seem, apart from the Honorary Oscar
the Academy awarded him in 2007,
in recognition no doubt of the fact
that, in light of the passing years,
they had better honor him before it
was too late, the composer had never
been awarded an Oscar proper. It
took Quentin Tarantino to supply the
opportunity for the Academy to finally
reward Morricone. Perhaps Tarantino's
greatest achievement, then, his finest
homage to film, is this: to have been
able to share this movie with his
idol and go all the way to the top
with him. And yet he did so with great
humility, the humility of the true
fan he has remained ever since the
days he spent roaming the aisles of
Video Archives. •

3- Ibid. • 4- Ibid.

ELVIS PRESLEY

God Save the King

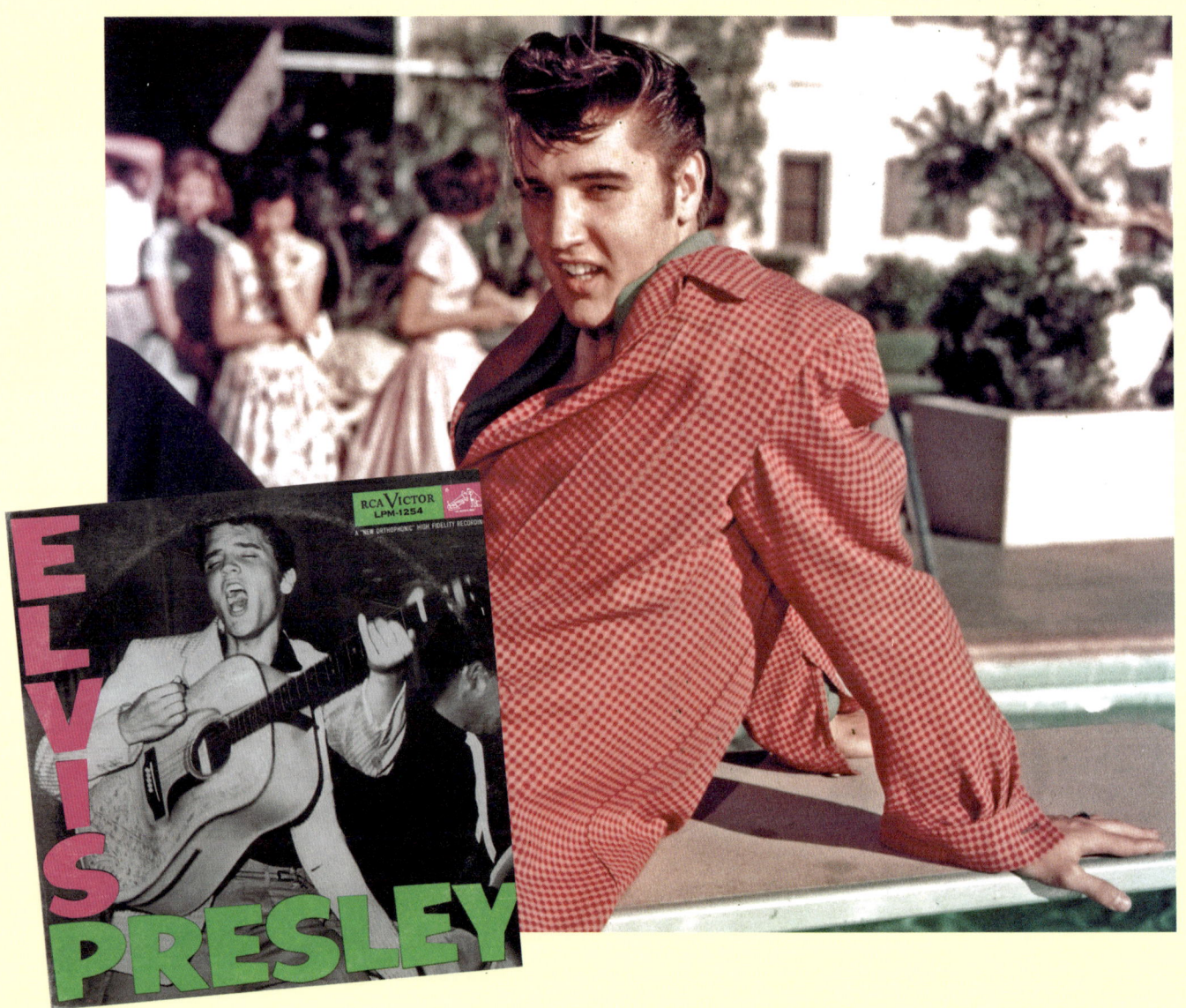

"Clarence, I like you. Always have, always will."

— Elvis Presley

Given that Quentin Tarantino enjoys nothing more than having a really good go at all the greatest American legends, there is no way that Elvis Presley could possibly escape his attention. And if the King occupies a particularly special place in Tarantino's heart, he obviously has to occupy every bit as big a space in our little record store.

"*I was into fifties rock 'n' roll*," Tarantino recalls.[1] The eighties saw the future filmmaker adopt a rockabilly devil look and strut around, by his own admission, dressed like his idol. Tarantino was desperately trying to break into acting at the time, and on the strength of a simple photo, he managed to land himself a small part—and not just any part, but a part as an Elvis impersonator—in an episode of the very popular sitcom *The Golden Girls*. Years later, on a late-night talk show, Tarantino regaled the audience with this anecdote, his recounting laced with a whole load of gestures and impersonation. "*You will notice, I'm not like the Vegas guy… in the jumpsuit. I'm the Sun Records Elvis*," he was careful to specify.[2] Most importantly, this little cameo (and the juicy residual royalties which came with the episode's numerous rebroadcasts) helped get a new project off the ground, this time with QT on the other side of the camera: *Reservoir Dogs*.

There are abundant references to Elvis Presley in Tarantino's movies—not in the soundtracks, where the King is notable by his absence, but in the core of the movies. The earliest is *My Best Friend's Birthday*, the very first movie the director made, back in 1987, which was shot in 16mm and in black and white, with whatever means he had available and the help of his coworkers at Video Archives. Tarantino, as a character named Clarence, delivered one of those tirades he does so well: "*I mean,*

he is rockabilly: mean, surly, nasty, rude. In that movie he couldn't give a fuck about anything except rockin' and rollin', livin' fast, dyin' young, and leaving a good corpse… I'd watch that hillbilly and I'd want to be him so bad. Elvis looked good. I'm no fag, but Elvis was good lookin'. He was fuckin' prettier than most women. I always said if ever I had to fuck a guy… I mean, had to cuz my life depended on it, I'd fuck Elvis." If this excerpt seems familiar, it's because it found its way into the script of *True Romance*, which Tarantino placed in the expert hands of director Tony Scott, and which *My Best Friend's Birthday* anticipates in many ways.

Of all the films in Quentin Tarantino's (extended) universe, it's definitely in *True Romance* that Elvis's influence comes across most clearly. In his

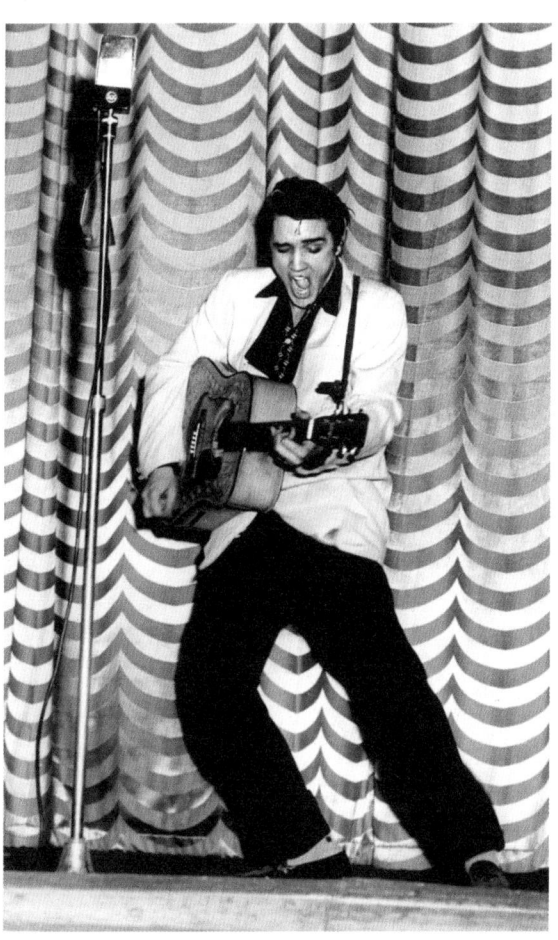

1– Quentin Tarantino, *Cinema Speculation* (Harper, 2022).
2– "Quentin Tarantino Reveals How *The Golden Girls* Helped Get *Reservoir Dogs* Made," *The Tonight Show Starring Jimmy Fallon*, January 9, 2020.

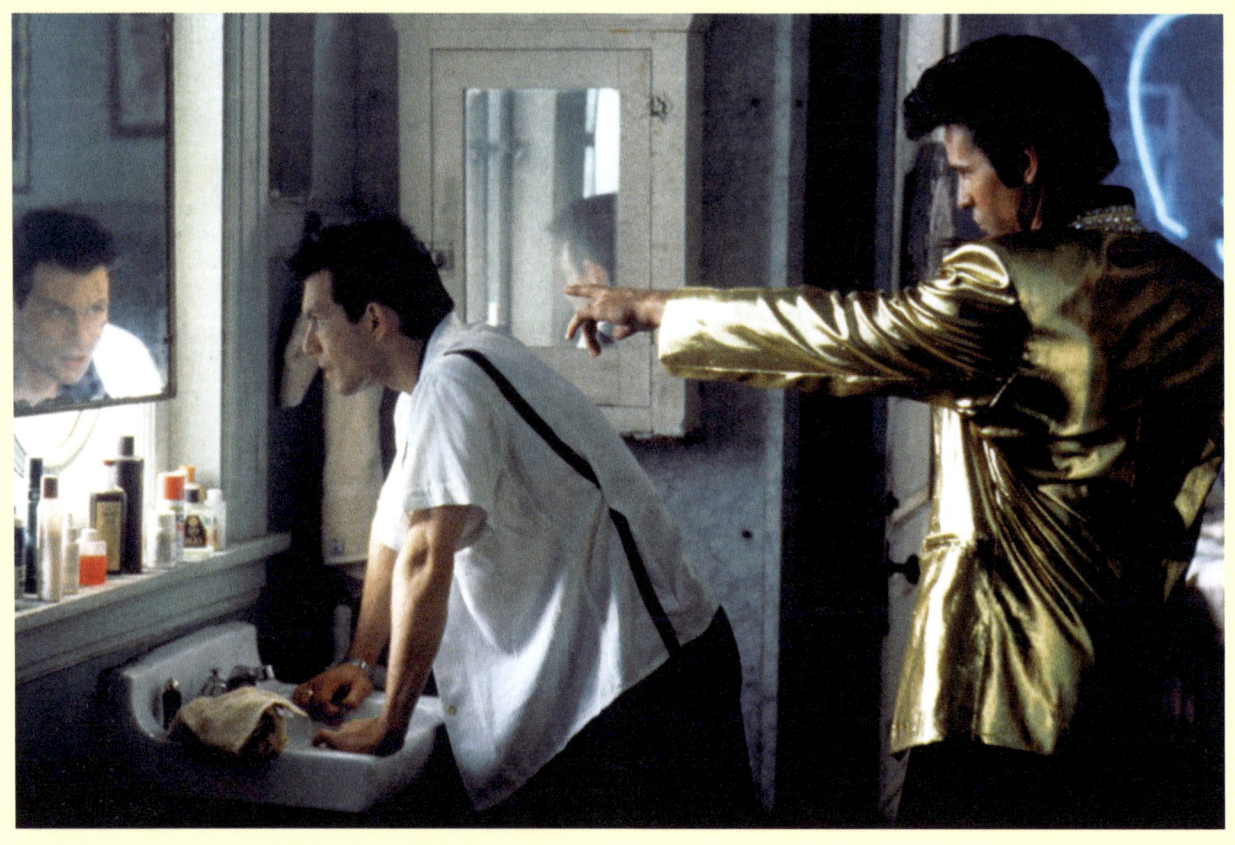

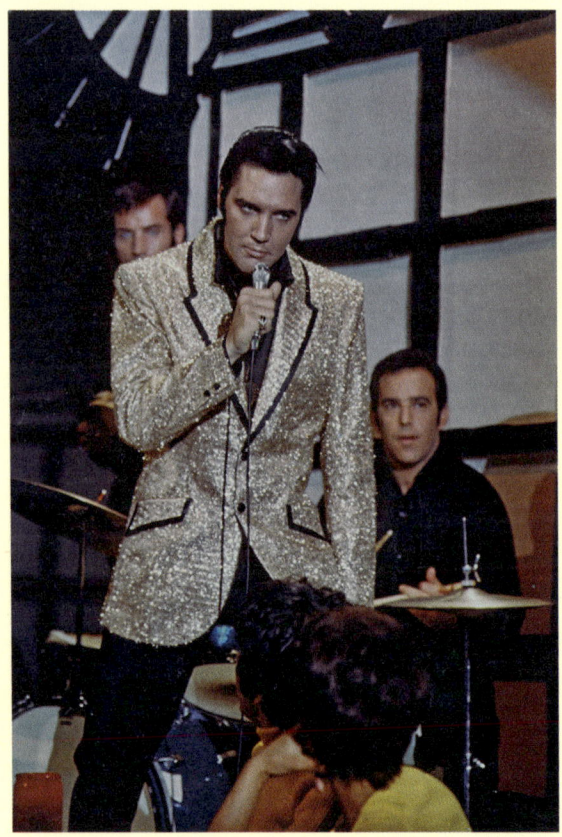

screenplay Tarantino even allows
himself the luxury of resurrecting
the King, played in the movie by
Val Kilmer, whose features we never
completely see. But the silhouette,
the smooth voice, the languid rhythm
and the gold jacket don't leave room
for any doubt. The star pays Clarence
a couple of visits from the other
side, in the privacy of the bathroom,
guiding our hero in his quest like
a mentor. Preoccupied with thoughts
of Drexl, Alabama's pimp, the young
man asks himself what Elvis Presley
would do. "*I'd kill him,*" the King
whispers in his ear. Has Clarence
completely lost his mind? Can anyone
with a shred of common sense take
Elvis Presley as their moral compass,
their guiding master, their religion?
Well, if you're going to be haunted
by anyone, it might as well be by the
King himself. As Tarantino remembers,
"*When I was young, I used to think
Elvis was the voice of truth. I don't
know what that means, but his voice…*

shit man, it sounded so fucking pure."
For the director, there was something
holy about the Elvis Presley of the
early days. "*Forget the Vegas period,*"
he goes on. "*If you really love Elvis,
you're ashamed of that man in Vegas.
You feel like he let you down. The
hillbilly cat never let you down.*"[3]
As always with Tarantino, the sacred
and the commonplace are never very
far apart: Modern legend that he is—
a symbol of American excess and a
mythic figure in a culture of desire
and consumption—Elvis Presley was
bound to heed the call when it came,
even if it meant coming back as
a ghost to haunt the bathroom. Of
course the King's influence is also
evident in other little touches in
True Romance, reminding us of the
movie's guiding force: in the white
bust Alabama brings down on Virgil's
head, for instance, and in the name
the lovers give their son in homage to
the king of rock 'n' roll.

We narrowly miss an encounter with
Elvis in *Pulp Fiction*, in a scene
which was cut from the movie in the
final edit. When Vincent Vega turns
up at the Wallaces' house to take
his boss's wife Mia out to dinner,
she originally greets him by turning
a little camcorder on him and
conducting an impromptu interview:
"*My theory is that when it comes
to important subjects, there's only
two ways a person can answer. Which
way they choose tells you who that
person is. For instance, there's only
two kinds of people in the world,
Beatles people and Elvis people. Now
Beatles people can like Elvis. And
Elvis people can like the Beatles.
But nobody likes them both equally.
Somewhere you have to make a choice.
And that choice tells you who you
are.*" Looking Vincent up and down, she
concludes: "*Well, now, obviously I'm
not going to ask you that one. Because
you're definitely an Elvis man.*" By the
same token, there's no need to ask
which kind of person Quentin Tarantino
is.

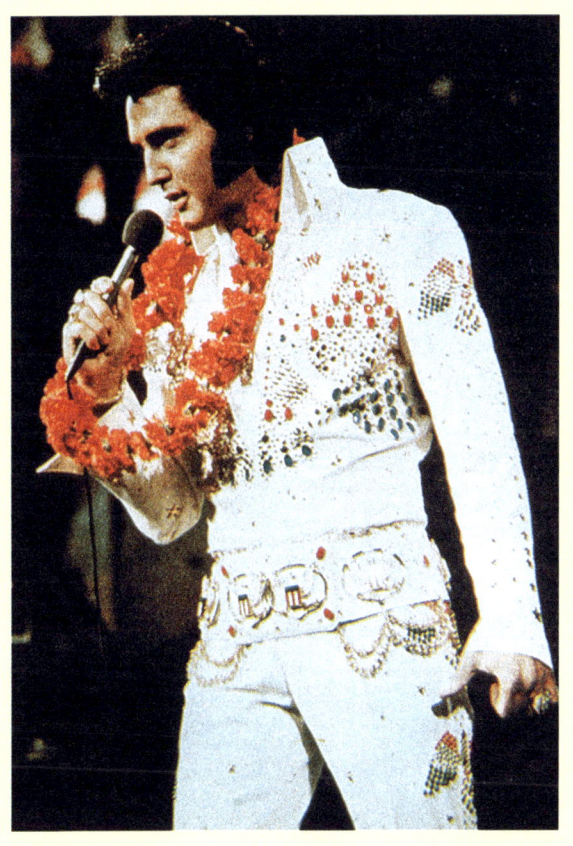

On another note, Elvis could well
be the key to one of the best-kept
secrets in Tarantino's world… What
exactly is inside that mysterious
briefcase in *Pulp Fiction*? We don't
know anything about the brown attaché
case the gangster Marsellus Wallace
sets such great store by, except that
whatever's inside dazzles and amazes
anyone who so much as glances at it.
Something gold, clearly, but that
doesn't get us very far. Unless, of
course… This MacGuffin will doubtless
long continue to prompt outlandish
theories of all kinds, but for a
few movie buffs, the answer couldn't
be more obvious: The case contains
nothing less than Elvis Presley's
gold suit. Careful not to add to the
mystery, Tarantino simply says the
case contains whatever viewers would
like it to contain. Well, then, as far
as we're concerned, there's no doubt
about it. •

3- Michael Bonner, "Quentin Tarantino Chooses His 10 Favourite Records," *Uncut*, August 2019.

RZA

Shaolin Ghetto Sound

It's the summer of 1995. The sweltering heat that hangs over the Big Apple finds its suffocating way onto the avenues of Manhattan, and New Yorkers protect themselves from the oppressive sun by covering their heads with the latest edition of *The New York Times*. The heat is reminiscent of Spike Lee's *Do the Right Thing*. The only thing missing is a throng of kids frolicking in jets of spray from the water hydrants, as captured in so many iconic images of New York in the seventies. The airwaves are dominated by Coolio's "Gangsta's Paradise" and Soundgarden's "Black Hole Sun." The sound that has been drilling into everyone's ears for the last year and a half in the city that never sleeps, however, has nothing to do with the present state of affairs, but harks back to the chilly days of November 1993.

Happy to stand on its own and never reluctant to step outside the mainstream, New York City vibrates to the rhythms of the Wu-Tang Clan. The group's first album, which came out in 1993, propelled them to fame and would redefine East Coast rap for decades. Behind everything was one man who steered the band from Staten Island like a conductor with his baton: Robert Fitzgerald Diggs, known as RZA, who shaped the sound of the Wu-Tang Clan and of all the solo albums of its various members which followed in the wake of that first album's phenomenal success. With its somber pianos, nervy violins, heavy beats, loops that get into your head, fragments of soul, and disturbing atmosphere, this sound sprang straight from the rough streets

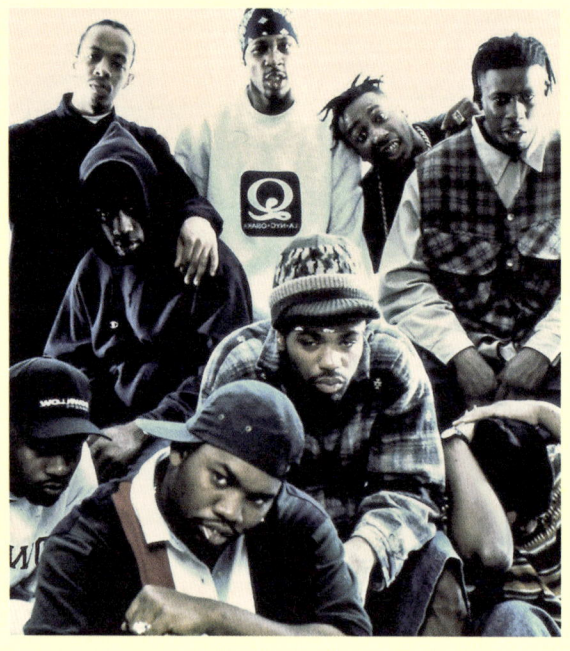

of New York—the ones that aren't included in the tourist guidebooks. It was so successful that it traveled beyond the rap world and became a real pop phenomenon, one which saw RZA collaborating on a magnificent remix of "Say What You Want (All Day, Every Day)" with the Scottish rock band Texas and their lead singer Sharleen Spiteri.

Steeped in the imagery of Hong Kong kung fu movies, the Wu-Tang Clan and RZA developed an entire world of their own which soon caught the eye of two movie directors… Jim Jarmusch, who was a distinguished connoisseur, a lover of rap, and a New Yorker through and through, was the first to enlist their help. In 1999 the group composed the original soundtrack for his film *Ghost Dog: The Way of the Samurai*, which is now forever linked with the momentous shift into the year 2000. Spare, radical, and hypnotic, the soundtrack gets to the very essence of the movie, and anyone who listens to it, headphones clamped on their head, will see themselves as Ghost Dog, played by a silent Forest Whitaker, pounding the sidewalks of their town, no matter where it is. A few years later, RZA was back, this time joining the credits for Tarantino's latest movie, the eagerly awaited *Kill Bill*. The Wu-Tang Clan nation was at its height, and an encounter between RZA, a huge fan of Asian film, and the director of *Reservoir Dogs* seemed inevitable. But they had to wait for the right project to come along, a movie in which RZA's distinctive soundscape and Quentin Tarantino's obsessive universe could be perfectly combined.

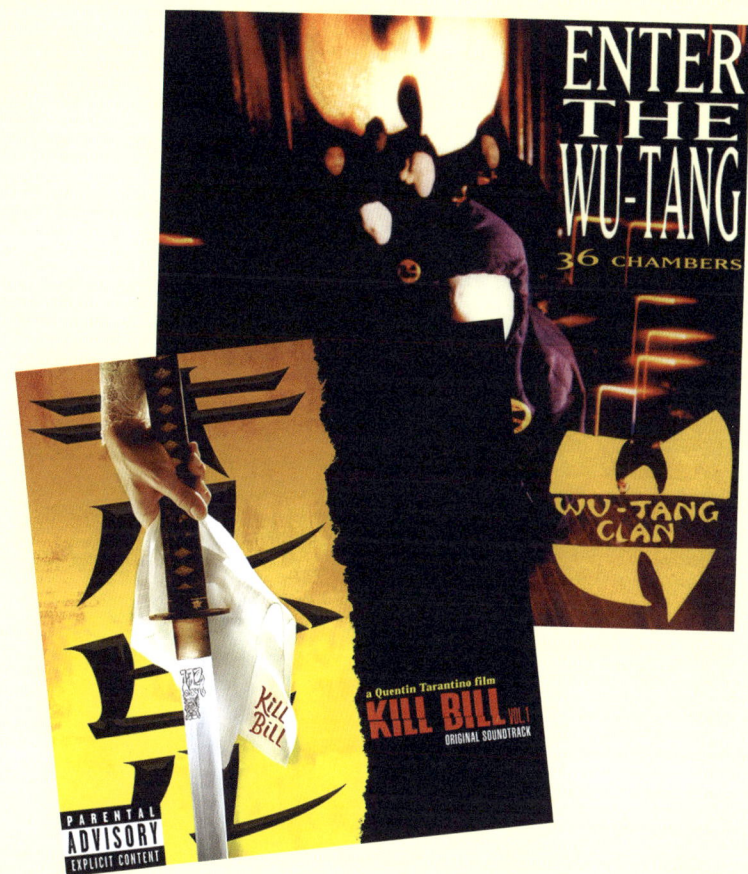

Mostly Tarantino's movies make use of existing music, comfortably adopting a piecemeal approach and selecting pieces as if from a jukebox. Original compositions are rare enough in his filmography to deserve special mention. In his quest for the ideal track list for his movie, Tarantino turned to the practice of collage, which was already a key element in his filmmaking. The musical equivalent was already there… In the world of rap and hip-hop, sampling—drawing pieces from a mass of references from every kind of music and even film—had become widespread in the eighties. Quentin Tarantino was bound to be attracted to this art of piecing references together in a musical jigsaw puzzle, since it so closely mirrored the approach he took in his filmmaking: sampling, combining radically different influences, incorporating a wide variety of diverse references. *Kill Bill* was a textbook case, pushing this art to the absolute limit and beyond.

The original score Tarantino and RZA worked on together inevitably had something of the *Ghost Dog* soundtrack to it, given that the sound RZA creates is so distinctive. In the

space of just a handful of tracks, some only a few seconds long, it lent *Kill Bill* a character which was very different from Tarantino's other films. The two men also worked hand in hand on the process of creating the soundtrack as a whole. For RZA, who is a huge movie buff, *Kill Bill* was in some ways like film school, with Quentin Tarantino as a mentor. "*He's also a music lover,*" he says. "*We all know that; you can tell in his films. He's actually a music producer who doesn't know how to use the equipment. And I was a director who didn't know the craft. And the goal was to exchange this knowledge with each other.*"[1] QT perhaps deliberately emphasizes the interconnection between their parallel worlds further in volume two by including a monologue from the movie *Shogun Assassin* which RZA used in 1995 to introduce the *Liquid Swords* album he produced for his cousin, Wu-Tang member GZA. These days we would describe this as "meta"; in 2003, we would have just said, "Motherfucking Wu-Tang!" •

1- Perri Nemiroff, "'Cut Throat City': The RZA Explains How Working with Quentin Tarantino Became His Film School," *Collider*, August 21, 2020.

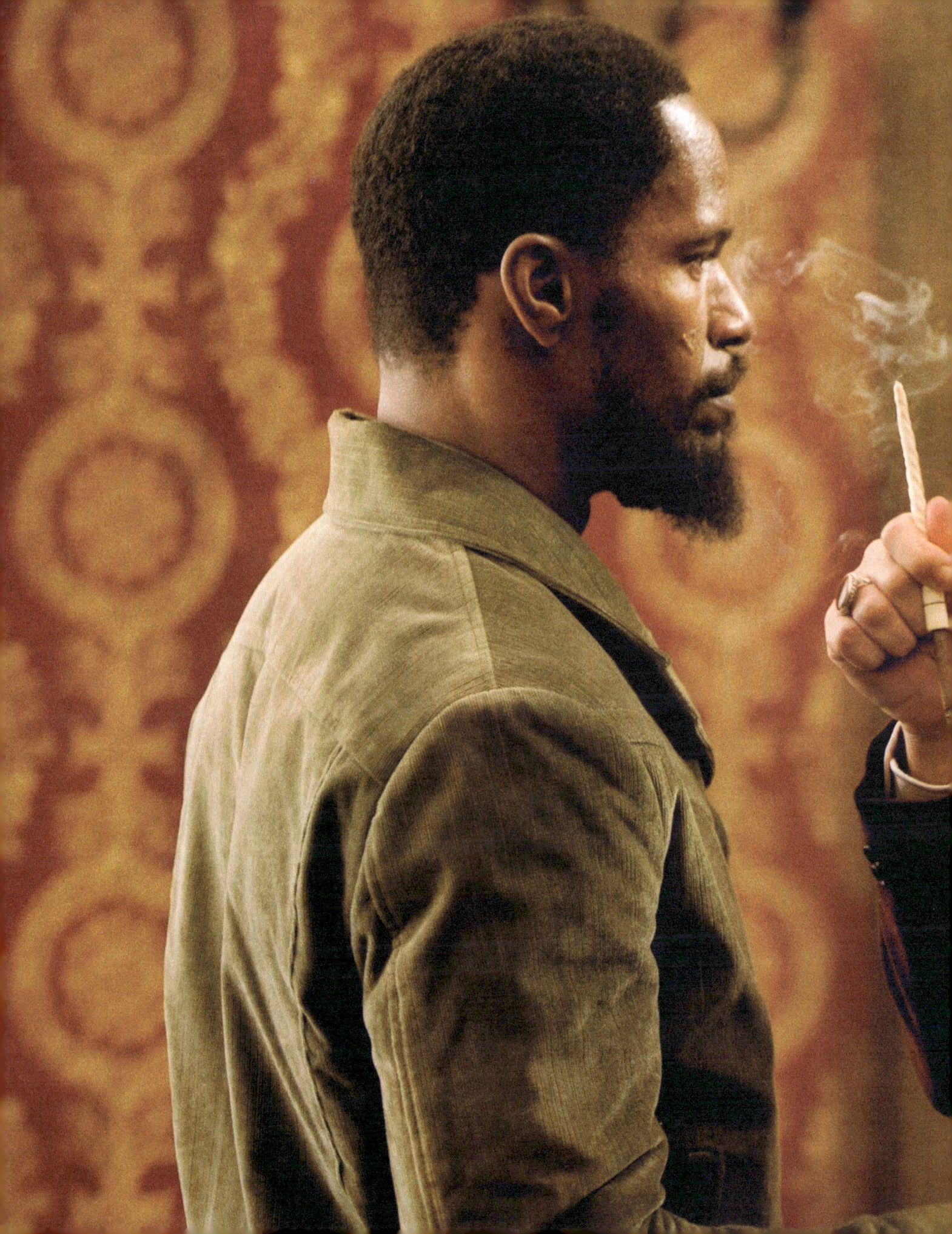

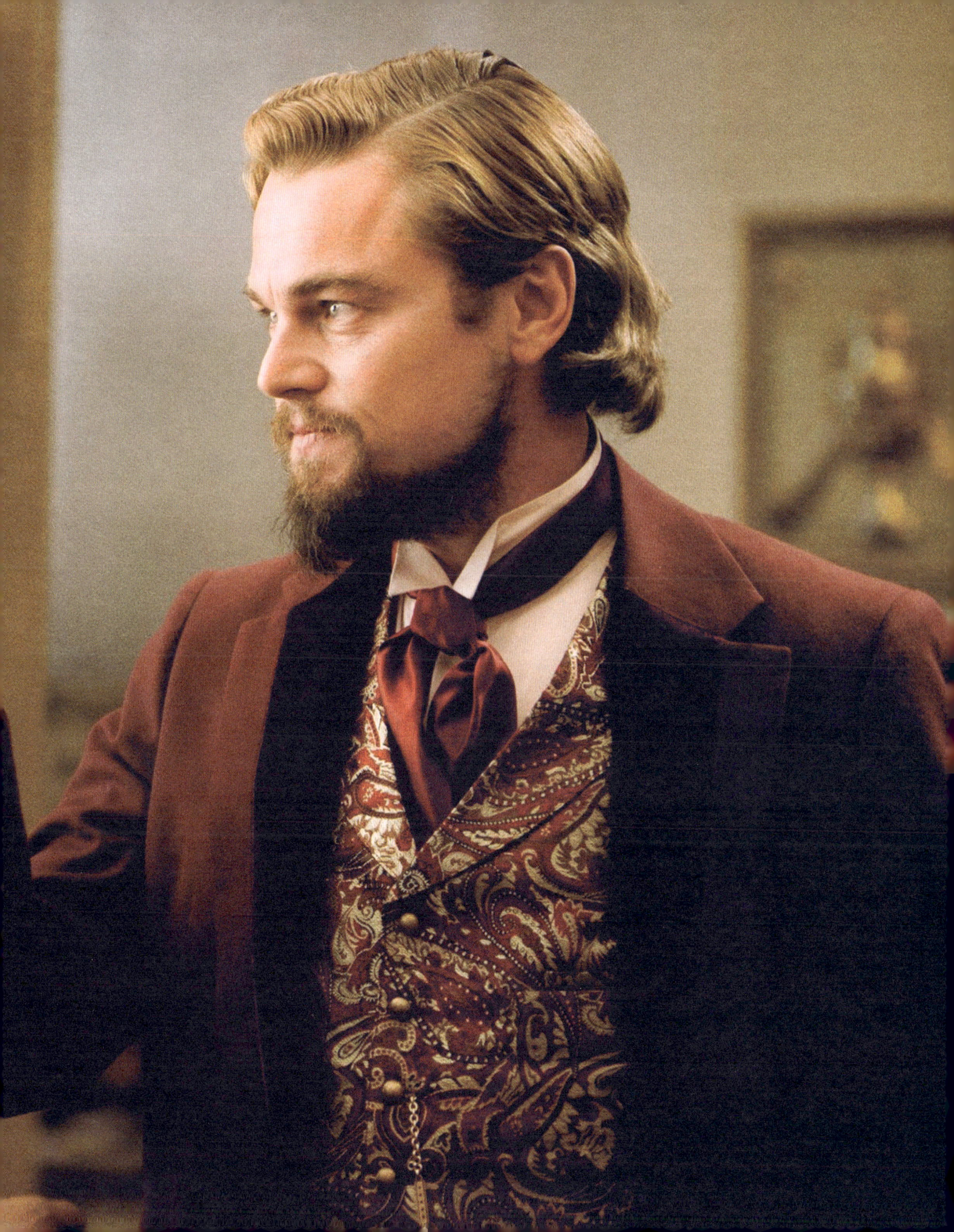

VIII
AT THE MOVIES

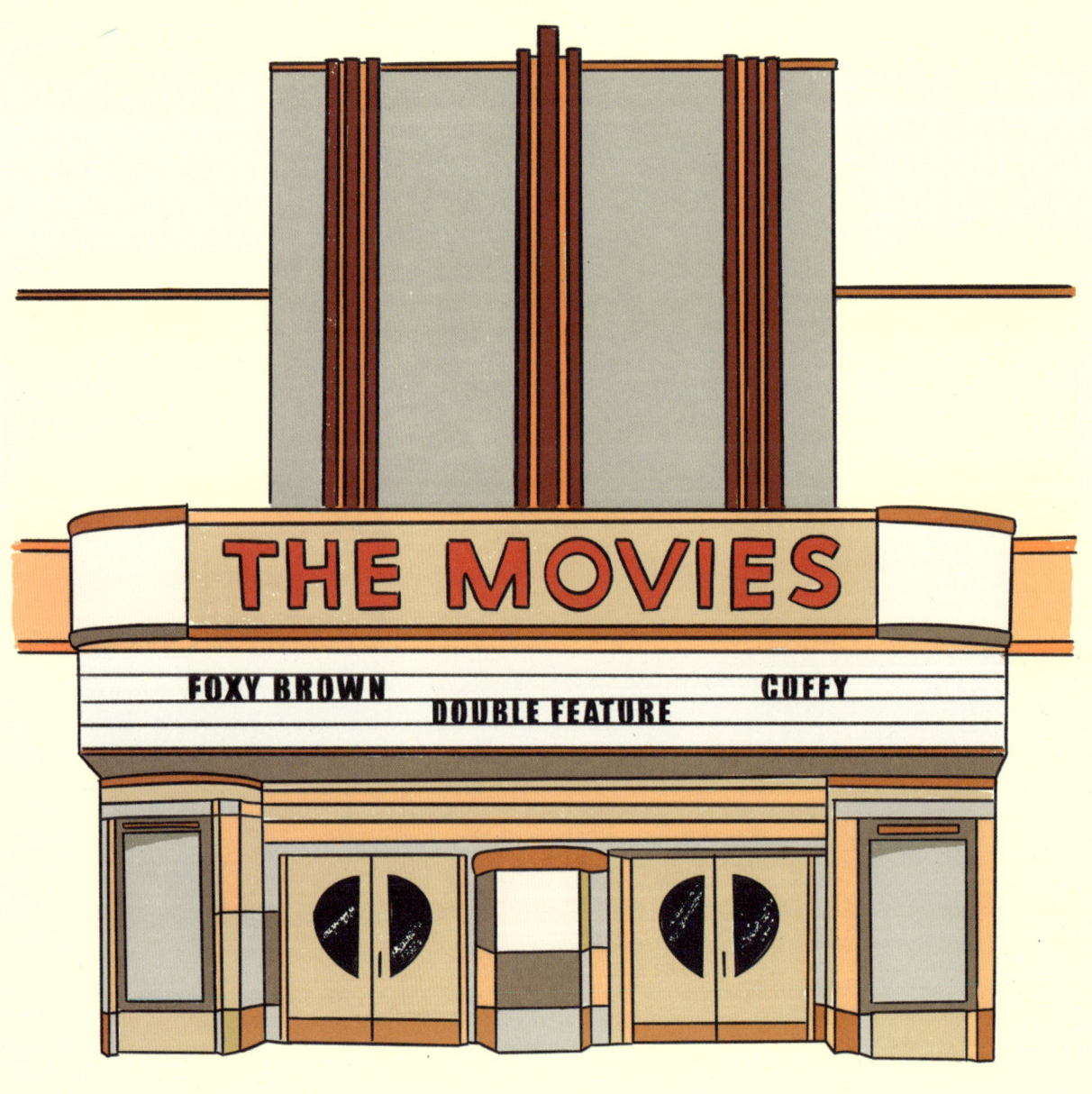

TARANTINO TOWN CINEMA
2301 R. DALTON BLVD.
ALL PROGRAMS PRESENTED ON 35 MM FILM!

Are you thinking you've already had your fill of movies from our video store? Well, you can't leave Tarantino Town without catching a film at the local theater. Renting a video or two is all well and good, but nothing beats a screening in a movie theater: getting a ticket at the desk, deciding where to sit, settling down into your seat… And then, as the lights go down, the magic begins.

Of course we can rewatch our favorite movies as many times as we like from the comfort of the couch, on video cassettes that have been carefully rewound, but there isn't a television set in the world that can substitute for the collective experience of a live screening. Quentin Tarantino knows this full well, having tirelessly worked his way around the movie theaters of Los Angeles. He's even come to the rescue of one or two of them, to ensure that the city doesn't lose this extra little bit of soul which makes it what it is. Having spent a lifetime sitting in the dark, as it were, in these magical places, feeding his insatiable appetite and developing an encyclopedic knowledge of film, the director is a passionate advocate of theater-going. *"You decide to go to see a film… and you buy a ticket, and you sit down, and you have an experience—you have an experience with a bunch of strangers. And at that moment, once the movie gets going, once the lights are down, you become a collective,"* he says. *"And… when you have a good experience, those are the things that stay in your mind and that you remember for the rest of your life, and they become indelible snapshots."*[1] So pick up a copy of the program in the foyer and enjoy a few carefully selected Tarantino classics. It might be an exploitation film, or it might be an art house movie: Our programming mashes everything up freely, just like the filmmaker's work. The popcorn is on the house, and you can follow it up with a piece of pie at the diner around the corner while you unpack the movie. You might be too lost in thought to touch your dessert, but head on down there anyway with our compliments: Show your ticket and you'll get fifteen percent off your bill. Enjoy the movie!

1 Quentin Tarantino, *The Late Show with Stephen Colbert*, CBS, November 9, 2021.

FASTER, PUSSYCAT! KILL! KILL!

Bad Girls

Ladies and gentlemen, welcome to violence: the word and the act. While violence cloaks itself in a plethora of disguises, its favorite mantle still remains… sex. Violence devours all it touches, its voracious appetite rarely fulfilled. Yet violence doesn't only destroy, it creates and molds as well. Let's examine closely, then, this dangerously evil creation, this new breed encased and contained within the supple skin of woman. The softness is there, the unmistakable smell of female, the surface shiny and silken, the body yielding yet wanton. But a word of caution: Handle with care, and don't drop your guard. This rapacious new breed prowls both alone and in packs, operating at any level, anytime, anywhere, and with anybody. Who are they? One might be your secretary, your doctor's receptionist, or a dancer in a go-go club…

Couched in suitably sensationalist terms, the voice-over at the beginning of the film effectively alerts us to what is in store. But does this somewhat paranoid preamble really constitute a warning? Surely not: Russ Meyer is not worried about the moral integrity of his viewers. Quite the opposite—he's whetting their appetites with a thinly disguised promise of things to come. Does depravity lurk under modern woman's silken skin and sweet perfume? It's an idea which could be construed as misogynistic, were it not for the sheer campy flamboyance of the violence perpetrated by these women, this "new breed" of beings, to whom we have yet to succumb. Alternately decried for objectifying the female body by exposing it to viewers' leering eyes and reclaimed as a genuine embodiment of feminism, *Faster, Pussycat! Kill! Kill!* revels gleefully in its contradictions. Hovering somewhere between the snarling anger of a riot grrrl and the dominating crack of a whip-wielding Bettie Page, *Faster, Pussycat! Kill! Kill!* claims an absolute right to depravity and nastiness.

Our heroines, three psychotic go-go girls, are driving at breakneck speed across the Mojave Desert, looking for trouble. Varla, Billie, and Rosie have hung up their sequined shorts and left the club where we watched them dance to the feverish appreciation of local

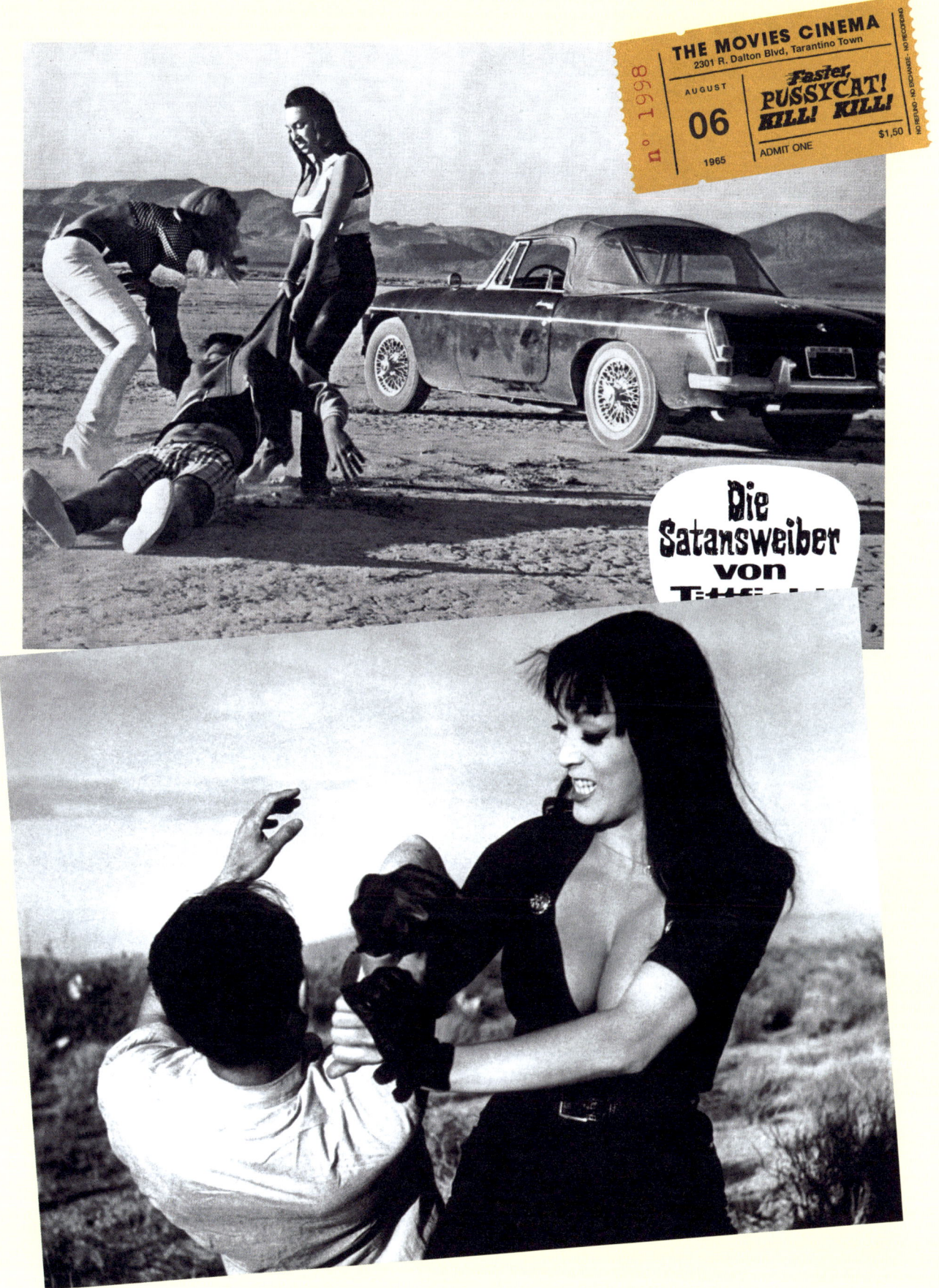

THE MOVIES CINEMA
2301 R. Dalton Blvd, Tarantino Town

n° 1998

AUGUST
06
1965

Faster, PUSSYCAT! KILL! KILL!

ADMIT ONE $1,50

Die Satansweiber von Tittfield

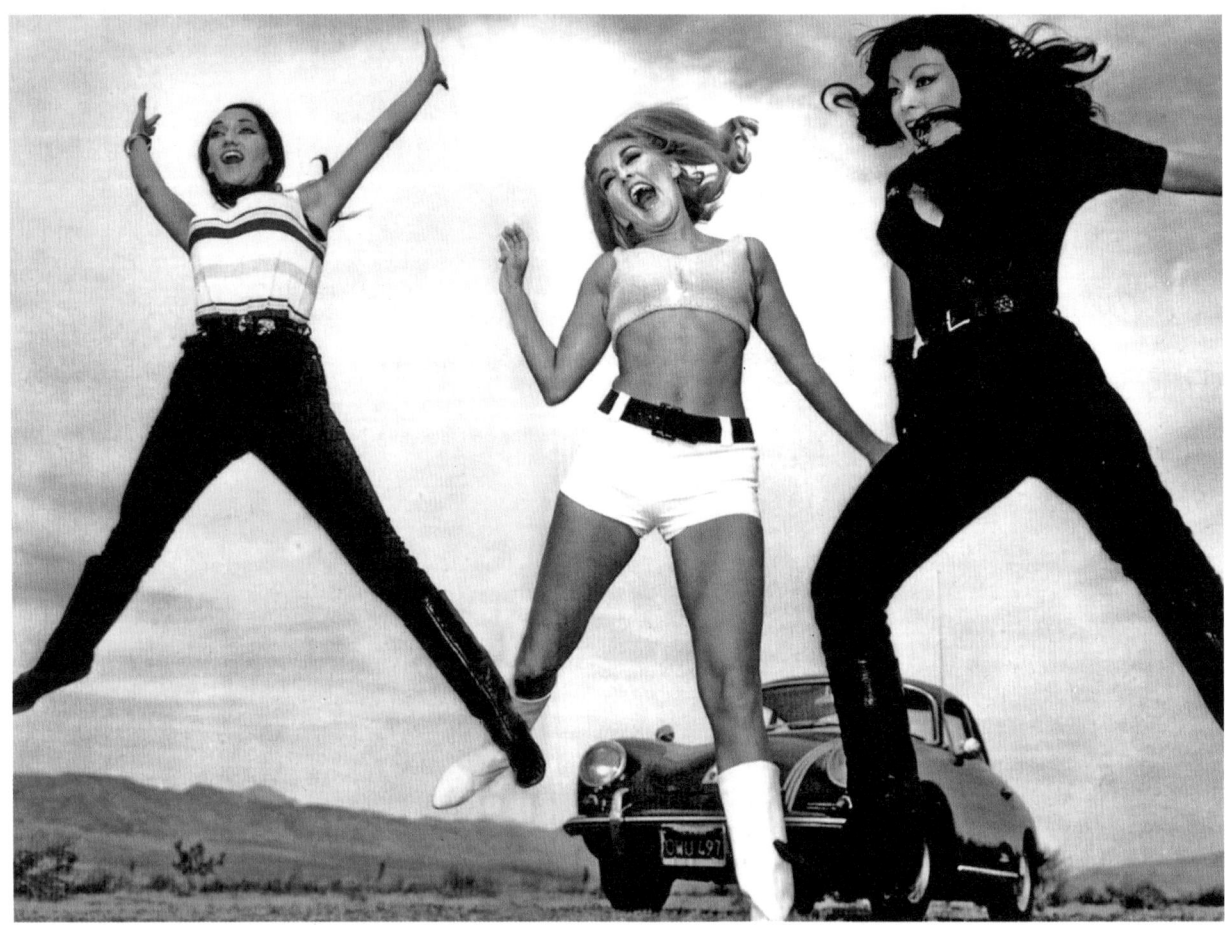

rednecks. Now they are in search of new adventures. Why not embark on a little crime spree, complete with murder and kidnapping? So begins a wild ride, led by the lush Varla (Tura Satana), the most venomous of our three vipers. Dressed from head to toe in black, complete with leather boots and gloves, she looks very much like someone who is not unfamiliar with sadomasochistic practices—and who wouldn't want to get their ass kicked by Tura Satana? On their travels they come across imbecilic, misogynist, and downright depraved men whom they never hesitate to outdo in cruelty. Russ Meyer's gently trashy movie is carried by the sight of these powerful Amazonian women we assume to be bisexual, with their terrifying instincts and voracious carnal appetites, pursuing a criminal chase at full tilt. Creatures like them

could only exist in the outrageous imagination of Meyer, high priest of the nudie, who shoots his sculptural antiheroines in comic-strip black and white, in which anything goes.

Despite its poor showing at the box office in 1965, *Faster, Pussycat! Kill! Kill!* became not only a must-see exploitation film, but also a flagship camp movie, a genre closely linked to queer counterculture, characterized by over-the-top performances and a delight in the grotesque. It's no surprise that director John Waters—who operates on the dirty fringes of film, adores freaks of every kind, and is gloriously queer and depraved to his very core—would be a tireless worshipper of the movie. In his book *Shock Value*, the Baltimore director (and the city's unofficial mayor) declared with customary moderation:

166

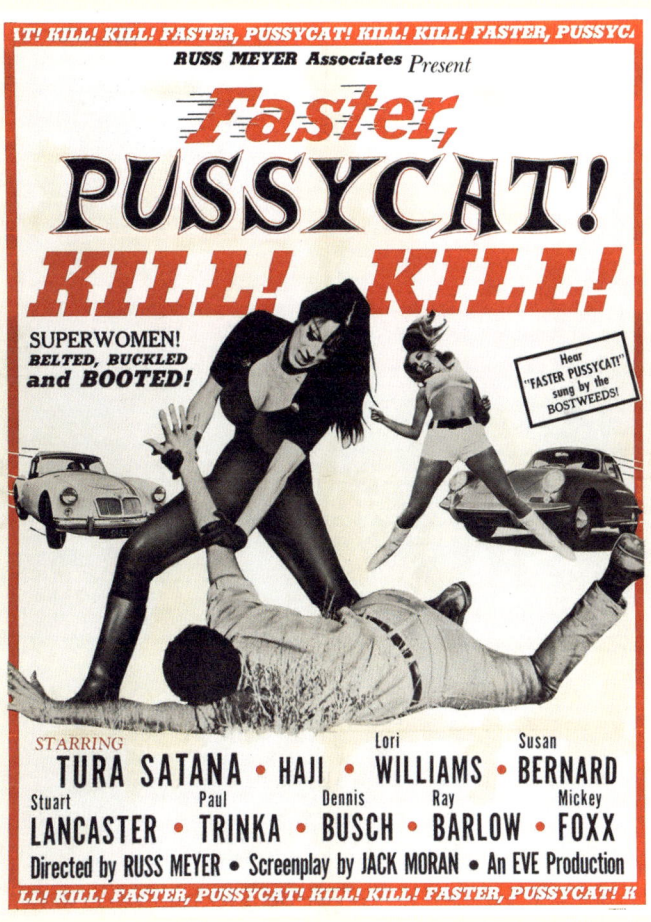

bare hands, is of course the final scene in which the three girlfriends dispatch Stuntman Mike by the side of the road in the middle of nowhere. Though the two films may be separated by time, Meyer's movie is connected to Tarantino's by the cathartic rage that drives the characters. Each in their own way, Varla and the *Death Proof* girls belong to that vast legendary class of angry women, ranging from the *Erinyes,* the goddesses of vengeance in Greek mythology, to the *bakeneko,* the cat-women who exact blind revenge in Japanese movies (in whose company the Bride would certainly be at home), to a number of blaxploitation movie heroines. In an interview, actress Tura Satana described how the part had allowed her to give full vent to the anger she had kept suppressed for far too long during a lifetime of abuse. It is perhaps precisely her expression of this anger that makes a feminist reappropriation of Russ Meyer's classic possible. In an interview before her death, Tarantino paid her a major compliment, saying: "*I would give up five years of my life to work with Tura Satana. She is Japanese, Cheyenne, and something else—awesome.*"[3]

"Faster, Pussycat! Kill! Kill! *is, beyond a doubt, the best movie ever made. It is possibly better than any film that will be made in the future.*" For Waters, Russ Meyer was nothing less than "*the Einstein of sex films.*" He found the characters' over-the-top bodies, unbridled sex drives, and violent tempers endlessly inspiring: "*Russ's nasty 'pussycats' became a 'role model' for all the characters in my productions—especially Divine.*"[1]

Other admirers of Meyer's indomitable pussycats, of course, include Quentin Tarantino, who is such a fan that rumors of a possible remake circulated for a time in the papers.[2] This hardly comes as much of a surprise, given that Tura Satana appears on Shanna's T-shirt in *Death Proof.* Echoing this image of Varla, ready to finish her adversary off with her

Finally, if *Faster, Pussycat! Kill! Kill!* is a fetishistic movie, it's not because of the swathes of naked flesh on show or its incendiary mix of eroticism and violence. It's because the film glorifies some of the greatest American fantasies: abundant feminine curves, roads burned dry by the sun and stretching straight ahead to the horizon, hip-hugging jeans, and gleaming bodywork… To this great panoramic vision of America, the director adds a few elements of his own: mean girls, karate moves, and outfits that are, frankly, indecently revealing. Awesome maniac and leading light of exploitation movies that he is, could Meyer ever be taken seriously as a writer? With a bit of luck, no, never. Blessed are those who depart from the norm! •

1- John Waters, *Shock Value* (Thunder's Mouth Press, 1981). • 2- Liz Smith, *Variety,* January 16, 2008.
3- Mary Kaye Schilling, "The Second Coming," *Entertainment Weekly,* April 16, 2004.

BANDE À PART

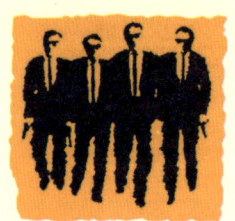
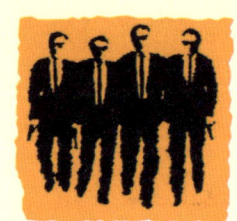

Love and Fighting

Every Tuesday afternoon, between a Spaghetti Western and a film noir classic, our little local movie theater shows off with a bit of art house. Showing this week is a French film.

A quick word of warning! Don't expect any of the stunning Technicolor you saw in *Le Mépris*, with its Mediterranean blue and Godard red: There may still be espadrilles, but in *Bande à part*, or *Band of Outsiders*, they're dragged through the suburbs of Paris and shot in black and white. A loose adaptation of a novel by Dolores Hitchens, *Fools' Gold*, which was published in France as *Pigeon vole* in 1959 as part of Marcel Duhamel's "Black Series," *Bande à part* was born of Godard's desire to turn out a movie quickly and simply, without all the glitz of *Le Mépris*, and perhaps in hopes of drawing his girlfriend, Anna Karina, out of the depression into which she was sinking. "*Le Mépris was shot in color, in CinemaScope, in Italy, with a star and American money,*" he explained. "*The best way for me to change direction was to impose constraints on myself. I couldn't do it any other way. I said to myself: 'I'm going to make* Bande à part *into a little Z movie like one of those American films I like so much.'*"[1]

When it came out in 1964, *Bande à part* was seen as a modest film, because of either its limited means or its limited success. Writing in the columns of *The New Republic* in 1966, the famous movie critic Pauline Kael underlined the paradox: "*Jean-Luc Godard intended to give the public what it wanted. His next film was going to be about a girl and a gun—'A sure-fire story which will sell a lot of tickets.'… He proceeded to make a work of art that sold fewer tickets than ever. What was to be a simple commercial movie about a robbery became* Band of Outsiders."[2] Two boys, a girl, a convertible, and a revolver. Love and fighting, especially fighting. This, in a few disjointed words— as befits Jean-Luc Godard's films— is exactly what his "*little Z movie*" is about.

Two years after *Jules et Jim*, as if in response to François Truffaut—another pillar of the French New Wave, with whom he had a turbulent friendship— Godard had a go at a threesome, setting off Karina with two young jokers, Claude Brasseur and Sami Frey. While Truffaut's movie was a marathon spanning almost two decades, requiring the emotions in it to be sustained over a considerable period, Godard's was a three-day sprint, a race against the clock. What starts out as a love triangle quickly turns into something darker, as the film enters the muddy realm of gangster movies. The two suitors enlist Odile's help in a robbery which reeks of amateurism. Their chaotic preparations soon give way to pure rushing about: The three young characters wander aimlessly

1- Jacques Bensimon, Christian Rasselet, and Pierre Théberge, "Les cravates rouges: Conversation avec Jean-Luc Godard," *Objectif* 65, no. 33, August–September 1965.
2- Pauline Kael, "Godard Among the Gangsters," *The New Republic*, September 10, 1966.

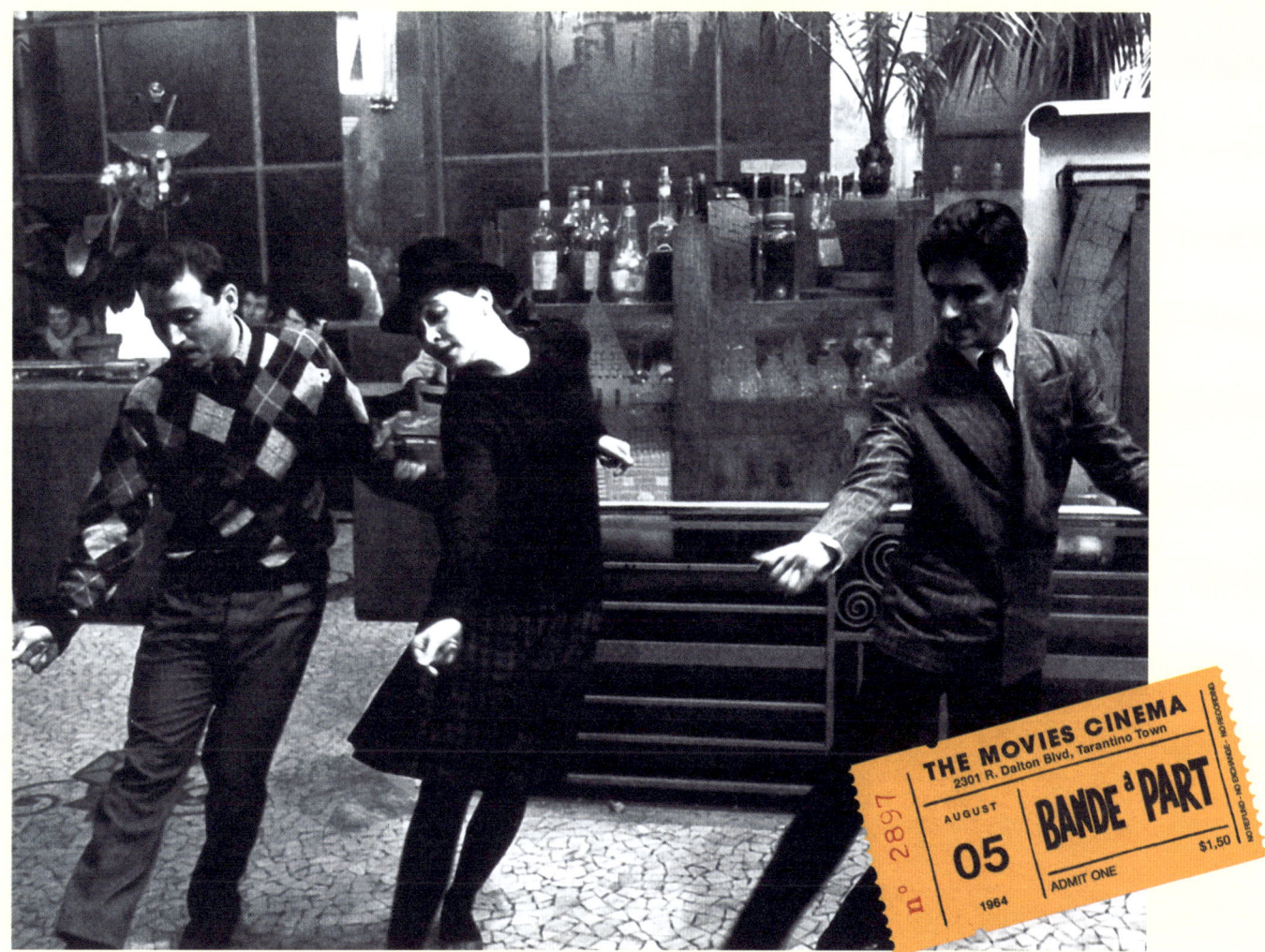

around Paris, from bistros to the metro, waiting for the inevitable fiasco to unfurl.

Stripped of all the complicated intrigues of film noir, *Bande à part* is a movie which happens entirely in gestures, in parentheses, in revealing moments: a game of musical chairs; a minute's silence; a poem by Louis Aragon sung in the metro, at Liberté station; a mad race through the Louvre; and, of course, a few steps of a made-up Madison dance. In her article, Pauline Kael talks about "*the casual way [Jean-Luc Godard] omits mechanical scenes that don't interest him so that the movie is all high points and marvelous 'little things.'*"[3] Kael here puts her finger on exactly what it was

about Godard's movie that would go on to capture the heart of a young movie buff named Quentin Tarantino. "*The one review Pauline Kael wrote that ended up meaning something to me in a big way,*" he recalls, "*was for* Band of Outsiders. *She said it was as if a bunch of movie-mad young French boys had taken a banal American crime novel and translated the poetry that they had read between the lines. It was like, 'That is my aesthetic right there! That's what I hope I can do!'*"[4] Quentin Tarantino shares a taste not just for digressing, going off-topic, with *Bande à part*, but also for smashing up genres. To help them with the famous twist scene in *Pulp Fiction*, Tarantino showed Uma Thurman and John Travolta the Madison dance scene.

3- Ibid.
4- *What She Said: The Art of Pauline Kael*, directed by Rob Garver, 2018.

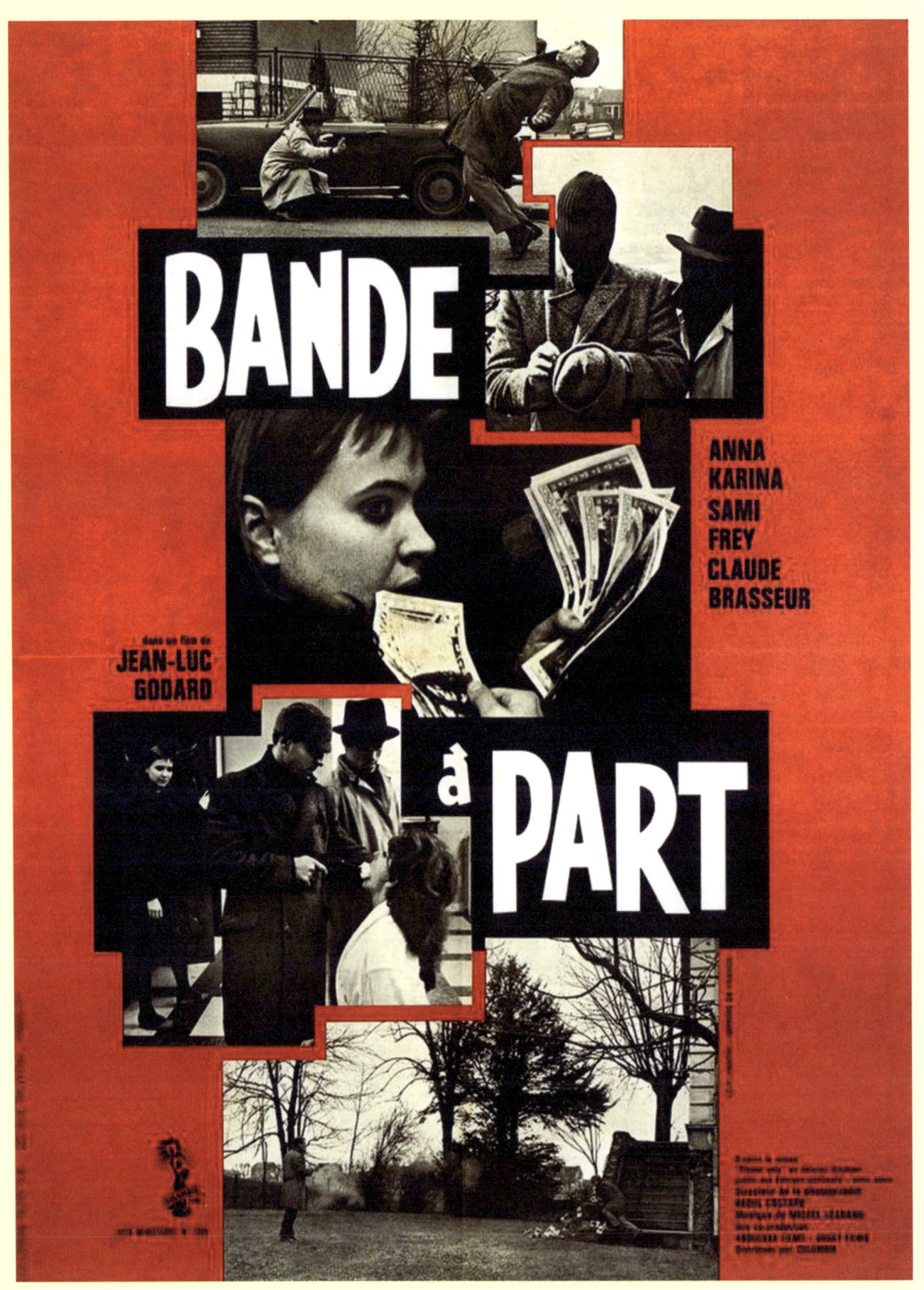

The actress was nervous about dancing opposite her partner, who was perhaps forever the legendary Tony Manero from *Saturday Night Fever* in her mind, and breathed a sigh of relief when she understood that Tarantino wasn't asking her to dance like a professional: "*I brought in the tape of* Band of Outsiders *and showed it to John and Uma as an inspiration of what I was looking for. Not choreographed dance movements, but people enjoying themselves to a jukebox and dancing with exuberance. They're not trained dancers, but in another way they're the best dancers in the world.*"[5] Like a true fan, Tarantino even called his production company "A Band Apart." Godard, for his part, permanently dented Tarantino's great admiration for him by attacking him in an interview, accusing him of borrowing his title without permission or payment. It was an astonishing admonition, given how well-known Godard's position vis-à-vis quotation and reference in his own movies was. As he said, "*For me, all quotations— whether they are pictorial or musical— belong to humanity.*"[6]

If there is one thing that Tarantino definitely shares with the older man, it is precisely this zest for reference, for the endless echoes of works made before him. What Pauline Kael said about Godard could equally well be applied to the young Tarantino's work: "*Godard's sense of the present is dominated by his movie past. This is what makes his movies… seem so new: for they are movies made by a generation bred on movies.*"[7] *Bande à part* is a movie shot through with references, often literary ones, but film ones too—to Chaplin, to Westerns, to B movies, to the French New Wave, and even to Jacques Demy's *Les Parapluies de Cherbourg*, which has similar music. We definitely don't believe it when Odile petulantly declares: "*I hate film.*" If there's one thing our band of outsiders excels in, it's the art of playing to the camera. These are children who dream

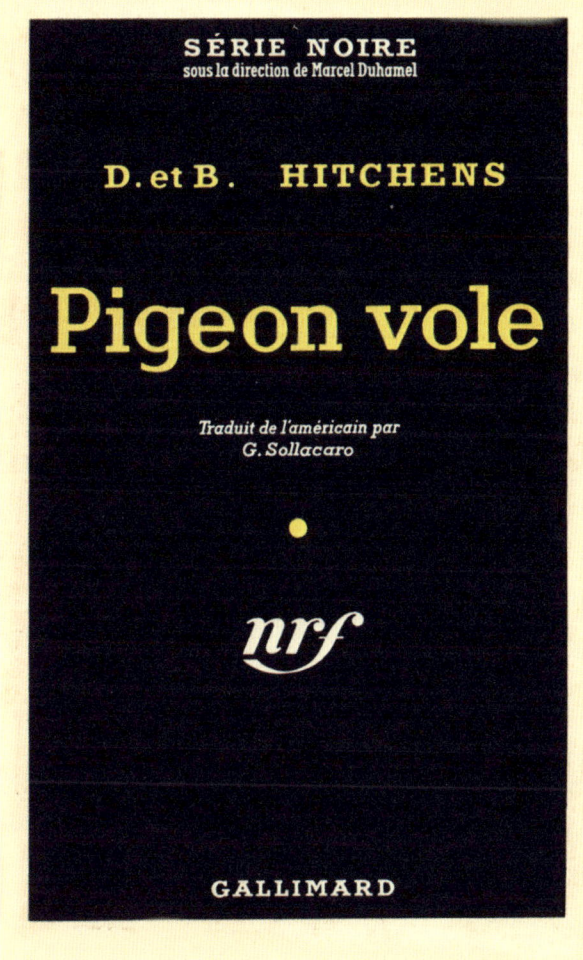

about American movies, who spend their time pretending to be petty film noir heroes and reenacting the death of Billy the Kid in Arthur Penn's *The Left Handed Gun*: Life is a game that is played for anything but real. But their fake shot brings about another, very real one at the end of a duel which proves every bit as fatal as the one between Billy the Kid and Pat Garrett. And while Godard may have wanted to make a little French-style American film and leave it at that, Tarantino, for his part, in some way tried to do the reverse with his first movie, to inject a New Wave feel into a profoundly American genre: "*When I did* Reservoir Dogs*, [I wanted to] do my version of a French New Wave crime film, but kind of go full circle with it, and bring it back with an American vernacular.*"[8] •

5- "Quentin Tarantino's Movie Mixtape," Radio 2, BBC, 2019.
6- "Jean-Luc Godard Press Conference," *Cahiers du cinéma*, no. 433, June 1990.
7- Pauline Kael, "Godard Among the Gangsters," *The New Republic*, September 10, 1966.
8- "Le Journal de 13 heures," Antenne 2, September 2, 1992.

VANISHING POINT

The Time You Have

1969 Dennis Hopper brought the sixties to a close with a monument to counterculture, the thundering *Easy Rider*. Several exceptional movies were to spring from this fertile ground, of which Richard C. Sarafian's *Vanishing Point* (1971) was by no means the least legendary. Based on a screenplay by Cuban writer Guillermo Cabrera Infante (under the pseudonym Guillermo Cain), *Vanishing Point* is a road movie with metaphysical leanings, a movie in which man himself is only passing through.

Fascinated by movement and speed, Sarafian was inspired by the writings of German theorist Carl Jacobi and his notion of elliptical functions. For the director, mankind is only passing through, at different speeds and on the way to different, unknown worlds. This idea may seem rather convoluted, but in the light of this almost magical angle, the movie gains an unexpected

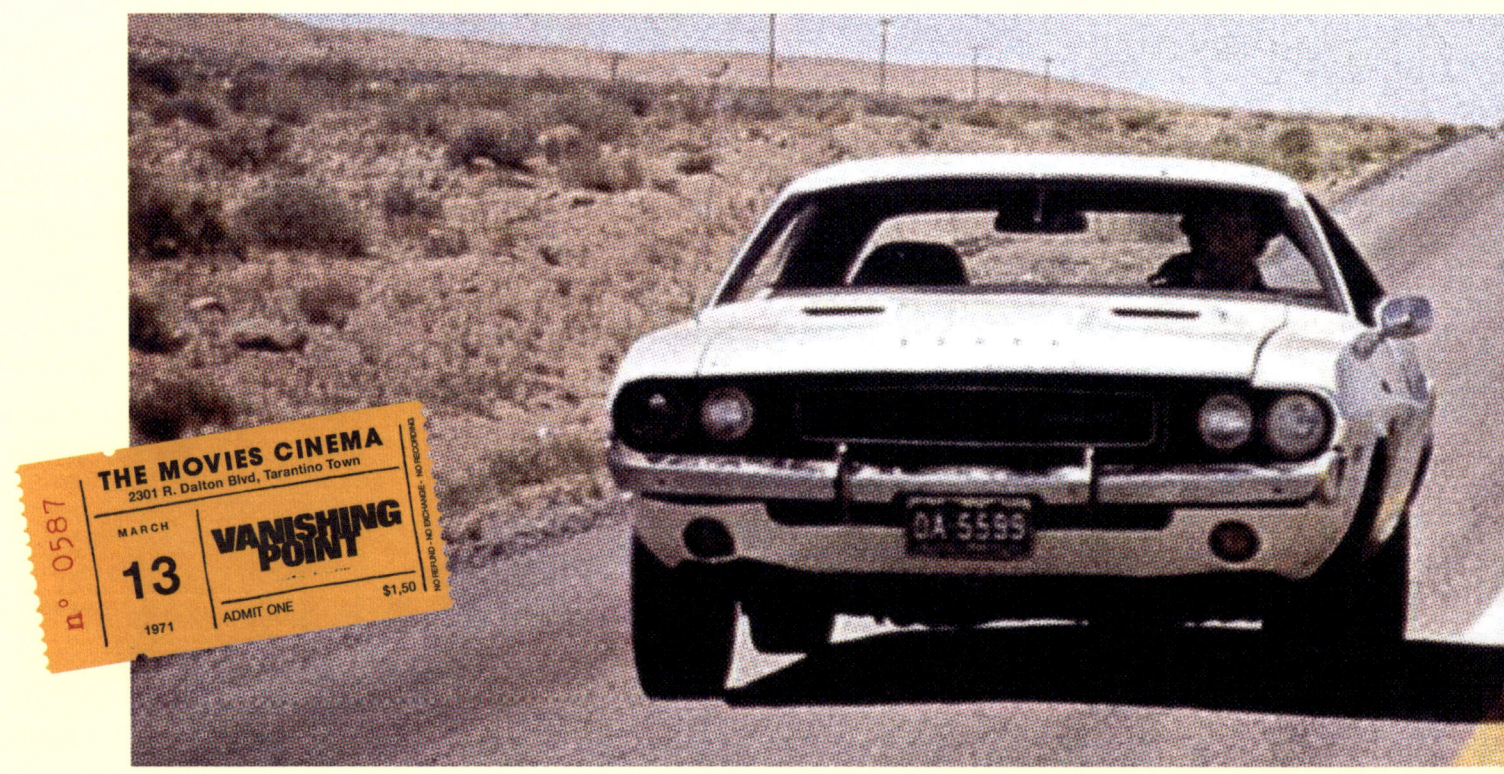

depth… Richard Sarafian has been called "*the most misunderstood writer in Hollywood.*"[1] The director wants to do nothing less than jump right into the engine, into the core of speed itself in order to experience it to the max, telling the story of a man who goes so fast that he spirals completely out of control, defying the laws of both men and physics. The movie's title says as much, describing as it does that extreme point of convergence, far in the horizon, where sky and earth merge. To make the movie, Sarafian traveled some ten thousand miles across the United States, crisscrossing the country's roads in search of locations and the road his hero would travel. All this traveling the length and breadth of the country might have made him hallucinate like his character, haunted by images from the past. Kowalski has powered through the previous decade at breakneck speed: An ex-cop with integrity, a Vietnam veteran, a race car driver, he is now adrift, lost in his memories, heading full tilt into the great nowhere at the wheel of a white Dodge Challenger which is destined to become legendary. As we cannot fail to notice, this is the same race car as the one that appears in *Death Proof*— the one that Quentin Tarantino's band of girlfriends is obsessed with, in homage to Sarafian's movie.

Vanishing Point came to epitomize Americana. The movie had its finger firmly on the nation's pulse, supplying it with a cross between a race and a chase into the West. In this modernized, motorized Western, the cowboys have run off and given way to hippies. Stretches of asphalt have replaced the untamable landscapes of America, giving the youth of the day a new style of American legend for their time, in which the infinite roads lend material form to an ideal of freedom. For this disenchanted generation, cars are the ultimate bastions of freedom, and speed is the ultimate life force, however close it may be to death. On the road, Kowalski comes across a number of marginal characters, the last remaining vestiges of the America of the days

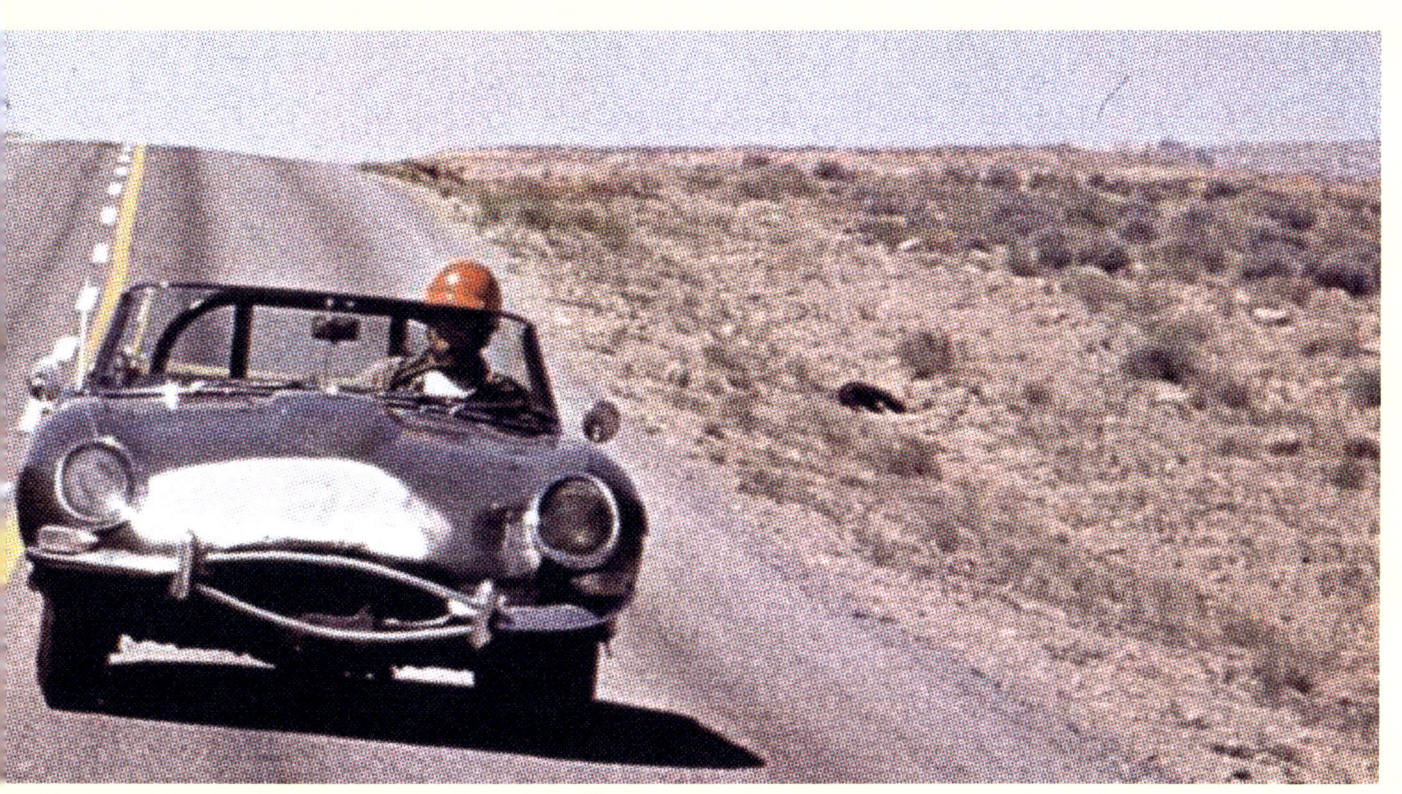

1- Jean-Baptiste Thoret and Bernard Bénoliel, *Road Movie, USA* (Hoebeke, 2011).

of the Summer of Love, whose illusions have come crumbling down in the desert sands. He makes one connection, however, with a character named Super Soul, a blind DJ on a local radio station. Like the chorus in a classical play, Super Soul follows our hero's progress, happy to play his part as a storyteller and recount Kowalski's great odyssey. The two men talk across time and space, via radio, in what seems like an ancient form of communication predating words. Once again, the story takes us into metaphysics and magic…

Similarly dear to the Armenian American director's heart is the theme of time. If you take a band and twist it, then let your fingers travel along its two opposite edges at once, you will go forward in space but backward in time. Sarafian explores this idea here, making the movie into a Möbius strip of its own: In *Vanishing Point,* roads have no beginnings or ends. There is only somewhere else, going off-piste, as Kowalski does all time, breaking free of his situation, surviving, perhaps, at another level. Sarafian clearly takes the cowboy playground that the desert once was and makes it into a place people come to die. In a scene which was cut by the producers from the final American version of the movie, our hero runs across a female hitchhiker, a ghostly, silent figure dressed entirely in black, played by the wonderful Charlotte Rampling. "*What's your name*?" Kowalski asks her. "*I'll tell you later,*" she replies mysteriously. "*I've been waiting for you for a long time. Oh, how I've waited for you,*" she goes on. "*Since when? Where?*" "*Oh, everywhere. Everywhere and since forever. Patiently.*" Kowalski's encounter with this angel of death ends with a kiss which may well seal his fate. *Vanishing Point* could of course have no happy ending (by order of the head of Fox Studios, Darryl Zanuck!), and its hero would not escape his fate. In his mad dash

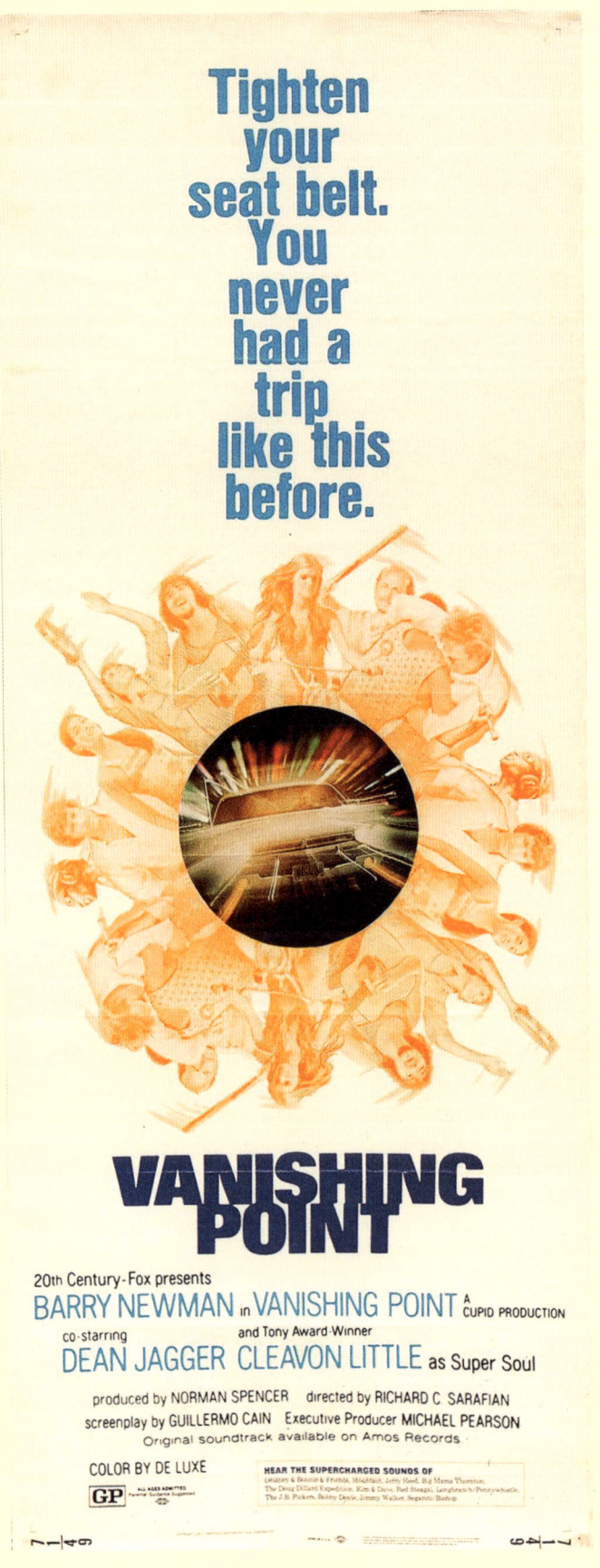

174

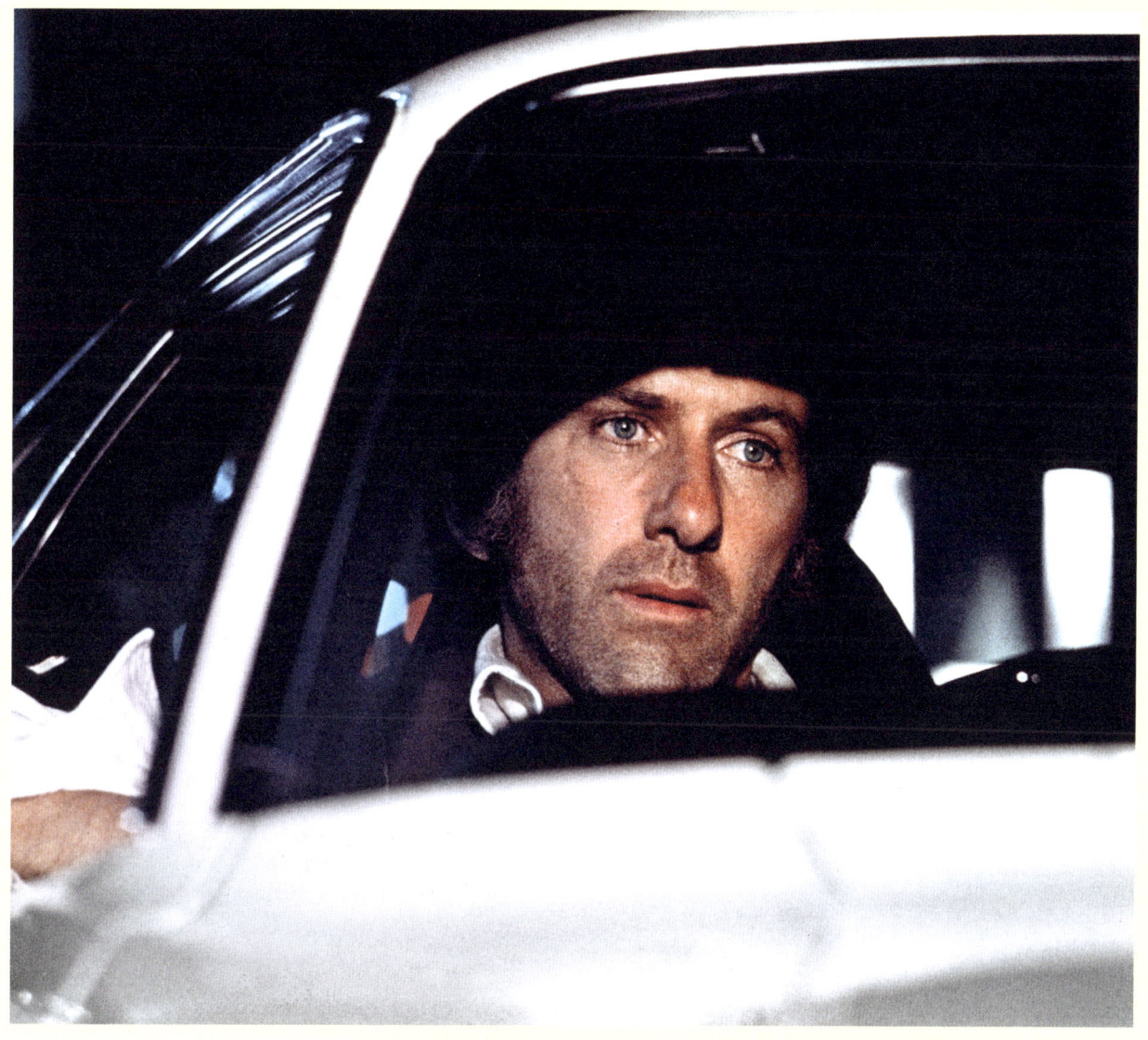

to the Great West, eating up the asphalt in his Dodge Challenger, Kowalski is, after all, "the last American hero."

Vanishing Point emerged at a tight bend in the road, when movies were pulling away sharply from the end of the sixties and heading off into the seventies under the inevitable influence of *Easy Rider*. Although Sarafian had initially hoped for Jack Nicholson to play the part of Kowalski, he was far from interested in creating the film equivalent of a B-side to the cult movie. Instead,

he created an antiestablishment, metaphysical, existential road-trip movie that was capable of abandoning the shores of reality and heading into the realm of legend at any given moment. Sarafian even wrote a sequel to his movie, called *Saint Mountain Symphony*, in which a virtuoso guitarist is able to travel through time and space thanks to the power of his music. He becomes an outlaw, pursued as Kowalski was before him, finally disappearing to the strains of a piece of guitar music. Bob Dylan wanted to write the music for the movie… •

LADY SNOWBLOOD

Lethal Snow

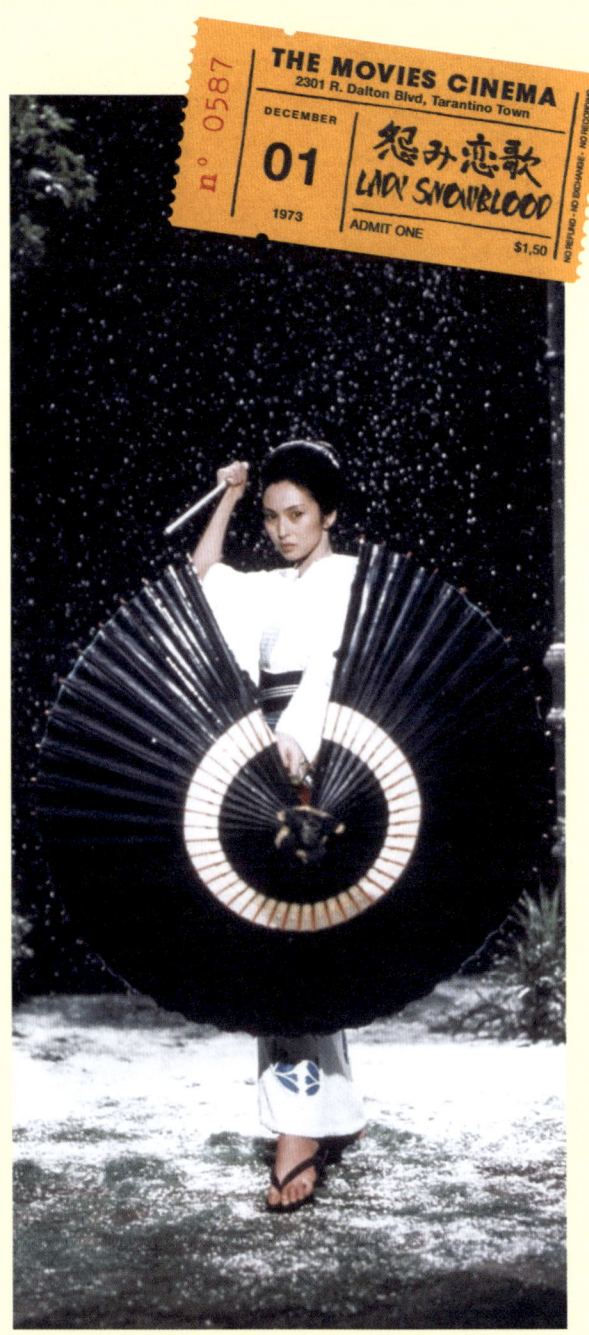

She inches forward, barefoot, across thick snow, in an alley, at night. From under her parasol, two cavernous eyes shine out from a pale, serious face. Lethal little Yuki, who is only twenty years old, waits in the shadows for her moment. As a group of men approaches, she draws a blade from her parasol and brings it down on them in a few deft movements, sending blood pouring onto the pristine snow. *Who are you?*," the last of them asks of the apparition before him. *Vengeance*," the young woman replies.

Directed by Toshiya Fujita in 1973 and based on a manga series by Kazuo Koike and Kazuo Kamimura, *Lady Snowblood* owes a great deal to the bottomless depths of the eyes of its leading actress, Meiko Kaji. For this exterminating angel, a child of snow and blood, everything begins in a frozen prison, buffeted by wind and snow, in nineteenth-century Japan: *"You are born for vengeance, poor child,"* her mother predicts as she breathes her last. Little Yuki is a flower sprung from diseased soil. Her sole inheritance is the hatred of a mother who has seen her husband and son murdered in front of her and has suffered every imaginable abuse herself, and who demands justice in the form of blood. Imprisoned for killing one of the men who raped her, the woman seeks to give birth to a child who will carry out her mission of revenge. The child is not the boy

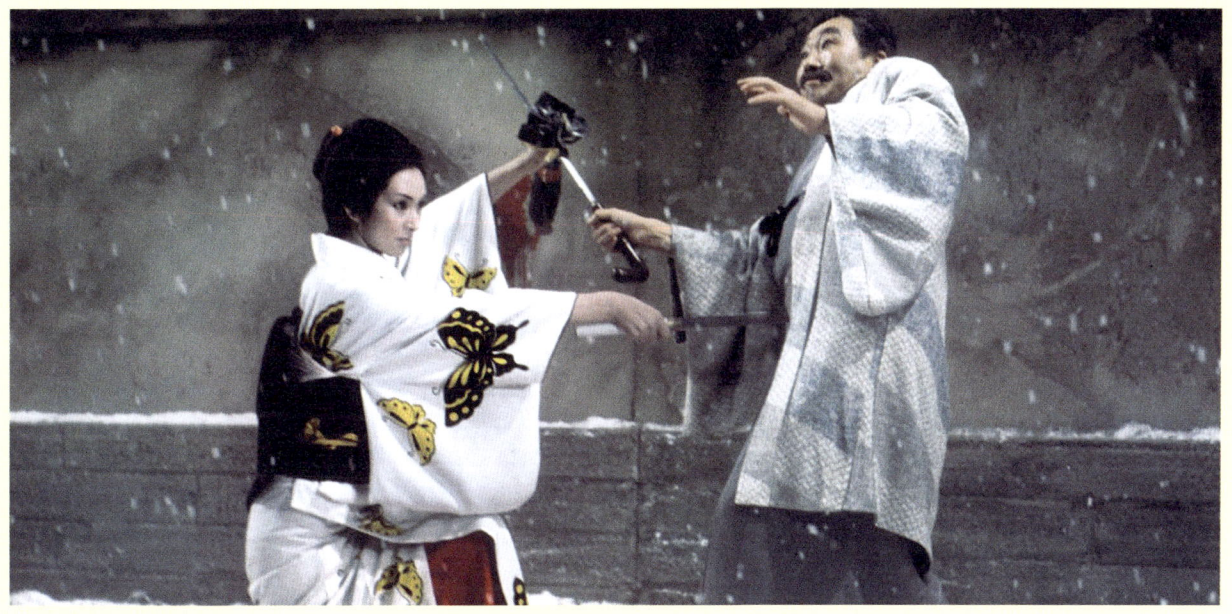

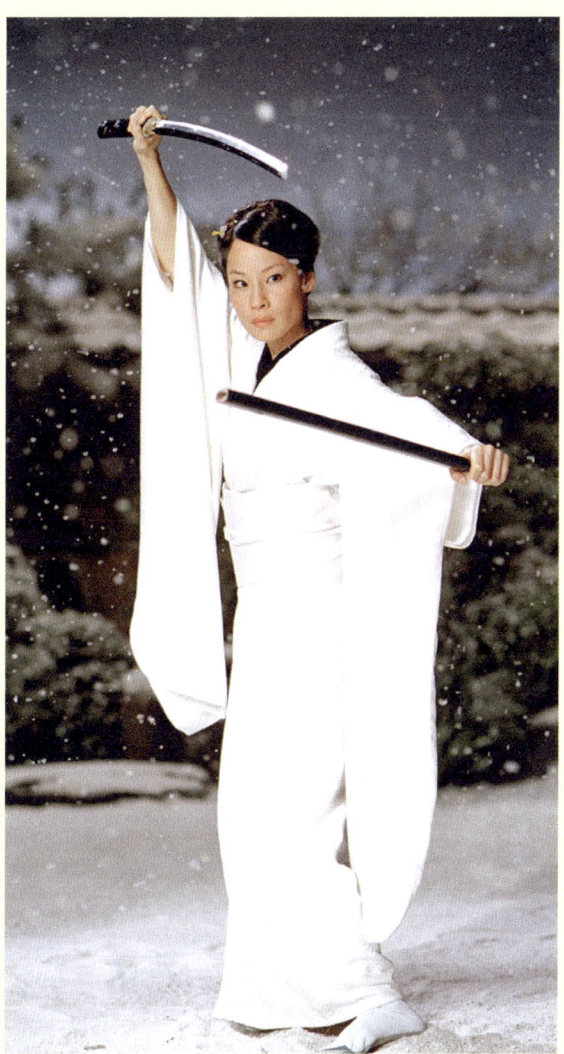

she had hoped for, but a little girl with dark eyes, born one winter night, who would go on to be called Yuki, "snow" in Japanese.

"*It is not pure, white snow that will cleanse this degenerate world, but the bright-red tainted snow of the netherworld*," proclaims the narrator. In *Lady Snowblood*, both physically and thematically, white calls forth red. The purity of the snow, the unbelievable pallor of Yuki's face, and the whiteness of her kimono are simply waiting to be covered in great sprays of blood. Tarantino will, of course, remember this lesson from *Lady Snowblood*. In *Kill Bill*, he dresses O-Ren Ishii in an immaculate kimono and chooses a snowy Japanese garden as the setting for the duel which pits her against the Bride. But the shadow of Yuki hangs over the whole of his two-parter: in the sprays of riotous red which spring from the edge of a sword; in the harsh training sequences; in the way the movie, just like the manga series, is divided into chapters, explicitly referencing Toshiya Fujita's film. Finally, the two heroines have the pursuit of a sweeping murderous itinerary in common. Beatrix and Yuki both have a list of targets to work through, retaliating for one crime after another until their merciless vengeance is complete.

Vengeance binds love and hate, as the first chapter of *Lady Snowblood* reminds us. In both films, it also forms an unbreakable bond between a mother and her daughter, a bond which transcends death (or at least so Beatrix Kiddo thinks…). Yuki is brought up to be an executioner: There is no redemption waiting for her at the end of her path of hate. "*You do not belong to our world*," her master lectures her. Utterly inscrutable, the young girl does not revel in her crimes; she exists simply as an instrument of revenge, forcing herself to put her allotted number of human beings

to sleep forever. Her specter-like appearance lends a mythical quality to the character, wrested as she is from her destiny as a woman and turned into an angel of death. With her ghostly presence, she occupies a place not unlike those monstrous cats known as *bakeneko* that haunt the Japanese imagination. From the stages of Kabuki theaters to the big screen, tales of these creatures tend to be couched in female terms and involve stories of revenge by scorned women. In the face of the atrocities committed against them, the emergence of a being thirsty for vengeance seems like a "necessary evil." Despite her strangeness, however, Yuki is very much a woman of flesh and blood, a tragic character caught between

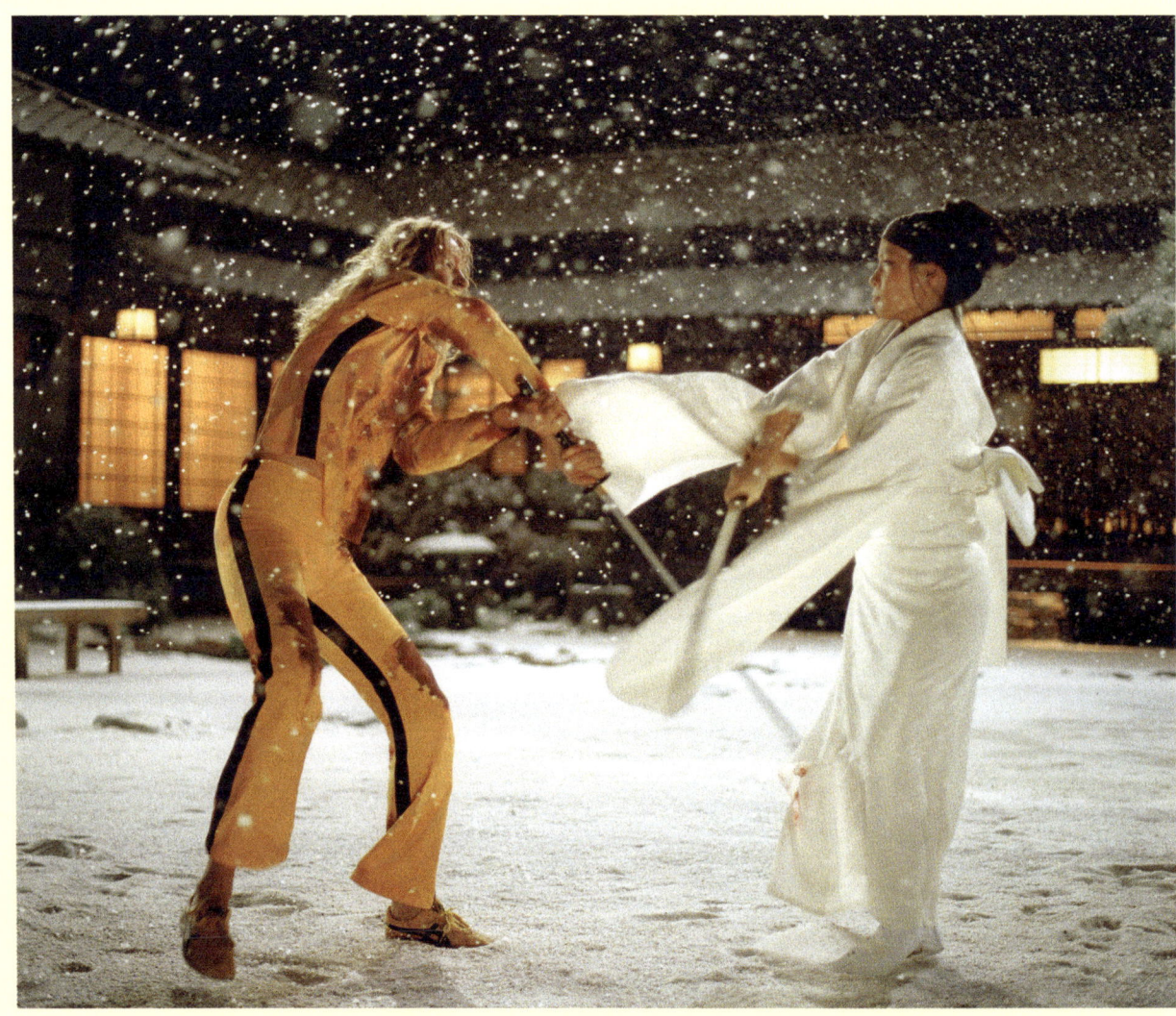

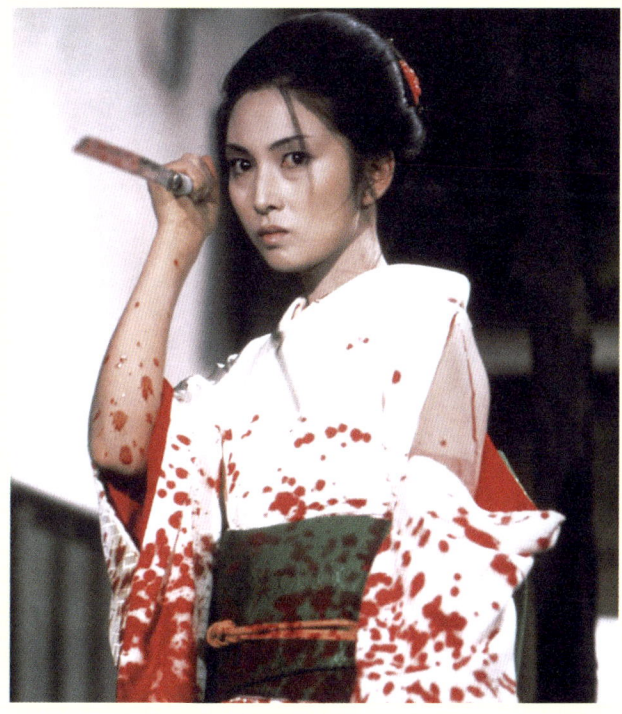

her humanity and a rage whose power overcomes her. As she is carrying out the final act of her mission, she is confronted by one of the victims created in its wake. This is the true cruelty of revenge tales: the endless cycle of destruction that springs from the original wrong, as violence feeds violence and blood calls for more blood. Wounded, stretched out on the snow in her blood-soaked kimono, Yuki finally has to face the absurdity of her vengeful destiny. As dawn breaks, all her vengeance finally appeased, she turns toward the rising sun, looking, perhaps, for a sign of hope. But can the tainted snow of the netherworld ever regain its purity? •

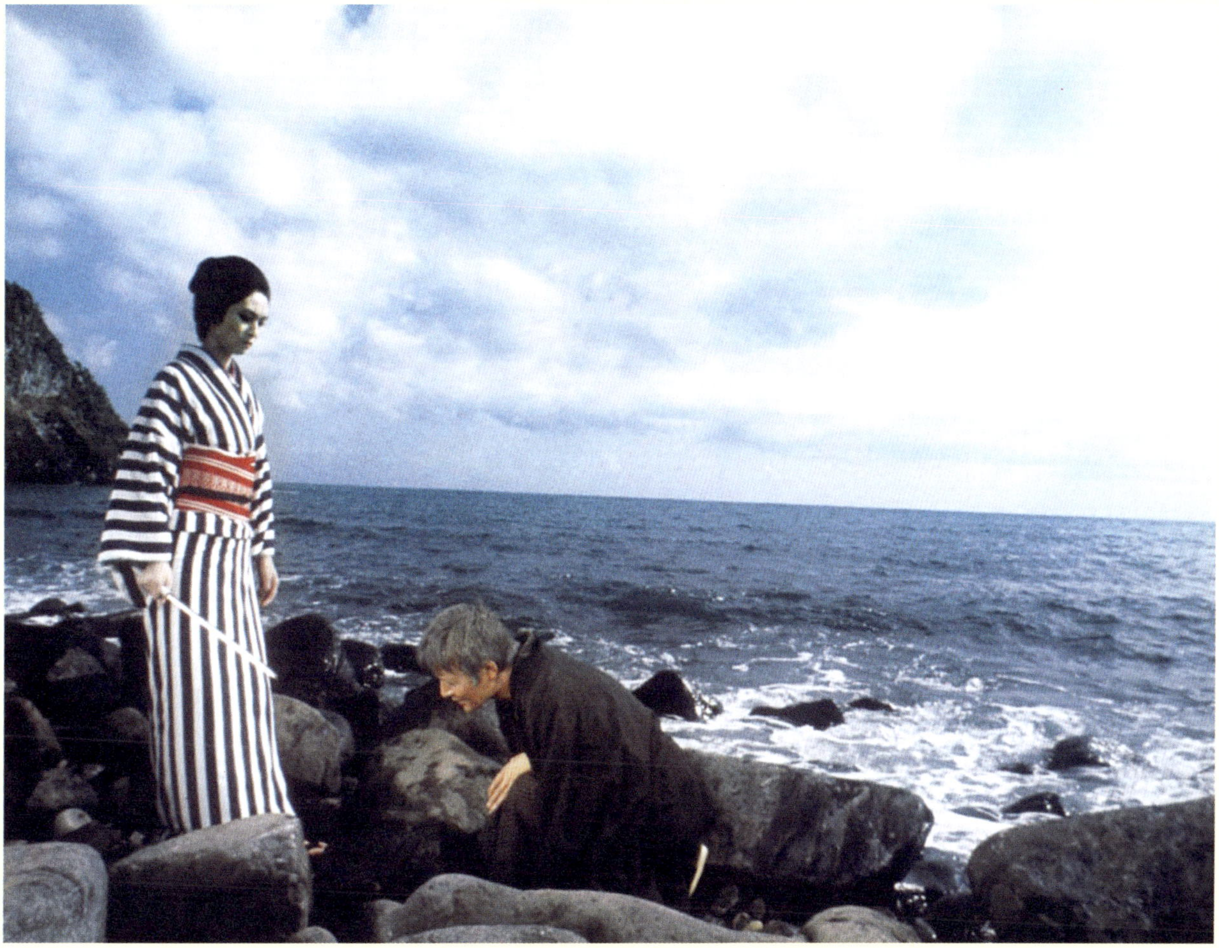

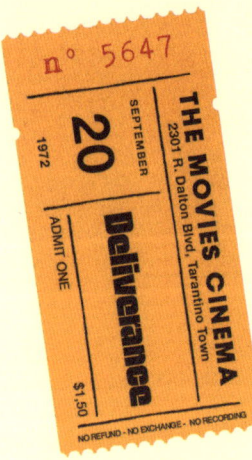

DELIVERANCE

One-Way River

"— We beat it, didn't we? Didn't we beat that?"
"— You don't beat it. You don't beat this river."
— Bobby Trippe & Lewis Medlock

Adapted from the novel of the same name by James Dickey, John Boorman's 1972 film *Deliverance* starts with a harmless weekend trip. Four friends from Atlanta leave town to grab a breath of fresh air and catch up with each other around a good old-fashioned campfire. It was still possible in the early seventies for Americans like them to play at being explorers: There were still places not yet colonized by man, even though the camera dwells on bulldozers digging up untouched landscapes as the opening credits roll. So Lewis, Ed, Bobby, and Drew have taken it into their heads to canoe down the tempestuous Cahulawassee River, soon to be dammed and disappear. Confident in the apparent power vested in them by the "American way of life"—which is itself an illusion already in decline—the men exude self-assurance. But no sooner have they arrived in this remote area, inhabited by a few souls who have remained cut off from the modern world, than something seems to throw our would-be conquering city boys' careful plans off course.

Bobby approaches the locals with a certain amount of condescension and a definite excess of arrogance. He's quick to talk down to and make sarcastic comments about the appearance of the first inhabitant he meets, to which the latter retorts that Bobby *"don't know nothin'."* Bobby even suggests the locals have *"genetic deficiencies,"* implying they are inbred. Meanwhile, Drew plays his guitar, dueling a boy who is picking his banjo. When their short but happy piece of improvisation comes to an end, Drew reaches his hand out to the young kid in a friendly way, but the boy dismisses the gesture and turns away. The duet ends there. From then on, an uncrossable line is drawn, separating the men from everything around them. While Bobby suggests leaving the boy a couple of bucks, a clear sign of his contempt for the local people, Lewis, for his part, watches the scene from afar. Wonderfully played by Burt Reynolds, Lewis is a survivalist—and even sports a patch saying just that on his jacket. Used to going on adventures armed with a bow and arrow, Lewis is the group's authority figure. He prides himself on being ready for anything when the time comes: *"The system's gonna fail,"* he says, and then the question will be *"survival. Who has the ability to survive?"* Lewis rails loudly and clearly against the ravages inflicted on nature by modern society: *"You push a little more power into Atlanta… a little more air conditioners for your smug little*

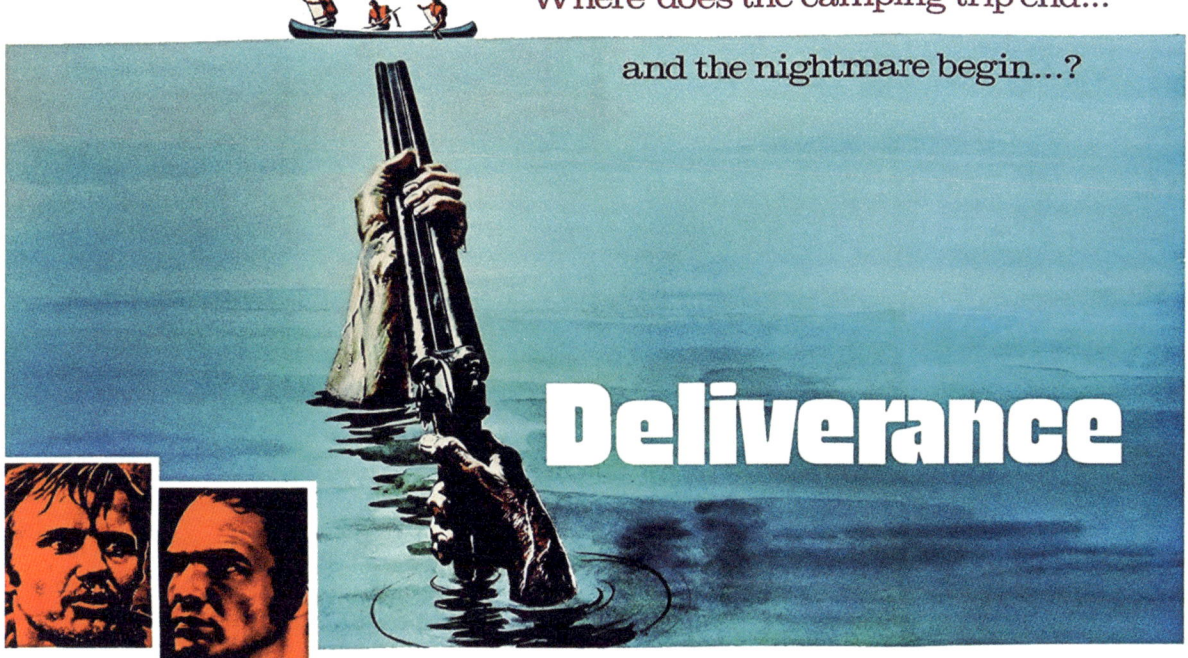

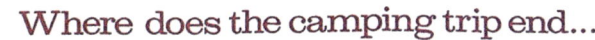

Where does the camping trip end...

and the nightmare begin...?

Deliverance

A JOHN BOORMAN FILM Starring **JON VOIGHT · BURT REYNOLDS** in "DELIVERANCE" x
Co-Starring NED BEATTY·RONNY COX · Screenplay by James Dickey Based on his novel·Produced and Directed by John Boorman
PANAVISION®·TECHNICOLOR®·From Warner Bros., A Warner Communications Company · Released by Columbia-Warner Distributors Ltd

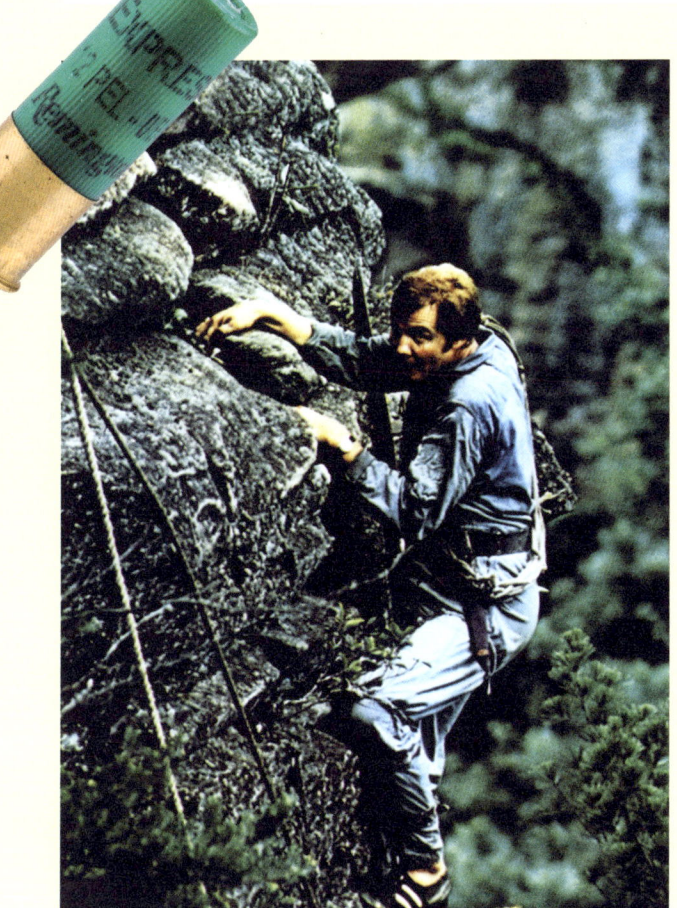

suburb… and you know what's gonna happen? We're gonna rape this whole goddamn landscape. We're gonna rape it."

This is the start of a nightmare weekend in which man will be forced to check his assumptions when confronted by untamable and unforgiving nature, in an America which hasn't gotten on board the bandwagon of progress and lives according to its own rules. The turning point of the movie comes in a shocking scene when Bobby and Ed find themselves suddenly face to face with two men who are armed with shotguns, and whose intentions look anything but good. The scene remains indelibly marked in the memory of anyone who has seen *Deliverance*. Quentin Tarantino, who first saw the movie at well below the recommended minimum age, is no exception. He recalls, *"Of all the double features I saw back then, none was as powerful, nor as controversial, as the time my mother took me with her on a date to see a double feature of* The Wild Bunch *and* Deliverance.*"*[1]

1- Quentin Tarantino, *Cinema Speculation* (Harper, 2022).

In this scene John Boorman confronts
the city boys with the terror of
a parallel, archaic America for
which they have no maps, a land of
forgotten regions, rednecks, and
hillbillies. Here, human law no
longer applies: It's no use hoping
for a helping hand from the local
sheriff, since he's bound to be the
cousin of one of their assailants—
according to Lewis, at least. We will
say no more about this scene, which
is both indescribable in its horror
and—paradoxically—beautifully lit
and shot by Hungarian-American chief
cameraman Vilmos Zsigmond. According
to Tarantino, viewers had a sense
that *something* was going to happen,
but nothing could have prepared them
for what it turned out to be: "*That
something is the most profound and
disturbing violent sequence in early
seventies studio cinema not directed
by Sam Peckinpah. It's also become
one of the most iconic.*"[2] Tarantino
is not someone we know to be readily
shocked, but for him *Deliverance* packs
a punch like no other movie. "*The film
begins veering away from standard
movie suspense to something we haven't
ever felt in* exactly *the same way in
a movie before. John Boorman doesn't
direct a suspense scene, he stages a
mind fuck,*" Tarantino goes on. "*The
way people were scared of going in the
water after* Jaws *was how I felt about
the prospect of going camping in the
woods after* Deliverance.*"[3]

The characters in *Deliverance* get to
experience a return to the basics of
life, a return to humility, which is
a far cry from the bourgeois fantasy
of abandoning, for a weekend, the
comforts of your "*nice job… nice
house… nice wife… nice kid,*" as Lewis
puts it to Ed, played by Jon Voight.
Ed retorts, "*I like my life*"—the
life of a man for whom the system has
worked well enough to feel satisfied,
replete with modern comforts,
sheltered from the world outside and
its violence. Ed, in particular,
will find himself forced to follow
a road which takes him the opposite

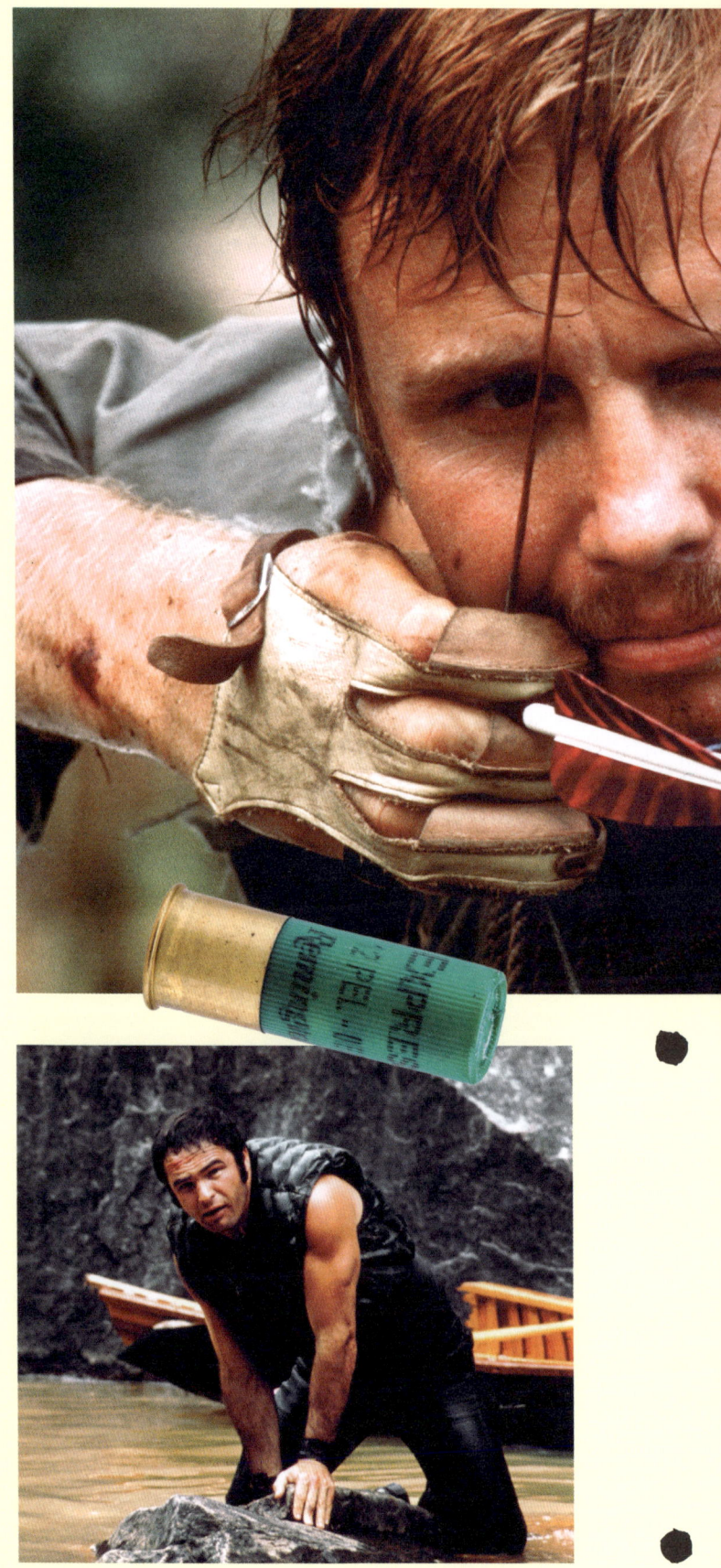

2- Ibid. • 3- Ibid.

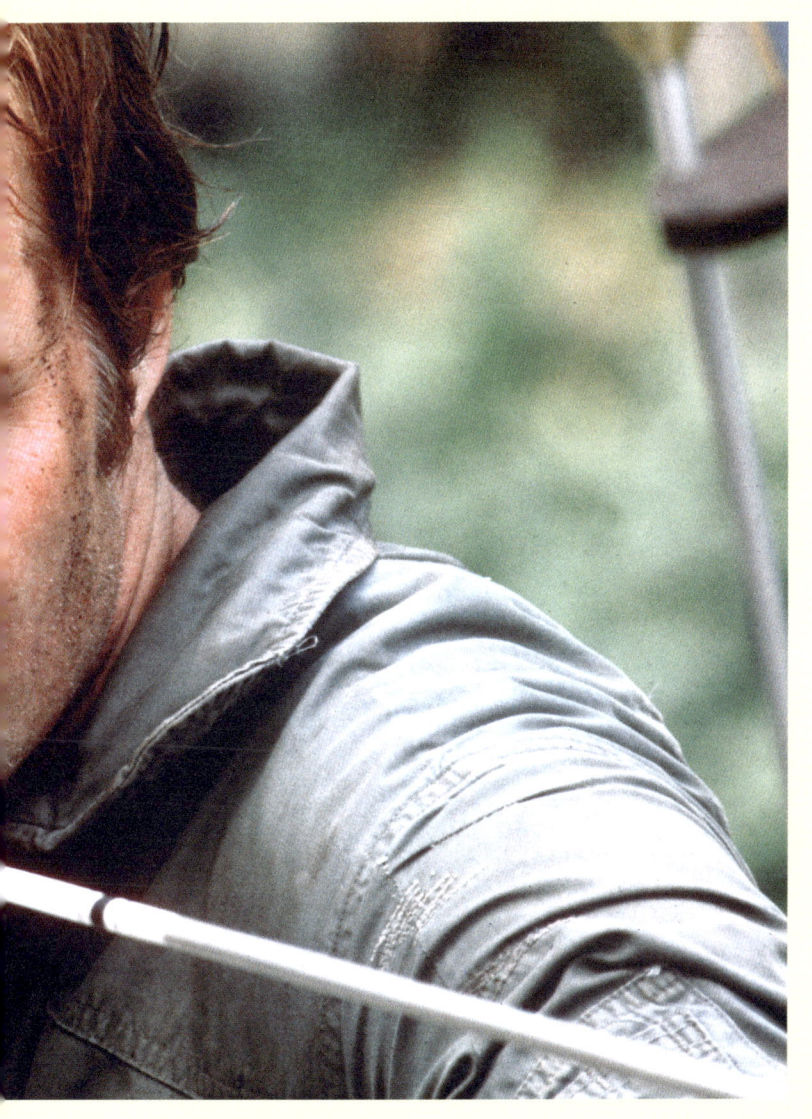

way, making him question his way of
living, thinking, even being, and
compelling him to tangle with a whole
range of big ideas about justice,
democracy, civilization, life, and
death. He will have to let go of his
civilized American habits and return
to the wild. In so doing, he literally
abandons his bucket hat and his pipe,
jettisoning all signs of himself as a
city nerd, a modern man. The guy who
can't shoot down a deer in the middle
of nature because of what he calls a
psychological "*loss of control*" finds
himself having to sacrifice everything
on the altar of his own survival, to
the point of holding a man's life at
the end of his arrow. As he stands
on the edge of the precipice, Ed
completes the trajectory which will
finally bring him to revise his own
moral principles. This is what John
Boorman's movie is all about: holding
up a mirror to the audience, placing
us in front of these moral dilemmas,
and in the end reminding us of our own
smallness—that we are nothing compared
with nature, and that nature will
always end up pursuing its own course,
knocking down any obstacles we put
in its way. •

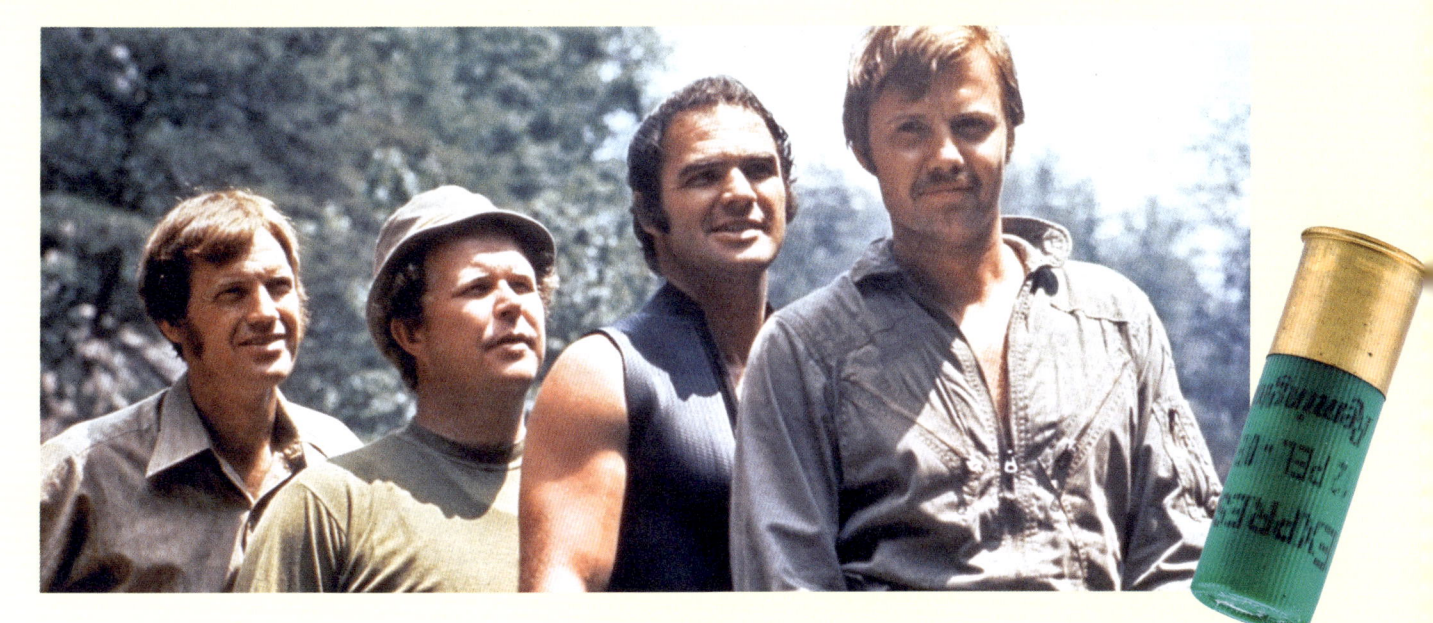

DJANGO

The Other Sergio

*N*ebraska what? Sergio who?" Rick Dalton stutters in response when Schwarz tells him that there could be a part for him in Sergio Corbucci's upcoming movie, *Nebraska Jim*. Corbucci is none other than the second-best director of Spaghetti Westerns, the agent assures the star. To convince him, Schwarz sets up a meeting between the two men in Rome, but the actor makes a cardinal error. Over the meal, he congratulates Sergio Corbucci on his wonderful achievement with Clint Eastwood in *A Fistful of Dollars*… by Sergio Leone. When Corbucci asks Dalton if he's seen any other Italian Westerns, there's only one he can think of, *Navajo Joe*, which he saw on the airplane and

thought was a total dud. "*A horrible movie with Burt Reynolds where he's wearing a wig that makes him look like Natalie Wood,*" he says sarcastically, not realizing that *Navajo Joe* is, of course, Corbucci's film. At the end of this catastrophic interview, the director says to Dalton: "*Why should I work with you?… You're an arrogant bastard. Nebraska Jim's an arrogant bastard, so I like that.*" And good old Rick replies: "*Sergio, I don't understand Italian Westerns… What does it matter if I don't get it? What does it matter if I like* Nebraska Jim *or not? I'm good in Westerns. I'm a good cowboy. You put a hat on my head, you put me in a cool costume, you put me on a horse, you're gonna like what I do.*" This legendary exchange, recounted by none other than

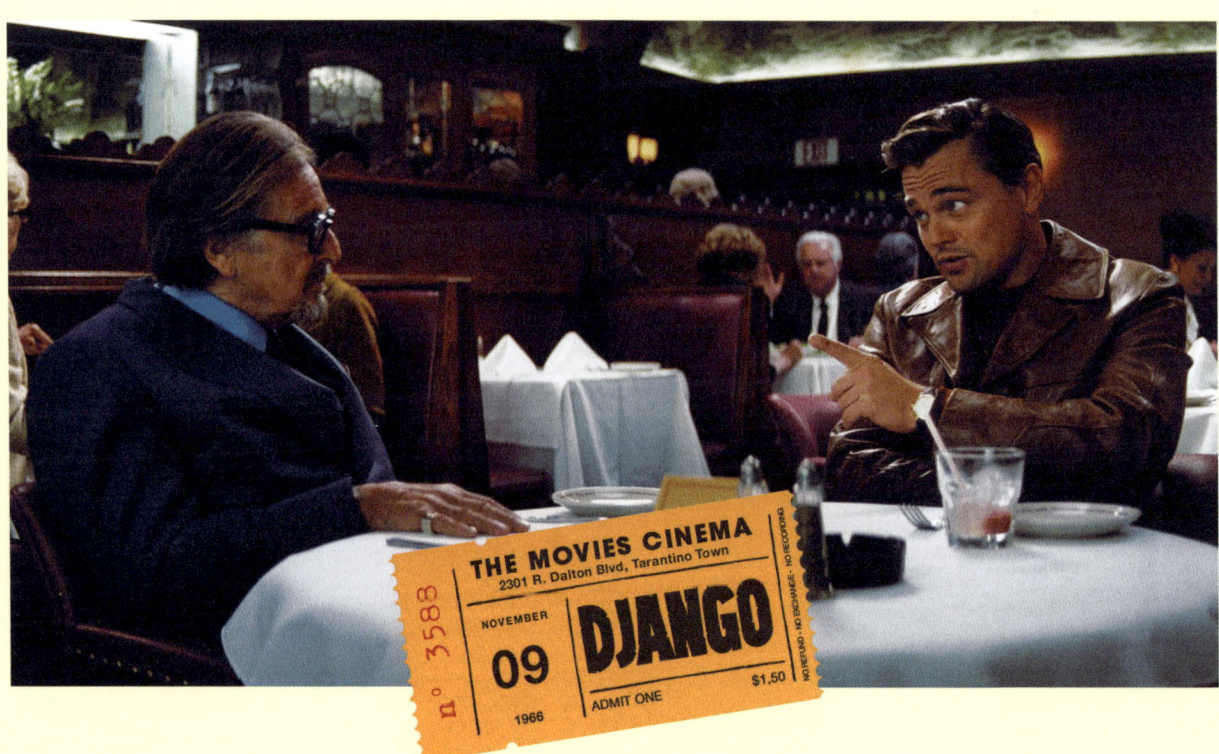

THE MOVIES CINEMA
2301 R. Dalton Blvd, Tarantino Town
NOVEMBER 09 1966
n° 3588
DJANGO
ADMIT ONE $1.50

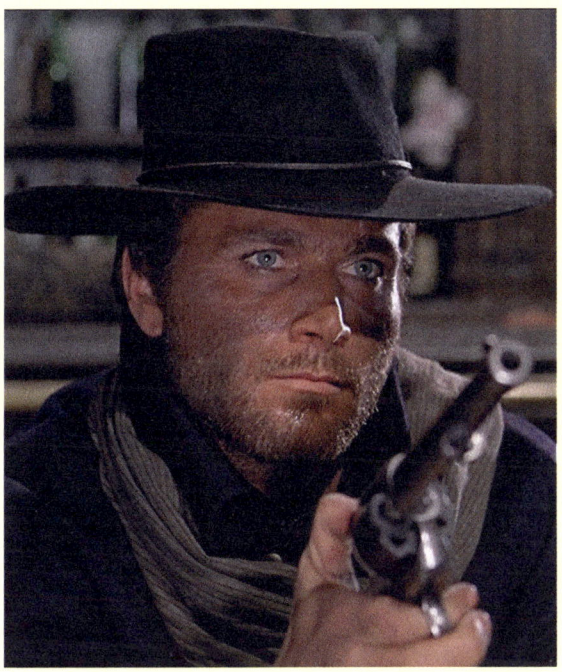

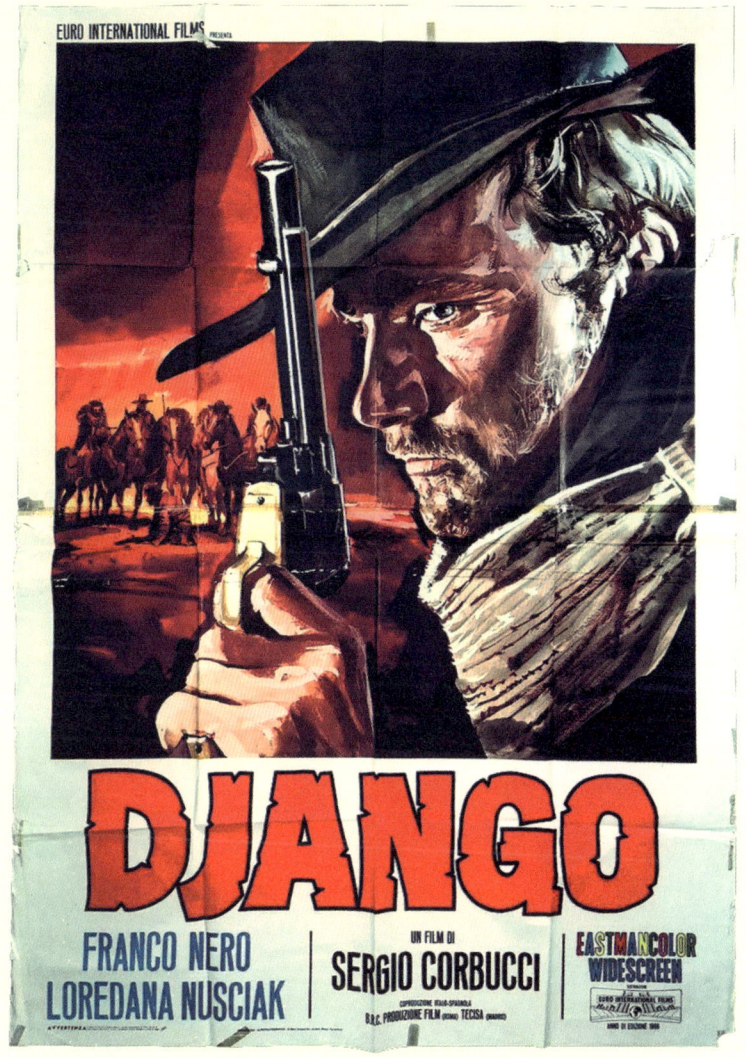

Quentin Tarantino himself,[1] finally cements the deal between Rick Dalton and the great Sergio… the other great Sergio, that is.

While he was in Tokyo to promote the release of *Inglourious Basterds*, Quentin Tarantino found himself scouring the racks in the record stores for Spaghetti Western music, a genre which was very popular in Japan. At around the same time, he had decided to embark on a critical essay about the master Italian Western movie director Corbucci, whose extravagant and sadistic vision of the West he found particularly impressive. While each of the great Western movie directors, from Anthony Mann and Sergio Leone to Sam Peckinpah, created their own particular version of the American West, for Tarantino, Corbucci's version stood out from all the others: "*His West was the most violent, surreal and pitiless landscape of any director in the history of the genre.*"[2] Somewhere in the crossfire of these disparate inspirations, *Django Unchained* was born. "*The Corbucci piece put all those images in my head. I was listening to spaghetti western soundtracks, and the first scene came to me.*"[3] In this way, *Django Unchained*, which was released in 2012, is a Western born under the influence—that of Corbucci and his 1966 movie, the original *Django,* from which Tarantino borrowed liberally, even going so far as to include the movie's theme song, composed by Luis Bacalov and sung by crooner Rocky Roberts.

A wanderer who drifts across desolate landscapes dragging a muddy coffin behind him, Django is a lone cowboy to whom actor Franco Nero lends a steely gaze. A former soldier on the Union side, he sets about settling scores with Major Jackson and his band of Confederate racists, who've come to sow terror in a rundown village which already has more than enough on its plate with a bunch of Mexican

1- Luca Rea, *Django & Django*, 2021.
2- Quentin Tarantino and Gavin Edwards, "Quentin Tarantino Tackles Old Dixie by Way of the Old West (by Way of Italy)," *The New York Times*, September 27, 2012.
3- Tom Shone, *Tarantino: A Retrospective* (Thames & Hudson, 2017).

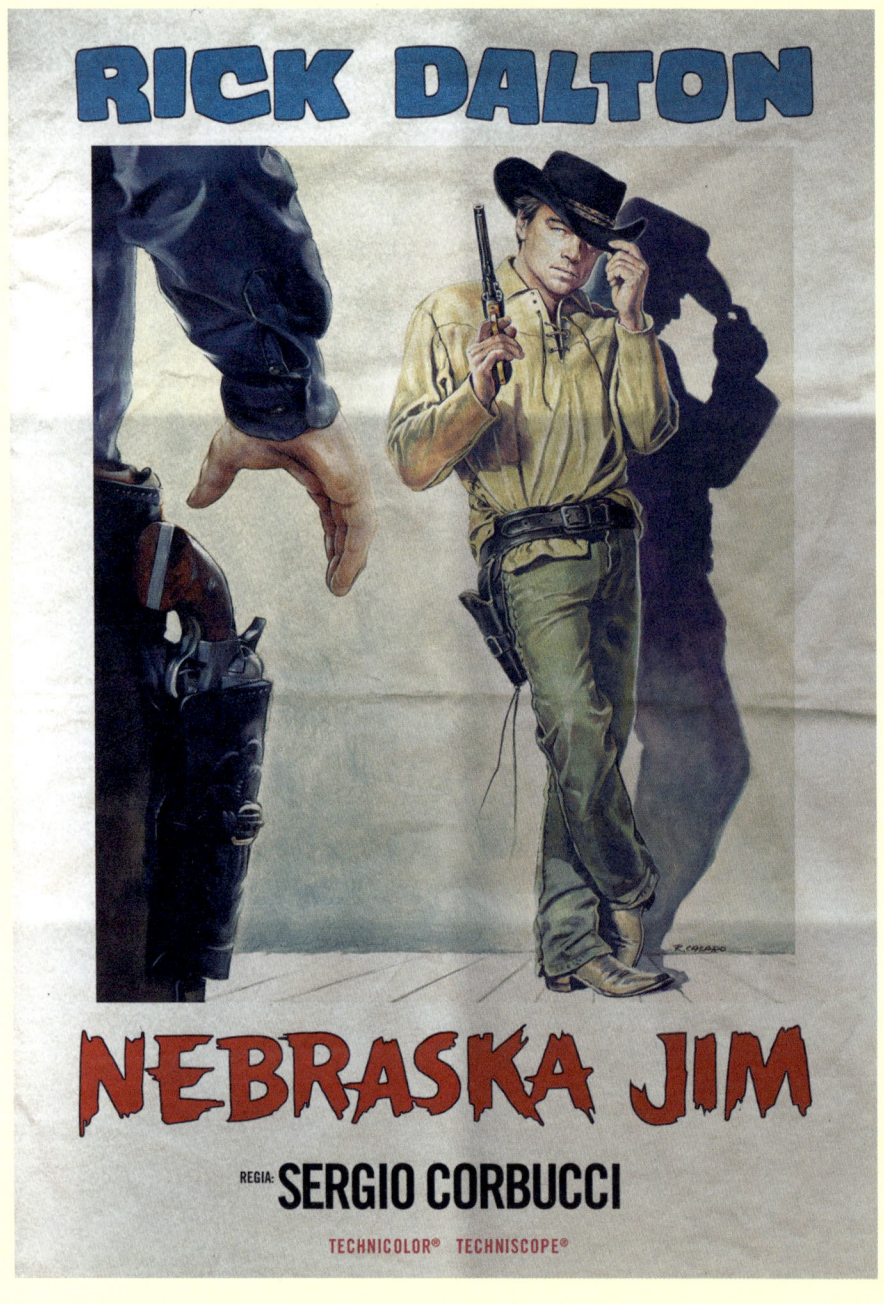

devil eat it…). "*I kill a lot of people*," Corbucci joked in an interview. "*I've killed more people than Nero and Caligula. But each time, it's more difficult for me to find a new method of murder. That's why I hate Westerns.*" When the interviewer asked him what sort of movie he would make next, the old fox replied: "*A Western, naturally.*"[4]

In this version of the West, where no excess is off-limits, inhabited by antiheroes who would blend in nicely in one of those comic books Corbucci loved, no one is safe. But beneath the hyperbolic bloodshed, Tarantino always finds a political subtext, carefully put in place by the director, that turns the violence into a metaphor for an evil that is gnawing away at the heart of his country. Born in 1926, Corbucci grew up in the Fascist Italy of World War II. "*And so I think the Westerns were all in response to that,*" Tarantino explains.[5] By bringing an Italian perspective to America's founding myths, Corbucci may succeed in exposing fanaticism in all its forms, but all the same, there is nothing heroic about his characters. They are trigger-happy avengers with dubious moral values. "*In another Western, they could be the villain,*"[6] Tarantino observes. For all his Christlike journey, Django himself is no angel of mercy. Despite its low budget and rudimentary sets, *Django* was a fantastic popular success, prompting a slew of unofficial sequels— distant cousins inspired to varying degrees by the original, sometimes doing little more than capitalizing on the name of Corbucci's *pistolero*. "Django" became the go-to name for

revolutionaries. In a display of violence on a truly operatic scale, which Tarantino of course retains, Django cleans up the town in great bursts of machine-gun fire. In a nice twist, his weapon was concealed in the coffin. Corbucci can be funny, but above all he knows how to be utterly bloodthirsty, executing extras in droves and cutting off a character's ear in a scene that would make Mr. Blonde blench (after all, he wasn't the kind to make the poor

4- Luca Rea, *Django & Django*, 2021.
5- Ibid. • 6- Ibid.

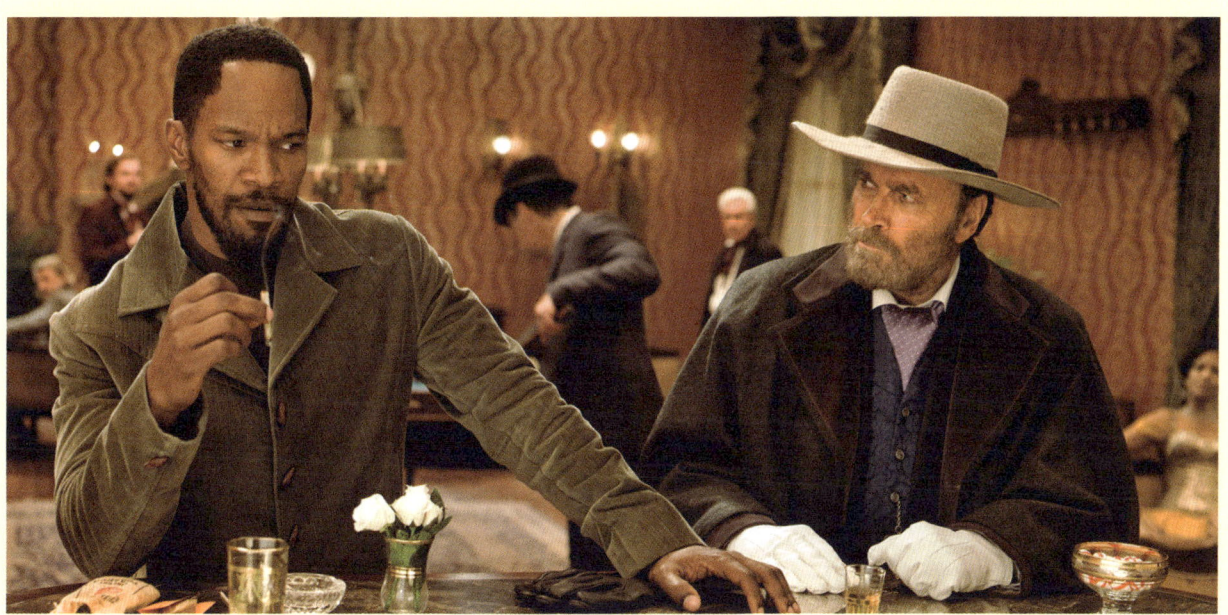

a whole host of tough cowboys, to the point of starting a little exploitation wave of its own. The character spilled out of the movie and turned into a legend, a film concept. It was no coincidence that Tarantino decided to make his freed slave one of the last variations of Corbucci's antihero, his Django unchained.

With his first Western—or Southern, as he likes to call it—Tarantino maintains the Italian director's legacy. The influence is even more palpable in *The Hateful Eight*, a paranoid Western plunged into the depths of a frozen winter worthy of *The Great Silence*, even if QT has no qualms about going off-piste and venturing into whodunit territory. "*I did* The Great Silence *for all those who believe in freedom and for all those who want to fight,*" Corbucci declared.[7] Like him, Tarantino gives his Westerns a social dimension: "Django *was definitely the beginning of my political side, and I think* The Hateful Eight *is the logical extension of that. In a weird way,* Django *was the question, and* The Hateful Eight *is the answer.*"[8] Tarantino continues his homage to Corbucci all the way to *Once Upon a Time… in Hollywood*, where

he incorporates him into his extended universe as he weaves an alternate history of film. Unlike Rick Dalton, who knows precious little about the film anyway, Tarantino has the greatest respect for *Navajo Joe* and unbridled admiration for Burt Reynolds's physical performance, wig or no wig. "*Before* The Wild Bunch *was released,* Navajo Joe *was the most violent movie that ever carried a Hollywood studio logo,*" he asserts.[9] And then there's the question of the great Sergio Leone and the eternal second fiddle our Sergio seems bound to play to him. Tarantino is similarly enthusiastic in his defense of Corbucci on this score: "*There's nothing wrong with the label 'second-best Spaghetti Western director after Leone,' all right. I don't believe Ford is the greatest of American Western directors, but if you take that thought, … then who's the second? Is it Peckinpah? Is it Hawks? Is it Raoul Walsh? Is it Delmer Daves? Who is it? Who's number two? All right? That's a dogfight. It's not a dogfight in Italy. Number two is fucking Corbucci.*"[10] •

7- Ibid.
8- Tom Shone, *Tarantino: A Retrospective* (Thames & Hudson, 2017).
9— Quentin Tarantino and Gavin Edwards, "Quentin Tarantino Tackles Old Dixie by Way of the Old West (by Way of Italy)," *The New York Times*, September 27, 2012.
10- Luca Rea, *Django & Django*, 2021.

COFFY & FOXY BROWN

Queen of the B's

Screening this evening at our little local movie theater is a furious double feature that will transport you back to the seventies. Pam Grier burst into the world of blaxploitation movies as the "*the black panther of Harlem*" in *Coffy*, written and directed by Jack Hill, in 1973, quickly followed by the eponymous *Foxy Brown* by the same director, in 1974. After this sensational debut, she rapidly established herself as the undisputed queen of the genre. "*She's the meanest chick in town,*" the poster for *Foxy Brown* warned. So grab yourself a big bucket of popcorn, settle in, and get ready for a double dose of Pam Grier. But be warned, it's no holds barred!

At the end of the workday, Coffy, a young nurse, sets aside her uniform to play the vigilante on the streets of Los Angeles. Determined to seek revenge on all and sundry for her sister's descent into drug addiction, Coffy wreaks havoc on pimps, dealers, shady cops, and corrupt politicians. As deadly with her retorts as she is with her sawed-off shotgun, Pam Grier landed her first iconic role with *Coffy*. The actress was anything but an amateur, however. After a brief appearance in *Beyond the Valley of the Dolls* by Russ Meyer in 1970, she got her big break when Roger Corman, who was the big cheese of B movies, cast her in *The Big Doll House* (1971) and *The Big Bird Cage* (1972), both produced

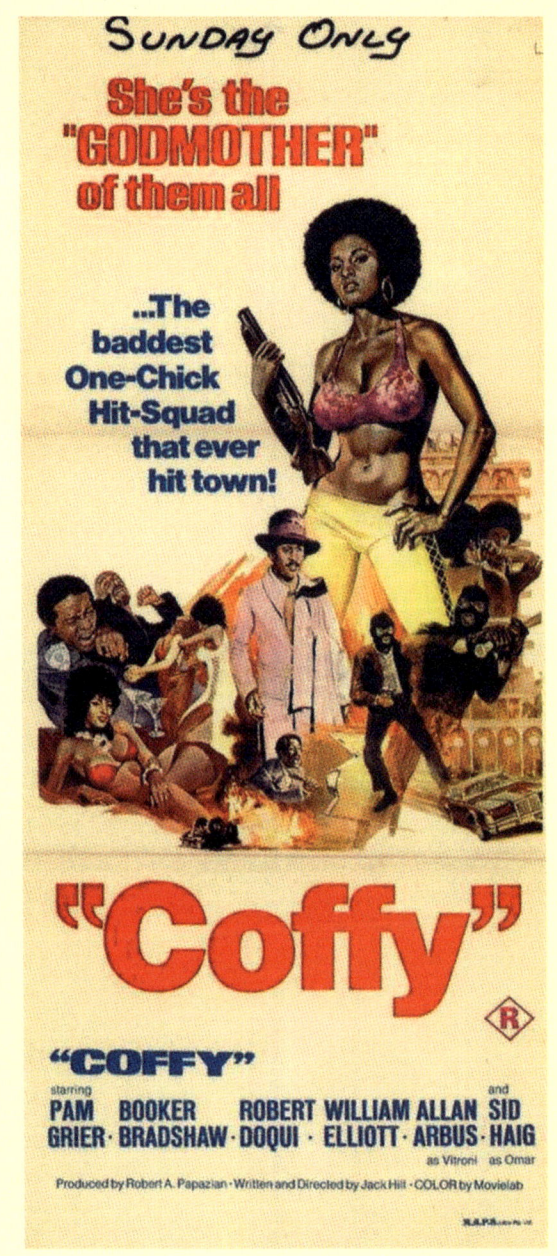

under the AIP (American International Pictures) banner. Both movies were directed by Jack Hill and belonged to a subgenre which was then all the rage: women-in-prison movies. The closed prison setting allowed filmmakers to combine violence and sweaty eroticism with shots of naked female prisoners, hints of lesbianism, and outbursts of all manner of cruelty. Pam Grier appeared in several other movies of this genre (*Women in Cages*, *Black Mama White Mama*…) and was already beginning to make a name for herself, both for her acting and for her sculpted physique. For Corman, it was a simple choice: The public was under her spell.

In her performance as Coffy, Pam Grier offers us a heroine with two different faces whose ambiguity enables her to go beyond the simplistic tropes typical of the genre. By day, Coffy is a paragon of virtue, a nurturing figure and a pillar of her community. At night, we see her turn into an exterminating angel, exacting revenge as if in a dream. With *Coffy*, Pam Grier kicked her

way into blaxploitation, a subgenre as ambivalent as Coffy herself, celebrated but also widely decried in African American communities, which have accused it of perpetuating caricatural representations. Despite the controversy it engendered, the wave of blaxploitation movies gave Black characters their own stories at a time when the only roles otherwise available were, according to Grier, "*practically invisible, or painfully stereotypical.*"[1] Confined for far too long to secondary roles as victims or stooges, male African American actors saw their horizons open up at this point in the early seventies. Early movie successes such as *Sweet Sweetback's Baadasssss Song,* directed by and starring Melvin Van Peebles, and *Shaft*, directed by Gordon Parks and produced by a major company, encouraged studios to invest. With the role of Coffy, Pam Grier broke the mold and showed herself to be the female equivalent of Shaft and the other muscular heroes of blaxploitation movies. As she observed, "*People had only seen African-American women*

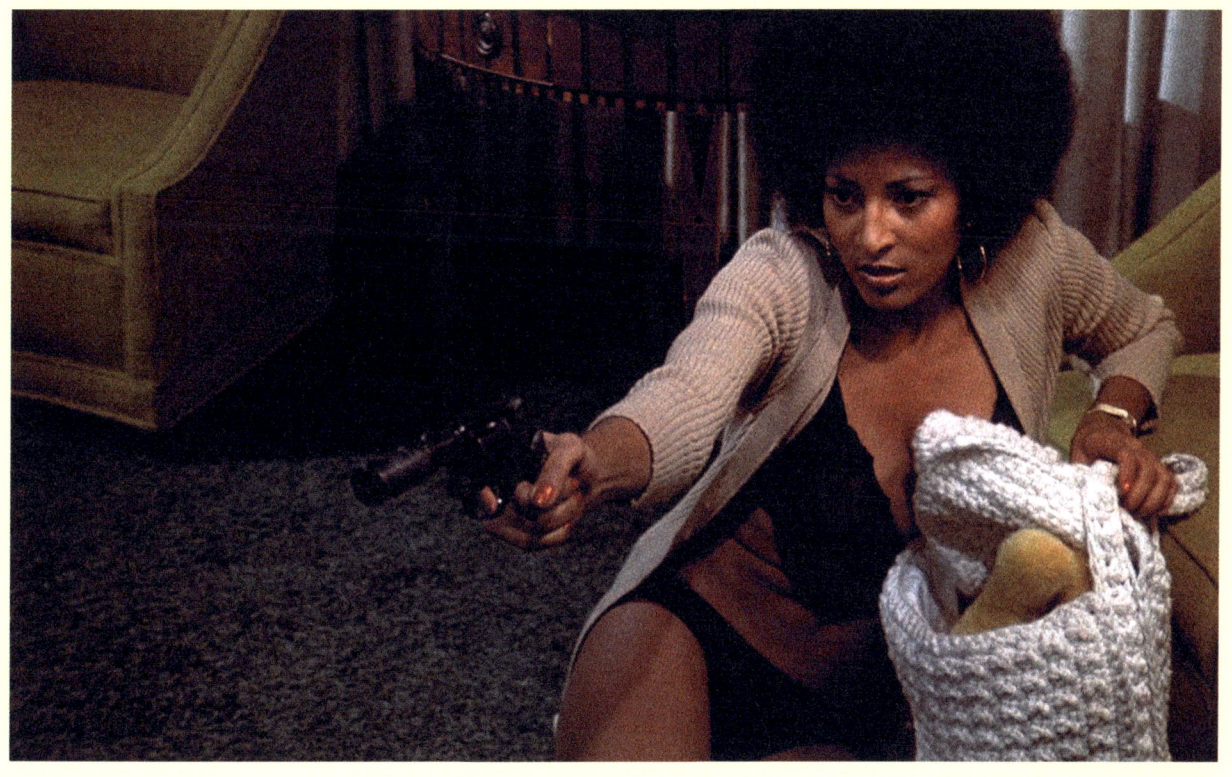

1- Shahesta Shaitly, "Pam Grier Takes Raunch to the Ranch," *The Guardian*, December 2011.

depicted a certain way in film and it was about time that changed."[2]

Following this urban thriller set against a backdrop of social injustice, Pam Grier found another role worthy of her in the character of Foxy Brown, righter of wrongs in the 1974 movie of the same name. When her federal agent boyfriend is murdered by drug dealers, Foxy decides to track down his killers. She quickly connects them to a purported modeling agency run by a couple who in fact supply prostitutes to people in power to encourage them to turn a blind eye to their trade. With *Foxy Brown*, Pam Grier pursued a course and nailed it: Already nicknamed the "*Queen of the B's*" by *Newsweek* magazine, she made a name for herself with these hard-boiled roles, from *Foxy Brown* to *Sheba, Baby*, and became one of the busiest actresses of the seventies. Other faces emerged, such as the model

Tamara Dobson in *Cleopatra Jones*, but Pam Grier dominated the genre.

Considered one of the sex symbols of the decade, she was known for her Afro hairstyle, shirts with bold patterns and dizzyingly low-cut necklines, and bell-bottom pants, but above all for her ferocious and legendary attitude, exemplified in the taglines for her movies. "*She's the 'GODMOTHER' of them all,*" we read in big letters across the top of the poster for *Coffy*. But blaxploitation was a loose term, and the lines between progressive movies and those that were purely commercial— between empowerment and outrageous sexism—were often blurred. Jack Hill's movies did not stint on eye-catching scenes and made the most of the actress's physical assets, but at the same time they seemed to take their heroines very seriously. Coffy and Foxy Brown seek a form of justice which goes beyond their individual quest

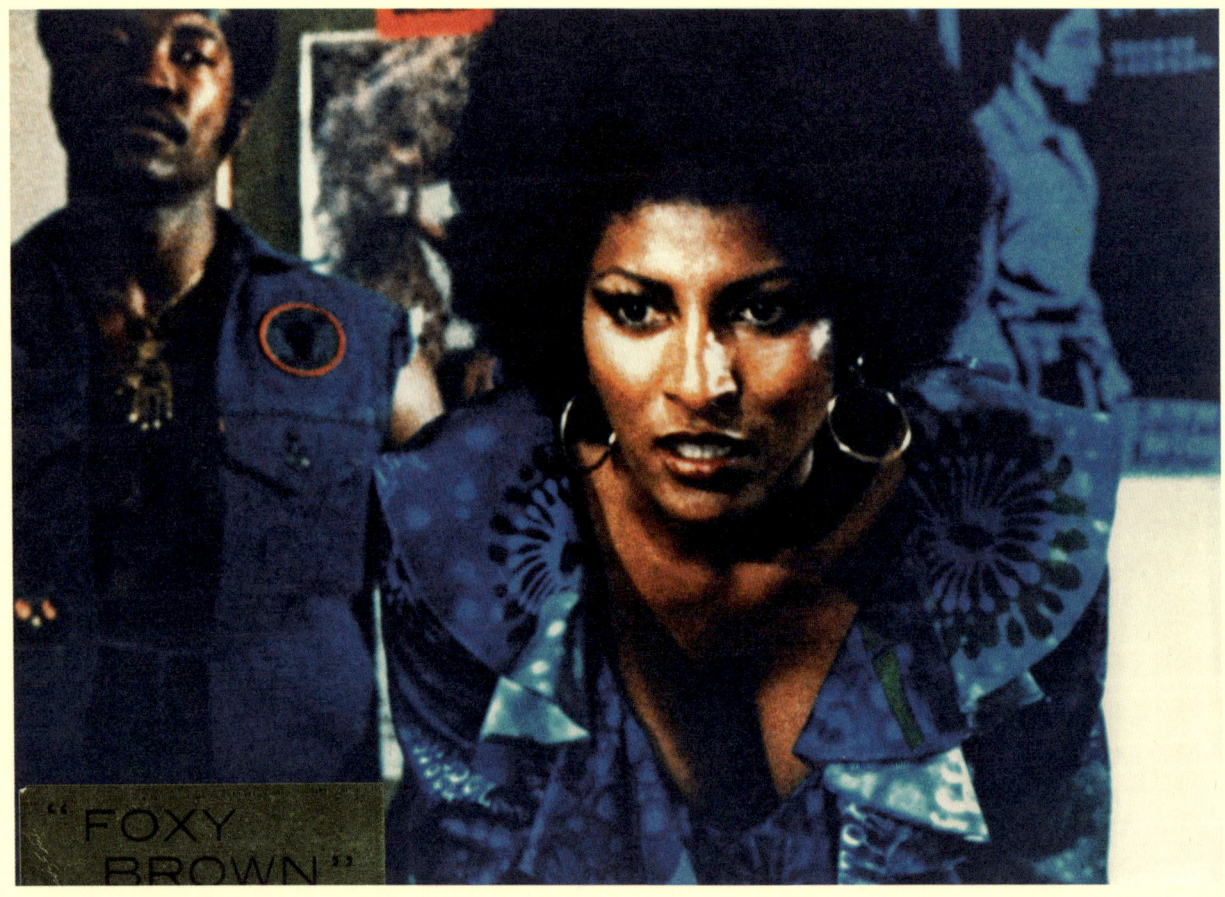

"FOXY BROWN"

2- Ibid.

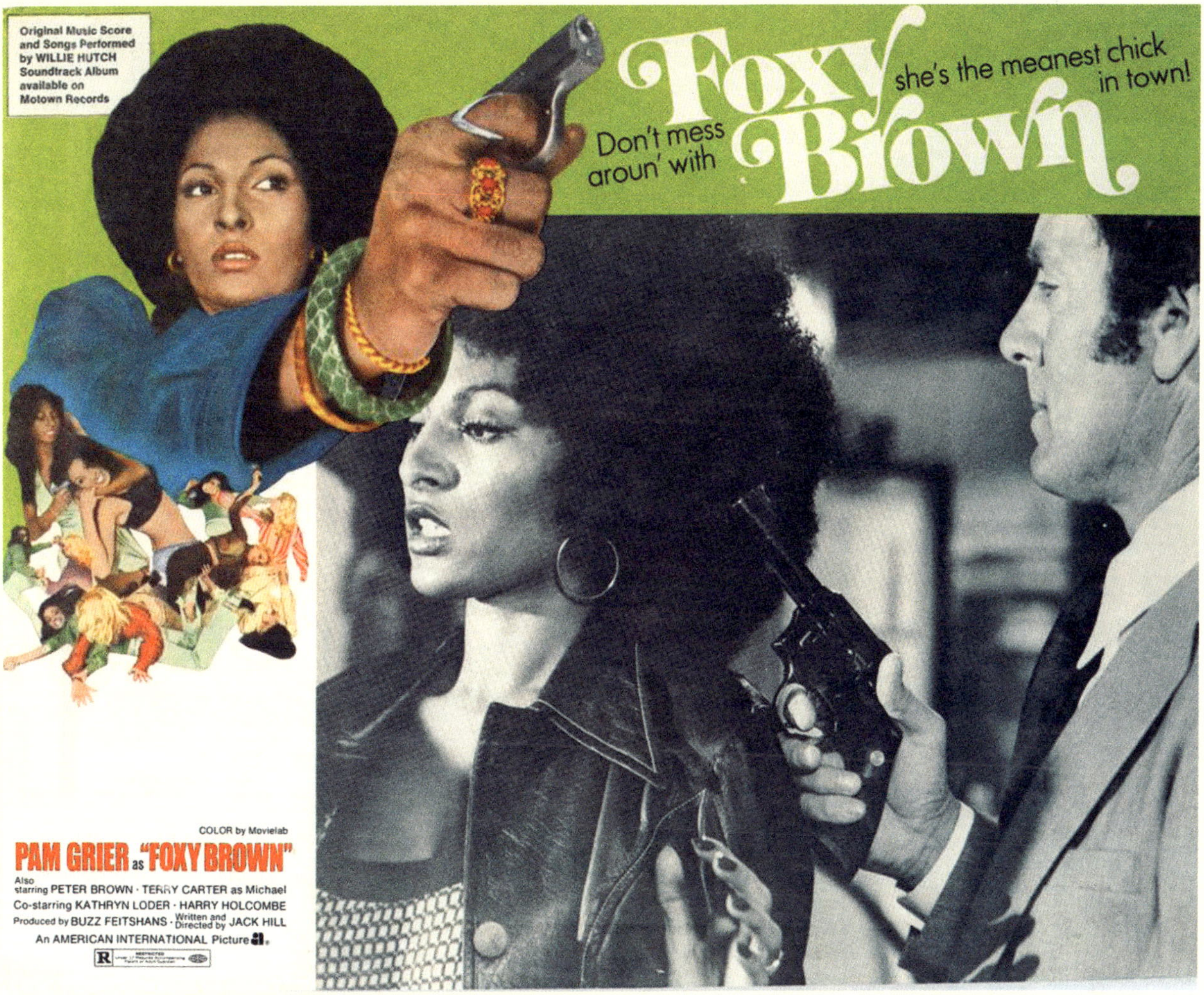

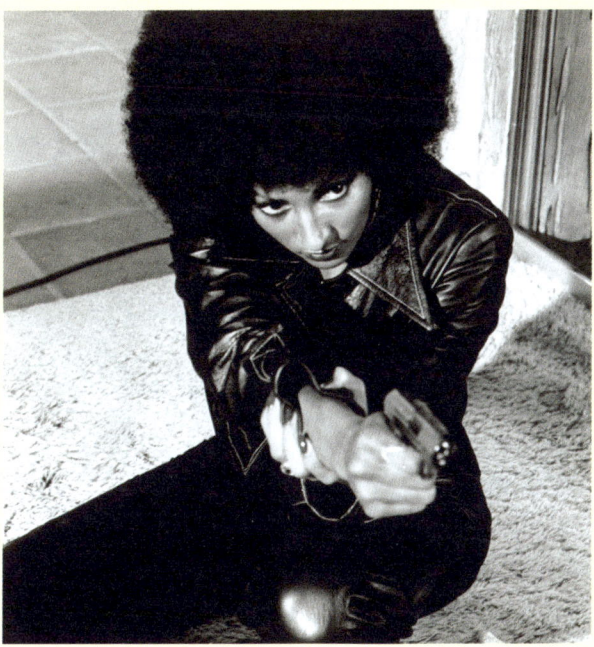

for revenge and assumes a broader social dimension. *"What is it you really want*?" a Black Panther look-alike asks Foxy. *"Justice." "For whom, your bother?" "Why not? It could be your brother, too. Or your sister. Or your children. I want justice for all of 'em. And I want justice for all the other people whose lives are bought and sold, so that a few big shots can climb up on their backs and laugh at the law and laugh at human decency."*

By playing these bold, aggressive characters—and as a martial arts practitioner herself, who performed her own stunts—Pam Grier established an image for herself as a tough, liberated woman capable of holding her own, an action heroine who embodied the struggles and hopes of African American women. For her, these roles were a reflection of all the women in the seventies who were looking for empowerment in their lives: "*All across the country, a lot of women were Foxy Brown and Coffy. They were independent, fighting to save their families, not accepting rape or being victimized… This was going on all across the country. I just happened to do it on film. I don't think it took any great genius or great imagination. I just exemplified it, reflecting it to society.*"[3] Having dipped its toes into every conceivable genre, from horror movies to sword-and-sandal historical ones (Pam Grier tried both, in *Scream Blacula Scream* and *The Arena*, respectively), blaxploitation petered out by the end of decade. Pam Grier made fewer and fewer appearances on screen, and the characters she played became less and less prominent. Although she never quite fell off the radar, the actress did gradually disappear from our screens… until 1997, when she suddenly returned to the spotlight in the role of a flight attendant who finds herself cornered and ready to go for broke by double-crossing both cops and gangsters.

With *Jackie Brown*, Quentin Tarantino penned an affectionate movie buff's tribute to all the heroines Grier has played. This extends even to the movie's funk and soul—inspired original soundtrack, which borrows from Roy Ayers's score for *Coffy*. The movie also helped offset criticism leveled at the filmmaker in the wake of his first two movies, which both gave pride of place to male characters. Far from following Hollywood conventions, *Jackie Brown* paints a sensitive portrait of a real woman, an intelligent, combative, forty-something Black woman. Just as he had done with John Travolta in *Pulp Fiction*, here Tarantino offered both Pam Grier and her fellow actor Robert Forster another lap around the track. "*Having the two of them*

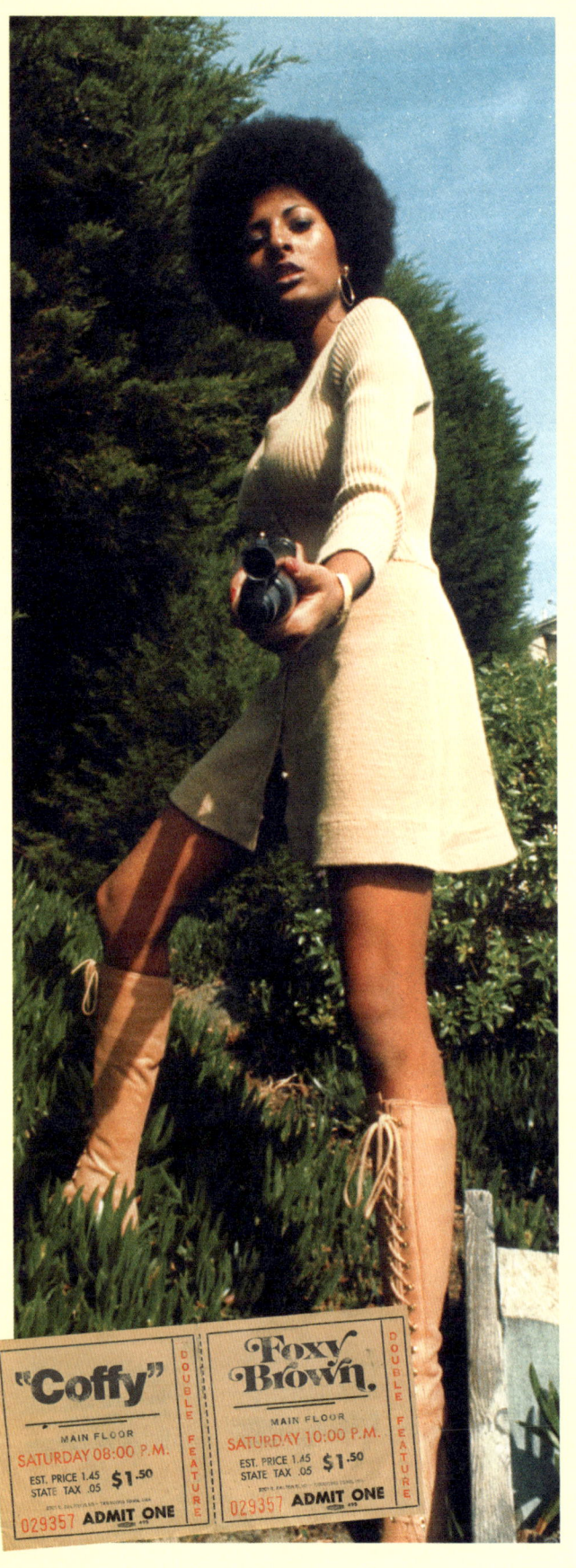

3- Yvonne D. Sims, *Women of Blaxploitation:
How the Black Action Film Heroine Changed American Popular Culture* (McFarland, 2006).

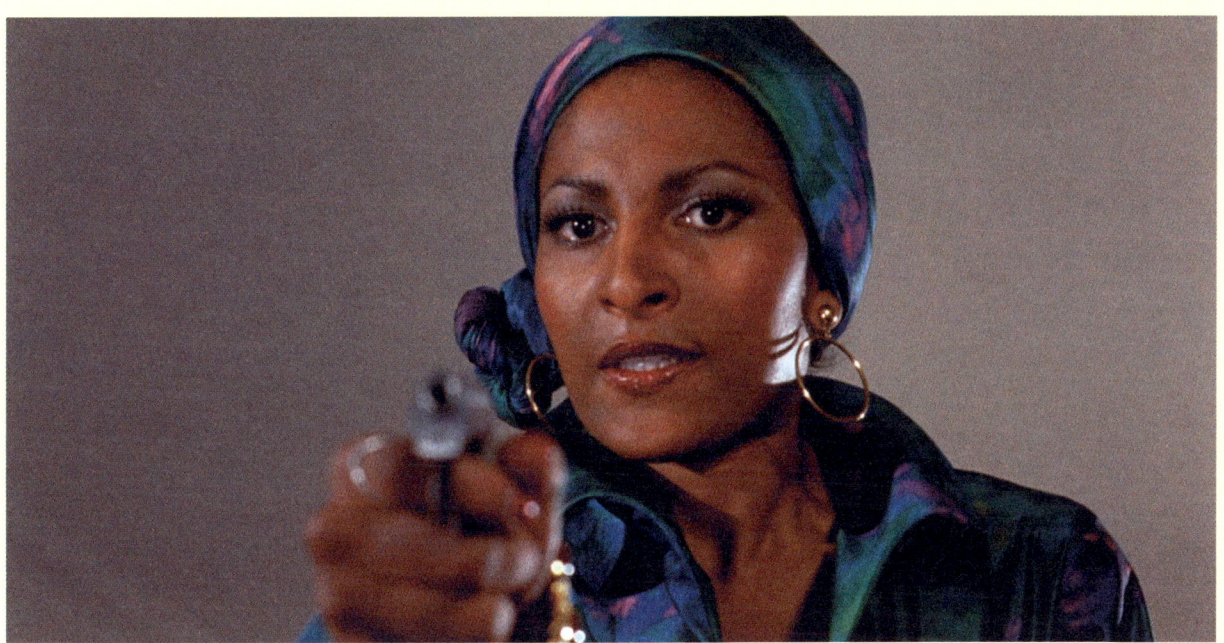

in it together," he explained, "*meant I had two actors who, in a quarter of a century in the business, had experienced both the highs and the lows, not stars like De Niro or Al Pacino who have always been at the top. Pam and Robert have both known real life, with all the trials that brings. They're like circus people, rodeo cowboys, or music-hall magicians: You can read the joy, despair, resentment, and suffering on their faces, just as you can on the faces of the characters they are playing.*"[4]

By casting Pam Grier in the title role, Tarantino conjured up a whole host of images from movies past. It was as if all the characters Grier had ever played were inextricably connected to her, and by playing Jackie (whose very surname connected her to those earlier heroines, through Foxy), she somehow extended their existence, manifesting and exploring an exhaustion and disillusionment to which, by implication, even our screen heroes are not immune. Older and wiser, moreover, Jackie is spared the usual Tarantino propensity for unnecessary chitchat and angry retorts. At forty-eight, the actress

appeared in a role which was both more mature and more subtle, and which Tarantino approached with a tenderness we had not witnessed in him before. The actress saw Jackie as the role of her life: "*What I know is that all my work before* Jackie Brown *prepared me for that part,*" she vouchsafed.[5] With this tailor-made part, she finally received the recognition as an actress that had eluded her in the seventies. Her performance was critically acclaimed, earning her several nominations as well as an award at the Golden Globes. With *Jackie Brown*, director and movie buff Tarantino reasserted his idol's achievements and her legacy as an actress who has fought back on screen, blow for blow, against all the racial and sexual violence and abuse her peers have endured in real life. "*I was part of a female cinematic revolution,*" she has said.[6] In her way, Pam Grier paved the way for Tarantino's future rebellious heroines. Before *Kill Bill* and its killer Bride, before the gang of angry girls in *Death Proof*, Coffy and Foxy were there, watching out fiercely and fearlessly. •

4- Michel Ciment and Hubert Niogret, "Entretien Quentin Tarantino: Je veux que le public voie mon 'nouveau' film et non mon film 'suivant,'" *Positif*, no. 446, April 1998.
5- Shahesta Shaitly, "Pam Grier Takes Raunch to the Ranch," *The Guardian*, December 2011.
6- Ryan Gilbey, "Pam Grier: 'I Was Part of a Female Cinematic Revolution,'" *The Guardian*, September 2022.

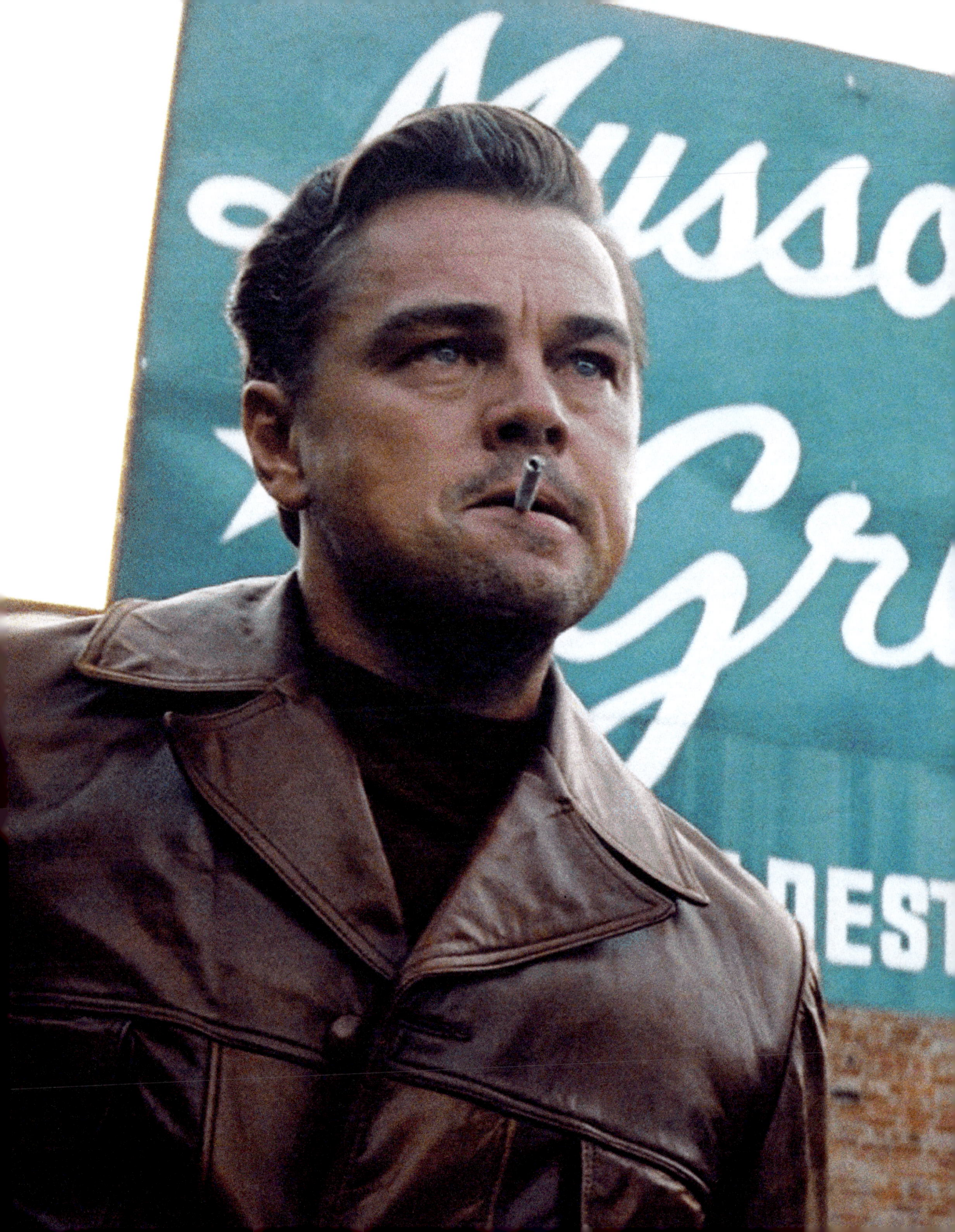

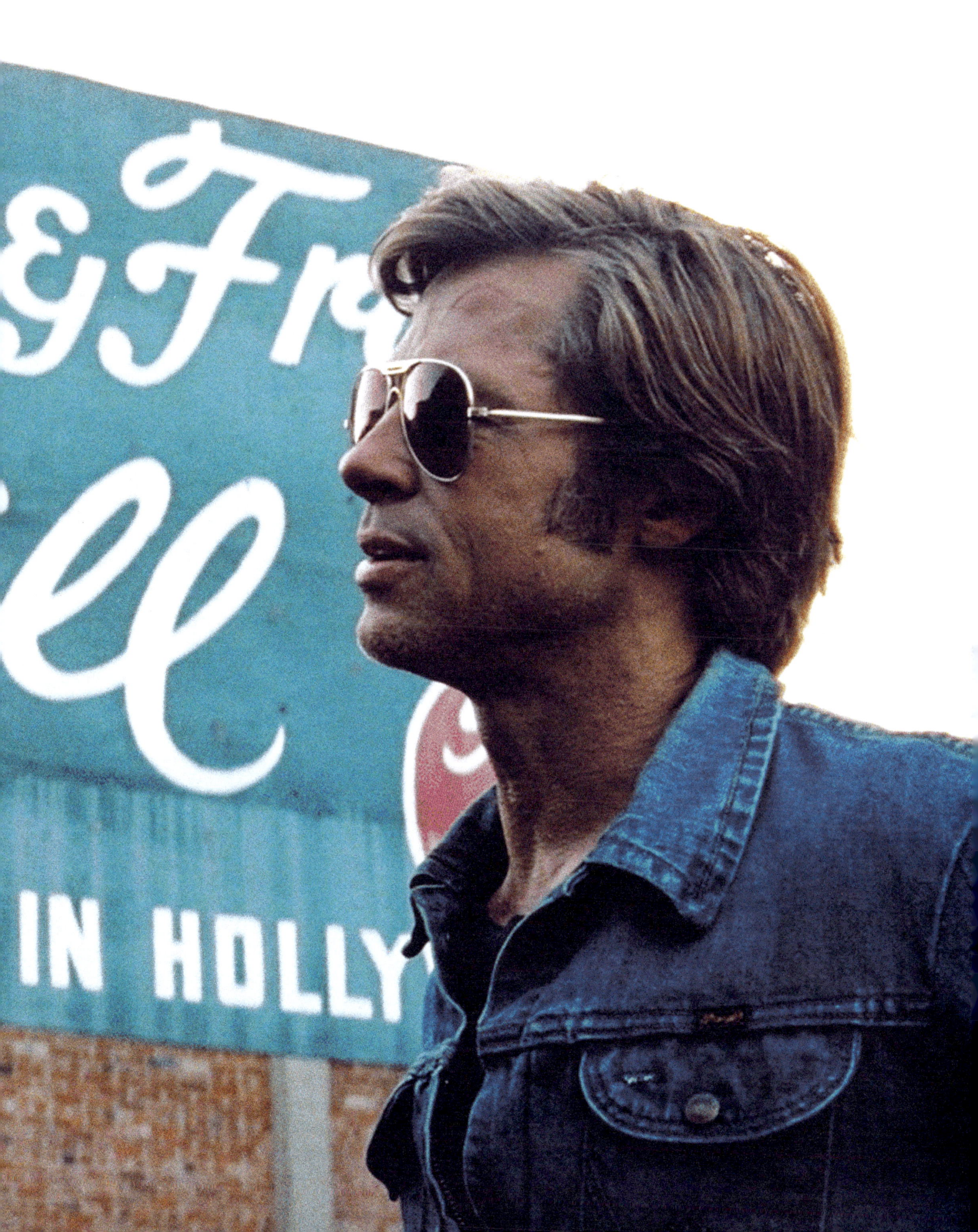

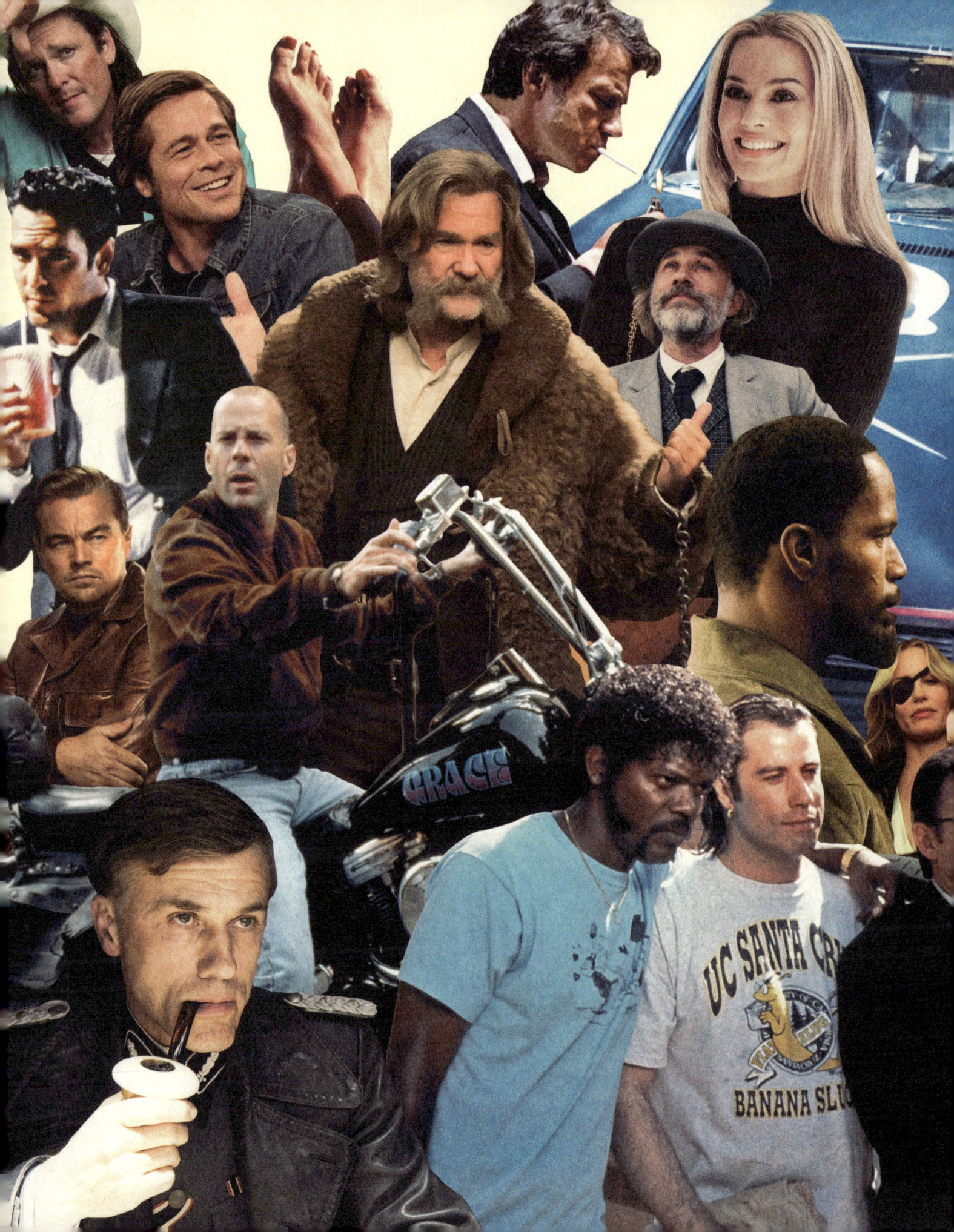

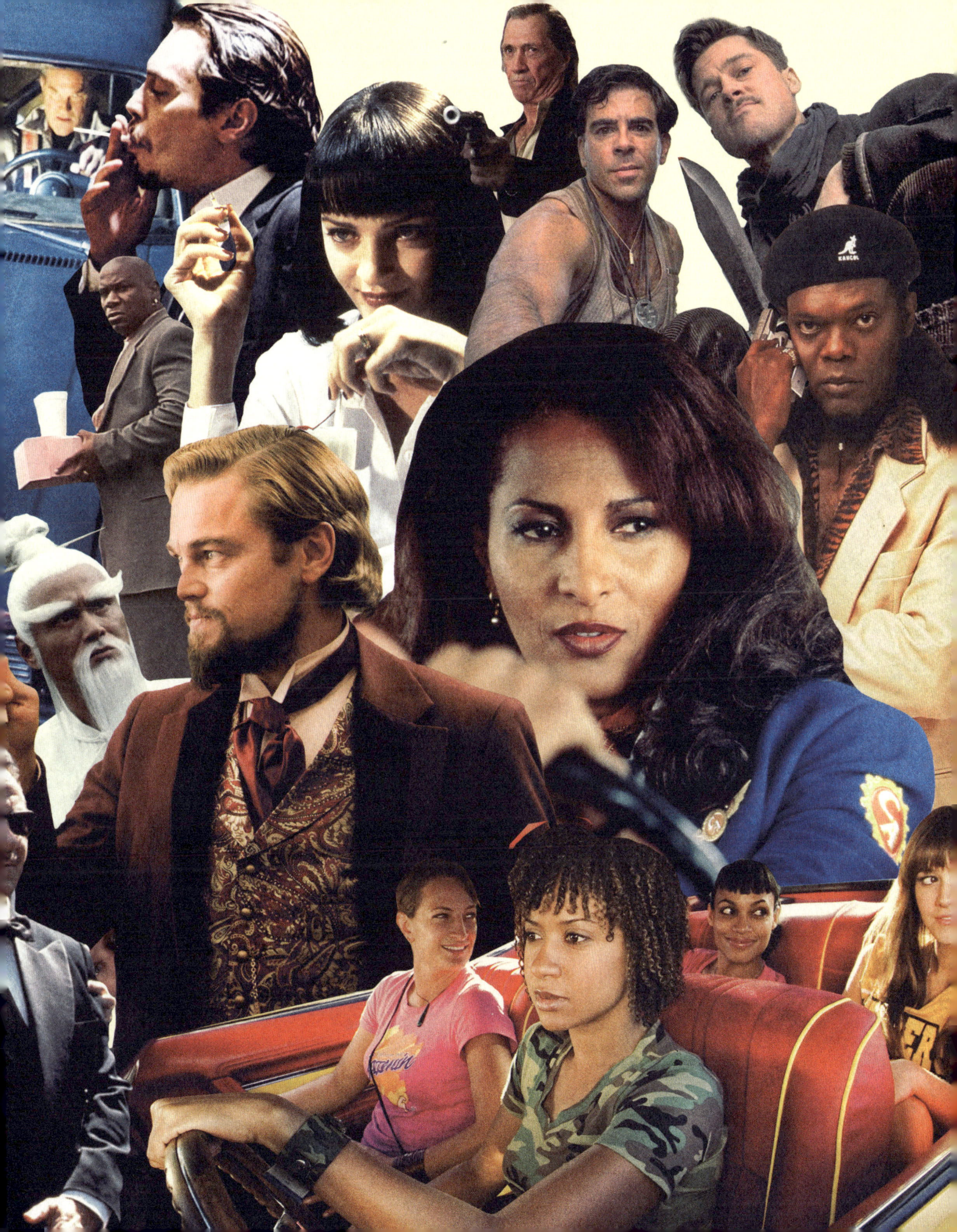

SEE YOU SOON!

★ ★

Your visit to Tarantino Town is drawing to a close. You've ordered everything on the diner menu, exhausted the program at the movie theater, entered into fierce debates with the employees of the video store, raided the aisles of the thrift store, and had a couple of memorable encounters in the corridors of the motel… and so here you are, ready to leave our little town. But are you sure it's time to go? Do you really think you've discovered everything there is to see? Aren't there a few corners left to explore in our town? Quentin Tarantino's universe, which reveals itself piece by piece through movies, books, records, and countless endlessly chatty interviews, is far too vast to lay out in all its detail here. And as for the influences and references entwined in his movies, they are infinite.

"I don't consider myself just as a director," Quentin Tarantino says, *"but as a movie man who has the whole treasure of the movies to choose from and take whatever gems I like, bring things together that have never been matched up before."*[1] His films could easily be described as postmodern: Aptly enough for an oeuvre in which so much eating goes on, his work reflects a carefully digested feast of film history, encompassing a whole spectrum, from well-documented movies to ones that have been forgotten, not to mention those consigned to the furthest reaches of what might be considered good taste. Tarantino is an insatiable movie buff, devouring movies and assimilating them into his own work, adding film to film. This is perhaps what is so shrewd about his movies: Rather than talking about life, they talk about other movies, as if his only way of apprehending the world were through the endless stream of film images which courses through his consciousness. Tarantino has earned a reputation as a thieving magpie, but rather than apologize for this, he embraces it like an article of faith, with that touch of cheerful impudence which is so typical of him. His exuberant pilfering and poaching of genres is always fired by the same burning passion, driven by the same instinct which sees him revive, celebrate, and share his memories of the movies he loves. While to his detractors he may be a tomb raider,

1- Tom Shone, *Tarantino: A Retrospective* (Thames & Hudson, 2017).

to his admirers, who are rather more numerous, he is one of the last keepers of the temple, the archivist and guardian of our collective film memory. There is nothing mausoleum-like about his movies, however: They are not edifices erected to the memory of a few defunct reels of celluloid, but constitute an exultant, inventive, living monument capable of bringing together the very newest cinema recruits and the most discerning movie buffs.

There is neither end nor limit to Tarantino Town, any more than there is to Tarantino's work, with its web of parallel stories and interwoven fictional worlds and the torrent of film images it brings with it. It's entirely up to you: You can stay as long as you want. So why not put your bags back down and book a few extra nights in the motel? Retrace your steps. Choose a few more movies to see at the theater, sample a new dish at the diner, lock horns with a few loudmouthed movie buffs at the video store. Put the world to rights with Jules and Vincent. Watch *Taxi Driver* for the hundredth time on the little TV set in your room, with some half-melted ice cream for company. Who wants to hurry home once they've set foot in Tarantino's universe? We certainly don't. So rewind the tape and watch the movie again, and again, and again.

THIS SPACE FOR WRITING

POSTCARD
THIS SPACE FOR ADDRESS ONLY

PLACE STAMP HERE

TARANTINO TOWN CARD, CO.

Bye Bye!

ACKNOWLEDGMENTS

Johan would like to dedicate this book to the video store in the Auchan shopping mall in Vaulx-en-Velin. Camille would like to dedicate it to all the movie buffs who like to talk their mouths off and gas on endlessly, and to reassure them that somewhere out there, Quentin Tarantino is talking even more than they are.

CREDITS: pp. 04-05: Landmark Media, Alamy / p. 07: Mayeul Longueville / p. 10: Live Entertainment, Dog Eat Dog Productions, RnB, Collection Christophel / p. 11: Compagnie Industrielle et Commerciale Cinématographique (CICC), Fida Cinematografica, Filmel, T.C. Productions, Collection Christophel / p. 12: Live Entertainment, Dog Eat Dog Productions, Collection Christophel / p. 15t: Miramax, Collection Christophel / p. 16: Miramax, A Band Apart, RnB, Collection Christophel / p. 17: Concord Productions, Golden Harvest, Collection Christophel / p. 18: Miramax, A Band Apart, RnB, Collection Christophel / p. 19: Columbia Pictures, Collection Christophel / p. 20: Andrew Cooper, Sony Pictures Entertainment, Heyday Films, Visiona Romantica, Collection Christophel / p. 21t: Maximul Films, Alamy / p. 21b: Live Entertainment, Dog Eat Dog Productions, Collection Christophel / p. 22t: ParamountPictures, RnB, Collection Christophel / p. 22b: Miramax, A Band Apart, Collection Christophel / p. 23: Pictorial Press Ltd, Alamy / p. 24: The Weinstein Company, Dimensions films, Collection Christophel / p. 25: The Weinstein Company, Dimensions films, Collection Christophel / p. 26t: The Weinstein Company, Dimensions films, Collection Christophel / p. 26b: Archives du 7eme Art, Photo12 via AFP / p. 27: The Weinstein Company, Dimensions films, Collection Christophel / p. 28: United Archives GmbH, Alamy / p. 29: The Weinstein Company, Dimensions films, Collection Christophel / pp. 30-31: Landmark Media, Alamy / p. 35t: Landmark Media, Alamy / p. 35b: Miramax, A Band Apart, Collection Christophel / pp. 36-37: Landmark Media, Alamy / p. 39: Miramax, A Band Apart, Collection Christophel / p. 41: The Weinstein Company, Dimensions films, Collection Christophel / p. 42: The Weinstein Company, Dimensions films, Collection Christophel / p. 43: The Weinstein Company, Dimensions films, Collection Christophel / p. 44: A Band Apart, Studio Babelsberg, Collection Christophel / p. 45t: Entertainment Pictures, Alamy / p. 45b: François Duhamel, Universal Pictures, The Weinstein Company, A Band Apart, Studio Babelsberg, Visiona Romantica, RnB, Collection Christophel / p. 46: A Band Apart, Studio Babelsberg, Collection Christophel / p. 47: A Band Apart, Studio Babelsberg, Collection Christophel / p. 49: Miramax, A Band Apart, RnB, Collection Christophel / p. 50t: Miramax, A Band Apart, Collection Christophel / p. 50b: Miramax, A Band Apart, Collection Christophel / p. 51: Landmark Media, Alamy / p. 52: Landmark Media, Alamy / p. 53: Landmark Media, Alamy / pp. 54-55: Landmark Media, Alamy / p. 56: Sony Pictures Entertainment, Heyday Films, Visiona Romantica, Collection Christophel / pp. 58-59: The Weinstein Company, Collection Christophel / p. 63: Miramax, RnB, Collection Christophel / p. 65: Landmark Media, Alamy / p. 67: Miramax, Collection Christophel / p. 68: Morgan Creek Entertainment, Davis Films, Collection Christophel / p. 71: The Weinstein Company, Dimensions films, Collection Christophel / p. 77: Michel Maurou, WWD, Penske Media via Getty Images / p. 78: 29Pictures, Good Wizard, MadPix, Collection Christophel / pp. 80-81: United Archives GmbH, Alamy / p. 89t: Miramax, A Band Apart, Collection Christophel / p. 89b: Landmark Media, Alamy / p. 97: Miramax, A Band Apart, Collection Christophel / p. 98: Landmark Media, Alamy / p. 99: Miramax, RnB, Collection Christophel / p. 100: Pictorial Press Ltd, Alamy / p. 102: Photo12, Alamy, PictureLux The Hollywood Archive / pp. 106-107: Entertainment Pictures, Alamy / p. 110: Cinema 77, Collection Christophel / p. 112: Columbia Pictures, Bill-Phillips, Italo-Judeo Productions, Collection Christophel / p. 116: View Askew Productions, Miramax, Collection Christophel / p. 117t: View Askew Productions, Miramax, Collection Christophel / p. 117b: View Askew Productions, Miramax, Collection Christophel / pp. 124-125: The Weinstein Company, Dimensions films, Collection Christophel / pp. 128, 130, 131: Boris Laplante / p. 129: Historic Collection, Alamy / p. 133: Alan Wylie, Alamy / p. 136: mauritius images GmbH, Alamy / p. 137: RGR Collection, Alamy / p. 138b: Everett, Shutterstock / p. 139: Albert L. Ortega, Getty Images / pp. 140-141: Miramax, A Band Apart, Collection Christophel / p. 145: Rights reserved / p. 148: Miramax, Collection Christophel / p. 150: Universal Images Group North America LLC, Alamy / p. 151: AJ Pics, Alamy / p. 152: United Archives GmbH, Alamy / p. 153: The Weinstein Company, Collection Christophel / p. 154: Pictorial Press Ltd, Alamy / p. 155: Allstar Picture Library Limited, Alamy / p. 156t: Morgan Creek, Davis Films, August, Collection Christophel / p. 156b: Pictorial Press Ltd, Alamy / p. 157: Pictorial Press Ltd, Alamy / p. 158: WENN Rights Ltd, Alamy / pp. 160-161: Pictorial Press Ltd, Alamy / p. 165t: United Archives GmbH, Alamy / p. 165b: The Weinstein Company, Dimensions films, Collection Christophel / p. 166: Pictorial Press Ltd, Alamy / p. 167: Archives du 7eme Art, Photo12 via AFP / p. 169: Anouchka films, Orsay films, Collection Christophel / pp. 172-173: United Archives GmbH, Alamy / p. 175: 20th Century Fox, Collection Christophel / p. 176: Collection Cinema, Photo12 via AFP / p. 177t: Collection Cinema, Photo12 via AFP / p. 177b: Miramax, A Band Apart, Collection Christophel / p. 178: Miramax, A Band Apart, Collection Christophel / p. 179t: Moviestore Collection Ltd, Alamy / p. 179b: Collection Cinema, Photo12 via AFP / p. 181t: Allstar Picture Library Limited, Alamy / p. 181b: Warner Bros., Archives du 7eme Art, Photo12 via AFP / p. 182t: Warner Bros., Archives du 7eme Art, Photo12 via AFP / p. 182b: Warner Bros., Collection Christophel / p. 183: Warner Bros.. Pictures, Elmer Enterprises, Collection Christophel / p. 184: Sony Pictures Entertainment, Heyday Films, Visiona Romantica, Collection Christophel / p. 185: Moviestore Collection Ltd, Alamy / p. 186: Sony Pictures Entertainment, Heyday Films, Visiona Romantica, Collection Christophel / p. 187: Archives du 7eme Art, Photo12 via AFP / p. 189: AIP Coffy, Collection Christophel / p. 190: Archives du 7eme Art, Photo12 via AFP / p. 191t: LMPC via Getty Images / p. 191b: PictureLux The Hollywood Archive, Alamy, Photo12 / p. 192: Entertainment Pictures, Alamy / p. 193: AIP, Collection Christophel / pp. 194-195: Sony Pictures Entertainment, Heyday Films, Visiona Romantica, Collection Christophel / p. 196: Mayeul Longueville / pp. 84, 85, 87, 93, 95, 101t, 103, 104, 105: Alain Charlot Collection / Other images: Rockyvision / Cover: Alain Charlot Collection / Endpapers: boarding pass and poster: Coolidge-Wilson Blue Robin Collectables, Alamy; other images: Rockyvision

Editorial direction: Claudia Schönecker
Project management: Veronika Brandt
Translation: Fabia Claris
Copyediting and typesetting: Weiß-Freiburg GmbH
Production management: Luisa Klose
Printing and binding: Toppan Leefung Printing Limited

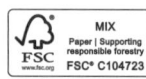

FSC MIX
Paper | Supporting responsible forestry
FSC® C104723

Penguin Random House Verlagsgruppe FSC® N001967

Printed in China

ISBN 978-3-7913-7628-8

www.prestel.com

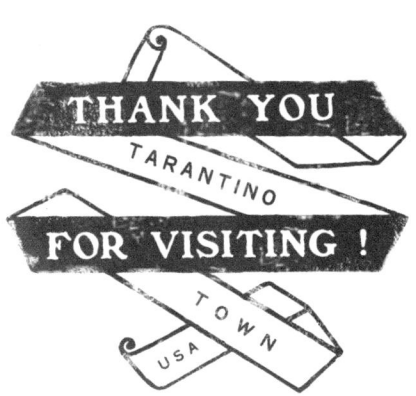

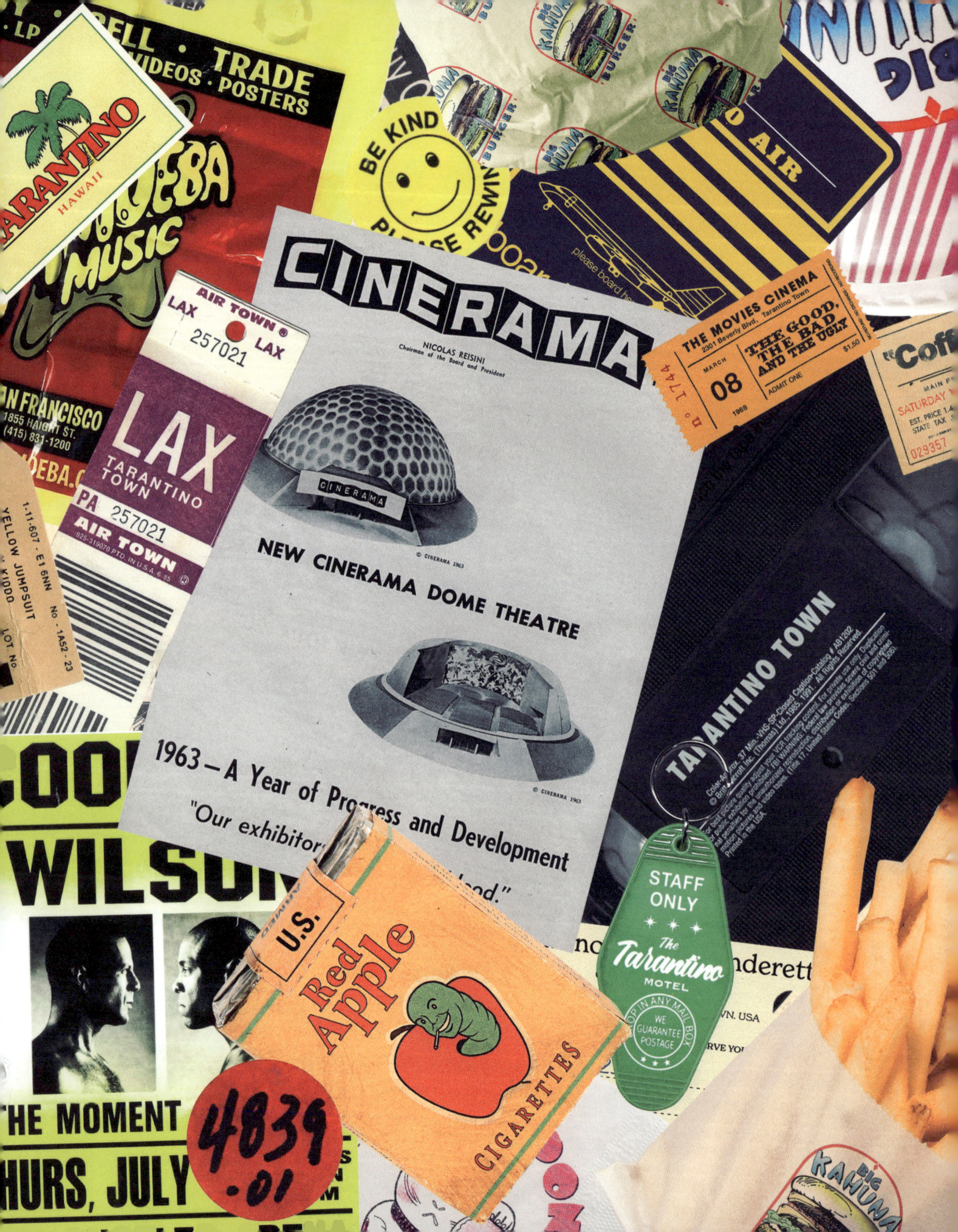